PENGUIN ⬤ CLASSICS

CONFESSIONS OF AN ENGL███ ███M-EATER
AND OTHER W████████

THOMAS DE QUINCEY was b██ ██ ██85 at Manchester. As a boy he was a brilliant Latin and █████ scholar, although he was unhappy both at home and at school. He ran away from Manchester Grammar School and went wandering through Wales, after which he went to London, where for several months he led an impoverished life. This period is vividly described in the *Confessions*. In 1804 he went to Worcester College, Oxford, but he failed to take his degree. It was there that he first began his correspondence with Wordsworth and also his opium addiction. From his early youth De Quincey had been a reverent admirer of Wordsworth and, to a lesser degree, Coleridge, and between 1809 and 1821 he rented Dove Cottage in Grasmere. His publication of the *Recollections of the Lakes and the Lake Poets* precipitated the end of his connection with the Wordsworths. In 1817 De Quincey married Margaret Simpson. He endeavoured to support their large family by writing for literary miscellanies but spent most of his adult life evading arrest for debt. *Confessions of an English Opium-Eater*, which ran through more than two dozen book editions by the end of the century, was first published in the *London Magazine* in 1821. But the majority of De Quincey's writing appeared in *Blackwood's Edinburgh Magazine*, which published two sequels to the *Confessions*: 'Suspiria de Profundis' in 1845 and 'The English Mail-Coach' in 1849. At the end of his life, De Quincey enjoyed a brief period as an eminent man of letters, receiving visits from international admirers and overseeing the first volumes of his collected works. He died in Edinburgh in 1859.

BARRY MILLIGAN is the author of *Pleasures and Pains: Opium and the Orient in Nineteenth-Century British Culture*. He has also published several essays on Romantic and Victorian literature and history and is co-editor, with Ghislaine McDayter and Guinn Batten, of *Romantic Generations: Essays in Honor of Robert F. Gleckner*. His research awards have included a Mellon Postdoctoral Fellowship in the Humanities and several visiting research fellowships at the Wellcome Institute for the History of Medicine, London. He has taught at Duke and Cornell Universities and currently teaches at Wright State University in Dayton, Ohio.

THOMAS DE QUINCEY

Confessions of an English Opium-Eater

AND OTHER WRITINGS

Edited with an Introduction and Notes by
BARRY MILLIGAN

PENGUIN BOOKS

PENGUIN BOOKS

Published by the Penguin Group
Penguin Books Ltd, 80 Strand, London WC2R ORL, England
Penguin Putnam Inc., 375 Hudson Street, New York, New York 10014, USA
Penguin Books Australia Ltd, 250 Camberwell Road, Camberwell, Victoria 3124, Australia
Penguin Books Canada Ltd, 10 Alcorn Avenue, Toronto, Ontario, Canada M4V 3B2
Penguin Books India (P) Ltd, 11, Community Centre, Panchsheel Park, New Delhi – 110 017, India
Penguin Books (NZ) Ltd, Cnr Rosedale and Airborne Roads, Albany, Auckland, New Zealand
Penguin Books (South Africa) (Pty) Ltd, 24 Sturdee Avenue, Rosebank 2196, South Africa

Penguin Books Ltd, Registered Offices: 80 Strand, London WC2R ORL, England

www.penguin.com

Confessions of an English Opium-Eater first published in *London Magazine* in 1821;
'Suspiria de Profundis' and 'The English Mail-Coach' first published in *Blackwood's
Edinburgh Magazine* in 1845 and 1849 respectively.
This selection published in Penguin Classics 2003

13

Editorial material copyright © Barry Milligan, 2003
All rights reserved

The moral right of the editor has been asserted

Set in 10.25/12.25 pt PostScript Adobe Sabon
Typeset by Rowland Phototypesetting Ltd, Bury St Edmunds, Suffolk
Printed in England by Clays Ltd, St Ives plc

ISBN-13: 978–0–140–43901–4
ISBN-10: 0–140–43901–3

www.greenpenguin.co.uk

Contents

Acknowledgements

The editor would like to thank Greg Anderson for substantial help with Latin and Greek passages and matters of Graeco-Roman culture in general, Sue Phillpott for her expert copy-editing and other significant contributions and Laura Barber, Carol Engelhardt, Michael Ferejohn, Henry Limouze, Grevel Lindop, Robert Mighall, Joan Milligan, Jennifer Spalding and Lindeth Vasey for various kinds of advice and assistance. Thanks are also due to the University Press of Virginia for permission to include a revised portion of the editor's *Pleasures and Pains: Opium and the Orient in Nineteenth-Century British Culture* (1995) in the Appendix. Finally, this edition is indebted to those editors who have gone before, especially Grevel Lindop and Alethea Hayter.

Chronology

1781 Posthumous publication of Jean-Jacques Rousseau's *Confessions*.

1785 15 August: birth of Thomas Penson Quincey in Manchester (his mother alters the name to the more aristocratic-sounding 'De Quincey' in 1796).

1788 Birth of Lord Byron.

1789 Storming of the Bastille marks the beginning of the French Revolution.

1792 Death of sister Elizabeth, the first great trauma of De Quincey's life. Birth of Percy Bysshe Shelley.

1793 Death of De Quincey's father.

1795 Embassy to Peking of Lord Macartney, charged with improving Anglo-Chinese trade relations. Birth of John Keats.

1796 De Quincey moves with his family to Bath and enters Bath Grammar School. Birth of Margaret Simpson, his future wife, at Grasmere in the Lake District.

1797 Samuel Taylor Coleridge drafts 'Kubla Khan' (published 1816).

1798 William Wordsworth and Samuel Taylor Coleridge's *Lyrical Ballads* published.

1799 De Quincey enters Winkfield School in Wiltshire. Wordsworth completes the first version of his autobiographical poem ultimately known as *The Prelude*.

1800 De Quincey enters Manchester Grammar School. France defeats Austria at the Battle of Marengo in Italy during the Napoleonic Wars.

1802 De Quincey runs away from school to ramble in Wales, then goes to London.

1803 Enters Worcester College, Oxford; writes to Wordsworth
for the first time. German pharmacist F. W. A. Sertürner
isolates a crystalline alkaloid of opium and dubs it
'morphium'.

1804 According to De Quincey's later claim in the *Confessions*,
he first takes opium this autumn.

1805 Britain's Navy defeats France's at the Battle of Trafalgar.
Wordsworth completes the second version of his autobiographical poem ultimately known as *The Prelude*.

1807 De Quincey meets Wordsworth at Grasmere.

1808 Leaves Oxford without taking a degree.

1809 Oversees publication of Wordsworth's pamphlet criticiz-
ing the Convention of Cintra, an agreement made between
the French, British and Portuguese during the Peninsular War
(1808–14). Moves into the Wordsworths' former home, the
cottage at Town End at Grasmere (later known as Dove
Cottage). Wellington's forces defeat Napoleon at the Battle
of Talavera in Spain during the Peninsular War. Birth of
Edgar Allan Poe.

1812 De Quincey reads law briefly. Wordsworth's daughter
Kate dies, plunging De Quincey into deep mourning. Wellington defeats French forces at the Battles of Badajoz and Salamanca in Spain, turning the tide towards ultimate British
victory in the Peninsular War. First two cantos of Byron's
Childe Harold's Pilgrimage published. Birth of Charles
Dickens.

1814 Sir Walter Scott's *Waverley* published.

1815 Wellington's forces defeat Napoleon's at the Battle of
Waterloo.

1816 Birth of son William to De Quincey and Margaret Simpson. Coleridge's *Christabel and Other Poems*, containing
'Kubla Khan' and 'The Pains of Sleep', published.

1817 De Quincey marries Margaret Simpson. David Ricardo's
On the Principles of Political Economy and Taxation
published.

1818 De Quincey is appointed editor of the *Westmorland
Gazette* (and dismissed the following year). Birth of daughter
Margaret.

1820 Birth of son Horace.

1821 De Quincey makes his first contributions to *Blackwood's Magazine*. *Confessions of an English Opium-Eater* published anonymously in two parts in the *London Magazine*. Death of Keats. Birth of French poet Charles Baudelaire. *Confessions* is widely reviewed; although some critics balk at the author's apparent egotism and immorality, there is consensus that both style and subject are remarkably original.

1822 Death of Shelley. First book edition of *Confessions* published.

1823 'On the Knocking at the Gate in Macbeth' published in the *London Magazine*. Birth of De Quincey's son Francis John. Second and third editions of *Confessions* published; also the anonymous *Advice to Opium-Eaters*, emulating *Confessions*. *Eclectic Review* notice of *Confessions* impugns De Quincey's credibility because he uses opium.

1824 De Quincey 'translates' the German imitation of Scott, *Walladmor*. Death of Byron.

1825 Publication of Charles Waterton's *Wanderings in South America* (describing his riding a cayman, to which De Quincey later alludes in 'The English Mail-Coach').

1826 Fourth edition of *Confessions*.

1827 'On Murder Considered as One of the Fine Arts' and 'The Last Days of Immanuel Kant' published in *Blackwood's*. Birth of De Quincey's son Paul Frederick and daughter Florence. Death of William Blake.

1829 Birth of De Quincey's son Julius. Robert Christison's *Treatise on Poisons* cites *Confessions* as 'a very poetical, but I believe also a very faithful, picture of the phenomena' accompanying opium use.

1830 De Quincey moves permanently to Edinburgh. Tennyson's *Poems, Chiefly Lyrical* published.

1832 De Quincey publishes gothic novel *Klosterheim*. Death of son Julius.

1833 Birth of daughter Emily. Evading arrest for debt, De Quincey takes up residence in Edinburgh's Holyrood Sanctuary. Thomas Carlyle's *Sartor Resartus* begins appearing in *Fraser's Magazine*.

1834 Death of De Quincey's son William. Death of Coleridge.

1837 De Quincey contributes articles on Goethe, Schiller, Shakespeare and Pope to *Encyclopaedia Britannica*. Death of his wife Margaret. Victoria's accession to the throne. First serial instalments of Dickens's *Pickwick Papers* published.

1839 First Opium War between Britain and China begins.

1840 Two articles by De Quincey on the First Opium War published in *Blackwood's*.

1842 Death of De Quincey's son Horace in military service in China. Treaty of Nanking ends First Opium War, with China ceding Hong Kong to Britain. William Blair's 'An Opium Eater in America' published.

1845 De Quincey's 'Suspiria de Profundis' and 'Coleridge on Opium Eating' published in *Blackwood's*, and 'On Wordsworth's Poetry' in *Tait's*. Fifth edition of *Confessions* published. Robert Gilfillan's *Gallery of Literary Portraits* praises De Quincey's 'pencil of fire', assesses his faculties as 'powerfully developed but not properly balanced'. *Medical Times & Gazette* avers that 'the law of his self-experience is paramount in the profession'.

1848 De Quincey receives an admiring Ralph Waldo Emerson on visit to Edinburgh.

1849 'The English Mail-Coach' published in *Blackwood's*. Death of Poe.

1850 Death of Wordsworth.

1851 Great Exhibition at Crystal Palace in London.

1851–9 Boston (Mass.) edition of De Quincey's *Writings* (20 vols.) published.

1853 De Quincey participates in publication of vols. 1 and 2 of *Selections Grave and Gay*, his collected works (14 vols.; last, 1860). Crimean War begins. Two new editions of *Confessions* published. Surge of critical interest in De Quincey accompanies publication of his collected works.

1854 London *Globe* prints large extracts from vol. 3 of *Selections Grave and Gay*; *Eclectic Review*: 'each personal pronoun is an algebraic symbol of great and general truths'; David Masson in *British Quarterly Review* praises De Quincey's innovative combination of subjective poetry and didactic prose. *Dublin University Magazine*: De Quincey's style is a 'figured Babylonian robe ... possibly plague-tainted'.

1856 Publication of *Selections Grave and Gay*, vol. 5, containing significantly revised *Confessions*. Second Opium War begins. Crimean War ends.

1857 The Indian Mutiny. *London Quarterly Review*: De Quincey's prose is 'haunted by the fiend of subjectivity'. Fitz Hugh Ludlow's *The Hashish Eater: Being Passages from the Life of a Pythagorean* published in the USA.

1858 Medical Act brings about unprecedented unity of British medical professions.

1859 7 December: Death of De Quincey in Edinburgh. *Athenaeum*: De Quincey's prose is 'steeped in egotism' and 'diseased introspection'.

1860 Second Opium War ends. Final volumes of *Selections Grave and Gay* published. Baudelaire's free French translation of sections from *Confessions* published in his *Les Paradise artificiels*.

Introduction

The addict has long been a familiar figure. The outlines may have shifted a bit over the years, but the core has remained much the same for at least a couple of centuries. Although there might at first seem to be little in common between an eighteenth-century English poem, the autobiography of a jazz musician and a glossy advertisement picturing a glowering, skinny youth, it is the deep similarities between these artifacts that reveal the advertisement as an example of 1990s 'junky chic' rather than a mere voyeuristic view of some undernourished teenager in designer jeans. And the guest on the daytime talk-show who says she was once unable to stop doing something – overeating, gambling, having dangerous sex – makes us pause for a moment before switching to another channel partly because she appeals to our notions of what an addict is, does and knows. But just what are those notions? What are addicts, and why are we convinced they have something compelling to say? What do supermodels have in common with Billie Holiday and Samuel Taylor Coleridge? And where did these associations come from in the first place?

Thomas De Quincey did not write about fashion models, jazz or daytime talk-shows, so it would be straining credulity to insist he has the answers to these questions. He did, however, establish many of the terms that make it possible to ask them in the first place. By cementing the connection between drug use and proto-psychedelic Oriental visions, he almost singlehandedly changed opium's popular status from the respectability of a useful medicine to the exoticism of a mind-altering drug. He forged the link between self-revelation and addiction that is a staple of today's booming self-help industry. He established the romantic figure of the drug addict as starving genius. He paved the way for the hippie rock concert experience by using drugs to enhance his enjoyment of live music. He was even a down-and-out junky in Edinburgh long before there was an Irvine Welsh. So even if his writings were not as engaging as they are, they would occupy a prominent position in the development of modern culture.

It is at least ironic, then, that this prominent position is an almost hidden one: his *magnum opus*, *Confessions of an English Opium-Eater*, is one of those books almost everyone has heard of but very few have read. This obscurity cannot be due to the quality of the writing, however. De Quincey's prose offers a quirky wit to rival Charles Dickens's and sensations equal to anything in a Wilkie Collins novel. If De Quincey has not enjoyed the enduring popularity of these contemporaries, it has more to do with the fact that he did not write novels (with the exception of a gothic potboiler even he regarded as a failure and a 'translation' of a hack German imitation of Walter Scott). His métier was the essay. Modern readers do not tend to ask one another whether they have read any good essays lately, nor do titles like 'Studies in the Essay' often appear in university course listings. But De Quincey's essays were widely read during his lifetime and exerted a powerful influence on such significant and diverse cultural developments as professional medicine, British imperial politics, French Symbolism, European concert music and Edgar Allan Poe's tales of terror, not to mention their more obviously formative role in so-called drug culture.

To trade one set of questions for another, then, who was this man, what were these essays and how did they come to be?

THE LITERARY TRADITION OF
SELF-INCRIMINATION

De Quincey inherited a legacy of warts-and-all confessional literature that goes back at least as far as the fourth-century *Confessions* of St Augustine, which tells of the author's early profligacy by way of contrast to his upright life after conversion to Christianity. A closer model for De Quincey, in both chronological and stylistic terms, came from one of the founders of the French Revolutionary sensibility, the Swiss writer Jean-Jacques Rousseau. His posthumously published *Confessions* (1781) similarly sought to explain his own philosophical development via brutally frank descriptions of his less commendable acts as well as his laudable ones. De Quincey's use of the word 'confessions' in his title thus clearly hearkens to these familiar precedents. As is so often the case with De Quincey, however, he pursues conflicting agendas at once; his title ensures that readers will compare his work to others', but he then insists in his first paragraph that no such comparison is warranted. His opening condemnation of the 'acts of gratuitous self-humiliation' characteristic of 'the spurious and defective sensibility of the French' is a not so subtle attempt to distance his autobiographical piece from Rousseau's. But both the form of his *Confessions* and the title beg for the analogy. In fact the most notable similarities between De Quincey's *Confessions* and Rousseau's are extended through the two other essays included in this volume, the 'sequels' to the *Confessions*, 'Suspiria de Profundis' and 'The English Mail-Coach'. One clearly stated goal of all three essays is to illustrate how the most troubling experiences of early life are repeatedly revisited by the sleeping mind, a trajectory that closely matches Rousseau's, developing an explanation of the author's present consciousness by analysing key moments in the process of its development.

An even more immediate influence, however, was the culminating masterwork of De Quincey's idol, the poet William Wordsworth. De Quincey was one of a small coterie with whom

Wordsworth shared parts of the autobiographical poem first drafted in 1799 but published only after his death in 1850 as *The Prelude*. This sprawling work traces the author's growth through key developmental incidents, and De Quincey's many direct quotations of Wordsworth show that he always had the great poet's example before him. In fact De Quincey called his discovery of *Lyrical Ballads* (1798) by Wordsworth and Samuel Taylor Coleridge 'the greatest event in the unfolding of my own mind',[1] and it ultimately drew him into the intimate circle of those poets in particular and a life of letters in general. De Quincey's self-effacing reverence especially for Wordsworth's poetry was surely a factor in his choice to concentrate on prose rather than verse – that and the fact that there was little money to be made from verse when he came to live by his pen.

The first half of the nineteenth century was a lively time for the essay as a genre. A boom in magazine publication was sparked by developments in several areas: new print technology made it easier and more economical to print large runs, faster and cheaper transportation made wider distribution practical, and a rise in literacy meant there was a broader base of consumers to support the growing industry. There was also a lot to write and read about. The raging Napoleonic Wars fuelled the political debates started by the French Revolution, and authors and audiences flocked to join the fray. Several great English essayists were in their heyday, including William Hazlitt and Charles Lamb (a.k.a. 'Elia'). The tone of all this debate was lively as well, given that British magazines were even more unapologetically biased in their politics then than they are now.

De Quincey served for a time as editor of a staunchly Tory newspaper, the *Westmorland Gazette*, and contributed several articles in that capacity. But he was out of his element as a political reporter and soon began publishing his own strange brand of conversational philosophizing. Such experiments were not ideally suited to the pages of a propaganda sheet but they were perfect for another arena. When De Quincey commenced his writing career in the late 1810s and early 1820s his good friend John Wilson was editing one of the most partisan and popular publications of the day, the Tory miscellany *Black-*

wood's Edinburgh Magazine, and it was with the contributions
Wilson invited that De Quincey grew into his own unique voice.
The bulk of his prose would first appear in *Blackwood's* over
the coming decades.

Another forum for De Quincey in the early days was the
London Magazine, which first published *Confessions of an
English Opium-Eater* in 1821. Less overtly political than *Blackwood's*, the *London Magazine* was an otherwise similar miscellany. In fact the two became arch-rivals, attacking one another
in print. The fight was so bitter at one point that a representative
of a *Blackwood's* contributor killed the *London's* editor in a
duel. De Quincey initially sided with his friends at *Blackwood's*,
but when his lifelong habit of procrastination brought relations
with them to a temporary crisis, he left Edinburgh for London,
where he contacted a connection at the *London Magazine*. Strug-
gling to recover from the death of their editor, the new managers
were eager for De Quincey's services and ready to pay hand-
somely for the 'opium article' he had begun for *Blackwood's*.
Progress was impeded by De Quincey's chronic health problems
and equally chronic financial ones, and periods of prostration
were punctuated by sudden changes of lodgings to avoid arrest
for debt (one hideout was in a building near Covent Garden that
now bears a plaque celebrating the distinction). But De Quincey
managed to stay just ahead of both deadlines and creditors, and
the first instalment made the September issue (with no byline) as
'Confessions of an English Opium-Eater: Being an Extract from
the Life of a Scholar'. It was such a commercial success that the
second part had pride of place in the October issue. A book edition followed in 1822 and the *Confessions* remained more or less
in print for the rest of the century.

De Quincey promised a third part of the *Confessions* and the
London Magazine even conveyed the pledge to its readers, but
true to his dilatory nature, he never delivered it. The closest he
came were the aforementioned sequels included in this volume,
both published decades later in *Blackwood's*: 'Suspiria de Profundis' ('Sighs from the Depths', 1845) and 'The English Mail-
Coach' (1849). These essays fully deserve to be called sequels
(as 'Suspiria' explicitly is in its subtitle), for they self-consciously

mine the same quarry, extending the most sustained strands of the *Confessions*. Through all three pieces, De Quincey maintains that the formative experiences of his early life, catalysed by the effects of opium, determined the fantastic content of his dream visions. He thus followed closely in the footsteps of his beloved Wordsworth, who held that youth was a state of purity and receptivity whereas age was youth's pale shadow. But De Quincey also anticipated some of the most influential insights of Sigmund Freud, who argued several generations later that recurrent patterns in dreams originate in unresolved conflicts from the individual's early development. The relationship between these entities – the experiences of youth, the dreaming mind and opium – is the organizing framework of all three essays. To call it 'organizing' is perhaps misleading, however, for it is the unpredictable, even chaotic interaction between the three factors that charts the path, thus foreshadowing the stream-of-consciousness mode of narrative regarded as avant-garde nearly a century later. Thus emerges the gem-like paradox at the heart of this trilogy of essays: not only can digression serve as structure; it in fact does constitute the very structure of human consciousness.

The second member of the trilogy, 'Suspiria de Profundis', seems the least organized, a trait determined as much by the circumstances of its publication as by its author's design. Those circumstances are the stuff of a long and convoluted story, but in short, De Quincey and the staff of *Blackwood's* disagreed about the form in which the piece would appear and how much space it would occupy. Consequently it was abridged, rearranged and concluded before the author regarded it as complete. De Quincey offered various and contradictory versions of what supposedly would have been the essay's scheme had he been allowed to finish it properly, but when preparing his fourteen-volume collected works, *Selections Grave and Gay*, at the end of his life he did not grasp what would seem to have been a golden opportunity to realize that scheme, instead pillaging 'Suspiria' for autobiographical fragments to include in other selections. In sum, De Quincey seems to have intended a series of dream narratives prefaced by an account of the early experiences revisited in the dreams, and what remains appears to be essentially the preface without the main body.

Perhaps the key to understanding the whole lies in the ingenious metaphor that provides the title for one of the sections, the palimpsest. Although it has been erased and overwritten again and again, the ancient sheet of vellum retains traces of all the words ever inscribed upon its surface, much as the mind holds on to vestiges of each past experience. And just as the previous written layers of the palimpsest can be brought into clearer focus with the application of modern chemicals, so can opium vividly restore to the dreaming mind such painful experiences as those recounted in the essay's first section, 'The Affliction of Childhood'. But never is the dreamer able to re-engage or resolve the traumas thus relived; instead, his past stands before him as an intangible spectre, magnified in the manner of the mirage-like apparition of the Brocken, which provides another section title. Such repeated, impotent encounters with the past beget a chronic melancholy, but that state of mind in turn yields the kind of profound insight available only through intense suffering, leading the author to regard the fantastic 'Levana and our Ladies of Sorrow' as his characteristic muses.

In 'The English Mail-Coach' De Quincey's digressive meditations have a more recognizable core, centring on his memorable experience of riding mail-coaches to and from Oxford when he was a student. The four parts of the piece were originally published by pairs in successive issues of *Blackwood's*, but De Quincey prefaced the second instalment with a note insisting that 'the reader is to understand this present paper . . . as connected with a previous paper on *The English Mail-Coach*', and he subsumed all four sections under the current title in *Selections Grave and Gay*, where he also claimed that he had originally intended the essay as a section of 'Suspiria'. (De Quincey's revisions for *Selections Grave and Gay* were often fussy and of questionable merit, as detailed below in relation to the *Confessions*, and 'The English Mail-Coach' is another case in point. Along with the essay's more defined centre comes a clearer organization. De Quincey claimed in 'Suspiria' that music exemplifies 'the confluence of the mighty and terrific discords with the subtle concords', the irresistible attraction between what appear to be opposing forces, and this conception becomes the backbone of 'The English Mail-Coach', surfacing most obviously in the concluding 'Dream-Fugue'. There De Quincey draws a provocative parallel between a dream's amalgamation of antagonistic images and the fugue's braiding of contrasting themes, thus suggesting again the crystalline structures concealed within apparent chaos. Some of the motifs are newly introduced, such as the mail-coach itself, which was the state-of-the-art conveyance in De Quincey's student days and the gold standard of speed. Riding atop the coach, according to De Quincey, one could not only experience the eponymous 'Glory of Motion' but also bask in the mail's grand duty and privilege of announcing British victories during the Napoleonic Wars. These become the chief themes of the first two sections, 'The English Mail-Coach' and 'Going Down with Victory'. The latter sections, 'The Vision of Sudden Death' and 'Dream-Fugue', deal with the darker side of the mail-coach's sublime speed, recounting near-disastrous collisions and the nightmares in which they subsequently resurfaced.

Throughout the essay, dreams also incorporate motifs already familiar from the *Confessions* and 'Suspiria'. Recalling the crocodiles with their 'cancerous kisses' that plagued the opium-eater's dreams in the *Confessions*, for instance, the intimidating coachman re-emerges in the mail-coach passenger's dreams 'with the form of a crocodile', exemplifying again 'the horrid inoculation upon each other of incompatible natures' – the one from England, the other emerging from the vast Orient of the author's imagination. The innocent young girl repeatedly menaced by the mail-coach throughout the 'Dream-Fugue' echoes the tragically lost Ann of the *Confessions*, the prematurely dead child-sister from the opening of 'Suspiria' and the young girl 'under a cloud of affliction' from its end. And opium's pivotal role is clear throughout: it is 'the taking of laudanum', says the 'Mail-Coach' narrator, that 'drew my attention to the fact that this coachman was a monster', and likewise in 'Suspiria' 'the grandeur of recovered life' emerges 'under the separate and the concurring inspirations of opium'.

De Quincey's final contribution to the genre of addict autobiography he originated came in 1856 in the form of an extensive revision of the original *Confessions* for *Selections Grave and Gay*. Critics will always disagree regarding whether an author's first or last words on a work are more authoritative, and the debate is all the more complicated in the arena of Romanticism, given that the patriarch of British Romanticism himself, Wordsworth, contradictorily prized both 'the spontaneous overflow of powerful feelings' and 'emotion recollected in tranquility'.[2] But even De Quincey was ambivalent towards the revision. His motivation in revising had more to do with quantity than quality: the publishers were determined that the *Confessions* would be a single volume of *Selections Grave and Gay* and sell for the same price as the others, and De Quincey felt the expensive book should at least be a thick one. That said, though, it is also true that he had never been satisfied with the piece's patchwork construction. He also seems to have looked back as an old man at the essay he had written as a relatively young one and seen an opportunity to soften, extenuate and otherwise recast his earlier judgements as well as disburden himself of the load of self-justification and philosophical speculation that remained within him.

The 1856 alterations comprise extensive additions and fussy expansions of already existing material. The chief focus of the newly added prose is a fuller account of the author's early life, which in 1856 fills nearly four times the space it did in 1821. Shadowy characters from the original are not only named in the revision but are often the subjects of mini-biographies, and many who had been summarily criticized in 1821 are lengthily excused in 1856. Many of the new additions, though, are questionably relevant. The charming tendency to digress apparent in the *London Magazine* becomes unnerving in *Selections Grave and Gay*, as the narrative repeatedly halts to make way for rambling disquisitions on subjects ranging from the opium use of contemporaries to the art of conversation. Sometimes De Quincey relegated these distracting musings to footnotes, but that was only when they were so wide of the subject at hand that he could not otherwise tie them in, and of these dozens of new notes several fill more than a page. Also, De Quincey's prose style had become more baroque in the decades since his *London Magazine* days, and he stretched several existing passages into rococo ramblings. An especially illustrative pair of examples is pinpointed by Ian Jack in his article 'De Quincey Revises his Confessions'.[3] Here is the 1821 original:

I have often been asked, how I first came to be a regular opium-eater; and have suffered, very unjustly, in the opinion of my acquaintance, from being reputed to have brought upon myself all the sufferings which I shall have to record, by a long course of indulgence in this practice purely for the sake of creating an artificial state of pleasurable excitement. This, however, is a misrepresentation of my case.

And the parallel passage as it appeared in 1856:

I have often been asked – how it was, and through what series of steps, that I became an opium-eater. Was it gradually, tentatively, mistrustingly, as one goes down a shelving beach into a deepening sea, and with a knowledge from the first of the dangers lying on that path; half-courting those dangers, in fact, whilst seeming to defy them? Or was it, secondly, in pure ignorance of such dangers, under the misleadings of mercenary fraud? Since oftentimes lozenges, for the relief of pulmonary affections, found their efficacy upon the opium which they contain, upon this, and this only, though clamorously disavowing so suspicious an alliance: and under such treacherous disguises, multitudes are seduced into a dependency which they had not foreseen upon a drug which they had not known; not known even by name, or by sight: and thus the case is not rare – that the chain of abject slavery is first detected when it has inextricably wound itself about the constitutional system. Thirdly, and lastly, was it [*Yes*, by passionate anticipation, I answer, before the question is finished] – was it on a sudden, overmastering impulse derived from bodily anguish? Loudly I repeat, *Yes*; loudly and indignantly – as in answer to a wilful calumny.

It is not difficult to see, then, how the revision stretched to twice the length of the original. Readers have almost unanimously agreed that the 1856 alterations clog the narrative flow and obscure what coherence the original had to offer.

Critical reception of the *Confessions* and its sequels has varied over the ages. When it first appeared in the *London Magazine*, the strange piece caused a considerable buzz. Although some balked at the author's apparent egotism and immorality, there was consensus that both the style and subject matter were remarkably original. Following the publication of the first book edition, the *Confessions* attracted even more notice from both critics and copycats (an anonymous *Advice to Opium-Eaters*, for instance, followed closely in 1823). An unsigned notice in the *Eclectic Review*, another literary miscellany, impugned De Quincey's credibility because he used opium excessively. At least one doctor expressed concern that readers would be tempted to follow the opium-eater's potentially dangerous example. (The medical profession's response to De Quincey is a subject unto itself, about which more in a moment.) After his initial fifteen minutes of fame, however, De Quincey receded from the limelight into the subcultural shadows for a whole generation. Although the opium-eater remained something of an idol for would-be Romantic visionaries, the fifth edition of the *Confessions* (1845) was not published until nearly two decades after the fourth (1826). And despite the reams of essays De Quincey produced during those years for *Blackwood's* and *Tait's Edinburgh Magazine* (a miscellany in the mould of *Blackwood's*) and a small but devoted following in the United States, he attracted almost no critical attention in print.

Following the appearance of both the fifth edition and the two sequels to the *Confessions*, however, De Quincey's popular fortunes climbed and he never strayed beyond the corner of the public eye until after the First World War. The 1850s saw the publication of two separate multivolume collected works in both Britain and the United States and a concomitant burst of literary criticism. The watershed separating those who loved De Quincey's prose style from those who hated it was the radically subjective point of view inherent in De Quincey's brand of confessional autobiography. Some respondents revered 'each personal pronoun [as] an algebraic symbol of great and general truths' while others scorned his prose as 'steeped in egotism' or 'haunted by the fiend of subjectivity'.[4] Previous misgivings that the opium-eater's example might spur others to adopt his habit were transmuted into vague fears of a more comprehensive contamination: a reviewer for the *Dublin University Magazine* both embraced and shunned De Quincey's style as a 'figured Babylonian robe . . . possibly plague-tainted'.

Twentieth-century literary critics typically treated De Quincey's essays as specimens of late Romanticism, emphasizing their similarities to the poetry of Lord Byron and Percy Bysshe Shelley, for instance. But since De Quincey's works are in prose rather than verse, they rarely rose above a second-class citizenship in the predominantly poetic canon of Romantic literature until the late twentieth century, when critics began to look beyond 'the Six' (Blake, Wordsworth, Coleridge, Byron, Shelley and Keats) and pay long-delayed attention to less enduringly famous but still important writers of the period.

Unlike many of these 'minor' figures, however, De Quincey had long enjoyed a sort of cult status as one of the fathers of 'drug literature'. Although his huge output ultimately included essays in literary criticism ('On the Knocking at the Gate in Macbeth' is often anthologized), satire ('On Murder Considered as One of the Fine Arts' remains one of the most engaging and ironic critiques of popular sensationalism), philosophy, economics and political commentary as well as several works of fiction, De Quincey's claim to fame has always rested most heavily upon his three related essays about his opium experiences, with the *Confessions* standing consistently at the head of the list. Apart from its literary status, the *Confessions* led a parallel life as supposed evidence in various ongoing debates. During the nineteenth century, it was marshalled as authoritative testimony in court cases regarding the impact of regular opium use upon longevity, cited as reliable data regarding opium consumption among Midland labourers and offered in medical literature as a compilation of clinical observations. It is ironic that the *Confessions* should have enjoyed such a robust life as representative testimony, given that the most recurrent negative criticisms indicted the author as a self-involved eccentric.

Whatever one's ultimate critical judgement of these works, however, there can be little doubt that the author was indeed idiosyncratic as well as somewhat narcissistic. Certainly he himself
would have agreed with that assessment, as it was his own inner-
most consciousness he explicitly sought to present and analyse.

THE CHILD IS FATHER OF THE MAN

An author's biography is always potentially interesting to
readers, but it is even more than that in the case of De Quincey,
for autobiography is at the heart of his best-remembered
writings. He was born on 15 August 1785, the fourth child and
second son of a prosperous Manchester textile merchant, and
christened Thomas Penson Quincey. His mother added the 'De'
later and Thomas kept it even after she had dropped it, claiming
it made the name sound more aristocratic. A sickly and pam-
pered child, he never exceeded five feet in height, and his unusual
smallness was the first thing most observers noted about him.
He spent his childhood on the family estate outside Manchester,
enjoying all the cultural advantages of the rising middle class.
The privileges of his boyhood included an abundance of what
was an even greater luxury then than now, books, and young
Thomas devoured them with astonishing speed and comprehen-
sion. In later life he was at least as addicted to books as he
was to opium, often going hungry in order to buy more and
ultimately collecting so many that they overflowed his cottage
in Grasmere.

For most of Thomas's youth, his father was away in warmer
climes nursing the tuberculosis that finally killed him, and
Thomas, left with only a cold and stern mother, attached himself
all the more tenaciously to his sisters and nursemaids. The death
of his eldest sister when he was seven years old was the first
great calamity of his life. His vivid memories of her death
chamber form the core of 'Suspiria de Profundis', and traumatic
separation from a nurturing female companion is a recurrent
motif in his autobiographical essays (his account in the *Confessions* of the lasting pain he suffered after inadvertently losing

track of his friend Ann is another notable case in point). Less traumatic was the death in the following year of the father he had barely known. Prosperous and prudent to the end, the elder Thomas Quincey made ample provision for the family he left behind and appointed his wife and four of his most trusted associates as official guardians to the Quincey children. After several years of private tutoring, young Thomas commenced a first-rate institutional education at Bath Grammar School when the family moved to the fashionable spa in 1796. Here Thomas manifested two traits that were to define him henceforth: his superior scholarship, especially a precocious facility with languages, and his disarming charm and tact. Almost everyone who commented on De Quincey in later years remarked upon his extreme politeness (immediately after noting his diminutive size; his intellect was, of course, the reason they bothered to comment on him in the first place). Although it was an asset in several obvious respects, De Quincey's exceptional intelligence also proved a liability in his early years. It ultimately earned the respect of his peers, but only after a period of alienation. These circumstances contributed to Thomas's sense of distance from those around him, which was initially discomfiting but which he grew to treasure as the lot of the 'pariah'. As a disgruntled seventeen-year-old at Manchester Grammar School, De Quincey discovered the cornerstone of English Romanticism, Lyrical Ballads, initially published in 1798 as the joint effort of William Wordsworth and Samuel Taylor Coleridge but associated more and more exclusively in subsequent editions with Wordsworth. De Quincey's passionate conversion to the Romantic sensibility rendered the factory-blackened atmosphere of Manchester even more oppressive and the pragmatic counsel of his evangelical mother and his guardians more irksome. He begged to be allowed to leave Manchester, either to attempt admission to a university or to study independently at home until he was eighteen. When his guardians persistently refused, he impetuously ran away to ramble through Wales.

In these solitary wanderings, De Quincey exercised his new-found Romantic sensibility and solidified his sense of himself as an outcast. Although he was not initially as estranged from

family and friends as he suggests in the original *Confessions* (he
was caught before leaving England and given grudging parental
consent and a meagre allowance), he ultimately chose to cut off
communication, forgo his allowance and truncate his planned
sojourn in Wales to hide out in London. His reasons for this
decision are obscure to say the least; he seems to have reached
an agreement with his guardians, so there was no clear need to
avoid them, and he would have been financially worse off in
London than in Wales even with his slim allowance, let alone
without it. This latter fact at least was clear to him: his first act
upon reaching the metropolis was to seek out a moneylender,
which promptly sank him into seemingly endless negotiations
via a shady lawyer in Soho who went by the probably assumed
name of Brunell (he resurfaces in both the *Confessions* and
'Suspiria'). When the protracted process consumed the last of
Thomas's already strained resources, Brunell allowed him to
stay in his dilapidated house in Greek Street in Soho, where
Thomas befriended a mysterious waif who seemed to live there,
possibly Brunell's illegitimate daughter.

The suffering associated with this period in the *Confessions*
was probably quite real, despite De Quincey's penchant for
heightened drama; the plight of a nearly penniless adolescent in
London of 1802 would have been a dire one. It clearly was so
in the case of De Quincey's most fondly remembered friend of
this period, the teenaged Ann, who fended off starvation as a
prostitute in Oxford Street. De Quincey claimed to have hovered
so near starvation himself during this period as to do permanent
damage to his digestive system, which he frequently offered as
the reason he took to regular use of opium years later. The real
mystery is why he chose to endure such hardship for so long
when he could easily have ended it with a word to his guardians.
But De Quincey often evinced a perversely self-destructive
streak, a paradoxical drive to demonstrate his will by voluntarily
submitting to miserable circumstances if not actively courting
them.

After more complex negotiations with both moneylenders
and his guardians, Thomas was uneasily reconciled with his
family and settled down enough to enter Worcester College,

Oxford, late in 1803. But ultimately more important to the course of his future life, he also made contact in that year with William Wordsworth by means of a worshipful but impressive letter begging for the honour of the poet's friendship. Wordsworth replied, inviting De Quincey to visit him at his Lake District home at Grasmere. Although Thomas could not immediately accept the offer, one of the great dreams of his youth had been realized: he had laid the groundwork for friendly relations with his idol and thus was born a relationship that was to exercise a powerful force upon the course of his life. De Quincey was reluctant for several years to meet the object of his reverence face to face, but he finally journeyed to Grasmere late in 1807, where he soon became a fixture in the Wordsworth household and assisted the great poet in his work. He was so woven into the family circle for a time that he was even entrusted with the education of the Wordsworths' daughter Kate, a somewhat awkward toddler of whom De Quincey was passionately fond. Her death before her fourth birthday in 1812 was another of the crushing blows of De Quincey's life, as he recounts in both the *Confessions* and 'Suspiria'.

In 1809, he moved into the Wordsworths' former home, the cottage at Town End (later known as Dove Cottage), and lived there for more than a decade. It was during this time that De Quincey met and courted a young local woman, Margaret Simpson. There was much scandal in Grasmere when she bore him a son in 1816 and most of De Quincey's friends regarded him as ruined when he married her the following year, though the marriage ultimately proved a happy one. De Quincey's personal relationship with the Wordsworth circle gradually soured for many reasons, including their disapproval of his opium habit, but he never lost his admiration for Wordsworth's poetry, even if he eventually came to find some fault with the man himself.

Besides his friendship with Wordsworth, the other profoundly influential relationship De Quincey formed during his Oxford days was with opium, whose psychoactive properties he first noted and began to enjoy when he took it on the recommendation of a fellow Worcester student for pain in his face. While at

Oxford, De Quincey managed to spend a good deal of time elsewhere, including London, where he discovered the joys of listening to opera and wandering the streets while under the influence of laudanum (opium dissolved in alcohol; see the Appendix for more detailed information about opiates). De Quincey's eventual habituation to the drug has been blamed upon as many of his misfortunes as it has been blamed for. It is true that, like his fellow opium-addicted writer and sometime friend Samuel Taylor Coleridge, De Quincey never quite fulfilled the extraordinary promise of his youth – at least not to his own satisfaction or that of his family and friends. Although he always dreamed of being a significant philosopher in the mould of Immanuel Kant, whose works deeply influenced his thought, he dragged out most of his adult life as a short-deadline magazine contributor on the run from creditors. But given that our under-standing of the phenomena subsumed under the rubric of 'addic-tion' is still far from perfect, it is difficult to say what in this whole drama was cause, what was effect, and what was neither.

There are only a few things we can say for certain about how De Quincey's opium habit fitted into his life. First, he took massive daily doses of laudanum and found it impossible to stop doing so until his death at seventy-four, a ripe old age in the mid-nineteenth century. Second, opium was both the subject and the inspiration for his most enduring works. De Quincey wrote an enormous number of prose pieces during his life, but the ones for which he is most remembered, and those that made the biggest splash in his own time, are the ones that most conspicuously address the consciousness-altering properties of opium. In order to understand opium's role in De Quincey's life and work, though, one must first understand its role in the culture of his day, a role that was in turn shaped significantly by De Quincey's work and its reception. The changing status of opium in nineteenth-century Britain is outlined in the Appendix. And one of the most telling examples of De Quincey's particular impact on that changing status is his vexed relationship with the medical professions.

THE DOCTORS VS. DE QUINCEY

With their increasing investment in the control of opium (see the Appendix), medical professionals began in the latter third of the century to perceive competing voices from outside the profession that had previously gone all but unnoticed. One of the most significant of these was that of De Quincey himself. Already the recognized popular authority on opium use since the early 1820s, De Quincey published his revision of *Confessions of an English Opium-Eater* in 1856, just as medical professionals were grasping for more control of opium. Even though De Quincey's experience was of what he dubbed 'opium-*eating*' rather than hypodermic injection of morphine (more precisely, his particular habit was opium-*drinking*, as he tippled laudanum), his growth in popularity and authority chronologically paralleled the evolution of hypodermic morphine injection, smoothing the public's intuitive transfer of his expertise from opium ingestion to opiate injection.

The *Confessions* appeared initially in 1821, just as morphine was making its way into mainstream medical practice, and the 'Opium-Eater', as the anonymous author styled himself in subsequent bylines, became both a cult idol for would-be visionaries and the de facto popular authority on all matters related to opium. Such reverence for the sage-like Opium-Eater was by no means confined to the lay public, either. Although at least one doctor spoke out early against the dangerous example the Opium-Eater set for potential imitators,[5] his regular appearances in medical discussions of opium during the first two-thirds of the century were more frequently as an authority on all imaginable aspects of the subject – from the highest endurable dose to affective responses under different circumstances to the rate of usage among Midland labourers. As one doctor attested in 1845, 'the law of his self-experience is paramount in the profession' and his 'is the only modern instance . . . of a non-medical writer submitting, upon a medical subject, an opinion which the whole profession has acknowledged as orthodox testimony'.[6]

Such veneration was not common among doctors late in the century, however, as a constellation of circumstances in addition to professional medicine's increased investment in the control of opium had rendered De Quincey a significant threat to medical authority. When he had claimed in 1821 that everything doctors had written about opium was 'lies! lies! lies!' because 'their experimental knowledge of its action is none at all', he was firing scattershot at a diffuse population of practitioners who did not have a particularly high stake in being right about the issue. But thirty-five years later, when he claimed in his revision not only that he alone pronounced 'the doctrine of the true church on the subject of opium' but also that he was that church's 'Pope (consequently infallible), and self-appointed *legate a latere* to all degrees of latitude and longitude', he was throwing down a gauntlet before a powerful and nearly unified profession with far more at stake than mere one-upmanship.

The consequent late-century medical opposition to De Quincey is well represented by physician Patrick Hehir's declaration in *Opium: Its Physical, Moral, and Social Effects* (1894) that 'the opinion of one man is not likely to be of much use in settling a question connected with a habit practised by millions of people' and that the 'language of the opium-eater must ... be read with that amount of allowance which we naturally concede to poetical writers, who aim at effect in the language they select, and are not afraid of the startling and uncommon'.[7] But even as doctors lined up to declare De Quincey wrong, they also tried to claim the authority so long granted him by the general public. This paradoxical agenda is especially well illustrated in the career of the American physician H. H. Kane: in 1881 he accused De Quincey of 'hand[ing] down to succeeding generations a mass of ingenious lies' and warned that 'such a book as [the *Confessions*] would create a longing and open the way to a road that has a certain ending in a life's bondage',[8] but these reservations did not deter him less than two decades later from calling his own programme for curing opiate addiction the 'De Quincey Home Method'.[9]

OPIATES AND THE MASSES

Prior to the rise of the public health movement in the 1830s, there was little or no institutionalized distinction between medical use and what might now be called recreational use of opium. Before the *Confessions*' publication, recreational use had been represented mainly in terms of exotic opium-eating and opium-smoking Orientals. In fact De Quincey's insistence on the adjective 'English' was probably meant in part to pre-empt the 'Oriental' that would otherwise have been automatically attached to 'Opium-Eater' (see the Appendix for discussion of the association between opium and the Orient). But the 1830s saw rising concern over opium poisonings, the practice of 'infant doping' and the supposed recreational use of opium among the working classes. The predominantly middle-class public health movement was most vocal about these supposed abuses, which were typically tagged as working-class evils. Concern seems to have been motivated largely by increasing class tensions in a recently industrialized society ever more apparently splitting into Disraeli's 'two nations'. This is not to say, however, that any of these condemned uses of opium was in fact confined to the working classes. Under any of the available criteria, De Quincey's practice of taking a dose of laudanum on Saturday nights to enhance his enjoyment of the opera, for instance, should have conspicuously qualified as recreational use.

The tendency to find the same behaviours fascinating in De Quincey and disgusting in the labourer may be due to a belief that De Quincey's opium use enhanced his literary talents and was therefore justified in a way that ostensibly did not apply to uneducated workers. But this only betrays once again a fairly transparent prejudice that De Quincey himself often shared. He famously proclaimed that 'if a man whose talk is of oxen should become an opium-eater, the probability is that (if he is not too dull to dream at all) he will dream of oxen', and he associated working-class opium use with already well-established negative stereotypes about drunkenness. 'The immediate occasion of [the prevalence of opium-eating among the working classes],' he says in the *Confessions*, 'was the lowness of wages, which, at that time, would not allow them to indulge in ale or spirits.' But he was inconsistent in his attitude, blurring class distinctions when he was justifying his own habit on the basis of its wide practice, in which case both he and the 'work-people' of Manchester belonged to the 'class of opium-eaters'.

There is plenty of reason to believe that such blurring was warranted, that habitual opium use was also common further up the socio-economic ladder. For verification, one need only scan the list of middle-class celebrities who were lifelong users: the parliamentarian and abolitionist William Wilberforce; the pioneer photographer and scion of a famous pottery dynasty, Tom Wedgwood; the novelist Wilkie Collins; and poets George Crabbe and Francis Thompson. Known frequent users who may or may not have been dependent at one time or another include Keats, Shelley, Byron, Sir Walter Scott, Elizabeth Barrett Browning, Jane Welsh Carlyle (wife of Thomas Carlyle) and Dickens. Robert Clive, Indian imperialist extraordinaire, and Lizzie Siddal, artist and model of the Pre-Raphaelite circle, both died of opium poisoning and it was widely presumed they committed suicide. The supposedly working-class evil of infant-doping was also a frequent if less publicized resort of more affluent parents; numerous opium-based preparations such as Godfrey's Cordial and Mrs Winslow's Soothing Syrup were staples of middle-class medicine chests throughout the century.

THE PHARMACOLOGICAL MUSE

It was also in the nineteenth century that opium became a mainstay of the bohemian image. The drug had cropped up now and then in artistic circles before De Quincey, but it was not generally considered the exotic agent of fantastic dreams until Coleridge published his famous preface to 'Kubla Khan' in 1816. There he claimed that several hundred lines of startling Oriental imagery had sprung fully formed into his mind upon his taking 'an anodyne' (rightly understood by all readers as a dose of opium) but had faded again when business interrupted his reverie. In the same volume, Coleridge also published 'The Pains of Sleep', a less glamorous portrayal of opium withdrawal as a state of frenzied paranoia. De Quincey more explicitly merged Oriental exotica and persecution mania in his *Confessions*, warning that the pleasures and pains of opium were inextricable from one another. But regardless of his ostensible intentions, his cautionary depictions of opium's pains usually failed to counterbalance his alluring representations of its pleasures, and the drug-induced sublime became a pillar of the post-Romantic aesthetic.

De Quincey's disciples were many and far-flung. In the United States, Edgar Allan Poe was the most successful of his admirers, clearly manifesting De Quinceyan style and content in phantasmagoric tales spun by confessional first-person narrators who often declare their opium use. Of less lasting fame were more slavish imitations such as William Blair's 'An Opium Eater in America' (1842) and Fitz Hugh Ludlow's *The Hashish Eater: Being Passages from the Life of a Pythagorean* (1857). The latter, as the title suggests, extends the De Quinceyan mode into the realm of the second most famous Oriental drug to make its mark on the West. On the Continent, the first knock-off of the *Confessions* to achieve lasting renown was not a literary but a musical composition: Hector Berlioz's 'Symphonie Fantastique' (1830) takes as its programme the laudanum-tippling composer's obsessive pursuit of his beloved through a series of fantastic dreamscapes, arguably rendering Berlioz the prototype of the visionary musician-addict who pervaded the twentieth-century jazz scene. De Quincey's more familiar legacy across the Channel, though, was French Symbolism. Born in the year of the *Confessions*' initial publication and first feeling its influence via the works of Poe, Charles Baudelaire borrowed liberally from De Quincey in *Les Paradis artificiels* (*Artificial Paradises*, 1860), which in turn influenced the next generation of French poets including Verlaine and Rimbaud.

Although De Quincey's influence was increasingly mediated through such channels as Poe and the French Symbolists, it can be clearly discerned throughout the culture of the twentieth century as well. The 'Beats', who emerged in the United States after the Second World War, evinced the Opium-Eater's influence in several ways, from Jack Kerouac's benzedrine-driven first-person narratives to William S. Burroughs's memoirs of the quasi-Oriental Manhattan subculture of 'junk'. The apartment of one of Burroughs's typical junkies 'looks like a chop suey joint', sporting 'a china Buddha with a votive candle in front of it'; groups of addicts swarm around a dealer 'like a crowd of Asiatic beggars'; and their archetype has a figurative 'place of origin [in] the Near East, probably Egypt'.[10] The colourful narrative of Burroughs's *Junky* (1953) gives way to the surreal heroin-drenched visions of his *Naked Lunch* (1959), recognizable descendants of De Quincey's dream encounters with Malays running amok, cancerous crocodiles and chattering parakeets.

Popular musicians have returned again and again to both De Quinceyan Orientalism and the idea – inspired though not endorsed by De Quincey – that artistic capacity is expanded by psychoactive drugs. The role of marijuana and opium in the creative process of jazz's early days is clearly documented by 'Mezz' Mezzrow, who compares a 1920s opium-smoking party to 'a scene straight out of the Arabian Nights, with the thieves and princes disguised in pinchback sports jackets',[11] and the rampancy of heroin addiction among the postwar bepop pioneers is a byword. In the 1960s those drugs were joined by LSD as major forces behind experimental rock, which spawned a subculture pervaded by a De Quinceyan conglomeration of Oriental imagery capable of transforming a San Francisco ballroom into 'a dope den with marijuana smoke swirling in the air' and peopled by dancers 'entranced by the Oriental tuning' of psychedelic rock anthems.[12]

The persistence of these ideas and images has led some readers to conclude that there is an essential property of opium itself that begets the patterns De Quincey described.[13] But the same patterns have also been associated with other very different drugs such as LSD and marijuana in the examples cited above, at least diluting the force of such an argument. Other similar examples abound. Experimenting with LSD, for instance, the critic and novelist Anaïs Nin saw 'the most delicate Persian designs' and 'murals which . . . were Oriental, fragile, and complete, but then . . . became actual Oriental cities, with pagodas, temples, rich Chinese gold and red altars, and Balinese music'.[14] One might attempt to extend the argument about chemical essences to account for this, to hypothesize that opium and LSD act similarly upon the brain and thus breed similar constellations of imagery and ideas. But other examples militate against such a hypothesis. The chemist who first synthesized LSD, for instance, gathered several colleagues at a Swiss castle to experiment with the new substance and found one dressed in 'a long, broad, dark blue striped kaftan-like garment . . . from Egypt' and another in 'a highly embroidered mandarin gown'.[15] The Oriental ambiance here clearly had nothing to do with the effects of LSD as neither man had yet experienced the drug, and it could have even less to do with the effects of opium.

The persistence of the patterns without regard to the specific chemical stimuli in question strongly suggests that much of what is commonly attributed to the effects of the drugs themselves has more to do with the cultural heritage surrounding them, a tradition that began with the essays in this volume. Writing at a particular moment in the evolution of medical therapy, the British Empire and confessional narrative, one highly imaginative and educated individual planted a seed of association between a psychoactive Oriental commodity and its geographic origin. That seed has taken root, blossomed and spawned new seedlings in the culture ever since. Thus Thomas De Quincey has been and continues to be a significant influence upon artists and audiences who might not even know his name.

NOTES

1. Thomas De Quincey, *Recollections of the Lakes and Lake Poets*, ed. David Wright (Penguin: Harmondsworth, 1970), p. 33.
2. William Wordsworth, 'Preface to the Second Edition of *Lyrical Ballads* (1800)', in *Selected Poems and Prefaces*, ed. Jack Stillinger (Houghton Mifflin: Boston, 1965), p. 460.

3. Ian Jack, 'De Quincey Revises His *Confessions*', *PMLA* 72 (1957), 134–5.

4. Respectively, *Eclectic Review* (1854), *Athenaeum* (1859), *London Quarterly Review* (1857) (quoted in Julian North, *De Quincey Reviewed: Thomas De Quincey's Critical Reception, 1821–1994* (Camden House: Columbia, S. Carolina, 1997, pp. 21–3). As North points out, the critics who scorned De Quincey's 'egotism' were in powerful company during the 1850s and thereafter, falling in line with the rising tide of anti-subjective aesthetics prominently represented by Matthew Arnold's preface to his *Poems* (1853).

5. Writing in the *Morning Chronicle* (22 May 1823), a doctor claimed to know of at least four imitators nearly poisoning themselves, and he damned the *Confessions* as 'of universal ill tendency' (quoted in Grevel Lindop's *The Opium-Eater: A Life of Thomas De Quincey* (Dent: London; Taplinger: New York, 1981), p. 248).

6. From an anonymous untitled article in *Medical Times and Gazette* 12 (1845), 128.

7. Patrick Hehir, *Opium: Its Physical, Moral, and Social Effects* (Baillière, Tindall & Cox: London, 1894), pp. 8–9, 264–6.

8. H. H. Kane, *Drugs That Enslave: The Opium, Morphine, Chloral and Hashisch Habits* (Presley, Blakiston: Philadelphia, 1881), pp. 22, 33.

9. Virginia Berridge and Griffith Edwards, *Opium and the People: Opiate Use in Nineteenth-Century England* (Yale University Press: New Haven, Conn., 1987), p. 163. Ironically, Kane also made a name for himself in another vein of the De Quinceyan tradition as a first-hand reporter on drug experiences; his 'A Hashish-House in New York: The Curious Adventures of an Individual Who Indulged in a Few Pipefuls of the Narcotic Hemp' (*Harper's Monthly* 67 (1883)), pp. 944–9, has become a cult classic.

10. William S. Burroughs, *Junky* (Penguin: Harmondsworth, 1977), pp. 5, 58, 111–12.

11. Milton 'Mezz' Mezzrow and Bernard Wolfe, *Really the Blues* (Random House: New York, 1946), p. 97.

12. John Densmore, *Riders on the Storm: My Life With Jim Morrison and the Doors* (Doubleday: New York, 1990), pp. 108–9.

13. This scenario is elaborated by M. H. Abrams in *The Milk of Paradise: The Effects of Opium Visions on the Works of De Quincey, Crabbe, Francis Thompson and Coleridge* (Harvard: Cambridge, Mass., 1934) and Alethea Hayter in *Opium and the Romantic Imagination* (University of California: Berkeley, 1968).

14. Anaïs Nin, 'from *The Diary of Anaïs Nin, 1947–1955*', in *The*

Drug User: Documents, 1840–1960, ed. John Strausbaugh and Donald Blaise (Blast Books: New York, 1991), p. 143.

15. Albert Hofmann, 'from *LSD: My Problem Child*', in *The Drug User*, ed. Strausbaugh and Blaise, p. 80.

Further Reading

WORKS

Lindop, Grevel (gen. ed.), *The Works of Thomas De Quincey*, 21 vols. (Pickering and Chatto: London and Brookfield, Vermont, 2000–)

Masson, David (ed.), *The Collected Writings of Thomas De Quincey*, 14 vols. (A. & C. Black: London, 1896–7)

Wright, David (ed.), [De Quincey,] *Recollections of the Lakes and Lake Poets* (Penguin: Harmondsworth, 1970)

BIOGRAPHY, REMINISCENCES

Eaton, Horace Ainsworth, *Thomas De Quincey: A Biography* (Oxford University Press: New York, 1936)

Findlay, John Ritchie, *Personal Recollections of Thomas De Quincey* (Adam & Charles Black: Edinburgh, 1886)

Lindop, Grevel, *The Opium-Eater: A Life of Thomas De Quincey* (Dent: London; Taplinger: New York, 1981)

Page, H. A. [A. H. Japp], *Thomas De Quincey: His Life and Writings, with Unpublished Correspondence* (Charles Scribner's Sons: New York, 1877)

CRITICISM

Barrell, John, *The Infection of Thomas De Quincey: A Psycho-pathology of Imperialism* (Yale University Press: New Haven, Conn., 1991)

Clej, Alina, *A Genealogy of the Modern Self: Thomas De Quincey and the Intoxication of Writing* (Stanford University Press: Stanford, Calif., 1995)

De Luca, V. A., *Thomas De Quincey: The Prose of Vision* (University of Toronto Press: Toronto, 1980)

Jack, Ian, 'De Quincey Revises His *Confessions*', *PMLA* 72 (1957), 122–46

Leask, Nigel, ' "Murdering One's Double": Thomas De Quincey and S. T. Coleridge, Autobiography, Opium and Empire in "Confessions of an English Opium Eater" and "Biographia Literaria" ', in *British Romantic Writers and the East: Anxieties of Empire* (Cambridge University Press: Cambridge, 1992), pp. 170–228

Lindop, Grevel, 'De Quincey and the Cursed Crocodile', *Essays in Criticism* 45/2 (April 1995), 121–40

—, 'De Quincey's "Immortal Druggist" and Wordsworth's "Power of Music" ', *Notes and Queries* 41 (1994), 341–3

—, 'De Quincey's Wordsworthian Quotations', *Wordsworth Circle* 26 (1995), 58–65

McDonagh, Josephine, *De Quincey's Disciplines* (Clarendon Press: Oxford, 1994)

Morrison, Robert, 'De Quincey and the Opium-Eater's Other Selves', *Romanticism* 5/1 (1999), 87–103

—, 'Opium-Eaters and Magazine Wars: De Quincey and Coleridge in 1821', *Victorian Periodicals Review* 30 (1997), 27–40

North, Julian, *De Quincey Reviewed: Thomas De Quincey's Critical Reception, 1821–1994* (Camden House: Columbia, S. Carolina, 1997)

Roberts, Daniel Sanjiv, 'Exorcising the Malay: Dreams and the Unconscious in Coleridge and De Quincey', *Wordsworth Circle* 24 (1993), 91–6

—, 'De Quincey's Discovery of *Lyrical Ballads*: The Politics of Reading', *Studies in Romanticism* 36 (1997), 511–40

Rzepka, Charles, 'De Quincey and the Malay: Dove Cottage Idolatry', *Wordsworth Circle* 24 (1993), 180–85

—, *Sacramental Commodities: Gift, Text, and the Sublime in De Quincey* (University of Massachusetts Press, Amherst, 1995)

Snyder, Robert Lance (ed.), *Thomas De Quincey: Bicentenary Studies* (University of Oklahoma Press: Norman, 1985)

DRUGS IN
NINETEENTH-CENTURY CULTURE

Berridge, Virginia, and Griffith Edwards, *Opium and the People: Opiate Use in Nineteenth-Century England* (Yale University Press: New Haven, Conn., 1987)

Booth, Martin, *Opium: A History* (St Martin's Press: New York, 1996)

Courtwright, David, *Forces of Habit: Drugs and the Making of the Modern World* (Harvard University Press: Cambridge, Mass., 2001)

Jay, Mike, *Artificial Paradises: A Drugs Reader* (Penguin: London, 1999)

—, *Emperors of Dreams: Drugs in the Nineteenth Century* (Dedalus: Sawtry, Cambs., 2000)

Latimer, Dean, and Jeff Goldberg, *Flowers in the Blood: The Story of Opium* (Franklin Watts: New York, 1981)

Milligan, Barry, *Pleasures and Pains: Opium and the Orient in Nineteenth-Century British Culture* (University Press of Virginia: Charlottesville, 1995)

Parssinen, Terry M., *Secret Passions, Secret Remedies: Narcotic Drugs in British Society 1820–1930* (Institute for the Study of Human Issues: Philadelphia, 1983)

Strausbaugh, John, and Donald Blaise, *The Drug User: Documents 1840–1960* (Blast Books: New York, 1991)

A Note on the Texts

The *Confessions* first appeared anonymously in two parts as 'Confessions of an English Opium-Eater: Being an Extract from the Life of a Scholar', in the September and October issues of the *London Magazine* for 1821 (vol. IV, pp. 293–312 and 353–79). The first book edition, with very minor revisions, followed from Taylor and Hessey, the publishers of the *London Magazine*, in 1822, and at least six more editions based on that text followed from 1822 to 1854. De Quincey revised the piece for his collected works, *Selections Grave and Gay*, in 1856 and more than doubled its length, predominantly with fussy alterations and distracting digressions. The text reproduced here is that of the original *London Magazine* publication, which critics are nearly unanimous in viewing as the authoritative version. When appropriate, important points about the 1856 revision are discussed in the explanatory notes.

'Suspiria de Profundis' has a tortured textual history, much of which is all but impossible to reconstruct. The key points, though, are that De Quincey and the staff of *Blackwood's* disagreed about the form and length of the piece and De Quincey was dissatisfied with it for the rest of his life. None the less, he bypassed the opportunity to realize his initial vision when revising his works for *Selections Grave and Gay*, choosing instead to incorporate excerpts from 'Suspiria' into other biographical pieces. The version reprinted here appeared in four parts in *Blackwood's Edinburgh Magazine* for March, April, June and July of 1845 (vol. LVII, pp. 269–85, 489–502, 739–51, and vol. LVIII, pp. 43–55).

'The English Mail-Coach' originally appeared in two parts as

'The English Mail-Coach, or the Glory of Motion' and 'The Vision of Sudden Death' in *Blackwood's* for October and December of 1849 (vol. LXVI, pp. 485–500 and 741–55). It too was revised for *Selections Grave and Gay*, but the revision suffers some of the same problems that beset the 1856 version of the *Confessions*, and the original *Blackwood's* version is the one reprinted here. There are a few passages in which the syntax is clearly garbled. One example is the sentence on p. 204 beginning 'Yet Fanny, as the loveliest young woman . . .'. Obviously something has been misplaced or omitted here, but this and other passages were completely recast in the revision. Thus it is impossible to reconstruct De Quincey's intended reading, so the sentence stands as it appears in the original.

Editorial alterations in general have been kept to a minimum. Title details repeated in later magazine instalments of the essays have been omitted. In all three essays, spelling remains unchanged excepting the occasional substitution of '-ize' for '-ise' in such words as 'realize', a point upon which the originals are inconsistent. Obvious and minor typographical errors have also been corrected. Original punctuation has been retained, with the following minor exceptions: double inverted commas have been made consistently single unless they appear in a phrase already within single inverted commas; full points have been removed from terms of address (e.g., Dr, Mr) and are also omitted from kings' numbers (e.g. George III) and some otherwise irregular section headings; dashes have been regularized according to their function, and strings of dashes sometimes marking the end of a section have been replaced with spaces; punctuation after italic words within otherwise roman text has been made consistently roman. De Quincey's own footnotes usually insert short dashes after the initial cue words, and those few that do not conform to this pattern have been regularized here.

De Quincey complained throughout his life about the erroneous typesetting of his frequent quotations of Greek, and he would have corrected such errors if he could have. But he often submitted his work so shortly before the publication deadline that he did not have the luxury of correcting proofs.

Furthermore, the type necessary to reproduce the Greek properly was probably unavailable to the magazine's compositors in many instances. Although we cannot be certain what specific corrections De Quincey would have made, he was an exceptional Greek scholar and almost certainly did not commit some of the errors that appear in the published versions of his works. Consequently, all Greek has been corrected here in accordance with standard orthography.

Confessions of an English Opium-Eater

AND OTHER WRITINGS

CONFESSIONS OF AN
ENGLISH OPIUM-EATER:

Being an Extract from the Life of a Scholar

To the Reader. – I here present you, courteous reader, with the record of a remarkable period in my life: according to my application of it, I trust that it will prove, not merely an interesting record, but, in a considerable degree, useful and instructive. In *that* hope it is, that I have drawn it up: and *that* must be my apology for breaking through that delicate and honourable reserve, which, for the most part, restrains us from the public exposure of our own errors and infirmities. Nothing, indeed, is more revolting to English feelings, than the spectacle of a human being obtruding on our notice his moral ulcers or scars, and tearing away that 'decent drapery,' which time, or indulgence to human frailty, may have drawn over them: accordingly, the greater part of *our* confessions (that is, spontaneous and extra-judicial confessions) proceed from demireps,[1] adventurers, or swindlers: and for any such acts of gratuitous self-humiliation from those who can be supposed in sympathy with the decent and self-respecting part of society, we must look to French literature, or to that part of the German, which is tainted with the spurious and defective sensibility of the French.[2] All this I feel so forcibly, and so nervously am I alive to reproach of this tendency, that I have for many months hesitated about the propriety of allowing this, or any part of my narrative, to come before the public eye, until after my death (when, for many reasons, the whole will be published): and it is not without an anxious review of the reasons, for and against this step, that I have, at last, concluded on taking it.

Guilt and misery shrink, by a natural instinct, from public notice: they court privacy and solitude: and, even in their choice of a grave, will sometimes sequester themselves from the general population of the churchyard, as if declining to claim fellowship with the great family of man, and wishing (in the affecting language of Mr Wordsworth)

> – Humbly to express
> A penitential loneliness.[3]

It is well, upon the whole, and for the interest of us all, that it should be so: nor would I willingly, in my own person, manifest a disregard of such salutary feelings; nor in act or word do anything to weaken them. But, on the one hand, as my self-accusation does not amount to a confession of guilt, so, on the other, it is possible that, if it *did*, the benefit resulting to others, from the record of an experience purchased at so heavy a price, might compensate, by a vast overbalance, for any violence done to the feelings I have noticed, and justify a breach of the general rule. Infirmity and misery do not, of necessity, imply guilt. They approach, or recede from, the shades of that dark alliance, in proportion to the probable motives and prospects of the offender, and the palliations, known or secret, of the offence: in proportion as the temptations to it were potent from the first, and the resistance to it, in act or in effort, was earnest to the last. For my own part, without breach of truth or modesty, I may affirm, that my life has been, on the whole, the life of a philosopher: from my birth I was made an intellectual creature: and intellectual in the highest sense my pursuits and pleasures have been, even from my school-boy days. If opium-eating be a sensual pleasure, and if I am bound to confess that I have indulged in it to an excess, not yet *recorded** of any other man, it is no less true, that I have struggled against this fascinating enthralment with a religious zeal, and have, at length, accomplished what I never yet heard attributed to any other man – have untwisted, almost to its final links, the accursed chain which fettered me.[4] Such a self-conquest may reasonably be set

---

* 'Not yet *recorded*,' I say: for there is one celebrated man[5] of the present day, who, if all be true which is reported of him, has greatly exceeded me in quantity.

off in counterbalance to any kind of degree of self-indulgence. Not to insist, that in my case, the self-conquest was unquestionable, the self-indulgence open to doubts of casuistry, according as that name shall be extended to acts aiming at the bare relief of pain, or shall be restricted to such as aim at the excitement of positive pleasure.

Guilt, therefore, I do not acknowledge: and, if I did, it is possible that I might still resolve on the present act of confession, in consideration of the service which I may thereby render to the whole class of opium-eaters. But who are they? Reader, I am sorry to say, a very numerous class indeed. Of this I became convinced some years ago, by computing, at that time, the number of those in one small class of English society (the class of men distinguished for talents, or of eminent station), who were known to me, directly or indirectly, as opium-eaters; such for instance, as the eloquent and benevolent ——, the late dean of ——; Lord ——; Mr ——, the philosopher; a late under-secretary of state (who described to me the sensation which first drove him to the use of opium, in the very same words as the dean of ——, viz. 'that he felt as though rats were gnawing and abrading the coats of his stomach'); Mr ——; and many others, hardly less known, whom it would be tedious to mention.[6] Now, if one class, comparatively so limited, could furnish so many scores of cases (and *that* within the knowledge of one single inquirer), it was a natural inference, that the entire population of England would furnish a proportionable number. The soundness of this inference, however, I doubted, until some facts became known to me, which satisfied me, that it was not incorrect. I will mention two: 1. Three respectable London druggists, in widely remote quarters of London, from whom I happened lately to be purchasing small quantities of opium, assured me, that the number of *amateur* opium-eaters (as I may term them) was, at this time, immense; and that the difficulty of distinguishing these persons, to whom habit had rendered opium necessary, from such as were purchasing it with a view to suicide, occasioned them daily trouble and disputes.[7] This evidence respected London only. But, 2. (which will possibly surprise the reader more,) some years ago, on passing through

Manchester, I was informed by several cotton-manufacturers, that their work-people were rapidly getting into the practice of opium-eating; so much so, that on a Saturday afternoon the counters of the druggists were strewed with pills of one, two, or three grains, in preparation for the known demand of the evening.[8] The immediate occasion of this practice was the low-ness of wages, which, at that time, would not allow them to indulge in ale or spirits: and, wages rising, it may be thought that this practice would cease: but, as I do not readily believe that any man, having once tasted the divine luxuries of opium, will afterwards descend to the gross and mortal enjoyments of alcohol, I take it for granted,

> That those eat now, who never ate before;
> And those who always ate, now eat the more.[9]

Indeed the fascinating powers of opium are admitted, even by medical writers, who are its greatest enemies: thus, for instance, Awsiter, apothecary to Greenwich-hospital, in his 'Essay on the Effects of Opium' (published in the year 1763), when attempting to explain, why Mead[10] had not been sufficiently explicit on the properties, counteragents, &c. of this drug, expresses himself in the following mysterious terms (φωνᾶντα συνετοῖσι):[11] 'perhaps he thought the subject of too delicate a nature to be made common; and as many people might then indiscriminately use it, it would take from that necessary fear and caution, which should prevent their experiencing the extensive power of this drug: *for there are many properties in it, if universally known, that would habituate the use, and make it more in request with us than the Turks themselves*:[12] the result of which knowledge,' he adds, 'must prove a general misfortune.' In the necessity of this conclusion I do not altogether concur: but upon that point I shall have occasion to speak at the close of my confessions, where I shall present the reader with the *moral* of my narrative.

[PART I]
PRELIMINARY CONFESSIONS

These preliminary confessions, or introductory narrative of the youthful adventures which laid the foundation of the writer's habit of opium-eating in after-life, it has been judged proper to premise, for three several reasons:

1. As forestalling that question, and giving it a satisfactory answer, which else would painfully obtrude itself in the course of the Opium-Confessions – 'How came any reasonable being to subject himself to such a yoke of misery, voluntarily to incur a captivity so servile, and knowingly to fetter himself with such a seven-fold chain?' – a question which, if not somewhere plausibly resolved, could hardly fail, by the indignation which it would be apt to raise as against an act of wanton folly, to interfere with that degree of sympathy which is necessary in any case to an author's purposes.

2. As furnishing a key to some parts of that tremendous scenery which afterwards peopled the dreams of the Opium-eater.

3. As creating some previous interest of a personal sort in the confessing subject, apart from the matter of the confessions, which cannot fail to render the confessions themselves more interesting. If a man 'whose talk is of oxen,'[13] should become an Opium-eater, the probability is, that (if he is not too dull to dream at all) – he will dream about oxen: whereas, in the case before him, the reader will find that the Opium-eater boasteth himself to be a philosopher: and accordingly, that the phantas-magoria of *his* dreams (waking or sleeping, day-dreams or night-dreams) is suitable to one who in that character,

Humani nihil a se alienum putat.[14]

For amongst the conditions which he deems indispensable to the sustaining of any claim to the title of philosopher, is not merely the possession of a superb intellect in its *analytic* functions (in which part of the pretension, however, England can for some generations show but few claimants; at least, he is not aware of any known candidate for this honour who can be styled emphatically *a subtle thinker*, with the exception of *Samuel Taylor Coleridge*, and in a narrower department of thought, with the recent illustrious exception* of *David Ricardo*)[15] – but also on such a constitution of the *moral* faculties, as shall give him an inner eye and power of intuition for the vision and the mysteries of our human nature: *that* constitution of faculties, in short, which (amongst all the generations of men that from the beginning of time have deployed into life, as it were, upon this planet) our English poets have possessed in the highest degree – and Scottish† Professors in the lowest.

I have often been asked, how I first came to be a regular opium-eater; and have suffered, very unjustly, in the opinion of my acquaintance, from being reputed to have brought upon myself all the sufferings which I shall have to record, by a long course of indulgence in this practice purely for the sake of creating an artificial state of pleasurable excitement. This, however, is a misrepresentation of my case. True it is, that for nearly ten years I did occasionally take opium, for the sake of the exquisite pleasure it gave me: but, so long as I took it with this view, I was effectually protected from all material bad consequences, by the necessity of interposing long intervals between the several acts of indulgence, in order to renew the

---

* A third exception[16] might perhaps have been added: and my reason for not adding that exception is chiefly because it was only in his juvenile efforts that the writer whom I allude to, expressly addressed himself to philosophical themes; his riper powers having been all dedicated (on very excusable and very intelligible grounds, under the present direction of the popular mind in England) to criticism and the Fine Arts. This reason apart, however, I doubt whether he is not rather to be considered an acute thinker than a subtle one. It is, besides, a great drawback on his mastery over philosophical subjects, that he has obviously not had the advantage of a regular scholastic education: he has not read Plato in his youth (which most likely was only his misfortune); but neither has he read Kant in his manhood (which is his fault).

† I disclaim any allusion to *existing* professors, of whom indeed I know only one.[17]

pleasurable sensations.[18] It was not for the purpose of creating pleasure, but of mitigating pain in the severest degree, that I first began to use opium as an article of daily diet. In the twenty-eighth year of my age, a most painful affection of the stomach, which I had first experienced about ten years before, attacked me in great strength. This affection had originally been caused by extremities of hunger, suffered in my boyish days. During the season of hope and redundant happiness which succeeded (that is, from eighteen to twenty-four) it had slumbered: for the three following years it had revived at intervals: and now, under unfavourable circumstances, from depression of spirits, it attacked me with a violence that yielded to no remedies but opium. As the youthful sufferings, which first produced this derangement of the stomach, were interesting in themselves, and in the circumstances that attended them, I shall here briefly retrace them.

My father died, when I was about seven years old, and left me to the care of four guardians. I was sent to various schools, great and small; and was very early distinguished for my classical attainments, especially for my knowledge of Greek. At thirteen, I wrote Greek with ease; and at fifteen my command of that language was so great, that I not only composed Greek verses in lyric metres, but could converse in Greek fluently, and without embarrassment – an accomplishment which I have not since met with in any scholar of my times, and which, in my case, was owing to the practice of daily reading off the newspapers into the best Greek I could furnish *extempore*: for the necessity of ransacking my memory and invention, for all sorts and combinations of periphrastic expressions, as equivalents for modern ideas, images, relations of things, &c. gave me a compass of diction which would never have been called out by a dull translation of moral essays, &c. 'That boy,' said one of my masters, pointing the attention of a stranger to me, 'that boy could harangue an Athenian mob, better than you or I could address an English one.' He who honoured me with this eulogy, was a scholar, 'and a ripe and good one:' and of all my tutors, was the only one whom I loved or reverenced. Unfortunately for me (and, as I afterwards learned, to this worthy man's great indignation), I was transferred to the care, first of a blockhead, who was in a perpetual panic, lest I should expose his ignorance; and finally, to that of a respectable scholar,[19] at the head of a great school on an ancient foundation. This man had been appointed to his situation by —— College, Oxford; and was a sound, well-built scholar, but (like most men, whom I have known from that college) coarse, clumsy, and inelegant. A miserable contrast he presented, in my eyes, to the Etonian brilliancy of my favourite master: and besides, he could not disguise from my hourly notice, the poverty and meagreness of his understanding. It is a bad thing for a boy to be, and to know himself, far beyond his tutors, whether in knowledge or in power of mind. This was the case, so far as regarded knowledge at least, not with myself only: for the two boys, who jointly with myself composed the first form, were better Grecians than the head-master, though not more elegant scholars, nor at all more accustomed to sacrifice to the graces. When I first entered, I remember that we read Sophocles; and it was a constant matter of triumph to us, the learned triumvirate of the first forms, to see our 'Archididascalus'[20] (as he loved to be called) conning our lesson before we went up, and laying a regular train, with lexicon and grammar, for blowing up and blasting (as it were) any difficulties he found in the choruses; whilst *we* never condescended to open our books, until the moment of going up, and were generally employed in writing epigrams upon his wig, or some such important matter. My two class-fellows were poor, and dependant for their future prospects at the university, on the recommendation of the head-master: but I, who had a small patrimonial property, the income of which was sufficient to support me at college, wished to be sent thither immediately. I made earnest representations on the subject to my guardians, but all to no purpose. One, who was more reasonable, and had more knowledge of the world than the rest, lived at a distance: two of the other three resigned all their authority into the hands of the fourth; and this fourth with whom I had to negotiate, was a worthy man, in his way, but haughty, obstinate, and intolerant of all opposition to his will. After a certain number of letters and personal interviews, I found that I had nothing to hope for, not even a compromise of the matter, from my guardian: unconditional submission was what he demanded: and I prepared myself, therefore, for other measures. Summer was now coming on with hasty steps, and my seventeenth birth-day was fast approaching; after which day I had sworn within myself, that I would no longer be numbered amongst school-boys. Money being what I chiefly wanted, I wrote to a woman of high rank,[21] who, though young herself, had known me from a child, and had latterly treated me with great distinction, requesting that she would 'lend' me five guineas. For upwards of a week no answer came; and I was beginning to despond, when, at length, a servant put into my hands a double letter, with a coronet on the seal. The letter was kind and obliging: the fair writer was on the sea-coast, and in that way the delay had arisen: she inclosed double of what I had asked, and good-naturedly hinted, that if I should *never* repay her, it would not absolutely ruin her. Now then, I was prepared for my scheme: ten guineas, added to about two which I had remaining from my pocket money, seemed to be sufficient for an indefinite length of time: and at that happy age, if no *definite* boundary can be assigned to one's power, the spirit of hope and pleasure makes it virtually infinite.

It is a just remark of Dr Johnson's (and what cannot often be said of his remarks, it is a very feeling one), that we never do any thing consciously for the last time (of things, that is, which we have long been in the habit of doing) without sadness of heart. This truth I felt deeply, when I came to leave ——,[22] a place which I did not love, and where I had not been happy. On the evening before I left —— for ever, I grieved when the ancient and lofty school-room resounded with the evening service, performed for the last time in my hearing; and at night, when the muster-roll of names was called over, and mine (as usual) was called first, I stepped forward, and, passing the head-master, who was standing by, I bowed to him, and looked earnestly in his face, thinking to myself, 'He is old and infirm, and in this world I shall not see him again.' I was right: I never *did* see him again, nor ever shall. He looked at me complacently, smiled good-naturedly, returned my salutation (or rather, my valediction), and we parted (though he knew it not) for ever. I could not reverence him intellectually: but he had been uniformly kind to me, and had allowed me many indulgencies: and I grieved at the thought of the mortification I should inflict upon him.

The morning came, which was to launch me into the world, and from which my whole succeeding life has, in many important points, taken its colouring. I lodged in the head-master's house, and had been allowed, from my first entrance, the indulgence of a private room, which I used both as a sleeping room and as a study. At half after three I rose, and gazed with deep emotion at the ancient towers of ——, 'drest in earliest light,'[23] and beginning to crimson with the radiant lustre of a cloudless July morning. I was firm and immoveable in my purpose: but yet agitated by anticipation of uncertain danger and troubles; and, if I could have foreseen the hurricane, and perfect hailstorm of affliction which soon fell upon me, well might I have been agitated. To this agitation the deep peace of the morning presented an affecting contrast, and in some degree a medicine. The silence was more profound than that of midnight: and to me the silence of a summer morning is more touching than all other silence, because, the light being broad and strong, as that of noon-day at other seasons of the year, it seems to differ from perfect day, chiefly because man is not yet abroad; and thus, the peace of nature, and of the innocent creatures of God, seems to be secure and deep, only so long as the presence of man, and his restless and unquiet spirit, are not there to trouble its sanctity. I dressed myself, took my hat and gloves, and lingered a little in the room. For the last year and a half this room had been my 'pensive citadel:'[24] here I had read and studied through all the hours of night: and, though true it was, that for the latter part of this time I, who was framed for love and gentle affections, had lost my gaiety and happiness, during the strife and fever of contention with my guardian; yet, on the other hand, as a boy, so passionately fond of books, and dedicated to intellectual pursuits, I could not fail to have enjoyed many happy hours in the midst of general dejection. I wept as I looked round on the chair, hearth, writing-table, and other familiar objects, knowing too certainly, that I looked upon them for the last time. Whilst

I write this, it is eighteen years ago: and yet, at this moment, I see distinctly as if it were yesterday, the lineaments and expression of the object on which I fixed my parting gaze: it was a picture of the lovely ——,[25] which hung over the mantle-piece; the eyes and mouth of which were so beautiful, and the whole countenance so radiant with benignity, and divine tranquillity, that I had a thousand times laid down my pen, or my book, to gather consolation from it, as a devotee from his patron saint. Whilst I was yet gazing upon it, the deep tones of —— clock proclaimed that it was four o'clock. I went up to the picture, kissed it, and then gently walked out, and closed the door for ever!

So blended and intertwisted in this life are occasions of laughter and of tears, that I cannot yet recal, without smiling, an incident which occurred at that time, and which had nearly put a stop to the immediate execution of my plan. I had a trunk of immense weight; for, besides my clothes, it contained nearly all my library. The difficulty was to get this removed to a carrier's: my room was at an aërial elevation in the house, and (what was worse) the stair-case, which communicated with this angle of the building, was accessible only by a gallery, which passed the head-master's chamber-door. I was a favourite with all the servants; and, knowing that any of them would screen me, and act confidentially, I communicated my embarrassment to a groom of the head-master's. The groom swore he would do any thing I wished; and, when the time arrived, went up stairs to bring the trunk down. This I feared was beyond the strength of any one man: however, the groom was a man –

> Of Atlantean shoulders, fit to bear
> The weight of mightiest monarchies;[26]

and had a back as spacious as Salisbury plain. Accordingly he persisted in bringing down the trunk alone, whilst I stood wait-ing at the foot of the last flight, in anxiety for the event. For some time I heard him descending with slow and firm steps: but, unfortunately, from his trepidation, as he drew near the dangerous quarter, within a few steps of the gallery, his foot slipped; and the mighty burden falling from his shoulders, gained such increase of impetus at each step of the descent, that, on reaching the bottom, it trundled, or rather leaped, right across, with the noise of twenty devils, against the very bed-room door of the archididascalus. My first thought was, that all was lost; and that my only chance for executing a retreat was to sacrifice my baggage. However, on reflection, I determined to abide the issue. The groom was in the utmost alarm, both on his own account and on mine: but, in spite of this, so irresistibly had the sense of the ludicrous, in this unhappy *contretems*,[27] taken possession of his fancy, that he sang out a long, loud, and canorous peal of laughter, that might have wakened the Seven Sleepers.[28] At the sound of this resonant merriment, within the very ears of insulted authority, I could not myself forbear joining in it: subdued to this, not so much by the unhappy *étourderie*[29] of the trunk, as by the effect it had upon the groom. We both expected, as a matter of course, that Dr —— would sally out of his room: for, in general, if but a mouse stirred, he sprang out like a mastiff from his kennel. Strange to say, however, on this occasion, when the noise of laughter had ceased, no sound, or rustling even, was to be heard in the bed-room. Dr —— had a painful complaint, which, sometimes keeping him awake, made his sleep, perhaps, when it *did* come, the deeper. Gathering courage from the silence, the groom hoisted his burden again, and accomplished the remainder of his descent without accident. I waited until I saw the trunk placed on a wheel-barrow, and on its road to the carrier's: then, 'with Providence my guide,'[30] I set off on foot, – carrying a small parcel, with some articles of dress, under my arm; a favourite English poet in one pocket; and a small 12mo. volume, containing about nine plays of Euripides, in the other.

It had been my intention originally to proceed to Westmoreland, both from the love I bore to that county, and on other personal accounts.[31] Accident, however, gave a different direction to my wanderings, and I bent my steps towards North Wales.

After wandering about for some time in Denbighshire,

Merionethshire, and Caernarvonshire, I took lodgings in a small neat house in B——.[32] Here I might have staid with great comfort for many weeks; for, provisions were cheap at B——, from the scarcity of other markets for the surplus produce of a wide agricultural district. An accident, however, in which, perhaps, no offence was designed, drove me out to wander again. I know not whether my reader may have remarked, but *I* have often remarked, that the proudest class of people in England (or at any rate, the class whose pride is most apparent) are the families of bishops. Noblemen, and their children, carry about with them, in their very titles, a sufficient notification of their rank. Nay, their very names (and this applies also to the children of many untitled houses) are often, to the English ear, adequate exponents of high birth, or descent. Sackville, Manners, Fitzroy, Paulet, Cavendish, and scores of others, tell their own tale. Such persons, therefore, find every where a due sense of their claims already established, except among those who are ignorant of the world, by virtue of their own obscurity: 'Not to know *them*, argues one's self unknown.'[33] Their manners take a suitable tone and colouring; and, for once that they find it necessary to impress a sense of their consequence upon others, they meet with a thousand occasions for moderating and tempering this sense by acts of courteous condescension. With the families of bishops it is otherwise: with them it is all up-hill work, to make known their pretensions: for the proportion of the episcopal bench, taken from noble families, is not at any time very large; and the succession to these dignities is so rapid, that the public ear seldom has time to become familiar with them, unless where they are connected with some literary reputation. Hence it is, that the children of bishops carry about with them an austere and repulsive air, indicative of claims not generally acknowledged, a sort of *noli me tangere*[34] manner, nervously apprehensive of too familiar approach, and shrinking with the sensitiveness of a gouty man, from all contact with the οἱ πολλοί.[35] Doubtless, a powerful understanding, or unusual goodness of nature, will preserve a man from such weakness: but, in general, the truth of my representation will be acknowledged: pride, if not of deeper root in such families, appears, at least, more upon the

surface of their manners. This spirit of manners naturally communicates itself to their domestics, and other dependants. Now,
my landlady had been a lady's maid, or a nurse, in the family of
the Bishop of ——;[36] and had but lately married away and
'settled' (as such people express it) for life. In a little town like
B——, merely to have lived in the bishop's family, conferred
some distinction: and my good landlady had rather more than
her share of the pride I have noticed on that score. What 'my
lord' said, and what 'my lord' did, how useful he was in parliament, and how indispensable at Oxford, formed the daily
burden of her talk. All this I bore very well: for I was too
good-natured to laugh in any body's face, and I could make an
ample allowance for the garrulity of an old servant. Of necessity,
however, I must have appeared in her eyes very inadequately
impressed with the bishop's importance: and, perhaps, to punish
me for my indifference, or possibly by accident, she one day
repeated to me a conversation in which I was indirectly a party
concerned. She had been to the palace to pay her respects to
the family; and, dinner being over, was summoned into the
dining-room. In giving an account of her household economy,
she happened to mention, that she had let her apartments.
Thereupon the good bishop (it seemed) had taken occasion to
caution her as to her selection of inmates: 'for,' said he, 'you
must recollect, Betty, that this place is in the high road to the
Head;[37] so that multitudes of Irish swindlers, running away from
their debts into England – and of English swindlers, running
away from their debts to the Isle of Man, are likely to take this
place in their route.' This advice was certainly not without
reasonable grounds: but rather fitted to be stored up for Mrs
Betty's private meditations, than specially reported to me. What
followed, however, was somewhat worse: – 'Oh, my lord,'
answered my landlady (according to her own representation of
the matter), 'I really don't think this young gentleman is a
swindler; because—:' 'You don't *think* me a swindler?' said I,
interrupting her, in a tumult of indignation: 'for the future I
shall spare you the trouble of thinking about it.' And without
delay I prepared for my departure. Some concessions the good
woman seemed disposed to make: but a harsh and contemptu-

ous expression, which I fear that I applied to the learned dignitary himself, roused *her* indignation in turn: and reconciliation then became impossible. I was, indeed, greatly irritated at the bishop's having suggested any grounds of suspicion, however remotely, against a person whom he had never seen: and I thought of letting him know my mind in Greek: which, at the same time that it would furnish some presumption that I was no swindler, would also (I hoped) compel the bishop to reply in the same language; in which case, I doubted not to make it appear, that if I was not so rich as his lordship, I was a far better Grecian. Calmer thoughts, however, drove this boyish design out of my mind: for I considered, that the bishop was in the right to counsel an old servant; that he could not have designed that his advice should be reported to me; and that the same coarseness of mind, which had led Mrs Betty to repeat the advice at all, might have coloured it in a way more agreeable to her own style of thinking, than to the actual expressions of the worthy bishop.

I left the lodgings the very same hour; and this turned out a very unfortunate occurrence for me: because, living henceforward at inns, I was drained of my money very rapidly. In a fortnight I was reduced to short allowance; that is, I could allow myself only one meal a-day. From the keen appetite produced by constant exercise, and mountain air, acting on a youthful stomach, I soon began to suffer greatly on this slender regimen; for the single meal, which I could venture to order, was coffee or tea. Even this, however, was at length withdrawn: and afterwards, so long as I remained in Wales, I subsisted either on blackberries, hips, haws, &c. or on the casual hospitalities which I now and then received, in return for such little services as I had an opportunity of rendering. Sometimes I wrote letters of business for cottagers, who happened to have relatives in Liverpool, or in London: more often I wrote love-letters to their sweethearts for young women who had lived as servants in Shrewsbury, or other towns on the English border. On all such occasions I gave great satisfaction to my humble friends, and was generally treated with hospitality: and once, in particular, near the village of Llan-y-styndw (or some such name),[38] in a sequestered part of Merionethshire, I was entertained for upwards of three days by a family of young people, with an affectionate and fraternal kindness that left an impression upon my heart not yet impaired. The family consisted, at that time, of four sisters, and three brothers, all grown up, and all remarkable for elegance and delicacy of manners. So much beauty, and so much native good-breeding and refinement, I do not remember to have seen before or since in any cottage, except once or twice in Westmorland and Devonshire. They spoke English: an accomplishment not often met with in so many members of one family, especially in villages remote from the high-road. Here I wrote, on my first introduction, a letter about prize-money,[39] for one of the brothers, who had served on board an English man of war; and more privately, two love-letters for two of the sisters. They were both interesting looking girls, and one of uncommon loveliness. In the midst of their confusion and blushes, whilst dictating, or rather giving me general instructions, it did not require any great penetration to discover that what they wished was, that their letters should be as kind as was consistent with proper maidenly pride. I contrived so to temper my expressions, as to reconcile the gratification of both feelings: and they were as much pleased with the way in which I had expressed their thoughts, as (in their simplicity) they were astonished at my having so readily discovered them. The reception one meets with from the women of a family, generally determines the tenor of one's whole entertainment. In this case, I had discharged my confidential duties as secretary, so much to the general satisfaction, perhaps also amusing them with my conversation, that I was pressed to stay with a cordiality which I had little inclination to resist. I slept with the brothers, the only unoccupied bed standing in the apartment of the young women: but in all other points, they treated me with a respect not usually paid to purses as light as mine; as if my scholarship were sufficient evidence, that I was of 'gentle blood.' Thus I lived with them for three days, and great part of a fourth: and, from the undiminished kindness which they continued to show me, I believe I might have staid with them up to this time, if their power had corresponded with their wishes. On the last morning, however,

I perceived upon their countenances, as they sate at breakfast, the expression of some unpleasant communication which was at hand; and soon after one of the brothers explained to me, that their parents had gone, the day before my arrival, to an annual meeting of Methodists, held at Caernarvon, and were that day expected to return; 'and if they should not be so civil as they ought to be,' he begged, on the part of all the young people, that I would not take it amiss. The parents returned, with churlish faces, and '*Dym Sassenach*' (*no English*), in answer to all my addresses. I saw how matters stood; and so, taking an affectionate leave of my kind and interesting young hosts, I went my way. For, though they spoke warmly to their parents in my behalf, and often excused the manner of the old people, by saying, that it was 'only their way,' yet I easily understood that my talent for writing love-letters would do as little to recommend me, with two grave sexagenarian Welsh Methodists, as my Greek Sapphics or Alcaics:[40] and what had been hospitality, when offered to me with the gracious courtesy of my young friends, would become charity, when connected with the harsh demeanour of these old people. Certainly, Mr Shelley is right in his notions about old age:[41] unless powerfully counteracted by all sorts of opposite agencies, it is a miserable corrupter and blighter to the genial charities of the human heart.

Soon after this, I contrived, by means which I must omit for want of room, to transfer myself to London. And now began the latter and fiercer stage of my long-sufferings; without using a disproportionate expression I might say, of my agony. For I now suffered, for upwards of sixteen weeks, the physical anguish of hunger in various degrees of intensity; but as bitter, perhaps, as ever any human being can have suffered who has survived it. I would not needlessly harass my reader's feelings, by a detail of all that I endured: for extremities such as these, under any circumstances of heaviest misconduct or guilt, cannot be contemplated, even in description, without a rueful pity that is painful to the natural goodness of the human heart. Let it suffice, at least on this occasion, to say, that a few fragments of bread from the breakfast-table of one individual (who supposed me to be ill, but did not know of my being in utter want), and these at uncertain intervals, constituted my whole support. During the former part of my sufferings (that is, generally in Wales, and always for the first two months in London) I was houseless, and very seldom slept under a roof. To this constant exposure to the open air I ascribe it mainly, that I did not sink under my torments. Latterly, however, when colder and more inclement weather came on, and when, from the length of my sufferings, I had begun to sink into a more languishing condition, it was, no doubt, fortunate for me, that the same person to whose breakfast-table I had access, allowed me to sleep in a large unoccupied house, of which he was tenant. Unoccupied, I call it, for there was no household or establishment in it; nor any furniture, indeed, except a table, and a few chairs. But I found, on taking possession of my new quarters, that the house already contained one single inmate, a poor friendless child, apparently ten years old; but she seemed hunger-bitten; and sufferings of that sort often make children look older than they are. From this forlorn child I learned, that she had slept and lived there alone, for some time before I came: and great joy the poor creature expressed, when she found that I was, in future, to be her companion through the hours of darkness. The house was large; and from the want of furniture, the noise of the rats made a prodigious echoing on the spacious stair-case and hall; and, amidst the real fleshly ills of cold, and, I fear, hunger, the forsaken child had found leisure to suffer still more (it appeared) from the self-created one of ghosts. I promised her protection against all ghosts whatsoever: but, alas! I could offer her no other assistance. We lay upon the floor, with a bundle of cursed law papers for a pillow: but with no other covering than a sort of large horseman's cloak: afterwards, however, we discovered, in a garret, an old sopha-cover, a small piece of rug, and some fragments of other articles, which added a little to our warmth. The poor child crept close to me for warmth, and for security against her ghostly enemies. When I was not more than usually ill, I took her into my arms, so that, in general, she was tolerably warm, and often slept when I could not: for, during the last two months of my sufferings, I slept much in the day-time, and was apt to fall into transient dozings at all hours. But my sleep

distressed me more than my watching: for, besides the tumultuousness of my dreams (which were only not so awful as those
which I shall have to describe hereafter as produced by opium),
my sleep was never more than what is called *dog-sleep*; so that
I could hear myself moaning, and was often, as it seemed to me,
wakened suddenly by my own voice; and, about this time, a
hideous sensation began to haunt me as soon as I fell into a
slumber, which has since returned upon me, at different periods
of my life, viz. a sort of twitching (I know not where, but
apparently about the region of the stomach), which compelled
me violently to throw out my feet for the sake of relieving it.
This sensation coming on as soon as I began to sleep, and the
effort to relieve it constantly awaking me, at length I slept only
from exhaustion; and from increasing weakness (as I said before)
I was constantly falling asleep, and constantly awaking. Meantime, the master of the house sometimes came in upon us suddenly, and very early, sometimes not till ten o'clock, sometimes
not at all. He was in constant fear of bailiffs: improving on the
plan of Cromwell,[42] every night he slept in a different quarter
of London; and I observed that he never failed to examine,
through a private window, the appearance of those who
knocked at the door, before he would allow it to be opened. He
breakfasted alone: indeed, his tea equipage would hardly have
admitted of his hazarding an invitation to a second person – any
more than the quantity of esculent *matériel*, which, for the most
part, was little more than a roll, or a few biscuits, which he had
bought on his road from the place where he had slept. Or, if he
had asked a party, as I once learnedly and facetiously observed
to him – the several members of it must have *stood* in the relation
to each other (not *sate* in any relation whatever) of succession,
as the metaphysicians have it, and not of co-existence; in the
relation of the parts of time, and not of the parts of space.
During his breakfast, I generally contrived a reason for lounging
in; and, with an air of as much indifference as I could assume,
took up such fragments as he had left – sometimes, indeed, there
were none at all. In doing this, I committed no robbery except
upon the man himself, who was thus obliged (I believe) now
and then to send out at noon for an extra biscuit; for, as to the

poor child, *she* was never admitted into his study (if I may give that name to his chief depositary of parchments, law writings, &c.); that room was to her the Blue-beard room of the house,[43] being regularly locked on his departure to dinner, about six o'clock, which usually was his final departure for the night. Whether this child were an illegitimate daughter of Mr ——,[44] or only a servant, I could not ascertain; she did not herself know; but certainly she was treated altogether as a menial servant. No sooner did Mr —— make his appearance, than she went below stairs, brushed his shoes, coat, &c.; and, except when she was summoned to run an errand, she never emerged from the dismal Tartarus[45] of the kitchens, &c. to the upper air, until my welcome knock at night called up her little trembling footsteps to the front door. Of her life during the day-time, however, I knew little but what I gathered from her own account at night; for, as soon as the hours of business commenced, I saw that my absence would be acceptable; and, in general, therefore, I went off and sate in the parks, or elsewhere, until night-fall.

But who, and what, meantime, was the master of the house himself? Reader, he was one of those anomalous practitioners in lower departments of the law, who – what shall I say? – who, on prudential reasons, or from necessity, deny themselves all indulgence in the luxury of too delicate a conscience: (a periphrasis which might be abridged considerably, but *that* I leave to the reader's taste:) in many walks of life, a conscience is a more expensive incumbrance, than a wife or a carriage; and just as people talk of 'laying down' their carriages, so I suppose my friend, Mr —— had 'laid down' his conscience for a time; meaning, doubtless, to resume it as soon as he could afford it. The inner economy of such a man's daily life would present a most strange picture, if I could allow myself to amuse the reader at his expense. Even with my limited opportunities for observing what went on, I saw many scenes of London intrigues, and complex chicanery, 'cycle and epicycle, orb in orb,'[46] at which I sometimes smile to this day – and at which I smiled then, in spite of my misery. My situation, however, at that time, gave me little experience, in my own person, of any qualities in Mr ——'s character but such as did him honour; and of his whole strange composition, I must forget every thing but that towards me he was obliging, and, to the extent of his power, generous.

That power was not, indeed, very extensive; however, in common with the rats, I sate rent free; and, as Dr Johnson has recorded, that he never but once in his life had as much wall-fruit as he could eat,[47] so let me be grateful, that on that single occasion I had as large a choice of apartments in a London mansion as I could possibly desire. Except the Blue-beard room, which the poor child believed to be haunted, all others, from the attics to the cellars, were at our service; 'the world was all before us;'[48] and we pitched our tent for the night in any spot we chose. This house I have already described as a large one; it stands in a conspicuous situation, and in a well-known part of London.[49] Many of my readers will have passed it, I doubt not, within a few hours of reading this. For myself, I never fail to visit it when business draws me to London; about ten o'clock, this very night, August 15, 1821, being my birth-day – I turned aside from my evening walk, down Oxford-street, purposely to take a glance at it: it is now occupied by a respectable family; and, by the lights in the front drawing-room, I observed a domestic party, assembled perhaps at tea, and apparently cheerful and gay. Marvellous contrast in my eyes to the darkness – cold – silence – and desolation of that same house eighteen years ago, when its nightly occupants were one famishing scholar, and a neglected child. – Her, by the bye, in after years, I vainly endeavoured to trace. Apart from her situation, she was not what would be called an interesting child: she was neither pretty, nor quick in understanding, nor remarkably pleasing in manners. But, thank God! even in those years I needed not the embellishments of novel-accessaries to conciliate my affections; plain human nature, in its humblest and most homely apparel, was enough for me: and I loved the child because she was my partner in wretchedness. If she is now living, she is probably a mother, with children of her own; but, as I have said, I could never trace her.

This I regret, but another person there was at that time, whom I have since sought to trace with far deeper earnestness, and with far deeper sorrow at my failure. This person was a young woman, and one of that unhappy class who subsist upon the wages of prostitution. I feel no shame, nor have any reason to feel it, in avowing, that I was then on familiar and friendly terms with many women in that unfortunate condition. The reader needs neither smile at this avowal, nor frown. For, not to remind my classical readers of the old Latin proverb – '*Sine Cerere*,' &c., it may well be supposed that in the existing state of my purse, my connexion with such women could not have been an impure one. But the truth is, that at no time of my life have I been a person to hold myself polluted by the touch or approach of any creature that wore a human shape: on the contrary, from my very earliest youth it has been my pride to converse familiarly, *more Socratico*,[50] with all human beings, man, woman, and child, that chance might fling in my way: a practice which is friendly to the knowledge of human nature, to good feelings, and to that frankness of address which becomes a man who would be thought a philosopher. For a philosopher should not see with the eyes of the poor limitary creature calling himself a man of the world, and filled with narrow and self-regarding prejudices of birth and education, but should look upon himself as a Catholic creature, and as standing in an equal relation to high and low – to educated and uneducated, to the guilty and the innocent. Being myself at that time of necessity a peripatetic, or a walker of the streets, I naturally fell in more frequently with those female peripatetics who are technically called Street-walkers. Many of these women had occasionally taken my part against watchmen who wished to drive me off the steps of houses where I was sitting. But one amongst them, the one on whose account I have at all introduced this subject – yet no! let me not class thee, Oh noble minded Ann ———, with that order of women; let me find, if it be possible, some gentler name to designate the condition of her to whose bounty and compassion, ministering to my necessities when all the world had forsaken me, I owe it that I am at this time alive. – For many weeks I had walked at nights with this poor friendless girl up and down Oxford Street, or had rested with her on steps and under the shelter of porticos. She could not be so old as myself: she told me, indeed, that she had not completed her sixteenth year. By such questions as my interest about her prompted, I had gradually drawn forth her simple history. Her's was a case of ordinary occurrence (as I have since had reason to think), and one in which, if London beneficence had better adapted its arrangements to meet it, the power of the law might oftener be interposed to protect, and to avenge. But the stream of London charity flows in a channel which, though deep and mighty, is yet noiseless and underground; not obvious or readily accessible to poor houseless wanderers: and it cannot be denied that the outside air and frame-work of London society is harsh, cruel, and repulsive. In any case, however, I saw that part of her injuries might easily have been redressed: and I urged her often and earnestly to lay her complaint before a magistrate: friendless as she was, I assured her that she would meet with immediate attention; and that English justice, which was no respecter of persons, would speedily and amply avenge her on the brutal ruffian who had plundered her little property. She promised me often that she would; but she delayed taking the steps I pointed out from time to time: for she was timid and dejected to a degree which showed how deeply sorrow had taken hold of her young heart: and perhaps she thought justly that the most upright judge, and the most righteous tribunals, could do nothing to repair her heaviest wrongs. Something, however, would perhaps have been done: for it had been settled between us at length, but unhappily on the very last time but one that I was ever to see her, that in a day or two we should go together before a magistrate, and that I should speak on her behalf. This little service it was destined, however, that I should never realize. Meantime, that which she rendered to me, and which was greater than I could ever have repaid her, was this: – One night, when we were pacing slowly along Oxford Street, and after a day when I had felt more than usually ill and faint, I requested her to turn off with me into Soho Square: thither we went; and we sate down on the steps of a house, which, to this hour, I never pass without a pang of grief, and an inner act of homage to the spirit of that unhappy girl, in memory of the noble action which she there performed. Suddenly, as we sate, I grew much worse: I had been leaning my head against her bosom; and all at once I sank from her arms and fell backwards on the steps. From the sensations I then had, I felt an inner conviction of the liveliest kind that without some powerful and reviving stimulus, I should either have died on the spot – or should at least have sunk to a point of exhaustion from which all reäscent under my friendless circumstances would soon have become hopeless. Then it was, at this crisis of my fate, that my poor orphan companion – who had herself met with little but injuries in this world – stretched out a saving hand to me. Uttering a cry of terror, but without a moment's delay, she ran off into Oxford Street, and in less time than could be imagined, returned to me with a glass of port wine and spices, that acted upon my empty stomach (which at that time would have rejected all solid food) with an instantaneous power of restoration: and for this glass the generous girl without a murmur paid out of her own humble purse at a time – be it remembered! – when she had scarcely wherewithal to purchase the bare necessaries of life, and when she could have no reason to expect that I should ever be able to reimburse her. – Oh! youthful benefactress! how often in succeeding years, standing in solitary places, and thinking of thee with grief of heart and perfect love, how often have I wished that, as in ancient times the curse of a father was believed to have a supernatural power, and to pursue its object with a fatal necessity of self-fulfilment, – even so the benediction of a heart oppressed with gratitude, might have a like prerogative; might have power given to it from above to chace – to haunt – to way-lay – to overtake – to pursue thee into the central darkness of a London brothel, or (if it were possible) into the darkness of the grave – there to awaken thee with an authentic message of peace and forgiveness, and of final reconciliation!

I do not often weep: for not only do my thoughts on subjects connected with the chief interests of man daily, nay hourly, descend a thousand fathoms 'too deep for tears;'[51] not only does the sternness of my habits of thought present an antagonism to the feelings which prompt tears – wanting of necessity to those who, being protected usually by their levity from any tendency to meditative sorrow, would by that same levity be made incapable of resisting it on any casual access of such feelings: –

but also, I believe that all minds which have contemplated such objects as deeply as I have done, must, for their own protection from utter despondency, have early encouraged and cherished some tranquilizing belief as to the future balances and the hieroglyphic meanings of human sufferings. On these accounts, I am cheerful to this hour: and, as I have said, I do not often weep. Yet some feelings, though not deeper or more passionate, are more tender than others: and often, when I walk at this time in Oxford Street by dreamy lamp-light, and hear those airs played on a barrel-organ which years ago solaced me and my dear companion (as I must always call her) I shed tears, and muse with myself at the mysterious dispensation which so suddenly and so critically separated us for ever. How it happened, the reader will understand from what remains of this introductory narration.

Soon after the period of the last incident I have recorded, I met, in Albemarle Street, a gentleman of his late Majesty's household.[52] This gentleman had received hospitalities, on different occasions, from my family: and he challenged me upon the strength of my family likeness. I did not attempt any disguise: I answered his questions ingenuously, – and, on his pledging his word of honor that he would not betray me to my guardians, I gave him an address to my friend the Attorney's. The next day I received from him a 10l.[53] Bank-note. The letter inclosing it was delivered with other letters of business to the Attorney: but, though his look and manner informed me that he suspected its contents, he gave it up to me honorably and without demur.

This present, from the particular service to which it was applied, leads me naturally to speak of the purpose which had allured me up to London, and which I had been (to use a forensic word) *soliciting* from the first day of my arrival in London, to that of my final departure.

In so mighty a world as London, it will surprise my readers that I should not have found some means of staving off the last extremities of penury: and it will strike them that two resources at least must have been open to me, – viz. either to seek assistance from the friends of my family, or to turn my youthful talents and attainments into some channel of pecuniary emolument. As to the first course, I may observe, generally, that what I dreaded

beyond all other evils was the chance of being reclaimed by my
guardians; not doubting that whatever power the law gave them
would have been enforced against me to the utmost; that is, to
the extremity of forcibly restoring me to the school which I had
quitted: a restoration which as it would in my eyes have been a
dishonor, even if submitted to voluntarily, could not fail, when
extorted from me in contempt and defiance of my known wishes
and efforts, to have been a humiliation worse to me than death,
and which would indeed have terminated in death. I was, therefore, shy enough of applying for assistance even in those quarters
where I was sure of receiving it – at the risk of furnishing my
guardians with any clue for recovering me. But, as to London
in particular, though, doubtless, my father had in his life-time
had many friends there, yet (as ten years had passed since his
death) I remembered few of them even by name: and never
having seen London before, except once for a few hours, I knew
not the address of even those few. To this mode of gaining help,
therefore, in part the difficulty, but much more the paramount
fear which I have mentioned, habitually indisposed me. In regard
to the other mode, I now feel half inclined to join my reader in
wondering that I should have overlooked it. As a corrector of
Greek proofs (if in no other way), I might doubtless have gained
enough for my slender wants. Such an office as this I could
have discharged with an exemplary and punctual accuracy that
would soon have gained me the confidence of my employers.
But it must not be forgotten that, even for such an office as this,
it was necessary that I should first of all have an introduction
to some respectable publisher: and this I had no means of
obtaining. To say the truth, however, it had never once occurred
to me to think of literary labours as a source of profit. No mode
sufficiently speedy of obtaining money had ever occurred to me,
but that of borrowing it on the strength of my future claims and
expectations. This mode I sought by every avenue to compass:
and amongst other persons I applied to a Jew named D——.*[54]

* To this same Jew, by the way, some eighteen months afterwards, I applied
again on the same business; and, dating at that time from a respectable college,
I was fortunate enough to gain his serious attention to my proposals. My
necessities had not arisen from any extravagance, or youthful levities (these my

To this Jew, and to other advertising money-lenders (some of whom were, I believe, also Jews), I had introduced myself with an account of my expectations; which account, on examining my father's will at Doctor's Commons, they had ascertained to be correct. The person there mentioned as the second son of ——,[55] was found to have all the claims (or more than all) that I had stated: but one question still remained, which the faces of the Jews pretty significantly suggested, – was *I* that person? This doubt had never occurred to me as a possible one: I had rather feared, whenever my Jewish friends scrutinized me keenly, that I might be too well known to be that person – and that some scheme might be passing in their minds for entrapping me and selling me to my guardians. It was strange to me to find my own self, *materialiter* considered (so I expressed it, for I doated on logical accuracy of distinctions), accused, or at least suspected, of counterfeiting my own self, *formaliter*[56] considered. However, to satisfy their scruples, I took the only course in my power. Whilst I was in Wales, I had received various letters from young friends: these I produced: for I carried them constantly in my pocket – being, indeed, by this time, almost the only relics of my personal incumbrances (excepting the clothes I wore) which

---

habits and the nature of my pleasures raised me far above), but simply from the vindictive malice of my guardian, who, when he found himself no longer able to prevent me from going to the university, had, as a parting token of his good nature, refused to sign an order for granting mc a shilling beyond the allowance made to me at school – viz. 100*l.* per ann. Upon this sum it was, in my time, barely possible to have lived in college; and not possible to a man who, though above the paltry affectation of ostentatious disregard for money, and without any expensive tastes, confided nevertheless rather too much in servants, and did not delight in the petty details of minute economy. I soon, therefore, became embarrassed: and at length, after a most voluminous negotiation with the Jew, (some parts of which, if I had leisure to rehearse them, would greatly amuse my readers), I was put in possession of the sum I asked for – on the 'regular' terms of paying the Jew seventeen and a half per cent. by way of annuity on all the money furnished; Israel, on his part, graciously resuming no more than about ninety guineas of the said money, on account of an Attorney's bill, (for what services, to whom rendered, and when, whether at the siege of Jerusalem – at the building of the Second Temple – or on some earlier occasion, I have not yet been able to discover). How many perches this bill measured I really forget: but I still keep it in a cabinet of natural curiosities; and sometime or other I believe I shall present it to the British Museum.

I had not in one way or other disposed of. Most of these letters were from the Earl of ——, who was at that time my chief (or rather only) confidential friend. These letters were dated from Eton. I had also some from the Marquis of ——, his father, who, though absorbed in agricultural pursuits, yet having been an Etonian himself, and as good a scholar as a nobleman needs to be – still retained an affection for classical studies, and for youthful scholars. He had, accordingly, from the time that I was fifteen, corresponded with me; sometimes upon the great improvements which he had made, or was meditating, in the counties of M—— and Sl——[57] since I had been there; sometimes upon the merits of a Latin poet; at other times, suggesting subjects to me on which he wished me to write verses.

On reading the letters, one of my Jewish friends agreed to furnish two or three hundred pounds on my personal security – provided I could persuade the young Earl, who was, by the way, not older than myself, to guarantee the payment on our coming of age: the Jew's final object being, as I now suppose, not the trifling profit he could expect to make by me, but the prospect of establishing a connection with my noble friend, whose immense expectations were well known to him. In pursuance of this proposal on the part of the Jew, about eight or nine days after I had received the 10*l.*, I prepared to go down to Eton. Nearly 3*l.* of the money I had given to my money-lending friend, on his alleging that the stamps must be bought, in order that the writings might be preparing whilst I was away from London. I thought in my heart that he was lying; but I did not wish to give him any excuse for charging his own delays upon me. A smaller sum I had given to my friend the attorney (who was connected with the money-lenders as their lawyer), to which, indeed, he was entitled for his unfurnished lodgings. About fifteen shillings I had employed in re-establishing (though in a very humble way) my dress. Of the remainder I gave one quarter to Ann, meaning on my return to have divided with her whatever might remain. These arrangements made, – soon after six o'clock, on a dark winter evening, I set off, accompanied by Ann, towards Piccadilly; for it was my intention to go down as far as Salt-hill on the Bath or Bristol Mail. Our course lay through a part of the town which has now all disappeared, so that I can no longer retrace its ancient boundaries: Swallow-street, I think it was called. Having time enough before us, however, we bore away to the left until we came into Golden-square: there, near the corner of Sherrard-street,[58] we sat down; not wishing to part in the tumult and blaze of Piccadilly. I had told her of my plans some time before: and I now assured her again that she should share in my good fortune, if I met with any; and that I would never forsake her, as soon as I had power to protect her. This I fully intended, as much from inclination as from a sense of duty: for, setting aside gratitude, which in any case must have made me her debtor for life, I loved her as affectionately as if she had been my sister: and at this moment, with seven-fold tenderness, from pity at witnessing her extreme dejection. I had, apparently, most reason for dejection, because I was leaving the saviour of my life: yet I, considering the shock my health had received, was cheerful and full of hope. She, on the contrary, who was parting with one who had had little means of serving her, except by kindness and brotherly treatment, was overcome by sorrow; so that, when I kissed her at our final farewell, she put her arms about my neck, and wept without speaking a word. I hoped to return in a week at farthest, and I agreed with her that on the fifth night from that, and every night afterwards, she should wait for me at six o'clock, near the bottom of Great Titchfield-street, which had been our customary haven, as it were, of rendezvous, to prevent our missing each other in the great Mediterranean of Oxford-street. This and other measures of precaution I took: one only I forgot. She had either never told me, or (as a matter of no great interest) I had forgotten, her surname. It is a general practice, indeed, with girls of humble rank in her unhappy condition, not (as novel-reading women of higher pretensions) to style themselves – *Miss Douglass*, *Miss Montague*, &c. but simply by their Christian names, *Mary*, *Jane*, *Frances*, &c. Her surname, as the surest means of tracing her hereafter, I ought now to have inquired: but the truth is, having no reason to think that our meeting could, in consequence of a short interruption, be more difficult or uncertain than it had been for so many weeks, I had scarcely for a moment adverted to it as necessary, or placed it amongst my memoranda against this parting interview: and, my final anxieties being spent in comforting her with hopes, and in pressing upon her the necessity of getting some medicines for a violent cough and hoarseness with which she was troubled, I wholly forgot it until it was too late to recal her.

It was past eight o'clock when I reached the Gloucester Coffee-house:[59] and, the Bristol Mail being on the point of going off, I mounted on the outside. The fine fluent motion* of this Mail soon laid me asleep: it is somewhat remarkable, that the first easy or refreshing sleep which I had enjoyed for some months, was on the outside of a Mail-coach – a bed which, at this day, I find rather an uneasy one. Connected with this sleep was a little incident, which served, as hundreds of others did at that time, to convince me how easily a man who has never been in any great distress, may pass through life without knowing, in his own person at least, anything of the possible goodness of the human heart – or, as I must add with a sigh, of its possible vileness. So thick a curtain of *manners* is drawn over the features and expression of men's *natures*, that to the ordinary observer, the two extremities, and the infinite field of varieties which lie between them, are all confounded – the vast and multitudinous compass of their several harmonies reduced to the meagre out-line of differences expressed in the gamut or alphabet of element-ary sounds. The case was this: for the first four or five miles from London, I annoyed my fellow passenger on the roof by occasionally falling against him when the coach gave a lurch to his side; and indeed, if the road had been less smooth and level than it is, I should have fallen off from weakness. Of this annoyance he complained heavily, as perhaps, in the same cir-cumstances most people would; he expressed his complaint, however, more morosely than the occasion seemed to warrant; and, if I had parted with him at that moment, I should have thought of him (if I had considered it worth while to think of him at all) as a surly and almost brutal fellow. However, I was

---

* The Bristol Mail is the best appointed in the kingdom – owing to the double advantage of an unusually good road, and of an extra sum for expences subscribed by the Bristol merchants.

conscious that I had given him some cause for complaint: and, therefore, I apologized to him, and assured him I would do what I could to avoid falling asleep for the future; and, at the same time, in as few words as possible, I explained to him that I was ill and in a weak state from long suffering; and that I could not afford at that time to take an inside place. The man's manner changed, upon hearing this explanation, in an instant: and when I next woke for a minute from the noise and lights of Hounslow (for in spite of my wishes and efforts I had fallen asleep again within two minutes from the time I had spoken to him) I found that he had put his arm round me to protect me from falling off: and for the rest of my journey he behaved to me with the gentleness of a woman, so that, at length, I almost lay in his arms: and this was the more kind, as he could not have known that I was not going the whole way to Bath or Bristol. Unfortunately, indeed, I *did* go rather farther than I intended: for so genial and refreshing was my sleep, that the next time, after leaving Hounslow that I fully awoke, was upon the sudden pulling up of the Mail (possibly at a Post-office); and, on inquiry, I found that we had reached Maidenhead – six or seven miles, I think, a-head of Salt-hill. Here I alighted: and for the half minute that the Mail stopped, I was entreated by my friendly companion (who, from the transient glimpse I had had of him in Piccadilly, seemed to me to be a gentleman's butler – or person of that rank) to go to bed without delay. This I promised, though with no intention of doing so: and in fact, I immediately set forward, or rather backward, on foot. It must then have been nearly midnight: but so slowly did I creep along, that I heard a clock in a cottage strike four before I turned down the lane from Slough to Eton. The air and the sleep had both refreshed me; but I was weary nevertheless. I remember a thought (obvious enough, and which has been prettily expressed by a Roman poet)[60] which gave me some consolation at that moment under my poverty. There had been some time before a murder commit- ted on or near Hounslow-heath. I think I cannot be mistaken when I say that the name of the murdered person was *Steele*, and that he was the owner of a lavender plantation in that neighbourhood. Every step of my progress was bringing me

nearer to the Heath: and it naturally occurred to me that I and
the accursed murderer, if he were that night abroad, might at
every instant be unconsciously approaching each other through
the darkness: in which case, said I, – supposing I, instead of
being (as indeed I am) little better than an outcast, –

> Lord of my learning and no land beside,

were, like my friend, Lord ———,[61] heir by general repute to
70,000*l*. per ann., what a panic should I be under at this moment
about my throat! – indeed, it was not likely that Lord ———
should ever be in my situation. But nevertheless, the spirit of the
remark remains true – that vast power and possessions make a
man shamefully afraid of dying: and I am convinced that many
of the most intrepid adventurers, who, by fortunately being
poor, enjoy the full use of their natural courage, would, if at the
very instant of going into action news were brought to them
that they had unexpectedly succeeded to an estate in England
of 50,000*l*. a year, feel their dislike to bullets considerably
sharpened* – and their efforts at perfect equanimity and self-
possession proportionably difficult. So true it is, in the language
of a wise man whose own experience had made him acquainted
with both fortunes, that riches are better fitted –

> To slacken virtue, and abate her edge,
> Than tempt her to do aught may merit praise.[62]
> *Parad. Regained.*

I dally with my subject because, to myself, the remembrance
of these times is profoundly interesting. But my reader shall not
have any further cause to complain: for I now hasten to its close.
– In the road between Slough and Eton, I fell asleep: and, just
as the morning began to dawn, I was awakened by the voice of
a man standing over me and surveying me. I know not what he

---

* It will be objected that many men, of the highest rank and wealth, have in
our own day, as well as throughout our history, been amongst the foremost in
courting danger in battle. True: but this is not the case supposed: long familiarity
with power has to them deadened its effect and its attractions.

was: he was an ill-looking fellow – but not therefore of necessity an ill-meaning fellow: or, if he were, I suppose he thought that no person sleeping out-of-doors in winter could be worth robbing. In which conclusion, however, as it regarded myself, I beg to assure him, if he should be among my readers, that he was mistaken. After a slight remark he passed on: and I was not sorry at his disturbance, as it enabled me to pass through Eton before people were generally up. The night had been heavy and lowering: but towards the morning it had changed to a slight frost: and the ground and the trees were now covered with rime. I slipped through Eton unobserved; washed myself, and, as far as possible, adjusted my dress at a little public-house in Windsor; and about eight o'clock went down towards Pote's.[63] On my road I met some junior boys of whom I made inquiries: an Etonian is always a gentleman; and, in spite of my shabby habiliments, they answered me civilly. My friend, Lord ——, was gone to the University of ——. 'Ibi omnis effusus labor!'[64] I had, however, other friends at Eton: but it is not to all who wear that name in prosperity that a man is willing to present himself in distress. On recollecting myself, however, I asked for the Earl of D——,[65] to whom, (though my acquaintance with him was not so intimate as with some others) I should not have shrunk from presenting myself under any circumstances. He was still at Eton, though I believe on the wing for Cambridge. I called, was received kindly, and asked to breakfast.

Here let me stop for a moment to check my reader from any erroneous conclusions: because I have had occasion incidentally to speak of various patrician friends, it must not be supposed that I have myself any pretensions to rank or high blood. I thank God that I have not: – I am the son of a plain English merchant, esteemed during his life for his great integrity, and strongly attached to literary pursuits (indeed, he was himself, anonymously, an author):[66] if he had lived, it was expected that he would have been very rich; but, dying prematurely, he left no more than about 30,000l. amongst seven different claimants. My mother I may mention with honour, as still more highly gifted. For, though unpretending to the name and honours of a *literary* woman, I shall presume to call her (what many literary

women are not) an *intellectual* woman: and I believe that if ever
her letters should be collected and published, they would be
thought generally to exhibit as much strong and masculine
sense, delivered in as pure 'mother English,' racy and fresh with
idiomatic graces, as any in our language – hardly excepting
those of lady M. W. Montague.[67] – These are my honours of
descent: I have no others: and I have thanked God sincerely that
I have not, because, in my judgment, a station which raises a
man too eminently above the level of his fellow-creatures is not
the most favourable to moral, or to intellectual qualities.

Lord D—— placed before me a most magnificent breakfast.
It was really so; but in my eyes it seemed trebly magnificent –
from being the first regular meal, the first 'good man's table,'[68]
that I had sate down to for months. Strange to say, however, I
could scarcely eat any thing. On the day when I first received
my 10*l*. Bank-note, I had gone to a baker's shop and bought a
couple of rolls: this very shop I had two months or six weeks
before surveyed with an eagerness of desire which it was almost
humiliating to me to recollect. I remembered the story about
Otway;[69] and feared that there might be danger in eating too
rapidly. But I had no need for alarm, my appetite was quite
sunk, and I became sick before I had eaten half of what I had
bought. This effect from eating what approached to a meal, I
continued to feel for weeks: or, when I did not experience any
nausea, part of what I ate was rejected, sometimes with acidity,
sometimes immediately, and without any acidity. On the present
occasion, at lord D——'s table, I found myself not at all better
than usual: and, in the midst of luxuries, I had no appetite. I
had, however, unfortunately at all times a craving for wine: I
explained my situation, therefore, to lord D——, and gave him
a short account of my late sufferings, at which he expressed
great compassion, and called for wine. This gave me a momentary relief and pleasure; and on all occasions when I had an
opportunity, I never failed to drink wine – which I worshipped
then as I have since worshipped opium. I am convinced, however, that this indulgence in wine contributed to strengthen my
malady; for the tone of my stomach was apparently quite sunk;
but by a better regimen it might sooner, and perhaps effectually,

have been revived. I hope that it was not from this love of wine that I lingered in the neighbourhood of my Eton friends: I persuaded myself *then* that it was from reluctance to ask of Lord D——, on whom I was conscious I had not sufficient claims, the particular service in quest of which I had come down to Eton. I was, however, unwilling to lose my journey, and – I asked it. Lord D——, whose good nature was unbounded, and which, in regard to myself, had been measured rather by his compassion perhaps for my condition, and his knowledge of my intimacy with some of his relatives, than by an over-rigorous inquiry into the extent of my own direct claims, faultered, nevertheless, at this request. He acknowledged that he did not like to have any dealings with money-lenders, and feared lest such a transaction might come to the ears of his connexions. Moreover, he doubted whether *his* signature, whose expectations were so much more bounded than those of ——, would avail with my unchristian friends. However, he did not wish, as it seemed, to mortify me by an absolute refusal: for after a little consideration, he promised, under certain conditions which he pointed out, to give his security. Lord D—— was at this time not eighteen years of age: but I have often doubted, on recollecting since the good sense and prudence which on this occasion he mingled with so much urbanity of manner (an urbanity which in him wore the grace of youthful sincerity), whether any statesman – the oldest and the most accomplished in diplomacy – could have acquitted himself better under the same circumstances. Most people, indeed, cannot be addressed on such a business, without surveying you with looks as austere and unpropitious as those of a Saracen's head.

Recomforted by this promise, which was not quite equal to the best, but far above the worst that I had pictured to myself as possible, I returned in a Windsor coach to London three days after I had quitted it. And now I come to the end of my story: – the Jews did not approve of Lord D——'s terms; whether they would in the end have acceded to them, and were only seeking time for making due inquiries, I know not; but many delays were made – time passed on – the small fragments of my bank note had just melted away; and before any conclusion could have been put to the business, I must have relapsed into my former state of wretchedness. Suddenly, however, at this crisis, an opening was made, almost by accident, for reconciliation with my friends. I quitted London, in haste, for a remote part of England: after some time, I proceeded to the university; and it was not until many months had passed away, that I had it in my power again to re-visit the ground which had become so interesting to me, and to this day remains so, as the chief scene of my youthful sufferings.

Meantime, what had become of poor Ann? For her I have reserved my concluding words: according to our agreement, I sought her daily, and waited for her every night, so long as I staid in London, at the corner of Titchfield-street. I inquired for her of every one who was likely to know her; and, during the last hours of my stay in London, I put into activity every means of tracing her that my knowledge of London suggested, and the limited extent of my power made possible. The street where she had lodged I knew, but not the house; and I remembered at last some account which she had given me of ill treatment from her landlord, which made it probable that she had quitted those lodgings before we parted. She had few acquaintance; most people, besides, thought that the earnestness of my inquiries arose from motives which moved their laughter, or their slight regard; and others, thinking I was in chase of a girl who had robbed me some trifles, were naturally and excusably indisposed to give me any clue to her, if, indeed, they had any to give. Finally, as my despairing resource, on the day I left London I put into the hands of the only person who (I was sure) must know Ann by sight, from having been in company with us once or twice, an address to —— in ——shire,[70] at that time the residence of my family. But, to this hour, I have never heard a syllable about her. This, amongst such troubles as most men meet with in this life, has been my heaviest affliction. – If she lived, doubtless we must have been sometimes in search of each other, at the very same moment, through the mighty labyrinths of London; perhaps, even within a few feet of each other – a barrier no wider in a London street, often amounting in the end to a separation for eternity! During some years, I hoped that she *did* live; and I suppose that, in the literal and unrhetorical use of the word *myriad*, I may say that on my different visits to London, I have looked into many, many myriads of female faces, in the hope of meeting her. I should know her again amongst a thousand, if I saw her for a moment; for, though not handsome, she had a sweet expression of countenance, and a peculiar and graceful carriage of the head. – I sought her, I have said, in hope. So it was for years; but now I should fear to see her; and her cough, which grieved me when I parted with her, is now my consolation. I now wish to see her no longer; but think of her, more gladly, as one long since laid in the grave; in the grave, I would hope, of a Magdalen; taken away, before injuries and cruelty had blotted out and transfigured her ingenuous nature, or the brutalities of ruffians had completed the ruin they had begun.[71]

PART II

So then, Oxford-street, stony-hearted step-mother! thou that listenest to the sighs of orphans, and drinkest the tears of children, at length I was dismissed from thee: the time was come at last that I no more should pace in anguish thy never-ending terraces; no more should dream, and wake in captivity to the pangs of hunger. Successors, too many, to myself and Ann, have, doubtless, since then trodden in our footsteps – inheritors of our calamities: other orphans than Ann have sighed: tears have been shed by other children: and thou, Oxford-street, hast since, doubtless, echoed to the groans of innumerable hearts. For myself, however, the storm which I had outlived seemed to have been the pledge of a long fair-weather; the premature sufferings which I had paid down, to have been accepted as a ransom for many years to come, as a price of long immunity from sorrow: and if again I walked in London, a solitary and contemplative man (as oftentimes I did), I walked for the most part in serenity and peace of mind. And, although it is true that the calamities of my noviciate in London had struck root so deeply in my bodily constitution that afterwards they shot up and flourished afresh, and grew into a noxious umbrage that has overshadowed and darkened my latter years, yet these second assaults of suffering were met with a fortitude more confirmed, with the resources of a maturer intellect, and with alleviations from sympathizing affection – how deep and tender!

Thus, however, with whatsoever alleviations, years that were far asunder were bound together by subtle links of suffering derived from a common root. And herein I notice an instance of the short-sightedness of human desires, that oftentimes on moonlight nights, during my first mournful abode in London, my consolation was (if such it could be thought) to gaze from Oxford-street up every avenue in succession which pierces through the heart of Marylebone to the fields and the woods; for *that*, said I, travelling with my eyes up the long vistas which lay part in light and part in shade, '*that* is the road to the North, and therefore to ——, and if I had the wings of a dove, *that* way I would fly for comfort.' Thus I said, and thus I wished, in my blindness; yet, even in that very northern region it was, even in that very valley, nay, in that very house[72] to which my erroneous wishes pointed, that this second birth of my sufferings began; and that they again threatened to besiege the citadel of life and hope. There it was, that for years I was persecuted by visions as ugly, and as ghastly phantoms as ever haunted the couch of an Orestes:[73] and in this unhappier than he, that sleep, which comes to all as a respite and a restoration, and to him especially, as a blessed* balm for his wounded heart and his haunted brain, visited me as my bitterest scourge. Thus blind was I in my desires; yet, if a veil interposes between the dim-sightedness of man and his future calamities, the same veil hides from him their alleviations; and a grief which had not been feared is met by consolations which had not been hoped. I, therefore, who participated, as it were, in the troubles of Orestes (excepting only in his agitated conscience), participated no less in all his supports: my Eumenides, like his, were at my bed-feet, and stared in upon me through the curtains: but, watching by my pillow, or defrauding herself of sleep to bear me company

* φίλον ὕπνου θέλγητρον, ἐπίκουρον νόσου.[74]

through the heavy watches of the night, sate my Electra: for thou, beloved M., dear companion of my later years, thou wast my Electra! and neither in nobility of mind nor in long-suffering affection, wouldst permit that a Grecian sister should excel an English wife. For thou thoughtst not much to stoop to humble offices of kindness, and to servile* ministrations of tenderest affection; – to wipe away for years the unwholesome dews upon the forehead, or to refresh the lips when parched and baked with fever; nor, even when thy own peaceful slumbers had by long sympathy become infected with the spectacle of my dread contest with phantoms and shadowy enemies that oftentimes bade me 'sleep no more!'[75] – not even then, didst thou utter a complaint or any murmur, nor withdraw thy angelic smiles, nor shrink from thy service of love more than Electra did of old. For she too, though she was a Grecian woman, and the daughter of the king† of men, yet wept sometimes, and hid her face‡ in her robe.

But these troubles are past: and thou wilt read these records of a period so dolorous to us both as the legend of some hideous dream that can return no more. Meantime, I am again in London: and again I pace the terraces of Oxford-street by night: and oftentimes, when I am oppressed by anxieties that demand all my philosophy and the comfort of thy presence to support, and yet remember that I am separated from thee by three hundred miles, and the length of three dreary months, – I look up the streets that run northwards from Oxford-street, upon moonlight nights, and recollect my youthful ejaculation of anguish; – and remembering that thou art sitting alone in that same valley, and mistress of that very house[76] to which my

* ἡδὺ δούλευμα. Eurip. Orest.[77]]

† ἄναξ ἀνδρῶν Ἀγαμέμνων.[78]

‡ ὄμμα θεῖσ᾽ εἴσω πέπλων.[79] The scholar will know that throughout this passage I refer to the early scenes of the Orestes; one of the most beautiful exhibitions of the domestic affections which even the drama of Euripides can furnish. To the English reader, it may be necessary to say, that the situation at the opening of the drama is that of a brother attended only by his sister during the demoniacal possession of a suffering conscience (or, in the mythology of the play, haunted by the Furies), and in circumstances of immediate danger from enemies, and of desertion or cold regard from nominal friends.

heart turned in its blindness nineteen years ago, I think that, though blind indeed, and scattered to the winds of late, the promptings of my heart may yet have had reference to a remoter time, and may be justified if read in another meaning: – and, if I could allow myself to descend again to the impotent wishes of childhood, I should again say to myself, as I look to the north, 'Oh, that I had the wings of a dove—' and with how just a confidence in thy good and gracious nature might I add the other half of my early ejaculation – 'And *that* way I would fly for comfort.'

THE PLEASURES OF OPIUM

It is so long since I first took opium, that if it had been a trifling incident in my life, I might have forgotten its date: but cardinal events are not to be forgotten; and from circumstances connected with it, I remember that it must be referred to the autumn of 1804. During that season I was in London, having come thither for the first time since my entrance at college. And my introduction to opium arose in the following way. From an early age I had been accustomed to wash my head in cold water at least once a day: being suddenly seized with tooth-ache, I attributed it to some relaxation caused by an accidental inter-mission of that practice; jumped out of bed; plunged my head into a bason of cold water; and with hair thus wetted went to sleep. The next morning, as I need hardly say, I awoke with excruciating rheumatic pains of the head and face, from which I had hardly any respite for about twenty days. On the twenty-first day, I think it was, and on a Sunday, that I went out into the streets; rather to run away, if possible, from my torments, than with any distinct purpose. By accident I met a college acquaint-ance who recommended opium. Opium! dread agent of unimaginable pleasure and pain! I had heard of it as I had of manna or of Ambrosia,[80] but no further: how unmeaning a sound was it at that time! what solemn chords does it now strike upon my heart! what heart-quaking vibrations of sad and happy remembrances! Reverting for a moment to these, I feel a mystic importance attached to the minutest circumstances connected with the place and the time, and the man (if man he was) that first laid open to me the Paradise of Opium-eaters. It was a Sunday afternoon, wet and cheerless: and a duller spectacle this earth of ours has not to show than a rainy Sunday in London. My road homewards lay through Oxford-street; and near 'the *stately* Pantheon,'[81] (as Mr Wordsworth has obligingly called it) I saw a druggist's shop. The druggist – unconscious minister of celestial pleasures! – as if in sympathy with the rainy Sunday, looked dull and stupid, just as any mortal druggist might be expected to look on a Sunday: and, when I asked for the tincture of opium,[82] he gave it to me as any other man might do: and furthermore, out of my shilling, returned me what seemed to be real copper halfpence, taken out of a real wooden drawer. Nevertheless, in spite of such indications of humanity, he has ever since existed in my mind as the beatific vision of an immortal druggist, sent down to earth on a special mission to myself. And it confirms me in this way of considering him, that, when I next came up to London, I sought him near the stately Pantheon, and found him not: and thus to me, who knew not his name (if indeed he had one) he seemed rather to have vanished from Oxford-street than to have removed in any bodily fashion. The reader may choose to think of him as, possibly, no more than a sublunary druggist: it may be so: but my faith is better: I believe him to have evanesced,* or evaporated. So unwillingly would I connect any mortal remembrances with that hour, and place, and creature, that first brought me acquainted with the celestial drug.

---

* *Evanesced.* – this way of going off the stage of life appears to have been well known in the 17th century, but at that time to have been considered a peculiar privilege of blood-royal, and by no means to be allowed to druggists. For about the year 1686, a poet of rather ominous name (and who, by the bye, did ample justice to his name), viz. *Mr Flat-man*, in speaking of the death of Charles II expresses his surprise that any prince should commit so absurd an act as dying; because, says he,

Kings should disdain to die, and only *disappear*.[83]

They should *abscond*, that is, into the other world.

Arrived at my lodgings, it may be supposed that I lost not a moment in taking the quantity prescribed. I was necessarily ignorant of the whole art and mystery of opium-taking: and, what I took, I took under every disadvantage. But I took it: – and in an hour, oh! Heavens! what a revulsion! what an upheaving, from its lowest depths, of the inner spirit! what an apocalypse of the world within me! That my pains had vanished, was now a trifle in my eyes: – this negative effect was swallowed up in the immensity of those positive effects which had opened before me – in the abyss of divine enjoyment thus suddenly revealed. Here was a panacea – a φάρμακον νηπενθές[84] for all human woes: here was the secret of happiness, about which philosophers had disputed for so many ages, at once discovered: happiness might now be bought for a penny, and carried in the waistcoat pocket: portable ecstacies might be had corked up in a pint bottle: and peace of mind could be sent down in gallons by the mail coach. But, if I talk in this way, the reader will think I am laughing: and I can assure him, that nobody will laugh long who deals much with opium: its pleasures even are of a grave and solemn complexion; and in his happiest state, the opium-eater cannot present himself in the character of *l'Allegro*: even then, he speaks and thinks as becomes *Il Penseroso*.[85] Nevertheless, I have a very reprehensible way of jesting at times in the midst of my own misery: and, unless when I am checked by some more powerful feelings, I am afraid I shall be guilty of this indecent practice even in these annals of suffering or enjoyment. The reader must allow a little to my infirm nature in this respect: and with a few indulgences of that sort, I shall endeavour to be as grave, if not drowsy, as fits a theme like opium, so anti-mercurial[86] as it really is, and so drowsy as it is falsely reputed.

And, first, one word with respect to its bodily effects: for upon all that has been hitherto written on the subject of opium, whether by travellers in Turkey (who may plead their privilege of lying as an old immemorial right), or by professors of medicine, writing *ex cathedra*,[87] – I have but one emphatic criticism to pronounce – Lies! lies! lies! I remember once, in passing a book-stall, to have caught these words from a page of some satiric author: – 'By this time I became convinced that the London newspapers spoke truth at least twice a week, viz. on Tuesday and Saturday,[88] and might safely be depended upon for – the list of bankrupts.' In like manner, I do by no means deny that some truths have been delivered to the world in regard to opium: thus it has been repeatedly affirmed by the learned, that opium is a dusky brown in colour; and this, take notice, I grant: secondly, that it is rather dear; which also I grant: for in my time, East-India opium has been three guineas a pound, and Turkey eight: and, thirdly, that if you eat a good deal of it, most probably you must – do what is particularly disagreeable to any man of regular habits, viz. die.* These weighty propositions are, all and singular, true: I cannot gainsay them: and truth ever was, and will be, commendable. But in these three theorems, I believe we have exhausted the stock of knowledge as yet accumulated by man on the subject of opium. And therefore, worthy doctors, as there seems to be room for further discoveries, stand aside, and allow me to come forward and lecture on this matter.

First, then, it is not so much affirmed as taken for granted, by all who ever mention opium, formally or incidentally, that it does, or can, produce intoxication. Now, reader, assure yourself, *meo periculo*,[89] that no quantity of opium ever did, or could intoxicate. As to the tincture of opium (commonly called laudanum) *that* might certainly intoxicate if a man could bear to take enough of it; but why? because it contains so much proof spirit, and not because it contains so much opium. But crude opium, I affirm peremptorily, is incapable of producing any state of body at all resembling that which is produced by alcohol; and not in *degree* only incapable, but even in *kind*: it is not in the quantity of its effects merely, but in the quality, that it differs altogether. The pleasure given by wine is always mounting, and tending to a crisis, after which it declines: that from opium,

---

* Of this, however, the learned appear latterly to have doubted: for in a pirated edition of Buchan's *Domestic Medicine*, which I once saw in the hands of a farmer's wife who was studying it for the benefit of her health, the Doctor was made to say – 'Be particularly careful never to take above five-and-twenty *ounces* of laudanum at once:' the true reading probably being five and twenty *drops*, which are held equal to about one grain of crude opium.

when once generated, is stationary for eight or ten hours: the first, to borrow a technical distinction from medicine, is a case of acute – the second, of chronic pleasure: the one is a flame, the other a steady and equable glow. But the main distinction lies in this, that whereas wine disorders the mental faculties, opium, on the contrary (if taken in a proper manner), introduces amongst them the most exquisite order, legislation, and harmony. Wine robs a man of his self-possession: opium greatly invigorates it. Wine unsettles and clouds the judgment, and gives a preternatural brightness, and a vivid exaltation to the contempts and the admirations, the loves and the hatreds, of the drinker: opium, on the contrary, communicates serenity and equipoise to all the faculties, active or passive: and with respect to the temper and moral feelings in general, it gives simply that sort of vital warmth which is approved by the judgment, and which would probably always accompany a bodily constitution of primeval or antediluvian health. Thus, for instance, opium, like wine, gives an expansion to the heart and the benevolent affections: but then, with this remarkable difference, that in the sudden development of kind-heartedness which accompanies inebriation, there is always more or less of a maudlin character, which exposes it to the contempt of the by-stander. Men shake hands, swear eternal friendship, and shed tears – no mortal knows why: and the sensual creature is clearly uppermost. But the expansion of the benigner feelings, incident to opium, is no febrile access, but a healthy restoration to that state which the mind would naturally recover upon the removal of any deep-seated irritation of pain that had disturbed and quarrelled with the impulses of a heart originally just and good. True it is, that even wine, up to a certain point, and with certain men, rather tends to exalt and to steady the intellect: I myself, who have never been a great wine-drinker, used to find that half a dozen glasses of wine advantageously affected the faculties – brightened and intensified the consciousness – and gave to the mind a feeling of being 'ponderibus librata suis:'[90] and certainly it is most absurdly said, in popular language, of any man, that he is *disguised* in liquor: for, on the contrary, most men are disguised by sobriety; and it is when they are drinking (as

some old gentleman says in Athenæus),[91] that men ἑαυτοὺς
ἐμφανίζουσιν οἵτινες εἰσίν[92] – display themselves in their true
complexion of character; which surely is not disguising themselves. But still, wine constantly leads a man to the brink of
absurdity and extravagance; and, beyond a certain point, it is
sure to volatilize and to disperse the intellectual energies:
whereas opium always seems to compose what had been agitated, and to concentrate what had been distracted. In short, to
sum up all in one word, a man who is inebriated, or tending to
inebriation, is, and feels that he is, in a condition which calls up
into supremacy the merely human, too often the brutal, part of
his nature: but the opium-eater (I speak of him who is not
suffering from any disease, or other remote effects of opium)
feels that the diviner part of his nature is paramount; that is, the
moral affections are in a state of cloudless serenity; and over all
is the great light of the majestic intellect.

This is the doctrine of the true church on the subject of opium:
of which church I acknowledge myself to be the only member[93]
– the alpha and the omega: but then it is to be recollected, that
I speak from the ground of a large and profound personal
experience: whereas most of the unscientific* authors who have

---

* Amongst the great herd of travellers, &c. who show sufficiently by their
stupidity that they never held any intercourse with opium, I must caution my
reader specially against the brilliant author of 'Anastasius.'[94] This gentleman,
whose wit would lead one to presume him an opium-eater, has made it impossible to consider him in that character from the grievous misrepresentation
which he gives of its effects, at p. 215–17, of vol. 1 – Upon consideration, it
must appear such to the author himself: for, waiving the errors I have insisted
on in the text, which (and others) are adopted in the fullest manner, he will
himself admit, that an old gentleman 'with a snow-white beard,' who eats
'ample doses of opium,' and is yet able to deliver what is meant and received as
very weighty counsel on the bad effects of that practice, is but an indifferent
evidence that opium either kills people prematurely, or sends them into a
madhouse. But, for my part, I see into this old gentleman and his motives: the
fact is, he was enamoured of 'the little golden receptacle of the pernicious drug'
which Anastasius carried about him; and no way of obtaining it so safe and so
feasible occurred, as that of frightening its owner out of his wits (which, by the
bye, are none of the strongest). This commentary throws a new light upon the
case, and greatly improves it as a story: for the old gentleman's speech, considered as a lecture on pharmacy, is highly absurd: but, considered as a hoax
on Anastasius, it reads excellently.

at all treated of opium, and even of those who have written expressly on the materia medica, make it evident, from the horror they express of it, that their experimental knowledge of its action is none at all. I will, however, candidly acknowledge that I have met with one person who bore evidence to its intoxicating power, such as staggered my own incredulity: for he was a surgeon,[95] and had himself taken opium largely. I happened to say to him, that his enemies (as I had heard) charged him with talking nonsense on politics, and that his friends apologized for him, by suggesting that he was constantly in a state of intoxication from opium. Now the accusation, said I, is not *primâ facie*,[96] and of necessity, an absurd one: but the defence *is*. To my surprise, however, he insisted that both his enemies and his friends were in the right: 'I will maintain,' said he, 'that I *do* talk nonsense; and secondly, I will maintain that I do not talk nonsense upon principle, or with any view to profit, but solely and simply, said he, solely and simply, – solely and simply (repeating it three times over), because I am drunk with opium; and *that* daily.' I replied that, as to the allegation of his enemies, as it seemed to be established upon such respectable testimony, seeing that the three parties concerned all agreed in it, it did not become me to question it; but the defence set up I must demur to. He proceeded to discuss the matter, and to lay down his reasons: but it seemed to me so impolite to pursue an argument which must have presumed a man mistaken in a point belonging to his own profession, that I did not press him even when his course of argument seemed open to objection: not to mention that a man who talks nonsense, even though 'with no view to profit,' is not altogether the most agreeable partner in a dispute, whether as opponent or respondent. I confess, however, that the authority of a surgeon, and one who was reputed a good one, may seem a weighty one to my prejudice: but still I must plead my experience, which was greater than his greatest by 7000 drops a day; and, though it was not possible to suppose a medical man unacquainted with the characteristic symptoms of vinous intoxication, it yet struck me that he might proceed on a logical error of using the word intoxication with too great latitude, and extending it generically to all modes of nervous excite-

amazon.co.uk

Thank you for shopping at Amazon.co.uk!

Invoice for
Your order of 31 July, 2011
Order ID 202-5389881-2875524
Invoice number DJWRXcRGN
Invoice date 31 July, 2011

Billing Address
William T. Graham
23 Withenfield Road
Northern Moor
Manchester, Greater Manchester M23 9BT
United Kingdom

Shipping Address
William T. Graham
23 Withenfield Road
Northern Moor
Manchester, Greater Manchester M23 9BT
United Kingdom

Qty.	Item	Our Price (excl. VAT)	VAT Rate	Total Price
1	**Confessions of an English Opium Eater (Penguin Classics)** Paperback. De Quincey, Thomas. 0140439013 (** P-1-A56C63 **)	£5.19	0%	£5.19
	Shipping charges	£0.00	0%	£0.00
	Subtotal (excl. VAT) 0%			£5.19
	Total VAT			£0.00
	Total			£5.19

Conversion rate - £1.00 : EUR 1,14

This shipment completes your order.

You can always check the status of your orders or change your account details from the "Your Account" link at the top of each page on our site.

Thinking of returning an item? PLEASE USE OUR ON-LINE RETURNS SUPPORT CENTRE.

Our Returns Support Centre (www.amazon.co.uk/returns-support) will guide you through our Returns Policy and provide you with a printable personalised return label. Please have your order number ready (you can find it next to your order summary, above). Our Returns Policy does not affect your statutory rights.

Amazon EU S.à r.l; 5, Rue Plaetis. L - 2338 Luxembourg
VAT number : GB727255821
Please note - this is not a returns address - for returns - please see above for details of our online returns centre

1/DKWsXcRGN/-1 of 1-//1AB1/premium-uk/5216818/0731-15:00/0731-10:05/wendya Pack Type : B1

ment, instead of restricting it as the expression for a specific sort of excitement, connected with certain diagnostics. Some people have maintained, in my hearing, that they have been drunk upon green tea: and a medical student in London, for whose knowledge in his profession I have reason to feel great respect, assured me, the other day, that a patient, in recovering from an illness, had got drunk on a beef-steak.

Having dwelt so much on this first and leading error, in respect to opium, I shall notice very briefly a second and a third; which are, that the elevation of spirits produced by opium is necessarily followed by a proportionate depression, and that the natural and even immediate consequence of opium is torpor and stagnation, animal and mental. The first of these errors I shall content myself with simply denying; assuring my reader, that for ten years, during which I took opium at intervals, the day succeeding to that on which I allowed myself this luxury was always a day of unusually good spirits.

With respect to the torpor supposed to follow, or rather (if we were to credit the numerous pictures of Turkish opium-eaters)[97] to accompany the practice of opium-eating, I deny that also. Certainly, opium is classed under the head of narcotics; and some such effect it may produce in the end: but the primary effects of opium are always, and in the highest degree, to excite and stimulate the system: this first stage of its action always lasted with me, during my noviciate, for upwards of eight hours; so that it must be the fault of the opium-eater himself if he does not so time his exhibition of the dose (to speak medically) as that the whole weight of its narcotic influence may descend upon his sleep. Turkish opium-eaters, it seems, are absurd enough to sit, like so many equestrian statues, on logs of wood as stupid as themselves. But that the reader may judge of the degree in which opium is likely to stupify the faculties of an Englishman, I shall (by way of treating the question illustratively, rather than argumentatively) describe the way in which I myself often passed an opium evening in London, during the period between 1804–1812. It will be seen, that at least opium did not move me to seek solitude, and much less to seek inactivity, or the torpid state of self-involution ascribed to the Turks. I give this account at the risk of being pronounced a crazy enthusiast or visionary: but I regard *that* little: I must desire my reader to bear in mind, that I was a hard student, and at severe studies for all the rest of my time: and certainly I had a right occasionally to relaxations as well as other people: these, however, I allowed myself but seldom.

The late Duke of —— [98] used to say, 'Next Friday, by the blessing of Heaven, I purpose to be drunk:' and in like manner I used to fix beforehand how often, within a given time, and when, I would commit a debauch of opium. This was seldom more than once in three weeks: for at that time I could not have ventured to call every day (as I did afterwards) for '*a glass of laudanum negus, warm, and without sugar.*' No: as I have said, I seldom drank laudanum, at that time, more than once in three weeks: this was usually on a Tuesday or a Saturday night; my reason for which was this. In those days Grassini[99] sang at the Opera: and her voice was delightful to me beyond all that I had ever heard. I know not what may be the state of the Opera-house now, having never been within its walls for seven or eight years, but at that time it was by much the most pleasant place of public resort in London for passing an evening. Five shillings admitted one to the gallery, which was subject to far less annoyance than the pit of the theatres: the orchestra was distinguished by its sweet and melodious grandeur from all English orchestras, the composition of which, I confess, is not acceptable to my ear, from the predominance of the clangorous instruments, and the absolute tyranny of the violin. The choruses were divine to hear: and when Grassini appeared in some interlude, as she often did, and poured forth her passionate soul as Andromache, at the tomb of Hector, &c. I question whether any Turk, of all that ever entered the Paradise of opium-eaters, can have had half the pleasure I had. But, indeed, I honour the Barbarians too much by supposing them capable of any pleasures approaching to the intellectual ones of an Englishman. For music is an intellectual or a sensual pleasure, according to the temperament of him who hears it. And, by the bye, with the exception of the fine extravaganza on that subject in Twelfth Night,[100] I do not recollect more than one thing said adequately on the subject of music in all literature: it is a passage in the *Religio Medici** of Sir T. Brown;[101] and, though chiefly remarkable for its sublimity, has also a philosophic value, inasmuch as it points to the true theory of musical effects. The mistake of most people is to suppose that it is by the ear they communicate with music, and, therefore, that they are purely passive to its effects. But this is not so: it is by the re-action of the mind upon the notices of the ear, (the *matter* coming by the senses, the *form* from the mind) that the pleasure is constructed: and therefore it is that people of equally good ear differ so much in this point from one another. Now opium, by greatly increasing the activity of the mind generally, increases, of necessity, that particular mode of its activity by which we are able to construct out of the raw material of organic sound an elaborate intellectual pleasure. But, says a friend, a succession of musical sounds is to me like a collection of Arabic characters: I can attach no ideas to them. Ideas! my good sir? there is no occasion for them: all that class of ideas, which can be available in such a case, has a language of representative feelings. But this is a subject foreign to my present purposes: it is sufficient to say, that a chorus, &c. of elaborate harmony, displayed before me, as in a piece of arras work, the whole of my past life – not, as if recalled by an act of memory, but as if present and incarnated in the music: no longer painful to dwell upon: but the detail of its incidents removed, or blended in some hazy abstraction; and its passions exalted, spiritualized, and sublimed. All this was to be had for five shillings. And over and above the music of the stage and the orchestra, I had all around me, in the intervals of the performance, the music of the Italian language talked by Italian women: for the gallery was usually crowded with Italians: and I listened with a pleasure such as that with which Weld the traveller[102] lay and listened, in Canada, to the sweet laughter of Indian women; for the less you understand of a language, the more sensible you are to the melody or harshness of its sounds: for such a purpose,

* I have not the book at this moment to consult: but I think the passage begins – 'And even that tavern music, which makes one man merry, another mad, in me strikes a deep fit of devotion,' &c.

therefore, it was an advantage to me that I was a poor Italian scholar, reading it but little, and not speaking it at all, nor understanding a tenth part of what I heard spoken.

These were my Opera pleasures: but another pleasure I had which, as it could be had only on a Saturday night, occasionally struggled with my love of the Opera; for, at that time, Tuesday and Saturday were the regular Opera nights. On this subject I am afraid I shall be rather obscure, but, I can assure the reader, not at all more so than Marinus in his life of Proclus,[103] or many other biographers and auto-biographers of fair reputation. This pleasure, I have said, was to be had only on a Saturday night. What then was Saturday night to me more than any other night? I had no labours that I rested from; no wages to receive: what needed I to care for Saturday night, more than as it was a summons to hear Grassini? True, most logical reader: what you say is unanswerable. And yet so it was and is, that, whereas different men throw their feelings into different channels, and most are apt to show their interest in the concerns of the poor, chiefly by sympathy, expressed in some shape or other, with their distresses and sorrows, I, at that time, was disposed to express my interest by sympathizing with their pleasures. The pains of poverty I had lately seen too much of; more than I wished to remember: but the pleasures of the poor, their consolations of spirit, and their reposes from bodily toil, can never become oppressive to contemplate. Now Saturday night is the season for the chief, regular, and periodic return of rest to the poor: in this point the most hostile sects unite, and acknowledge a common link of brotherhood: almost all Christendom rests from its labours. It is a rest introductory to another rest: and divided by a whole day and two nights from the renewal of toil. On this account I feel always, on a Saturday night, as though I also were released from some yoke of labour, had some wages to receive, and some luxury of repose to enjoy. For the sake, therefore, of witnessing, upon as large a scale as possible, a spectacle with which my sympathy was so entire, I used often, on Saturday nights, after I had taken opium, to wander forth, without much regarding the direction or the distance, to all the markets, and other parts of London, to which the poor resort on a Saturday night, for laying out their wages. Many a family party, consisting of a man, his wife, and sometimes one or two of his children, have I listened to, as they stood consulting on their ways and means, or the strength of their exchequer, or the price of household articles. Gradually I became familiar with their wishes, their difficulties, and their opinions. Sometimes there might be heard murmurs of discontent: but far oftener expressions on the countenance, or uttered in words, of patience, hope, and tranquillity. And taken generally, I must say, that, in this point at least, the poor are far more philosophic than the rich – that they show a more ready and cheerful submission to what they consider as irremediable evils, or irreparable losses. Whenever I saw occasion, or could do it without appearing to be intrusive, I joined their parties; and gave my opinion upon the matter in discussion, which, if not always judicious, was always received indulgently. If wages were a little higher, or expected to be so, or the quartern loaf a little lower, or it was reported that onions and butter were expected to fall, I was glad: yet, if the contrary were true, I drew from opium some means of consoling myself. For opium (like the bee, that extracts its materials indiscriminately from roses and from the soot of chimneys)[104] can overrule all feelings into a compliance with the master key. Some of these rambles led me to great distances: for an opium-eater is too happy to observe the motion of time. And sometimes in my attempts to steer homewards, upon nautical principles, by fixing my eye on the pole-star, and seeking ambitiously for a north-west passage, instead of circumnavigating all the capes and head-lands I had doubled in my outward voyage, I came suddenly upon such knotty problems of alleys, such enigmatical entries, and such sphynx's riddles of streets without thoroughfares, as must, I conceive, baffle the audacity of porters, and confound the intellects of hackney-coachmen. I could almost have believed, at times, that I must be the first discoverer of some of these *terrae incognitae*,[105] and doubted, whether they had yet been laid down in the modern charts of London. For all this, however, I paid a heavy price in distant years, when the human face tyrannized over my dreams, and the perplexities of my steps in London came back and haunted my sleep, with the feeling of perplexities moral or intellectual, that brought confusion to the reason, or anguish and remorse to the conscience.

Thus I have shown that opium does not, of necessity, produce inactivity or torpor; but that, on the contrary, it often led me into markets and theatres. Yet, in candour, I will admit that markets and theatres are not the appropriate haunts of the opium-eater, when in the divinest state incident to his enjoyment. In that state, crowds become an oppression to him; music even, too sensual and gross. He naturally seeks solitude and silence, as indispensable conditions of those trances, or profoundest reveries, which are the crown and consummation of what opium can do for human nature. I, whose disease it was to meditate too much, and to observe too little, and who, upon my first entrance at college, was nearly falling into a deep melancholy, from brooding too much on the sufferings which I had witnessed in London, was sufficiently aware of the tendencies of my own thoughts to do all I could to counteract them. – I was, indeed, like a person who, according to the old legend, had entered the cave of Trophonius:[106] and the remedies I sought were to force myself into society, and to keep my understanding in continual activity upon matters of science. But for these remedies, I should certainly have become hypochondriacally melancholy. In after years, however, when my cheerfulness was more fully re-established, I yielded to my natural inclination for a solitary life. And, at that time, I often fell into these reveries upon taking opium; and more than once it has happened to me, on a summer-night, when I have been at an open window, in a room from which I could overlook the sea at a mile below me, and could command a view of the great town of L——,[107] at about the same distance, that I have sate, from sun-set to sunrise, motionless, and without wishing to move.

I shall be charged with mysticism, Behmenism, quietism, &c. but *that* shall not alarm me. Sir H. Vane, the younger,[108] was one of our wisest men: and let my readers see if he, in his philosophical works, be half as unmystical as I am. – I say, then, that it has often struck me that the scene itself was somewhat typical of what took place in such a reverie. The town of L——

represented the earth, with its sorrows and its graves left behind, yet not out of sight, nor wholly forgotten. The ocean, in everlasting but gentle agitation, and brooded over by a dove-like calm, might not unfitly typify the mind and the mood which then swayed it. For it seemed to me as if then first I stood at a distance, and aloof from the uproar of life; as if the tumult, the fever, and the strife, were suspended; a respite granted from the secret burthens of the heart; a sabbath of repose; a resting from human labours. Here were the hopes which blossom in the paths of life, reconciled with the peace which is in the grave; motions of the intellect as unwearied as the heavens, yet for all anxieties a halcyon calm: a tranquillity that seemed no product of inertia, but as if resulting from mighty and equal antagonisms; infinite activities, infinite repose.

Oh! just, subtle, and mighty opium! that to the hearts of poor and rich alike, for the wounds that will never heal, and for 'the pangs that tempt the spirit to rebel,'[109] bringest an assuaging balm; eloquent opium! that with thy potent rhetoric stealest away the purposes of wrath; and to the guilty man, for one night givest back the hopes of his youth, and hands washed pure from blood; and to the proud man, a brief oblivion for

Wrongs unredress'd, and insults unavenged;[110]

that summonest to the chancery of dreams, for the triumphs of suffering innocence, false witnesses; and confoundest perjury; and dost reverse the sentences of unrighteous judges: – thou buildest upon the bosom of darkness, out of the fantastic imagery of the brain, cities and temples, beyond the art of Phidias and Praxiteles – beyond the splendour of Babylon and Hekatómpylos: and 'from the anarchy of dreaming sleep,' callest into sunny light the faces of long-buried beauties, and the blessed household countenances, cleansed from the 'dishonours of the grave.'[111] Thou only givest these gifts to man; and thou hast the keys of Paradise, oh, just, subtle, and mighty opium!

INTRODUCTION TO THE PAINS OF OPIUM

Courteous, and, I hope, indulgent reader (for all *my* readers must be indulgent ones, or else, I fear, I shall shock them too much to count on their courtesy), having accompanied me thus far, now let me request you to move onwards, for about eight years; that is to say, from 1804 (when I have said that my acquaintance with opium first began) to 1812. The years of academic life are now over and gone – almost forgotten: – the student's cap no longer presses my temples; if my cap exist at all, it presses those of some youthful scholar, I trust, as happy as myself, and as passionate a lover of knowledge. My gown is, by this time, I dare to say, in the same condition with many thousands of excellent books in the Bodleian,[112] viz. diligently perused by certain studious moths and worms: or departed, however (which is all that I know of its fate), to that great reservoir of *somewhere*, to which all the tea-cups, tea-caddies, tea-pots, tea-kettles, &c. have departed (not to speak of still frailer vessels, such as glasses, decanters, bed-makers, &c.)[113] which occasional resemblances in the present generation of tea-cups, &c. remind me of having once possessed, but of whose departure and final fate I, in common with most gownsmen of either university, could give, I suspect, but an obscure and conjectural history. The persecutions of the chapel-bell, sounding its unwelcome summons to six o'clock matins, interrupts my slumbers no longer: the porter who rang it, upon whose beautiful nose (bronze, inlaid with copper) I wrote, in retaliation, so many Greek epigrams, whilst I was dressing, is dead, and has ceased to disturb any body: and I, and many others, who suffered much from his tintinnabulous propensities, have now agreed to overlook his errors, and have forgiven him. Even with the bell I am now in charity: it rings, I suppose, as formerly, thrice a-day: and cruelly annoys, I doubt not, many worthy gentlemen, and disturbs their peace of mind: but as to me, in this year 1812, I regard its treacherous voice no longer (treacherous, I call it, for, by some refinement of malice, it spoke in as sweet and silvery tones as if it had been inviting one to a party):

its tones have no longer, indeed, power to reach me, let the wind sit as favourable as the malice of the bell itself could wish: for I am 250 miles away from it, and buried in the depth of mountains. And what am I doing amongst the mountains? Taking opium. Yes, but what else? Why, reader, in 1812, the year we are now arrived at, as well as for some years previous, I have been chiefly studying German metaphysics, in the writings of Kant, Fichte, Schelling,[114] &c. And how, and in what manner, do I live? in short, what class or description of men do I belong to? I am at this period, viz. in 1812, living in a cottage; and with a single female servant (honi soit qui mal y pense),[115] who, amongst my neighbours, passes by the name of my 'housekeeper.' And, as a scholar and a man of learned education, and in that sense a gentleman, I may presume to class myself as an unworthy member of that indefinite body called *gentlemen*. Partly on the ground I have assigned, perhaps; partly because, from my having no visible calling or business, it is rightly judged that I must be living on my private fortune; I am so classed by my neighbours: and, by the courtesy of modern England, I am usually addressed on letters, &c. *esquire*, though having, I fear, in the rigorous construction of heralds, but slender pretensions to that distinguished honour: yes, in popular estimation, I am X. Y. Z., esquire, but not Justice of the Peace, nor Custos Rotulorum.[116] Am I married? Not yet. And I still take opium? On Saturday nights. And, perhaps, have taken it unblushingly ever since 'the rainy Sunday,' and 'the stately Pantheon,' and 'the beatific druggist' of 1804? – Even so. And how do I find my health after all this opium-eating? in short, how do I do? Why, pretty well, I thank you, reader: in the phrase of ladies in the straw,[117] 'as well as can be expected.' In fact, if I dared to say the real and simple truth, though, to satisfy the theories of medical men, I *ought* to be ill, I never was better in my life than in the spring of 1812; and I hope sincerely, that the quantity of claret, port, or 'particular Madeira,' which, in all probability, you, good reader, have taken, and design to take, for every term of eight years, during your natural life, may as little disorder your health as mine was disordered by the opium I had taken for the eight years, between 1804 and 1812. Hence you may see again the danger of taking any medical advice from *Anastasius*; in divinity, for aught I know, or law, he may be a safe counsellor; but not in medicine. No: it is far better to consult Dr Buchan;[118] as I did: for I never forgot that worthy man's excellent sugges- tion: and I was 'particularly careful not to take above five-and- twenty ounces of laudanum.' To this moderation and temperate use of the article, I may ascribe it, I suppose, that as yet, at least, (*i.e.* in 1812,) I am ignorant and unsuspicious of the avenging terrors which opium has in store for those who abuse its lenity. At the same time, it must not be forgotten, that hitherto I have been only a dilettante eater of opium: eight years' practice even, with the single precaution of allowing sufficient intervals between every indulgence, has not been sufficient to make opium necessary to me as an article of daily diet. But now comes a different era. Move on, if you please, reader, to 1813. In the summer of the year we have just quitted, I had suffered much in bodily health from distress of mind connected with a very melancholy event.[119] This event, being no ways related to the subject now before me, further than through the bodily illness which it produced, I need not more particularly notice. Whether this illness of 1812 had any share in that of 1813, I know not: but so it was, that in the latter year, I was attacked by a most appalling irritation of the stomach, in all respects the same as that which had caused me so much suffering in youth, and accompanied by a revival of all the old dreams. This is the point of my narrative on which, as respects my own self-justification, the whole of what follows may be said to hinge. And here I find myself in a perplexing dilemma: – Either, on the one hand, I must exhaust the reader's patience, by such a detail of my malady, and of my struggles with it, as might suffice to establish the fact of my inability to wrestle any longer with irritation and constant suffering: or, on the other hand, by passing lightly over this critical part of my story, I must forego the benefit of a stronger impression left on the mind of the reader, and must lay myself open to the misconstruction of having slipped by the easy and gradual steps of self-indulging persons, from the first to the final stage of opium-eating (a misconstruction to which there will be a lurking predisposition in most readers, from my previous acknowledgments.) This is the dilemma: the first horn of which would be sufficient to toss and gore any column of patient readers, though drawn up sixteen deep and constantly relieved by fresh men: consequently *that* is not to be thought of. It remains then, that I *postulate* so much as is necessary for my purpose. And let me take as full credit for what I postulate as if I had demonstrated it, good reader, at the expense of your patience and my own. Be not so ungenerous as to let me suffer in your good opinion through my own forbearance and regard for your comfort. No: believe all that I ask of you, viz. that I could resist no longer, believe it liberally, and as an act of grace: or else in mere prudence: for, if not, then in the next edition of my Opium Confessions revised and enlarged, I will make you believe and tremble: and *à force d'ennuyer*, by mere dint of pandiculation[120] I will terrify all readers of mine from ever again questioning any postulate that I shall think fit to make.

This then, let me repeat, I postulate – that, at the time I began to take opium daily, I could not have done otherwise. Whether, indeed, afterwards I might not have succeeded in breaking off the habit, even when it seemed to me that all efforts would be unavailing, and whether many of the innumerable efforts which I *did* make, might not have been carried much further, and my gradual reconquests of ground lost might not have been followed up much more energetically – these are questions which I must decline. Perhaps I might make out a case of palliation; but, shall I speak ingenuously? I confess it, as a besetting infirmity of mine, that I am too much of an Eudæmonist:[121] I hanker too much after a state of happiness, both for myself and others: I cannot face misery, whether my own or not, with an eye of sufficient firmness: and am little capable of encountering present pain for the sake of any reversionary benefit. On some other matters, I can agree with the gentlemen in the cotton-trade* at Manchester in affecting the Stoic

---

* A handsome news-room, of which I was very politely made free in passing through Manchester by several gentlemen of that place, is called, I think, *The Porch*: whence I, who am a stranger in Manchester, inferred that the subscribers meant to profess themselves followers of Zeno. But I have been since assured that this is a mistake.

philosophy:[122] but not in this. Here I take the liberty of an
Eclectic philosopher, and I look out for some courteous and
considerate sect that will condescend more to the infirm condition of an opium-eater; that are 'sweet men,' as Chaucer says,
'to give absolution,'[123] and will show some conscience in the
penances they inflict, and the efforts of abstinence they exact,
from poor sinners like myself. An inhuman moralist I can no
more endure in my nervous state than opium that has not been
boiled.[124] At any rate, he, who summons me to send out a large
freight of self-denial and mortification upon any cruising voyage
of moral improvement, must make it clear to my understanding
that the concern is a hopeful one. At my time of life (six and
thirty years of age) it cannot be supposed that I have much
energy to spare: in fact, I find it all little enough for the intellectual labours I have on my hands: and, therefore, let no man
expect to frighten me by a few hard words into embarking any
part of it upon desperate adventures of morality.

Whether desperate or not, however, the issue of the struggle
in 1813 was what I have mentioned; and from this date, the
reader is to consider me as a regular and confirmed opium-eater,
of whom to ask whether on any particular day he had or
had not taken opium, would be to ask whether his lungs had
performed respiration, or the heart fulfilled its functions. – You
understand now, reader, what I am: and you are by this time
aware, that no old gentleman, 'with a snow-white beard,' will
have any chance of persuading me to surrender 'the little golden
receptacle of the pernicious drug.'[125] No: I give notice to all,
whether moralists or surgeons, that, whatever be their pretensions and skill in their respective lines of practice, they must not
hope for any countenance from me, if they think to begin by
any savage proposition for a Lent or Ramadan[126] of abstinence
from opium. This then being all fully understood between us,
we shall in future sail before the wind. Now then, reader, from
1813, where all this time we have been sitting down and loitering
– rise up, if you please, and walk forward about three years
more. Now draw up the curtain, and you shall see me in a new
character.

If any man, poor or rich, were to say that he would tell us

what had been the happiest day in his life, and the why, and the wherefore, I suppose that we should all cry out – Hear him! Hear him! – As to the happiest *day*, that must be very difficult for any wise man to name: because any event, that could occupy so distinguished a place in a man's retrospect of his life, or be entitled to have shed a special felicity on any one day, ought to be of such an enduring character, as that (accidents apart) it should have continued to shed the same felicity, or one not distinguishably less, on many years together. To the happiest *lustrum*, however, or even to the happiest *year*, it may be allowed to any man to point without discountenance from wisdom. This year, in my case, reader, was the one which we have now reached; though it stood, I confess, as a parenthesis between years of a gloomier character. It was a year of brilliant water (to speak after the manner of jewellers), set as it were, and insulated, in the gloom and cloudy melancholy of opium. Strange as it may sound, I had a little before this time descended suddenly, and without any considerable effort, from 320 grains of opium (i.e. eight* thousand drops of laudanum) per day, to forty[127] grains, or one eighth part. Instantaneously, and as if by magic, the cloud of profoundest melancholy which rested upon my brain, like some black vapours that I have seen roll away from the summits of mountains, drew off in one day (νυχθήμερον);[128] passed off with its murky banners as simultaneously as a ship that has been stranded, and is floated off by a spring tide –

That moveth altogether, if it move at all.[129]

Now, then, I was again happy: I now took only 1000 drops of laudanum per day: and what was that? A latter spring had

* I here reckon twenty-five drops of laudanum as equivalent to one grain of opium, which, I believe, is the common estimate. However, as both may be considered variable quantities (the crude opium varying much in strength, and the tincture still more), I suppose that no infinitesimal accuracy can be had in such a calculation. Tea-spoons vary as much in size as opium in strength. Small ones hold about 100 drops: so that 8000 drops are about eighty times a tea-spoonful. The reader sees how much I kept within Dr Buchan's indulgent allowance.

come to close up the season of youth: my brain performed its functions as healthily as ever before: I read Kant again; and again I understood him, or fancied that I did. Again my feelings of pleasure expanded themselves to all around me: and if any man from Oxford or Cambridge, or from neither had been announced to me in my unpretending cottage, I should have welcomed him with as sumptuous a reception as so poor a man could offer. Whatever else was wanting to a wise man's happiness, – of laudanum I would have given him as much as he wished, and in a golden cup. And, by the way, now that I speak of giving laudanum away, I remember, about this time, a little incident, which I mention, because, trifling as it was, the reader will soon meet it again in my dreams, which it influenced more fearfully than could be imagined. One day a Malay knocked at my door. What business a Malay could have to transact amongst English mountains, I cannot conjecture: but possibly he was on his road to a sea-port about forty miles distant.

The servant who opened the door to him was a young girl born and bred amongst the mountains, who had never seen an Asiatic dress of any sort: his turban, therefore, confounded her not a little: and, as it turned out, that his attainments in English were exactly of the same extent as hers in the Malay, there seemed to be an impassable gulph fixed between all communication of ideas, if either party had happened to possess any. In this dilemma, the girl, recollecting the reputed learning of her master (and, doubtless, giving me credit for a knowledge of all the languages of the earth, besides, perhaps, a few of the lunar ones), came and gave me to understand that there was a sort of demon below, whom she clearly imagined that my art could exorcise from the house. I did not immediately go down: but, when I did, the group which presented itself, arranged as it was by accident, though not very elaborate, took hold of my fancy and my eye in a way that none of the statuesque attitudes exhibited in the ballets at the Opera House, though so ostentatiously complex, had ever done. In a cottage kitchen, but panelled on the wall with dark wood that from age and rubbing resembled oak, and looking more like a rustic hall of entrance than a kitchen, stood the Malay – his turban and loose trowsers of dingy white relieved upon the dark panelling: he had placed himself nearer to the girl than she seemed to relish; though her native spirit of mountain intrepidity contended with the feeling of simple awe which her countenance expressed as she gazed upon the tiger-cat before her. And a more striking picture there could not be imagined, than the beautiful English face of the girl, and its exquisite fairness, together with her erect and independent attitude, contrasted with the sallow and bilious skin of the Malay, enamelled or veneered with mahogany, by marine air, his small, fierce, restless eyes, thin lips, slavish gestures and adorations. Half-hidden by the ferocious looking Malay, was a little child from a neighbouring cottage who had crept in after him, and was now in the act of reverting its head, and gazing upwards at the turban and the fiery eyes beneath it, whilst with one hand he caught at the dress of the young woman for protection. My knowledge of the Oriental tongues is not remarkably extensive, being indeed confined to two words – the Arabic word for barley, and the Turkish for opium (madjoon), which I have learnt from Anastasius. And, as I had neither a Malay dictionary, nor even Adelung's *Mithridates*,[130] which might have helped me to a few words, I addressed him in some lines from the Iliad; considering that, of such languages as I possessed, Greek, in point of longitude, came geographically nearest to an Oriental one. He worshipped me in a most devout manner, and replied in what I suppose was Malay. In this way I saved my reputation with my neighbours: for the Malay had no means of betraying the secret. He lay down upon the floor for about an hour, and then pursued his journey. On his departure, I presented him with a piece of opium. To him, as an Orientalist, I concluded that opium must be familiar: and the expression of his face convinced me that it was. Nevertheless, I was struck with some little consternation when I saw him suddenly raise his hand to his mouth, and (in the school-boy phrase) bolt the whole, divided into three pieces, at one mouthful. The quantity was enough to kill three dragoons and their horses: and I felt some alarm for the poor creature: but what could be done? I had given him the opium in compassion for his solitary life, on recollecting that if he had travelled on foot from London, it must be nearly three weeks since he could have exchanged a thought with any human being. I could not think of violating the laws of hospitality, by having him seized and drenched with an emetic, and thus frightening him into a notion that we were going to sacrifice him to some English idol. No: there was clearly no help for it: – he took his leave: and for some days I felt anxious: but as I never heard of any Malay being found dead, I became convinced that he was used* to opium: and that I must have done him the service I designed, by giving him one night of respite from the pains of wandering.

This incident I have digressed to mention, because this Malay (partly from the picturesque exhibition he assisted to frame, partly from the anxiety I connected with his image for some days) fastened afterwards upon my dreams, and brought other Malays with him worse than himself, that ran 'a-muck'† at me, and led me into a world of troubles. – But to quit this episode, and to return to my intercalary year of happiness. I have said already, that on a subject so important to us all as happiness, we should listen with pleasure to any man's experience or experiments, even though he were but a plough-boy, who cannot be supposed to have ploughed very deep into such an intractable soil as that of human pains and pleasures, or to have conducted his researches upon any very enlightened principles. But I, who have taken happiness, both in a solid and a liquid shape, both boiled and unboiled, both East India and Turkey – who have

* This, however, is not a necessary conclusion: the varieties of effect produced by opium on different constitutions are infinite. A London Magistrate (Harriott's *Struggles through Life*, vol. iii. p. 391, Third Edition), has recorded that, on the first occasion of his trying laudanum for the gout, he took *forty* drops, the next night *sixty*, and on the fifth night *eighty*, without any effect whatever: and this at an advanced age. I have an anecdote from a country surgeon, however, which sinks Mr Harriott's case into a trifle; and in my projected medical treatise on opium, which I will publish, provided the College of Surgeons will pay me for enlightening their benighted understandings upon this subject, I will relate it: but it is far too good a story to be published gratis.

† See the common accounts in any Eastern traveller or voyager of the frantic excesses committed by Malays who have taken opium, or are reduced to desperation by ill luck at gambling.

conducted my experiments upon this interesting subject with a sort of galvanic battery – and have, for the general benefit of the world, inoculated myself, as it were, with the poison of 8000 drops of laudanum per day (just, for the same reason, as a French surgeon inoculated himself lately with cancer – an English one, twenty years ago, with plague – and a third, I know not of what nation, with hydrophobia),[131] – *I* (it will be admitted) must surely know what happiness is, if any body does. And, therefore, I will here lay down an analysis of happiness; and as the most interesting mode of communicating it, I will give it, not didactically, but wrapt up and involved in a picture of one evening, as I spent every evening during the intercalary year when laudanum, though taken daily, was to me no more than the elixir of pleasure. This done, I shall quit the subject of happiness altogether, and pass to a very different one – the *pains of opium*.

Let there be a cottage, standing in a valley, 18 miles from any town – no spacious valley, but about two miles long, by three quarters of a mile in average width; the benefit of which provision is, that all the families resident within its circuit will compose, as it were, one larger household personally familiar to your eye, and more or less interesting to your affections. Let the mountains be real mountains, between 3 and 4000 feet high; and the cottage, a real cottage; not (as a witty author has it) 'a cottage with a double coach-house:'[132] let it be, in fact (for I must abide by the actual scene), a white cottage, embowered with flowering shrubs, so chosen as to unfold a succession of flowers upon the walls, and clustering round the windows through all the months of spring, summer, and autumn – beginning, in fact, with May roses, and ending with jasmine. Let it, however, *not* be spring, nor summer, nor autumn – but winter, in his sternest shape. This is a most important point in the science of happiness. And I am surprised to see people overlook it, and think it matter of congratulation that winter is going; or, if coming, is not likely to be a severe one. On the contrary, I put up a petition annually, for as much snow, hail, frost, or storm, of one kind or other, as the skies can possibly afford us. Surely every body is aware of the divine pleasures which attend a winter fire-side: candles at four o'clock, warm hearth-rugs, tea, a fair tea-maker, shutters closed, curtains flowing in ample draperies on the floor, whilst the wind and rain are raging audibly without,

> And at the doors and windows seem to call,
> As heav'n and earth they would together mell;
> Yet the least entrance find they none at all;
> Whence sweeter grows our rest secure in massy hall.[133]
> – *Castle of Indolence.*

All these are items in the description of a winter evening, which must surely be familiar to every body born in a high latitude. And it is evident, that most of these delicacies, like ice-cream, require a very low temperature of the atmosphere to produce them: they are fruits which cannot be ripened without weather stormy or inclement, in some way or other. I am not '*particular*,' as people say, whether it be snow, or black frost, or wind so strong, that (as Mr —— says) 'you may lean your back against it like a post.'[134] I can put up even with rain, provided it rains cats and dogs: but something of the sort I must have: and, if I have it not, I think myself in a manner ill-used: for why am I called on to pay so heavily for winter, in coals, and candles, and various privations that will occur even to gentlemen, if I am not to have the article good of its kind? No: a Canadian winter for my money: or a Russian one, where every man is but a co-proprietor with the north wind in the fee-simple[135] of his own ears. Indeed, so great an epicure am I in this matter, that I cannot relish a winter night fully if it be much past St Thomas's day,[136] and have degenerated into disgusting tendencies to vernal appearances: no: it must be divided by a thick wall of dark nights from all return of light and sunshine. – From the latter weeks of October to Christmas-eve, therefore, is the period during which happiness is in season, which, in my judgment, enters the room with the tea-tray: for tea, though ridiculed by those who are naturally of coarse nerves, or are become so from wine-drinking, and are not susceptible of influence from so refined a stimulant, will always be the favourite beverage of the intellectual: and, for my part, I would have joined Dr Johnson in a *bellum internecinum* against Jonas Hanway,[137]

or any other impious person, who should presume to disparage
it. – But here, to save myself the trouble of too much verbal
description, I will introduce a painter; and give him directions
for the rest of the picture. Painters do not like white cottages,
unless a good deal weatherstained: but as the reader now under-
stands that it is a winter night, his services will not be required,
except for the inside of the house.

Paint me, then, a room seventeen feet by twelve, and not more
than seven and a half feet high. This, reader, is somewhat
ambitiously styled, in my family, the drawing-room: but, being
contrived 'a double debt to pay,'[138] it is also, and more justly,
termed the library; for it happens that books are the only article
of property in which I am richer than my neighbours. Of these,
I have about five thousand, collected gradually since my eighteenth year. Therefore, painter, put as many as you can into this
room. Make it populous with books: and, furthermore, paint
me a good fire; and furniture, plain and modest, befitting the
unpretending cottage of a scholar. And, near the fire, paint me
a tea-table; and (as it is clear that no creature can come to see
one such a stormy night,) place only two cups and saucers
on the tea-tray: and, if you know how to paint such a thing
symbolically, or otherwise, paint me an eternal tea-pot – eternal
à parte ante, and *à parte post*;[139] for I usually drink tea from
eight o'clock at night to four o'clock in the morning. And, as it
is very unpleasant to make tea, or to pour it out for oneself,
paint me a lovely young woman, sitting at the table. Paint her
arms like Aurora's, and her smiles like Hebe's:[140] – But no, dear
M., not even in jest let me insinuate that thy power to illuminate
my cottage rests upon a tenure so perishable as mere personal
beauty; or that the witchcraft of angelic smiles lies within the
empire of any earthly pencil. Pass, then, my good painter, to
something more within its power: and the next article brought
forward should naturally be myself – a picture of the Opium-
eater, with his 'little golden receptacle of the pernicious drug,'
lying beside him on the table. As to the opium, I have no
objection to see a picture of *that*, though I would rather see the
original: you may paint it, if you choose; but I apprize you, that
no 'little' receptacle would, even in 1816, answer *my* purpose,

who was at a distance from the 'stately Pantheon,' and all
druggists (mortal or otherwise). No: you may as well paint the
real receptacle, which was not of gold, but of glass, and as much
like a wine-decanter as possible. Into this you may put a quart
of ruby-coloured laudanum: that, and a book of German metaphysics placed by its side, will sufficiently attest my being in the
neighbourhood; but, as to myself, – there I demur. I admit that,
naturally, I ought to occupy the foreground of the picture; that
being the hero of the piece, or (if you choose) the criminal at the
bar, my body should be had into court. This seems reasonable:
but why should I confess, on this point, to a painter? or why
confess at all? If the public (into whose private ear I am confidentially whispering my confessions, and not into any painter's)
should chance to have framed some agreeable picture for itself,
of the Opium-eater's exterior, – should have ascribed to him,
romantically, an elegant person, or a handsome face, why should
I barbarously tear from it so pleasing a delusion – pleasing both
to the public and to me? No: paint me, if at all, according to
your own fancy: and, as a painter's fancy should teem with
beautiful creations, I cannot fail, in that way, to be a gainer.
And now, reader, we have run through all the ten categories of
my condition, as it stood about 1816–17: up to the middle of
which latter year I judge myself to have been a happy man: and
the elements of that happiness I have endeavoured to place
before you, in the above sketch of the interior of a scholar's
library, in a cottage among the mountains, on a stormy winter
evening.

But now farewell – a long farewell to happiness – winter or
summer! farewell to smiles and laughter! farewell to peace of
mind! farewell to hope and to tranquil dreams, and to the
blessed consolations of sleep! for more than three years and a
half I am summoned away from these: I am now arrived at an
Iliad of woes: for I have now to record

THE PAINS OF OPIUM

– as when some great painter dips
His pencil in the gloom of earthquake and eclipse.[141]
  Shelley's Revolt of Islam.

Reader, who have thus far accompanied me, I must request your attention to a brief explanatory note on three points:

1. For several reasons, I have not been able to compose the notes for this part of my narrative into any regular and connected shape. I give the notes disjointed as I find them, or have now drawn them up from memory. Some of them point to their own date; some I have dated; and some are undated. Whenever it could answer my purpose to transplant them from the natural or chronological order, I have not scrupled to do so. Sometimes I speak in the present, sometimes in the past tense. Few of the notes, perhaps, were written exactly at the period of time to which they relate; but this can little affect their accuracy; as the impressions were such that, they can never fade from my mind. Much has been omitted. I could not, without effort, constrain myself to the task of either recalling, or constructing into a regular narrative, the whole burthen of horrors which lies upon my brain. This feeling partly I plead in excuse, and partly that I am now in London, and am a helpless sort of person, who cannot even arrange his own papers without assistance; and I am separated from the hands which are wont to perform for me the offices of an amanuensis.[142]

2. You will think, perhaps, that I am too confidential and communicative of my own private history. It may be so. But my way of writing is rather to think aloud, and follow my own humours, than much to consider who is listening to me; and, if I stop to consider what is proper to be said to this or that person, I shall soon come to doubt whether any part at all is proper. The fact is, I place myself at a distance of fifteen or twenty years ahead of this time, and suppose myself writing to those who will be interested about me hereafter; and wishing to have some record of a time, the entire history of which no one can know

but myself, I do it as fully as I am able with the efforts I am now capable of making, because I know not whether I can ever find time to do it again.

3. It will occur to you often to ask, why did I not release myself from the horrors of opium, by leaving it off, or diminishing it? To this I must answer briefly: it might be supposed that I yielded to the fascinations of opium too easily; it cannot be supposed that any man can be charmed by its terrors. The reader may be sure, therefore, that I made attempts innumerable to reduce the quantity. I add, that those who witnessed the agonies of those attempts, and not myself, were the first to beg me to desist. But could not I have reduced it a drop a day, or by adding water, have bisected or trisected a drop? A thousand drops bisected would thus have taken nearly six years to reduce; and that way would certainly not have answered. But this is a common mistake of those who know nothing of opium experimentally; I appeal to those who do, whether it is not always found that down to a certain point it can be reduced with ease and even pleasure, but that, after that point, further reduction causes intense suffering. Yes, say many thoughtless persons, who know not what they are talking of, you will suffer a little low spirits and dejection for a few days. I answer, no; there is nothing like low spirits; on the contrary, the mere animal spirits are uncommonly raised: the pulse is improved: the health is better. It is not there that the suffering lies. It has no resemblance to the sufferings caused by renouncing wine. It is a state of unutterable irritation of stomach (which surely is not much like dejection), accompanied by intense perspirations, and feelings such as I shall not attempt to describe without more space at my command.[143]

I shall now enter '*in medias res*,' and shall anticipate, from a time when my opium pains might be said to be at their *acmé*,[144] an account of their palsying effects on the intellectual faculties.

My studies have now been long interrupted. I cannot read to myself with any pleasure, hardly with a moment's endurance. Yet I read aloud sometimes for the pleasure of others; because, reading is an accomplishment of mine; and, in the slang use of the word *accomplishment* as a superficial and ornamental attainment, almost the only one I possess: and formerly, if I had any vanity at all connected with any endowment or attainment of mine, it was with this; for I had observed that no accomplishment was so rare. Players are the worst readers of all: —— reads vilely: and Mrs ——,[145] who is so celebrated, can read nothing well but dramatic compositions: Milton she cannot read sufferably. People in general either read poetry without any passion at all, or else overstep the modesty of nature,[146] and read not like scholars. Of late, if I have felt moved by any thing in books, it has been by the grand lamentations of Samson Agonistes, or the great harmonies of the Satanic speeches in Paradise Regained, when read aloud by myself. A young lady sometimes comes and drinks tea with us: at her request and M.'s I now and then read W——'s[147] poems to them. (W., by the bye, is the only poet I ever met who could read his own verses: often indeed he reads admirably.)

For nearly two years I believe that I read no book but one: and I owe it to the author, in discharge of a great debt of gratitude, to mention what that was. The sublimer and more passionate poets I still read, as I have said, by snatches, and occasionally. But my proper vocation, as I well knew, was the exercise of the analytic understanding. Now, for the most part, analytic studies are continuous, and not to be pursued by fits and starts, or fragmentary efforts. Mathematics, for instance, intellectual philosophy, &c. were all become insupportable to me; I shrunk from them with a sense of powerless and infantine feebleness that gave me an anguish the greater from remembering the time when I grappled with them to my own hourly delight; and for this further reason, because I had devoted the labour of my whole life, and had dedicated my intellect, blossoms and fruits, to the slow and elaborate toil of constructing one single work, to which I had presumed to give the title of an unfinished work of Spinosa's; viz. *De emendatione humani intellectûs*.[148] This was now lying locked up, as by frost, like any Spanish bridge or aqueduct, begun upon too great a scale for the resources of the architect; and, instead of surviving me as a monument of wishes at least, and aspirations, and a life of labour devoted to the exaltation of human nature in that way in which God had best fitted me to promote so great an object, it was likely to stand a memorial to my children of hopes defeated, of baffled efforts, of materials uselessly accumulated, of foundations laid that were never to support a superstructure, – of the grief and the ruin of the architect. In this state of imbecility, I had, for amusement, turned my attention to political economy; my understanding, which formerly had been as active and restless as a hyena, could not, I suppose (so long as I lived at all) sink into utter lethargy; and political economy offers this advantage to a person in my state, that though it is eminently an organic science (no part, that is to say, but what acts on the whole, as the whole again re-acts on each part); yet the several parts may be detached and contemplated singly. Great as was the prostration of my powers at this time, yet I could not forget my knowledge; and my understanding had been for too many years intimate with severe thinkers, with logic, and the great masters of knowledge, not to be aware of the utter feebleness of the main herd of modern economists. I had been led in 1811 to look into loads of books and pamphlets on many branches of economy; and, at my desire, M. sometimes read to me chapters from more recent works, or parts of parliamentary debates. I saw that these were generally the very dregs and rinsings of the human intellect; and that any man of sound head, and practised in wielding logic with a scholastic adroitness, might take up the whole academy of modern economists, and throttle them between heaven and earth with his finger and thumb, or bray their fungus heads to powder with a lady's fan. At length, in 1819, a friend in Edinburgh sent me down Mr Ricardo's book: and recurring to my own prophetic anticipation of the advent of some legislator for this science, I said, before I had finished the first chapter, 'Thou art the Man!'[149] Wonder and curiosity were emotions that had long been dead in me. Yet I wondered once more: I wondered at myself that I could once again be stimulated to the effort of reading: and much more I wondered at the book. Had this profound work been really written in England during the nineteenth century? Was it possible? I supposed thinking* had been extinct in England. Could it be that an Englishman, and he not in academic bowers, but oppressed by mercantile and senatorial cares, had accomplished what all the universities of Europe, and a century of thought, had failed even to advance by one hair's breadth? All other writers had been crushed and overlaid by the enormous weight of facts and documents; Mr Ricardo had deduced, *à priori*,[150] from the understanding itself, laws which first gave a ray of light into the unwieldy chaos of materials, and had constructed what had been but a collection of tentative discussions into a science of regular proportions, now first standing on an eternal basis.

Thus did one single work of a profound understanding avail to give me a pleasure and an activity which I had not known for years: – it roused me even to write, or, at least, to dictate, what M. wrote for me. It seemed to me, that some important truths had escaped even 'the inevitable eye'[151] of Mr Ricardo: and, as these were, for the most part, of such a nature that I could express or illustrate them more briefly and elegantly by algebraic symbols than in the usual clumsy and loitering diction of economists, the whole would not have filled a pocket-book; and being so brief, with M. for my amanuensis, even at this time, incapable as I was of all general exertion, I drew up my *Prolegomena to all future Systems of Political Economy*. I hope it will not be found redolent of opium; though, indeed, to most people, the subject itself is a sufficient opiate.

This exertion, however, was but a temporary flash; as the sequel showed – for I designed to publish my work: arrangements were made at a provincial press, about eighteen miles distant, for printing it. An additional compositor was retained, for some days, on this account. The work was even twice advertised: and I was, in a manner, pledged to the fulfilment of my intention. But I had a preface to write; and a dedication, which

---

* The reader must remember what I here mean by *thinking*: because, else this would be a very presumptuous expression. England, of late, has been rich to excess in fine thinkers, in the departments of creative and combining thought; but there is a sad dearth of masculine thinkers in any analytic path. A Scotchman of eminent name has lately told us,[152] that he is obliged to quit even mathematics, for want of encouragement.

I wished to make a splendid one, to Mr Ricardo. I found myself quite unable to accomplish all this. The arrangements were countermanded: the compositor dismissed: and my 'Prolegomena' rested peacefully by the side of its elder and more dignified brother.

I have thus described and illustrated my intellectual torpor, in terms that apply, more or less, to every part of the four years during which I was under the Circean spells of opium. But for misery and suffering, I might, indeed, be said to have existed in a dormant state. I seldom could prevail on myself to write a letter; an answer of a few words, to any that I received, was the utmost that I could accomplish; and often *that* not until the letter had lain weeks, or even months, on my writing table. Without the aid of M. all records of bills paid, or *to be* paid, must have perished: and my whole domestic economy, whatever became of Political Economy, must have gone into irretrievable confusion. – I shall not afterwards allude to this part of the case: it is one, however, which the opium-eater will find, in the end, as oppressive and tormenting as any other, from the sense of incapacity and feebleness, from the direct embarrassments incident to the neglect or procrastination of each day's appropriate duties, and from the remorse which must often exasperate the stings of these evils to a reflective and conscientious mind. The opium-eater loses none of his moral sensibilities, or aspirations: he wishes and longs, as earnestly as ever, to realize what he believes possible, and feels to be exacted by duty; but his intellectual apprehension of what is possible infinitely outruns his power, not of execution only, but even of power to attempt. He lies under the weight of incubus and night-mare: he lies in sight of all that he would fain perform, just as a man forcibly confined to his bed by the mortal languor of a relaxing disease, who is compelled to witness injury or outrage offered to some object of his tenderest love: – he curses the spells which chain him down from motion: – he would lay down his life if he might but get up and walk; but he is powerless as an infant, and cannot even attempt to rise.

I now pass to what is the main subject of these latter confessions, to the history and journal of what took place in my dreams; for these were the immediate and proximate cause of my acutest suffering.

The first notice I had of any important change going on in this part of my physical economy, was from the re-awakening of a state of eye generally incident to children, or exalted states of irritability. I know not whether my reader is aware that many children, perhaps most, have a power of painting, as it were, upon the darkness, all sorts of phantoms; in some, that power is simply a mechanic affection of the eye; others have a voluntary, or a semi-voluntary power to dismiss or to summon them; or, as a child once said to me when I questioned him on this matter, 'I can tell them to go, and they go; but sometimes they come, when I don't tell them to come.' Whereupon I told him that he had almost as unlimited a command over apparitions, as a Roman centurion over his soldiers. – In the middle of 1817, I think it was, that this faculty became positively distressing to me: at night, when I lay awake in bed, vast processions passed along in mournful pomp; friezes of never-ending stories, that to my feelings were as sad and solemn as if they were stories drawn from times before Œdipus or Priam – before Tyre – before Memphis.[153] And, at the same time, a corresponding change took place in my dreams; a theatre seemed suddenly opened and lighted up within my brain, which presented nightly spectacles of more than earthly splendour. And the four following facts may be mentioned, as noticeable at this time:

1. That, as the creative state of the eye increased, a sympathy seemed to arise between the waking and the dreaming states of the brain in one point – that whatsoever I happened to call up and to trace by a voluntary act upon the darkness was very apt to transfer itself to my dreams; so that I feared to exercise this faculty; for, as Midas turned all things to gold, that yet baffled his hopes and defrauded his human desires, so whatsoever things capable of being visually represented I did but think of it in the darkness, immediately shaped themselves into phantoms of the eye; and, by a process apparently no less inevitable, when thus once traced in faint and visionary colours, like writings in sympathetic ink, they were drawn out by the fierce chemistry of my dreams, into insufferable splendour that fretted my heart.

2. For this, and all other changes in my dreams, were accompanied by deep-seated anxiety and gloomy melancholy, such as are wholly incommunicable by words. I seemed every night to descend, not metaphorically, but literally to descend, into chasms and sunless abysses, depths below depths, from which it seemed hopeless that I could ever re-ascend. Nor did I, by waking, feel that I *had* re-ascended. This I do not dwell upon; because the state of gloom which attended these gorgeous spectacles, amounting at last to utter darkness, as of some suicidal despondency, cannot be approached by words.

3. The sense of space, and in the end, the sense of time, were both powerfully affected. Buildings, landscapes, &c. were exhibited in proportions so vast as the bodily eye is not fitted to receive. Space swelled, and was amplified to an extent of unutterable infinity. This, however, did not disturb me so much as the vast expansion of time; I sometimes seemed to have lived for 70 or 100 years in one night; nay; sometimes had feelings representative of a millenium passed in that time, or, however, of a duration far beyond the limits of any human experience.

4. The minutest incidents of childhood, or forgotten scenes of later years, were often revived: I could not be said to recollect them; for if I had been told of them when waking, I should not have been able to acknowledge them as parts of my past experience. But placed as they were before me, in dreams like intuitions, and clothed in all their evanescent circumstances and accompanying feelings. I *recognized* them instantaneously. I was once told by a near relative of mine, that having in her childhood fallen into a river, and being on the very verge of death but for the critical assistance which reached her, she saw in a moment her whole life, in its minutest incidents, arrayed before her simultaneously as in a mirror; and she had a faculty developed as suddenly for comprehending the whole and every part. This, from some opium experiences of mine, I can believe; I have, indeed, seen the same thing asserted twice in modern books, and accompanied by a remark which I am convinced is true; viz. that the dread book of account, which the Scriptures speak of, is, in fact, the mind itself of each individual. Of this at least, I feel assured, that there is no such thing as *forgetting*

possible to the mind; a thousand accidents may, and will inter-
pose a veil between our present consciousness and the secret
inscriptions on the mind; accidents of the same sort will also
rend away this veil; but alike, whether veiled or unveiled, the
inscription remains for ever; just as the stars seem to withdraw
before the common light of day, whereas, in fact, we all know
that it is the light which is drawn over them as a veil – and that
they are waiting to be revealed when the obscuring daylight
shall have withdrawn.

Having noticed these four facts as memorably distinguishing
my dreams from those of health, I shall now cite a case illustrative of the first fact; and shall then cite any others that I remember, either in their chronological order, or any other that may
give them more effect as pictures to the reader.

I had been in youth, and even since, for occasional amusement, a great reader of Livy,[154] whom, I confess, that I prefer,
both for style and matter, to any other of the Roman historians:
and I had often felt as most solemn and appalling sounds, and
most emphatically representative of the majesty of the Roman
people, the two words so often occurring in Livy – *Consul
Romanus*; especially when the consul is introduced in his military character. I mean to say, that the words king – sultan –
regent, &c. or any other titles of those who embody in their
own persons the collective majesty of a great people, had less
power over my reverential feelings. I had also, though no great
reader of history, made myself minutely and critically familiar
with one period of English history, viz. the period of the Parliamentary War,[155] having been attracted by the moral grandeur
of some who figured in that day, and by the many interesting
memoirs which survive those unquiet times. Both these parts of
my lighter reading, having furnished me often with matter of
reflection, now furnished me with matter for my dreams. Often
I used to see, after painting upon the blank darkness a sort of
rehearsal whilst waking, a crowd of ladies, and perhaps a festival, and dances. And I heard it said, or I said to myself, 'these
are English ladies from the unhappy times of Charles I. These
are the wives and the daughters of those who met in peace, and
sate at the same tables, and were allied by marriage or by blood;

and yet, after a certain day in August, 1642, never smiled upon each other again, nor met but in the field of battle; and at Marston Moor, at Newbury, or at Naseby,[156] cut asunder all ties of love by the cruel sabre, and washed away in blood the memory of ancient friendship.' – The ladies danced, and looked as lovely as the court of George IV. Yet I knew, even in my dream, that they had been in the grave for nearly two centuries. – This pageant would suddenly dissolve: and, at a clapping of hands, would be heard the heart-quaking sound of *Consul Romanus*: and immediately came 'sweeping by,' in gorgeous paludaments,[157] Paulus or Marius, girt round by a company of centurions, with the crimson tunic hoisted on a spear, and followed by the *alalagmos*[158] of the Roman legions.

Many years ago, when I was looking over Piranesi's Antiquities of Rome, Mr Coleridge, who was standing by, described to me a set of plates by that artist, called his *Dreams*,[159] and which record the scenery of his own visions during the delirium of a fever. Some of them (I describe only from memory of Mr Coleridge's account) represented vast Gothic halls: on the floor of which stood all sorts of engines and machinery, wheels, cables, pulleys, levers, catapults, &c. &c. expressive of enormous power put forth, and resistance overcome. Creeping along the sides of the walls, you perceived a staircase; and upon it, groping his way upwards, was Piranesi himself: follow the stairs a little further, and you perceive it come to a sudden abrupt termination, without any balustrade, and allowing no step onwards to him who had reached the extremity, except into the depths below. Whatever is to become of poor Piranesi, you suppose, at least, that his labours must in some way terminate here. But raise your eyes, and behold a second flight of stairs still higher: on which again Piranesi is perceived, but this time standing on the very brink of the abyss. Again elevate your eye, and a still more aerial flight of stairs is beheld: and again is poor Piranesi busy on his aspiring labours: and so on, until the unfinished stairs and Piranesi both are lost in the upper gloom of the hall. – With the same power of endless growth and self-reproduction did my architecture proceed in dreams. In the early stage of my malady, the splendours of my dreams were indeed chiefly architectural: and I beheld such pomp of cities and palaces as was never yet beheld by the waking eye, unless in the clouds. From a great modern poet I cite part of a passage which describes, as an appearance actually beheld in the clouds, what in many of its circumstances I saw frequently in sleep:

> The appearance, instantaneously disclosed,
> Was of a mighty city – boldly say
> A wilderness of building, sinking far
> And self-withdrawn into a wondrous depth,
> Far sinking into splendor – without end!
> Fabric it seem'd of diamond, and of gold,
> With alabaster domes, and silver spires,
> And blazing terrace upon terrace, high
> Uplifted; here, serene pavilions bright
> In avenues disposed; there towers begirt
> With battlements that on their restless fronts
> Bore stars – illumination of all gems!
> By earthly nature had the effect been wrought
> Upon the dark materials of the storm
> Now pacified; on them, and on the coves,
> And mountain-steeps and summits, whereunto
> The vapours had receded, – taking there
> Their station under a cerulean sky. &c. &c.[160]

The sublime circumstance – 'battlements that on their *restless* fronts bore stars,' – might have been copied from my architectural dreams, for it often occurred. – We hear it reported of Dryden, and of Fuseli in modern times, that they thought proper to eat raw meat for the sake of obtaining splendid dreams: how much better for such a purpose to have eaten opium, which yet I do not remember that any poet is recorded to have done, except the dramatist Shadwell: and in ancient days, Homer[161] is, I think, rightly reputed to have known the virtues of opium.

To my architecture succeeded dreams of lakes – and silvery expanses of water: – these haunted me so much, that I feared (though possibly it will appear ludicrous to a medical man) that

some dropsical state or tendency of the brain might thus be
making itself (to use a metaphysical word) *objective*; and the
sentient organ *project* itself as its own object. – For two months
I suffered greatly in my head, – a part of my bodily structure
which had hitherto been so clear from all touch or taint of
weakness (physically, I mean), that I used to say of it, as the last
Lord Orford[162] said of his stomach, that it seemed likely to
survive the rest of my person. – Till now I had never felt a
head-ache even, or any the slightest pain, except rheumatic pains
caused by my own folly. However, I got over this attack, though
it must have been verging on something very dangerous.

The waters now changed their character, – from translucent
lakes, shining like mirrors, they now became seas and oceans.
And now came a tremendous change, which, unfolding itself
slowly like a scroll, through many months, promised an abiding
torment; and, in fact, it never left me until the winding up of my
case. Hitherto the human face had mixed often in my dreams,
but not despotically, nor with any special power of tormenting.
But now that which I have called the tyranny of the human face
began to unfold itself. Perhaps some part of my London life
might be answerable for this.[163] Be that as it may, now it was
that upon the rocking waters of the ocean the human face began
to appear: the sea appeared paved with innumerable faces,
upturned to the heavens: faces, imploring, wrathful, despairing,
surged upwards by thousands, by myriads, by generations, by
centuries: – my agitation was infinite, – my mind tossed – and
surged with the ocean.

May, 1818.

The Malay has been a fearful enemy for months. I have been
every night, through his means, transported into Asiatic scenes.
I know not whether others share in my feelings on this point;
but I have often thought that if I were compelled to forego
England, and to live in China, and among Chinese manners and
modes of life and scenery, I should go mad. The causes of my
horror lie deep; and some of them must be common to others.
Southern Asia, in general, is the seat of awful images and associations. As the cradle of the human race, it would alone have a

dim and reverential feeling connected with it. But there are other reasons. No man can pretend that the wild, barbarous, and capricious superstitions of Africa, or of savage tribes elsewhere, affect him in the way that he is affected by the ancient, monumental, cruel, and elaborate religions of Indostan, &c. The mere antiquity of Asiatic things, of their institutions, histories, modes of faith, &c. is so impressive, that to me the vast age of the race and name overpowers the sense of youth in the individual. A young Chinese seems to me an antediluvian man renewed. Even Englishmen, though not bred in any knowledge of such institutions, cannot but shudder at the mystic sublimity of *castes* that have flowed apart, and refused to mix, through such immemorial tracts of time; nor can any man fail to be awed by the names of the Ganges, or the Euphrates. It contributes much to these feelings, that southern Asia is, and has been for thousands of years, the part of the earth most swarming with human life; the great *officina gentium*.[164] Man is a weed in those regions. The vast empires also, into which the enormous population of Asia has always been cast, give a further sublimity to the feelings associated with all oriental names or images. In China, over and above what it has in common with the rest of southern Asia, I am terrified by the modes of life, by the manners, and the barrier of utter abhorrence, and want of sympathy, placed between us by feelings deeper than I can analyze. I could sooner live with lunatics, or brute animals. All this, and much more than I can say, or have time to say, the reader must enter into before he can comprehend the unimaginable horror which these dreams of oriental imagery, and mythological tortures, impressed upon me. Under the connecting feeling of tropical heat and vertical sun-lights, I brought together all creatures, birds, beasts, reptiles, all trees and plants, usages and appearances, that are found in all tropical regions, and assembled them together in China or Indostan. From kindred feelings, I soon brought Egypt and all her gods under the same law. I was stared at, hooted at, grinned at, chattered at, by monkeys, by paroquets, by cockatoos. I ran into pagodas: and was fixed, for centuries, at the summit, or in secret rooms; I was the idol; I was the priest; I was worshipped; I was sacrificed. I fled from the wrath of Brama through all the forests of Asia: Vishnu hated me: Seeva laid wait for me. I came suddenly upon Isis and Osiris:[165] I had done a deed, they said, which the ibis and the crocodile trembled at. I was buried, for a thousand years, in stone coffins, with mummies and sphynxes, in narrow chambers at the heart of eternal pyramids. I was kissed, with cancerous kisses, by crocodiles; and laid, confounded with all unutterable slimy things, amongst reeds and Nilotic mud.

I thus give the reader some slight abstraction of my oriental dreams, which always filled me with such amazement at the monstrous scenery, that horror seemed absorbed, for a while, in sheer astonishment. Sooner or later, came a reflux of feeling that swallowed up the astonishment, and left me, not so much in terror, as in hatred and abomination of what I saw. Over every form, and threat, and punishment, and dim sightless incarceration, brooded a sense of eternity and infinity that drove me into an oppression as of madness. Into these dreams only, it was, with one or two slight exceptions, that any circumstances of physical horror entered. All before had been moral and spiritual terrors. But here the main agents were ugly birds, or snakes, or crocodiles; especially the last. The cursed crocodile became to me the object of more horror than almost all the rest. I was compelled to live with him; and (as was always the case almost in my dreams) for centuries. I escaped sometimes, and found myself in Chinese houses, with cane tables, &c. All the feet of the tables, sophas, &c. soon became instinct with life: the abominable head of the crocodile, and his leering eyes, looked out at me, multiplied into a thousand repetitions: and I stood loathing and fascinated. And so often did this hideous reptile haunt my dreams, that many times the very same dream was broken up in the very same way: I heard gentle voices speaking to me (I hear every thing when I am sleeping); and instantly I awoke: it was broad noon; and my children were standing, hand in hand, at my bed-side; come to show me their coloured shoes, or new frocks, or to let me see them dressed for going out. I protest that so awful was the transition from the damned crocodile, and the other unutterable monsters and abortions of my dreams, to the sight of innocent *human* natures and of infancy, that, in the mighty and sudden revulsion of mind, I wept, and could not forebear it, as I kissed their faces.

June, 1819.

I have had occasion to remark, at various periods of my life, that the deaths of those whom we love, and indeed the contemplation of death generally, is (*cæteris paribus*)[166] more affecting in summer than in any other season of the year. And the reasons are these three, I think: first, that the visible heavens in summer appear far higher, more distant, and (if such a solecism may be excused) more infinite; the clouds, by which chiefly the eye expounds the distance of the blue pavilion stretched over our heads, are in summer more voluminous, massed, and accumulated in far grander and more towering piles: secondly, the light and the appearances of the declining and the setting sun are much more fitted to be types and characters of the Infinite: and, thirdly, (which is the main reason) the exuberant and riotous prodigality of life naturally forces the mind more powerfully upon the antagonist thought of death, and the wintry sterility of the grave. For it may be observed, generally, that wherever two thoughts stand related to each other by a law of antagonism, and exist, as it were, by mutual repulsion, they are apt to suggest each other. On these accounts it is that I find it impossible to banish the thought of death when I am walking alone in the endless days of summer; and any particular death, if not more affecting, at least haunts my mind more obstinately and besiegingly in that season. Perhaps this cause, and a slight incident which I omit, might have been the immediate occasions of the following dream; to which, however, a predisposition must always have existed in my mind; but having been once roused, it never left me, and split into a thousand fantastic varieties, which often suddenly re-united, and composed again the original dream.

I thought that it was a Sunday morning in May, that it was Easter Sunday, and as yet very early in the morning. I was standing, as it seemed to me, at the door of my own cottage. Right before me lay the very scene which could really be commanded from that situation, but exalted, as was usual, and

solemnized by the power of dreams. There were the same mountains, and the same lovely valley at their feet; but the mountains
were raised to more than Alpine height, and there was interspace
far larger between them of meadows and forest lawns; the
hedges were rich with white roses; and no living creature was to
be seen, excepting that in the green church-yard there were cattle
tranquilly reposing upon the verdant graves, and particularly
round about the grave of a child whom I had tenderly loved,[167]
just as I had really beheld them, a little before sun-rise in the
same summer, when that child died. I gazed upon the well-
known scene, and I said aloud (as I thought) to myself, 'it yet
wants much of sun-rise; and it is Easter Sunday; and that is the
day on which they celebrate the first fruits of resurrection. I will
walk abroad; old griefs shall be forgotten to-day; for the air is
cool and still, and the hills are high, and stretch away to Heaven;
and the forest-glades are as quiet as the church-yard; and, with
the dew, I can wash the fever from my forehead, and then I shall
be unhappy no longer.' And I turned, as if to open my garden
gate; and immediately I saw upon the left a scene far different;
but which yet the power of dreams had reconciled into harmony
with the other. The scene was an oriental one; and there also it
was Easter Sunday, and very early in the morning. And at a vast
distance were visible, as a stain upon the horizon, the domes
and cupolas of a great city – an image or faint abstraction,
caught perhaps in childhood from some picture of Jerusalem.
And not a bow-shot from me, upon a stone, and shaded by
Judean palms, there sat a woman; and I looked; and it was –
Ann! She fixed her eyes upon me earnestly; and I said to her at
length: 'So then I have found you at last.' I waited: but she
answered me not a word. Her face was the same as when I saw
it last, and yet again how different! Seventeen years ago, when
the lamp-light fell upon her face, as for the last time I kissed her
lips (lips, Ann, that to me were not polluted), her eyes were
streaming with tears: the tears were now wiped away; she
seemed more beautiful than she was at that time, but in all other
points the same, and not older. Her looks were tranquil, but
with unusual solemnity of expression; and I now gazed upon
her with some awe, but suddenly her countenance grew dim,

and, turning to the mountains, I perceived vapours rolling between us; in a moment, all had vanished; thick darkness came on; and, in the twinkling of an eye, I was far away from mountains, and by lamp-light in Oxford-street, walking again with Ann – just as we walked seventeen years before, when we were both children.

As a final specimen, I cite one of a different character, from 1820.

The dream commenced with a music which now I often heard in dreams – a music of preparation and of awakening suspense; a music like the opening of the Coronation Anthem,[168] and which, like *that*, gave the feeling of a vast march – of infinite cavalcades filing off – and the tread of innumerable armies. The morning was come of a mighty day – a day of crisis and of final hope for human nature, then suffering some mysterious eclipse, and labouring in some dread extremity. Somewhere, I knew not where – somehow, I knew not how – by some beings, I knew not whom – a battle, a strife, an agony, was conducting, – was evolving like a great drama, or piece of music; with which my sympathy was the more insupportable from my confusion as to its place, its cause, its nature, and its possible issue. I, as is usual in dreams (where, of necessity, we make ourselves central to every movement), had the power, and yet had not the power, to decide it. I had the power, if I could raise myself, to will it; and yet again had not the power, for the weight of twenty Atlantics was upon me, or the oppression of inexpiable guilt. 'Deeper than ever plummet sounded,'[169] I lay inactive. Then, like a chorus, the passion deepened. Some greater interest was at stake; some mightier cause than ever yet the sword had pleaded, or trumpet had proclaimed. Then came sudden alarms: hurryings to and fro: trepidations of innumerable fugitives, I knew not whether from the good cause or the bad: darkness and lights: tempest and human faces; and at last, with the sense that all was lost, female forms, and the features that were worth all the world to me, and but a moment allowed, – and clasped hands, and heart-breaking partings, and then – everlasting farewells! and with a sigh, such as the caves of hell sighed when the incestuous mother uttered the abhorred name of death,[170] the sound was reverberated – everlasting farewells! and again, and yet again reverberated – everlasting farewells!

And I awoke in struggles, and cried aloud – 'I will sleep no more!'

But I am now called upon to wind up a narrative which has already extended to an unreasonable length. Within more spacious limits, the materials which I have used might have been better unfolded; and much which I have not used might have been added with effect. Perhaps, however, enough has been given. It now remains that I should say something of the way in which this conflict of horrors was finally brought to its crisis. The reader is already aware (from a passage near the beginning of the introduction to the first part) that the opium-eater has, in some way or other, 'unwound, almost to its final links, the accursed chain which bound him.' By what means? To have narrated this, according to the original intention, would have far exceeded the space which can now be allowed. It is fortunate, as such a cogent reason exists for abridging it, that I should, on a maturer view of the case, have been exceedingly unwilling to injure, by any such unaffecting details, the impression of the history itself, as an appeal to the prudence and the conscience of the yet unconfirmed opium-eater – or even (though a very inferior consideration) to injure its effect as a composition. The interest of the judicious reader will not attach itself chiefly to the subject of the fascinating spells, but to the fascinating power. Not the opium-eater, but the opium, is the true hero of the tale; and the legitimate centre on which the interest revolves. The object was to display the marvellous agency of opium, whether for pleasure or for pain: if that is done, the action of the piece has closed.

However, as some people, in spite of all laws to the contrary, will persist in asking what became of the opium-eater, and in what state he now is, I answer for him thus: The reader is aware that opium had long ceased to found its empire on spells of pleasure; it was solely by the tortures connected with the attempt to abjure it, that it kept its hold. Yet, as other tortures, no less it may be thought, attended the non-abjuration of such a tyrant, a choice only of evils was left; and *that* might as well have been adopted, which, however terrific in itself, held out a prospect of final restoration to happiness. This appears true; but good logic gave the author no strength to act upon it. However, a crisis arrived for the author's life, and a crisis for other objects still dearer to him – and which will always be far dearer to him than his life, even now that it is again a happy one. – I saw that I must die if I continued the opium: I determined, therefore, if that should be required, to die in throwing it off. How much I was at that time taking I cannot say; for the opium which I used had been purchased for me by a friend who afterwards refused to let me pay him; so that I could not ascertain even what quantity I had used within the year. I apprehend, however, that I took it very irregularly: and that I varied from about fifty or sixty grains, to 150 a-day. My first task was to reduce it to forty, to thirty, and, as fast as I could, to twelve grains.

I triumphed: but think not, reader, that therefore my sufferings were ended; nor think of me as of one sitting in a *dejected* state. Think of me as of one, even when four months had passed, still agitated, writhing, throbbing, palpitating, shattered; and much, perhaps, in the situation of him who has been racked, as I collect the torments of that state from the affecting account of them left by a most innocent sufferer* (of the times of James I). Meantime, I derived no benefit from any medicine, except one prescribed to me by an Edinburgh surgeon of great eminence,[171] viz. ammoniated tincture of Valerian. Medical account, therefore, of my emancipation I have not much to give: and even that little, as managed by a man so ignorant of medicine as myself, would probably tend only to mislead. At all events, it would be misplaced in this situation. The moral of the narrative is addressed to the opium-eater; and therefore, of necessity, limited in its application. If he is taught to fear and tremble, enough has been effected. But he may say, that the issue of my case is at least a proof that opium, after a seventeen years' use, and an eight years' abuse of its powers, may still be renounced:[172] and

---

* William Lithgow:[173] his book (Travels, &c.) is ill and pedantically written: but the account of his own sufferings on the rack at Malaga is overpoweringly affecting.

that *he* may chance to bring to the task greater energy than I did, or that with a stronger constitution than mine he may obtain the same results with less. This may be true: I would not presume to measure the efforts of other men by my own: I heartily wish him more energy: I wish him the same success. Nevertheless, I had motives external to myself which he may unfortunately want: and these supplied me with conscientious supports which mere personal interests might fail to supply to a mind debilitated by opium.

Jeremy Taylor[174] conjectures that it may be as painful to be born as to die: I think it probable: and, during the whole period of diminishing the opium, I had the torments of a man passing out of one mode of existence into another. The issue was not death, but a sort of physical regeneration: and I may add, that ever since, at intervals, I have had a restoration of more than youthful spirits, though under the pressure of difficulties, which, in a less happy state of mind, I should have called misfortunes.

One memorial of my former condition still remains: my dreams are not yet perfectly calm: the dread swell and agitation of the storm have not wholly subsided: the legions that encamped in them are drawing off, but not all departed: my sleep is still tumultuous, and, like the gates of Paradise to our first parents when looking back from afar, it is still (in the tremendous line of Milton) –

With dreadful faces throng'd and fiery arms.[175]

SUSPIRIA DE PROFUNDIS:[1]

Being a Sequel to the Confessions of an English Opium-Eater

Introductory Notice

In 1821, as a contribution to a periodical work – in 1822, as a separate volume – appeared the 'Confessions of an English Opium-Eater.' The object of that work was to reveal something of the grandeur which belongs *potentially* to human dreams. Whatever may be the number of those in whom this faculty of dreaming splendidly can be supposed to lurk, there are not perhaps very many in whom it is developed. He whose talk is of oxen, will probably dream of oxen: and the condition of human life, which yokes so vast a majority to a daily experience incompatible with much elevation of thought, oftentimes neutralizes the tone of grandeur in the reproductive faculty of dreaming, even for those whose minds are populous with solemn imagery. Habitually to dream magnificently, a man must have a constitutional determination to reverie. This in the first place; and even this, where it exists strongly, is too much liable to disturbance from the gathering agitation of our present English life. Already, in this year 1845, what by the procession through fifty years of mighty revolutions amongst the kingdoms of the earth, what by the continual development of vast physical agencies – steam in all its applications, light getting under harness as a slave for man,* powers from heaven descending upon education and accelerations of the press, powers from hell (as it might seem, but these also celestial) coming round upon artillery and the forces of destruction – the eye of the calmest observer

* Daguerreotype, &c.[2]

is troubled; the brain is haunted as if by some jealousy of ghostly beings moving amongst us; and it becomes too evident that, unless this colossal pace of advance can be retarded, (a thing not to be expected,) or, which is happily more probable, can be met by counter-forces of corresponding magnitude, forces in the direction of religion or profound philosophy, that shall radiate centrifugally against this storm of life so perilously centripetal towards the vortex of the merely human, left to itself the natural tendency of so chaotic a tumult must be to evil; for some minds to lunacy, for others to a reagency of fleshly torpor. How much this fierce condition of eternal hurry, upon an arena too exclusively human in its interests, is likely to defeat the grandeur which is latent in all men, may be seen in the ordinary effect from living too constantly in varied company. The word *dissipation*, in one of its uses, expresses that effect; the action of thought and feeling is too much dissipated and squandered. To reconcentrate them into meditative habits, a necessity is felt by all observing persons for sometimes retiring from crowds. No man ever will unfold the capacities of his own intellect who does not at least chequer his life with solitude. How much solitude, so much power. Or, if not true in that rigour of expression, to this formula undoubtedly it is that the wise rule of life must approximate.

Among the powers in man which suffer by this too intense life of the *social* instincts, none suffers more than the power of dreaming. Let no man think this a trifle. The machinery for dreaming planted in the human brain was not planted for nothing. That faculty, in alliance with the mystery of darkness, is the one great tube through which man communicates with the shadowy. And the dreaming organ, in connexion with the heart, the eye, and the ear, compose the magnificent apparatus which forces the infinite into the chambers of a human brain, and throws dark reflections from eternities below all life upon the mirrors of the sleeping mind.

But if this faculty suffers from the decay of solitude, which is becoming a visionary idea in England, on the other hand, it is certain that some merely physical agencies can and do assist the faculty of dreaming almost preternaturally. Amongst these is intense exercise; to some extent at least, and for some persons: but beyond all others is opium, which indeed seems to possess a *specific* power in that direction; not merely for exalting the colours of dream-scenery, but for deepening its shadows; and, above all, for strengthening the sense of its fearful *realities*.

The *Opium Confessions* were written with some slight secondary purpose of exposing this specific power of opium upon the faculty of dreaming, but much more with the purpose of displaying the faculty itself; and the outline of the work travelled in this course. Supposing a reader acquainted with the true object of the Confessions as here stated, viz. the revelation of dreaming, to have put this question: –

'But how came you to dream more splendidly than others?'

The answer would have been: – 'Because (*præmissis præmittendis*)[3] I took excessive quantities of opium.'

Secondly, suppose him to say, 'But how came you to take opium in this excess?'

The answer to *that* would be, 'Because some early events in my life had left a weakness in one organ which required (or seemed to require) that stimulant.'

Then, because the opium dreams could not always have been understood without a knowledge of these events, it became necessary to relate them. Now, these two questions and answers exhibit the *law* of the work, *i.e.* the principle which determined its form, but precisely in the inverse or regressive order. The work itself opened with the narration of my early adventures. These, in the natural order of succession, led to the opium as a resource for healing their consequences; and the opium as naturally led to the dreams. But in the synthetic order of presenting the facts, what stood last in the succession of development, stood first in the order of my purposes.

At the close of this little work, the reader was instructed to believe – and *truly* instructed – that I had mastered the tyranny of opium. The fact is, that *twice* I mastered it, and by efforts even more prodigious, in the second of these cases, than in the first. But one error I committed in both. I did not connect with the abstinence from opium – so trying to the fortitude under *any* circumstances – that enormity of exercise which (as I have since learned) is the one sole resource for making it endurable. I overlooked, in those days, the one *sine quâ non*[4] for making the triumph permanent. Twice I sank – twice I rose again. A third time I sank; partly from the cause mentioned, (the oversight as to exercise,) partly from other causes, on which it avails not now to trouble the reader. I could moralize if I chose; and perhaps *he* will moralize whether I choose it or not. But, in the mean time, neither of us is acquainted properly with the circumstances of the case; I, from natural bias of judgment, not altogether acquainted; and he (with his permission) not at all.

During this third prostration before the dark idol, and after some years, new and monstrous phenomena began slowly to arise. For a time, these were neglected as accidents, or palliated by such remedies as I knew of. But when I could no longer conceal from myself that these dreadful symptoms were moving forward for ever, by a pace steadily, solemnly, and equably increasing, I endeavoured, with some feeling of panic, for a third time to retrace my steps. But I had not reversed my motions for many weeks, before I became profoundly aware that this was impossible. Or, in the imagery of my dreams, which translated every thing into their own language, I saw through vast avenues of gloom those towering gates of ingress which hitherto had always seemed to stand open, now at last barred against my retreat, and hung with funeral crape.

As applicable to this tremendous situation, (the situation of one escaping by some refluent current from the maelstrom roaring for him in the distance, who finds suddenly that this current is but an eddy, wheeling round upon the same maelstrom,) I have since remembered a striking incident in a modern novel.[5] A lady abbess of a convent, herself suspected of Protestant leanings, and in that way already disarmed of all effectual power, finds one of her own nuns (whom she knows to be innocent) accused of an offence leading to the most terrific of punishments. The nun will be immured alive if she is found guilty; and there is no chance that she will not – for the evidence against her is strong – unless something were made known that cannot be made known; and the judges are hostile. All follows in the order of the reader's fears. The witnesses depose; the evidence is without effectual contradiction; the conviction is declared; the judgment is delivered; nothing remains but to see execution done. At this crisis the abbess, alarmed too late for effectual interposition, considers with herself that, according to the regular forms, there will be one single night open during which the prisoner cannot be withdrawn from her own separate jurisdiction. This one night, therefore, she will use, at any hazard to herself, for the salvation of her friend. At midnight, when all is hushed in the convent, the lady traverses the passages which lead to the cells of prisoners. She bears a master-key under her professional habit. As this will open every door in every corridor, – already, by anticipation, she feels the luxury of holding her emancipated friend within her arms. Suddenly she has reached the door; she descries a dusky object; she raises her lamp; and, ranged within the recess of the entrance, she beholds the funeral banner of the Holy Office,[6] and the black robes of its inexorable officials.

I apprehend that, in a situation such as this, supposing it a real one, the lady abbess would not start, would not show any marks externally of consternation or horror. The case was beyond *that*. The sentiment which attends the sudden revelation that *all is lost*! silently is gathered up into the heart; it is too deep for gestures or for words; and no part of it passes to the outside. Were the ruin conditional, or were it in any point doubtful, it would be natural to utter ejaculations, and to seek sympathy. But where the ruin is understood to be absolute, where sympathy cannot be consolation, and counsel cannot be hope, this is otherwise. The voice perishes; the gestures are frozen; and the spirit of man flies back upon its own centre. I, at least, upon seeing those awful gates closed and hung with draperies of woe, as for a death already past, spoke not, nor started, nor groaned. One profound sigh ascended from my heart, and I was silent for days.

It is the record of this third, or final stage of opium, as one differing in something more than degree from the others, that I am now undertaking. But a scruple arises as to the true interpretation of these final symptoms. I have elsewhere explained, that it was no particular purpose of mine, and *why* it was no particular purpose, to warn other opium-eaters. Still, as some few persons may use the record in that way, it becomes a matter of interest to ascertain how far it is likely, that, even with the same excesses, other opium-eaters could fall into the same condition. I do not mean to lay a stress upon any supposed idiosyncrasy in myself. Possibly every man has an idiosyncrasy. In some things, undoubtedly, he has. For no man ever yet resembled another man so far, as not to differ from him in features innumerable of his inner nature. But what I point to are not peculiarities of temperament or of organization, so much as peculiar circumstances and incidents through which my own separate experience had revolved. Some of these were of a nature to alter the whole economy of my mind. Great convulsions, from whatever cause, from conscience, from fear, from grief, from struggles of the will, sometimes, in passing away themselves, do not carry off the changes which they have worked. *All* the agitations of this magnitude which a man may have threaded in his life, he neither ought to report, nor *could* report. But one which affected my childhood is a privileged exception. It is privileged as a proper communication for a stranger's ear; because, though relating to a man's proper self, it is a self so far removed from his present self as to wound no feelings of delicacy or just reserve. It is privileged also as a proper subject for the sympathy of the narrator. An adult sympathizes with himself in childhood because he *is* the same, and because (being the same) yet he is *not* the same. He acknowledges the deep, mysterious identity between himself, as adult and as infant, for the ground of his sympathy; and yet, with this general agreement, and necessity of agreement, he feels the differences between his two selves as the main quickeners of his sympathy. He pities the infirmities, as they arise to light in his young forerunner, which now perhaps he does not share; he looks indulgently upon errors of the understanding, or limitations of view which now he has long survived; and sometimes, also, he honours in the infant that rectitude of will which, under *some* temptations, he may since have felt it so difficult to maintain.

The particular case to which I refer in my own childhood, was one of intolerable grief; a trial, in fact, more severe than many people at *any* age are called upon to stand. The relation in which the case stands to my latter opium experiences, is this: – Those vast clouds of gloomy grandeur which overhung my dreams at all stages of opium, but which grew into the darkest of miseries in the last, and that haunting of the human face, which latterly towered into a curse – were they not partly derived from this childish experience? It is certain that, from the essential solitude in which my childhood was passed; from the depth of my sensibility; from the exaltation of this by the resistance of an intellect too prematurely developed, it resulted that the terrific grief which I passed through, drove a shaft for me into the worlds of death and darkness which never again closed, and through which it might be said that I ascended and descended at will, according to the temper of my spirits. Some of the phenomena developed in my dream-scenery, undoubtedly, do but repeat the experiences of childhood; and others seem likely to have been growths and fructifications from seeds at that time sown.

The reasons, therefore, for prefixing some account of a 'passage' in childhood, to this record of a dreadful visitation from opium excess, are – 1st, That, in colouring, it harmonizes with that record, and, therefore, is related to it at least in point of feeling; 2dly, That possibly it was in part the origin of some features in that record, and so far is related to it in logic; 3dly, That, the final assault of opium being of a nature to challenge the attention of medical men, it is important to clear away all doubts and scruples which can gather about the roots of such a malady. Was it opium, or was it opium in combination with something else, that raised these storms?

Some cynical reader will object – that for this last purpose it would have been sufficient to state the fact, without rehearsing *in extenso*[7] the particulars of that case in childhood. But the reader of more kindness (for a surly reader is always a bad critic) will also have more discernment; and he will perceive that it is not for the mere facts that the case is reported, but because these facts move through a wilderness of natural thoughts or feelings; some in the child who suffers; some in the man who reports; but all so far interesting as they relate to solemn objects.

Meantime, the objection of the sullen critic reminds me of a scene sometimes beheld at the English lakes. Figure to yourself an energetic tourist, who protests every where that he comes only to see the lakes. He has no business whatever; he is not searching for any recreant indorser of a bill, but simply in search of the picturesque. Yet this man adjures every landlord, 'by the virtue of his oath,' to tell him, and as he hopes for peace in this world to tell him truly, which is the *nearest* road to Keswick. Next, he applies to the postilions – the Westmoreland postilions always fly down hills at full stretch without locking – but nevertheless, in the full career of their fiery race, our picturesque man lets down the glasses, pulls up four horses and two postilions, at the risk of six necks and twenty legs, adjuring them to reveal whether they are taking the *shortest* road. Finally, he descries my unworthy self upon the road; and, instantly stopping his flying equipage, he demands of me (as one whom he believes to be a scholar and a man of honour) whether there is not, in the possibility of things, a *shorter* cut to Keswick. Now, the answer which rises to the lips of landlord, two postilions, and myself, is this – 'Most excellent stranger, as you come to the lakes simply to see their loveliness, might it not be as well to ask after the most beautiful road, rather than the shortest? Because, if abstract shortness, if τὸ brevity[8] is your object, then the shortest of all possible tours would seem, with submission – never to have left London.' On the same principle, I tell my critic that the whole course of this narrative resembles, and was meant to resemble, a *caduceus*[9] wreathed about with meandering ornaments, or the shaft of a tree's stem hung round and surmounted with some vagrant parasitical plant. The mere medical subject of the opium answers to the dry withered pole, which shoots all the rings of the flowering plants, and seems to do so by some dexterity of its own; whereas, in fact, the plant and its tendrils have curled round the sullen cylinder by mere luxuriance of *theirs*. Just as in Cheapside,[10] if you look right and left, the streets so narrow, that lead off at right angles, seemed quarried and blasted out of some Babylonian brick kiln; bored, not raised artificially by the builder's hand. But, if you enquire of the worthy men who live in that neighbourhood, you will find it unanimously deposed – that not the streets were quarried out of the bricks, but, on the contrary, (most ridiculous as it seems,) that the bricks have supervened upon the streets.

The streets did not intrude amongst the bricks, but those cursed bricks came to imprison the streets. So, also, the ugly pole – hop pole, vine pole, espalier, no matter what – is there only for support. Not the flowers are for the pole, but the pole is for the flowers. Upon the same analogy view me, as one (in the words of a true and most impassioned poet*) '*viridantem floribus hastas*'[11] – making verdant, and gay with the life of flowers, murderous spears and halberts – things that express death in their origin, (being made from dead substances that once had lived in forests,) things that express ruin in their use. The true object in my 'Opium Confessions' is not the naked physiological theme – on the contrary, *that* is the ugly pole, the murderous spear, the halbert – but those wandering musical variations upon the theme – those parasitical thoughts, feelings, digressions, which climb up with bells and blossoms round about the arid stock; ramble away from it at times with perhaps too rank a luxuriance; but at the same time, by the external interest attached to the *subjects* of these digressions, no matter what were the execution, spread a glory over incidents that for themselves would be – less than nothing.

PART I

THE AFFLICTION OF CHILDHOOD

It is so painful to a lover of open-hearted sincerity, that any indirect traits of vanity should even *seem* to creep into records of profound passion; and yet, on the other hand, it is so impossible, without an unnatural restraint upon the freedom of the narrative, to prevent oblique gleams reaching the reader from such circumstances of luxury or elegance as did really surround my childhood, that on all accounts I think it better to tell him from

* Valerius Flaccus.

the first, with the simplicity of truth, in what order of society
my family moved at the time from which this preliminary narrative is dated. Otherwise it would happen that, merely by moving
truly and faithfully through the circumstances of this early
experience, I could hardly prevent the reader from receiving an
impression as of some higher rank than did really belong to my
family. My father was a merchant; not in the sense of Scotland,
where it means a man who sells groceries in a cellar, but in the
English sense, a sense severely exclusive – viz. he was a man
engaged in *foreign* commerce, and no other; therefore, in *wholesale* commerce, and no other, – which last circumstance it is
important to mention, because it brings him within the benefit
of Cicero's condescending distinction* – as one to be despised,
certainly, but not too intensely to be despised even by a Roman
senator. He, this imperfectly despicable man, died at an early
age, and very soon after the incidents here recorded, leaving
to his family, then consisting of a wife and six children, an
unburthened estate producing exactly £1600 a-year. Naturally,
therefore, at the date of my narrative, if narrative it can be
called, he had an income still larger, from the addition of current
commercial profits. Now, to any man who is acquainted with
commercial life, but above all, with such life in England, it will
readily occur that in an opulent English family of that class –
opulent, though not rich in a mercantile estimate – the domestic
economy is likely to be upon a scale of liberality altogether
unknown amongst the corresponding orders in foreign nations.
Whether as to the establishment of servants, or as to the provision made for the comfort of all its members, such a household
not uncommonly eclipses the scale of living even amongst the
poorer classes of our nobility, though the most splendid in
Europe – a fact which, since the period of my infancy, I have
had many personal opportunities for verifying both in England
and in Ireland. From this peculiar anomaly affecting the domestic economy of merchants, there arises a disturbance upon

---

* Cicero, in a well-known passage of his *Ethics*,[12] speaks of trade as irredeem-
ably base, if petty; but as not so absolutely felonious if wholesale. He gives a
real merchant (one who is such in the English sense) leave to think himself a
shade above small-beer.

the general scale of outward signs by which we measure the relations of rank. The equation, so to speak, between one order of society and another, which usually travels in the natural line of their comparative expenditure, is here interrupted and defeated, so that one rank would be collected from the name of the occupation, and another rank, much higher, from the splendour of the domestic *ménage*. I warn the reader, therefore, (or rather, my explanation has already warned him,) that he is not to infer from any casual gleam of luxury or elegance a corresponding elevation of rank.

We, the children of the house, stood in fact upon the very happiest tier in the scaffolding of society for all good influences. The prayer of Agar[13] – 'Give me neither poverty nor riches' – was realized for us. That blessing had we, being neither too high nor too low; high enough we were to see models of good manners; obscure enough to be left in the sweetest of solitudes. Amply furnished with the nobler benefits of wealth, *extra* means of health, of intellectual culture, and of elegant enjoyment, on the other hand, we knew nothing of its social distinctions. Not depressed by the consciousness of privations too sordid, not tempted into restlessness by the consciousness of privileges too aspiring, we had no motives for shame, we had none for pride. Grateful also to this hour I am, that, amidst luxuries in all things else, we were trained to a Spartan simplicity of diet – that we fared, in fact, very much less sumptuously than the servants. And if (after the model of the emperor Marcus Aurelius)[14] I should return thanks to Providence for all the separate blessings of my early situation, these four I would single out as chiefly worthy to be commemorated – that I lived in the country; that I lived in solitude; that my infant feelings were moulded by the gentlest of sisters, not by horrid pugilistic brothers; finally, that I and they were dutiful children of a pure, holy, and magnificent church.

The earliest incidents in my life which affected me so deeply as to be rememberable at this day, were two, and both before I could have completed my second year, viz. a remarkable dream of terrific grandeur about a favourite nurse, which is interesting for a reason to be noticed hereafter; and secondly, the fact of having connected a profound sense of pathos with the re-appearance, very early in spring, of some crocuses. This I mention as inexplicable, for such annual resurrections of plants and flowers affect us only as memorials, or suggestions of a higher change, and therefore in connexion with the idea of death; but of death I could, at that time, have had no experience whatever.

This, however, I was speedily to acquire. My two eldest sisters – eldest of three *then* living, and also elder than myself – were summoned to an early death. The first who died was Jane[15] – about a year older than myself. She was three and a half, I two and a half, *plus* or *minus* some trifle that I do not recollect. But death was then scarcely intelligible to me, and I could not so properly be said to suffer sorrow as a sad perplexity. There was another death in the house about the same time, viz. of a maternal grandmother; but as she had in a manner come to us for the express purpose of dying in her daughter's society, and from illness had lived perfectly secluded, our nursery party knew her but little, and were certainly more affected by the death (which I witnessed) of a favourite bird, viz. a kingfisher who had been injured by an accident. With my sister Jane's death [though otherwise, as I have said, less sorrowful than unintelligible] there was, however, connected an incident which made a most fearful impression upon myself, deepening my tendencies to thoughtfulness and abstraction beyond what would seem credible for my years. If there was one thing in this world from which, more than from any other, nature had forced me to revolt, it was brutality and violence. Now a whisper arose in the family, that a woman-servant, who by accident was drawn off from her proper duties to attend my sister Jane for a day or two, had on one occasion treated her harshly, if not brutally; and – as this ill treatment happened within two days of her death – so that the occasion of it must have been some fretfulness in the poor child caused by her sufferings – naturally there was a sense of awe diffused through the family. I believe the story never reached my mother, and possibly it was exaggerated; but upon me the effect was terrific. I did not often see the person charged with this cruelty; but, when I did, my eyes sought the ground;

nor could I have borne to look her in the face – not through anger; and as to vindictive thoughts, how could these lodge in a powerless infant? The feeling which fell upon me was a shuddering awe, as upon a first glimpse of the truth that I was in a world of evil and strife. Though born in a large town, I had passed the whole of my childhood, except for the few earliest weeks, in a rural seclusion. With three innocent little sisters for playmates, sleeping always amongst them, and shut up for ever in a silent garden from all knowledge of poverty, or oppression, or outrage, I had not suspected until this moment the true complexion of the world in which myself and my sisters were living. Henceforward the character of my thoughts must have changed greatly; for so *representative* are some acts, that one single case of the class is sufficient to throw open before you the whole theatre of possibilities in that direction. I never heard that the woman, accused of this cruelty, took it at all to heart, even after the event, which so immediately succeeded, had reflected upon it a more painful emphasis. On the other hand, I knew of a case, and will pause to mention it, where a mere semblance and shadow of such cruelty, under similar circumstances, inflicted the grief of self-reproach through the remainder of life. A boy, interesting in his appearance, as also from his remarkable docility, was attacked, on a cold day of spring, by a complaint of the trachea – not precisely croup, but like it. He was three years old, and had been ill perhaps for four days; but at intervals had been in high spirits, and capable of playing. This sunshine, gleaming through dark clouds, had continued even on the fourth day; and from nine to eleven o'clock at night, he had showed more animated pleasure than ever. An old servant, hearing of his illness, had called to see him; and her mode of talking with him had excited all the joyousness of his nature. About midnight his mother, fancying that his feet felt cold, was muffling them up in flannels; and, as he seemed to resist her a little, she struck lightly on the sole of one foot as a mode of admonishing him to be quiet. He did not repeat his motion; and in less than a minute his mother had him in her arms with his face looking upwards. 'What is the meaning,' she exclaimed, in sudden affright, 'of this strange repose settling upon his features?' She called loudly to a servant in another room; but before the servant could reach her, the child had drawn two inspirations – deep, yet gentle – and had died in his mother's arms. Upon this the poor afflicted lady made the discovery that those struggles, which she had supposed to be expressions of resistance to herself, were the struggles of departing life. It followed, or seemed to follow, that with these final struggles had blended an expression, on *her* part, of displeasure. Doubtless the child had not distinctly perceived it; but the mother could never look back to the incident without self-reproach. And seven years after, when her own death happened, no progress had been made in reconciling her thoughts to that which only the depth of love could have viewed as any offence.

So passed away from earth one out of those sisters that made up my nursery playmates; and so did my acquaintance (if such it could be called) commence with mortality. Yet, in fact, I knew little more of mortality than that Jane had disappeared. She had gone away; but, perhaps, she would come back. Happy interval of heaven-born ignorance! Gracious immunity of infancy from sorrow disproportioned to its strength! I was sad for Jane's absence. But still in my heart I trusted that she would come again. Summer and winter came again – crocuses and roses; why not little Jane?

Thus easily was healed, then, the first wound in my infant heart. Not so the second. For thou, dear, noble Elizabeth, around whose ample brow, and often as thy sweet countenance rises upon the darkness, I fancy a tiara of light or a gleaming *aureola* in token of thy premature intellectual grandeur – thou whose head, for its superb developments, was the astonishment of science* – thou

* *'The astonishment of science.'* – Her medical attendants were Dr Percival, a well-known literary physician, who had been a correspondent of Condorcet, D'Alembert, &c., and Mr Charles White,[16] a very distinguished surgeon. It was he who pronounced her head to be the finest in its structure and development of any that he had ever seen – an assertion which, to my own knowledge, he repeated in after years, and with enthusiasm. That he had some acquaintance with the subject may be presumed from this, that he wrote and published a work on the human skull, supported by many measurements which he had made of heads selected from all varieties of the human species. Meantime, as I would be loth that any trait of what might seem vanity should creep into this

next, but after an interval of happy years, thou also wert summoned away from our nursery; and the night which, for me, gathered upon that event, ran after my steps far into life; and perhaps at this day I resemble little for good or for ill that which else I should have been. Pillar of fire, that dist go before me to guide and to quicken – pillar of darkness, when thy countenance was turned away to God, that didst too truly shed the shadow of death over my young heart – in what scales should I weigh thee? Was the blessing greater from thy heavenly presence, or the blight which followed thy departure? Can a man weigh off and value the glories of dawn against the darkness of hurricane? Or, if he could, how is it that, when a memorable love has been followed by a memorable bereavement, even suppose that God would replace the sufferer in a point of time anterior to the entire experience, and offer to cancel the woe, but so that the sweet face which had caused the woe should also be obliterated – vehemently would every man shrink from the exchange! In the *Paradise Lost*, this strong instinct of man – to prefer the heavenly, mixed and polluted with the earthly, to a level experience offering neither one nor the other – is divinely commemorated. What worlds of pathos are in that speech of Adam's – 'If God should make another Eve,'[17] &c. – that is, if God should replace him in his primitive state, and should condescend to bring again a second Eve, one that would listen to no temptation – still that original partner of his earliest solitude –

> 'Creature in whom excell'd
> Whatever can to sight or thought be form'd,
> Holy, divine, good, amiable, or sweet' –

---

record, I will candidly admit that she died of hydrocephalus; and it has been often supposed that the premature expansion of the intellect in cases of that class, is altogether morbid – forced on, in fact, by the mere stimulation of the disease. I would, however, suggest, as a possibility, the very inverse order of relation between the disease and the intellectual manifestations. Not the disease may always have caused the preternatural growth of the intellect, but, on the contrary, this growth coming on spontaneously, and outrunning the capacities of the physical structure, may have caused the disease.

even now, when she appeared in league with an eternity of woe, and ministering to his ruin, could not be displaced for him by any better or happier Eve. 'Loss of thee!' he exclaims in this anguish of trial –

> 'Loss of thee
> Would never from my heart; no, no, I feel
> The link of nature draw me; flesh of flesh,
> Bone of my bone thou art; and from thy state
> Mine never shall be parted, bliss or woe.'*

But what was it that drew my heart, by gravitation so strong, to my sister? Could a child, little above six years of age, place any special value upon her intellectual forwardness? Serene and capacious as her mind appeared to me upon after review, was *that* a charm for stealing away the heart of an infant? Oh, no! I think of it *now* with interest, because it lends, in a stranger's ear, some justification to the excess of my fondness. But then it was lost upon me; or, if not lost, was but dimly perceived. Hadst thou been an idiot, my sister, not the less I must have loved thee – having that capacious heart overflowing, even as mine overflowed, with tenderness, and stung, even as mine was stung, by the necessity of being loved. This it was which crowned thee with beauty –

> 'Love, the holy sense,
> Best gift of God, in thee was most intense.'[18]

---

* Amongst the oversights in the *Paradise Lost*, some of which have not yet been perceived, it is certainly *one* – that, by placing in such overpowering light of pathos the sublime sacrifice of Adam to his love for his frail companion, he has too much lowered the guilt of his disobedience to God. All that Milton can say afterwards, does not, and cannot, obscure the beauty of that action: reviewing it calmly, we condemn – but taking the impassioned station of Adam at the moment of temptation, we approve in our hearts. This was certainly an oversight; but it was one very difficult to redress. I remember, amongst the many exquisite thoughts of John Paul, (Richter,)[19] one which strikes me as peculiarly touching upon this subject. He suggests – not as any grave theological comment, but as the wandering fancy of a poetic heart – that, had Adam conquered the anguish of separation as a pure sacrifice of obedience to God, his reward would have been the pardon and reconciliation of Eve, together with her restoration to innocence.

That lamp lighted in Paradise was kindled for me which shone so steadily in thee; and never but to thee only, never again since thy departure, *durst* I utter the feelings which possessed me. For I was the shiest of children; and a natural sense of personal dignity held me back at all stages of life, from exposing the least ray of feelings which I was not encouraged *wholly* to reveal.

It would be painful, and it is needless, to pursue the course of that sickness which carried off my leader and companion. She (according to my recollection at this moment) was just as much above eight years as I above six. And perhaps this natural precedency in authority of judgment, and the tender humility with which she declined to assert it, had been amongst the fascinations of her presence. It was upon a Sunday evening, or so people fancied, that the spark of fatal fire fell upon that train of predispositions to a brain-complaint which had hitherto slumbered within her. She had been permitted to drink tea at the house of a labouring man, the father of an old female servant. The sun had set when she returned in the company of this servant through meadows reeking with exhalations after a fervent day. From that time she sickened. Happily a child in such circumstances feels no anxieties. Looking upon medical men as people whose natural commission it is to heal diseases, since it is their natural function to profess it, knowing them only as *ex-officio*[20] privileged to make war upon pain and sickness – I never had a misgiving about the result. I grieved indeed that my sister should lie in bed: I grieved still more sometimes to hear her moan. But all this appeared to me no more than a night of trouble on which the dawn would soon arise. Oh! moment of darkness and delirium, when a nurse awakened me from that delusion, and launched God's thunderbolt at my heart in the assurance that my sister *must* die. Rightly it is said of utter, utter misery, that it 'cannot be *remembered*.'* Itself, as a remembrable thing, is swallowed up in its own chaos. Mere anarchy and confusion of

* 'I stood in unimaginable trance
And agony, which cannot be remember'd.'
   – *Speech of Alhadra in Coleridge's Remorse.*[21]

mind fell upon me. Deaf and blind I was, as I reeled under the revelation. I wish not to recal the circumstances of that time, when *my* agony was at its height, and hers in another sense was approaching. Enough to say – that all was soon over; and the morning of that day had at last arrived which looked down upon her innocent face, sleeping the sleep from which there is no awaking, and upon me sorrowing the sorrow for which there is no consolation.

On the day after my sister's death, whilst the sweet temple of her brain was yet unviolated by human scrutiny, I formed my own scheme for seeing her once more. Not for the world would I have made this known, nor have suffered a witness to accompany me. I had never heard of feelings that take the name of 'sentimental,' nor dreamed of such a possibility. But grief even in a child hates the light, and shrinks from human eyes. The house was large; there were two staircases; and by one of these I knew that about noon, when all would be quiet, I could steal up into her chamber. I imagine that it was exactly high noon when I reached the chamber door; it was locked; but the key was not taken away. Entering, I closed the door so softly, that, although it opened upon a hall which ascended through all the stories, no echo ran along the silent walls. Then turning round, I sought my sister's face. But the bed had been moved; and the back was now turned. Nothing met my eyes but one large window wide open, through which the sun of midsummer at noonday was showering down torrents of splendour. The weather was dry, the sky was cloudless, the blue depths seemed the express types of infinity; and it was not possible for eye to behold or for heart to conceive any symbols more pathetic of life and the glory of life.

Let me pause for one instant in approaching a remembrance so affecting and revolutionary for my own mind, and one which (if any earthly remembrance) will survive for me in the hour of death, – to remind some readers, and to inform others, that in the original *Opium Confessions* I endeavoured to explain the reason*

---

* Some readers will question the *fact*, and seek no reason. But did they ever suffer grief at *any* season of the year?

why death, *cæteris paribus*, is more profoundly affecting in summer than in other parts of the year; so far at least as it is liable to any modification at all from accidents of scenery or season. The reason, as I there suggested, lies in the antagonism between the tropical redundancy of life in summer and the dark sterilities of the grave. The summer we see, the grave we haunt with our thoughts; the glory is around us, the darkness is within us. And, the two coming into collision, each exalts the other into stronger relief. But in my case there was even a subtler reason why the summer had this intense power of vivifying the spectacle or the thoughts of death. And, recollecting it, often I have been struck with the important truth – that far more of our deepest thoughts and feelings pass to us through perplexed combinations of *concrete* objects, pass to us as *involutes* (if I may coin that word) in compound experiences incapable of being disentangled, than ever reach us *directly*, and in their own abstract shapes. It had happened that amongst our nursery collection of books was the Bible illustrated with many pictures. And in long dark evenings, as my three sisters with myself sate by the firelight round the *guard*[22] of our nursery, no book was so much in request amongst us. It ruled us and swayed us as mysteriously as music. One young nurse, whom we all loved, before any candle was lighted, would often strain her eyes to read it for us; and sometimes, according to her simple powers, would endeavour to explain what we found obscure. We, the children, were all constitutionally touched with pensiveness; the fitful gloom and sudden lambencies of the room by fire-light, suited our evening state of feelings; and they suited also the divine revelations of power and mysterious beauty which awed us. Above all, the story of a just man, – man and yet *not* man, real above all things and yet shadowy above all things, who had suffered the passion of death in Palestine, slept upon our minds like early dawn upon the waters. The nurse knew and explained to us the chief differences in Oriental climates; and all these differences (as it happens) express themselves in the great varieties of summer. The cloudless sunlights of Syria – those seemed to argue everlasting summer; the disciples plucking the ears of corn – that *must* be summer; but, above all, the very name of Palm Sunday, (a festival in the English church,) troubled me like an anthem. 'Sunday!' what was *that*? That was the day of peace which masqued another peace deeper than the heart of man can comprehend. 'Palms!' – what were they? *That* was an equivocal word: palms, in the sense of trophies, expressed the pomps of life: palms, as a product of nature, expressed the pomps of summer. Yet still even this explanation does not suffice: it was not merely by the peace and by the summer, by the deep sound of rest below all rest, and of ascending glory, – that I had been haunted. It was also because Jerusalem stood near to those deep images both in time and in place. The great event of Jerusalem was at hand when Palm Sunday came; and the scene of that Sunday was near in place to Jerusalem. Yet what then was Jerusalem? Did I fancy it to be the *omphalos* (navel) of the earth? That pretension had once been made for Jerusalem, and once for Delphi; and both pretensions had become ridiculous, as the figure of the planet became known. Yes; but if not of the earth, for earth's tenant Jerusalem was the *omphalos* of mortality. Yet how? there on the contrary it was, as we infants understood, that mortality had been trampled under foot. True; but for that very reason there it was that mortality had opened its very gloomiest crater. There it was indeed that the human had risen on wings from the grave; but for that reason there also it was that the divine had been swallowed up by the abyss: the lesser star could not rise, before the greater would submit to eclipse. Summer, therefore, had connected itself with death not merely as a mode of antagonism, but also through intricate relations to Scriptural scenery and events.

Out of this digression, which was almost necessary for the purpose of showing how inextricably my feelings and images of death were entangled with those of summer, I return to the bedchamber of my sister. From the gorgeous sunlight I turned round to the corpse. There lay the sweet childish figure, there the angel face: and, as people usually fancy, it was said in the house that no features had suffered any change. Had they not? The forehead indeed, the serene and noble forehead, *that* might be the same; but the frozen eyelids, the darkness that seemed to steal from beneath them, the marble lips, the stiffening hands, laid palm to palm, as if repeating the supplications of closing anguish, could these be mistaken for life? Had it been so, wherefore did I not spring to those heavenly lips with tears and never-ending kisses? But so it was *not*. I stood checked for a moment; awe, not fear, fell upon me; and, whilst I stood, a solemn wind began to blow – the most mournful that ear ever heard. Mournful! that is saying nothing. It was a wind that had swept the fields of mortality for a hundred centuries. Many times since, upon a summer day, when the sun is about the hottest, I have remarked the same wind arising and uttering the same hollow, solemn, Memnonian,[23] but saintly swell: it is in this world the one sole *audible* symbol of eternity. And three times in my life I have happened to hear the same sound in the same circumstances, viz. when standing between an open window and a dead body on a summer day.

Instantly, when my ear caught this vast Æolian intonation,[24] when my eye filled with the golden fulness of life, the pomps and glory of the heavens outside, and turning when it settled upon the frost which overspread my sister's face, instantly a trance fell upon me. A vault seemed to open in the zenith of the far blue sky, a shaft which ran up for ever. I in spirit rose as if on billows that also ran up the shaft for ever; and the billows seemed to pursue the throne of God; but *that* also ran before us and fled away continually. The flight and the pursuit seemed to go on for ever and ever. Frost, gathering frost, some Sarsar wind of death,[25] seemed to repel me; I slept – for how long I cannot say; slowly I recovered my self-possession, and found myself standing, as before, close to my sister's bed.

Oh* flight of the solitary child to the solitary God – flight from the ruined corpse to the throne that could not be ruined! – how rich wert thou in truth for after years. Rapture of grief, that, being too mighty for a child to sustain, foundest a happy oblivion in a heaven-born sleep, and within that sleep didst conceal a dream, whose meanings in after years, when slowly I deciphered, suddenly there flashed upon me new light; and even

---

* φυγὴ μόνου πρὸς μόνον.[26] – PLOTINUS.

by the grief of a child, as I will show you reader hereafter, were confounded the falsehoods of philosophers.*

In the *Opium Confessions* I touched a little upon the extra-ordinary power connected with opium (after long use) of ampli-fying the dimensions of time. Space also it amplifies by degrees that are sometimes terrific. But time it is upon which the exalting and multiplying power of opium chiefly spends its operation. Time becomes infinitely elastic, stretching out to such immeasur-able and vanishing termini, that it seems ridiculous to compute the sense of it on waking by expressions commensurate to human life. As in starry fields one computes by diameters of the earth's orbit, or of Jupiter's, so in valuing the *virtual* time lived during some dreams, the measurement by generations is ridiculous – by millennia is ridiculous: by æons, I should say, if æons were more determinate, would be also ridiculous. On this single occasion, however, in my life, the very inverse phenom-enon occurred. But why speak of it in connexion with opium? Could a child of six years old have been under that influence? No, but simply because it so exactly reversed the operation of opium. Instead of a short interval expanding into a vast one, upon this occasion a long one had contracted into a minute. I have reason to believe that a *very* long one had elapsed during this wandering or suspension of my perfect mind. When I returned to myself, there was a foot (or I fancied so) on the stairs. I was alarmed. For I believed that, if any body should detect me, means would be taken to prevent my coming again. Hastily, therefore, I kissed the lips that I should kiss no more, and slunk like a guilty thing with stealthy steps from the room. Thus perished the vision, loveliest amongst all the shows which earth has revealed to me; thus mutilated was the parting which should have lasted for ever; thus tainted with fear was the farewell sacred to love and grief, to perfect love and perfect grief.

Oh, Ahasuerus, everlasting Jew!†[27] fable or not a fable, thou

---

* The thoughts referred to will be given in final notes;[28] as at this point they seemed too much to interrupt the course of the narrative.

† 'Everlasting Jew!' – *der ewige Jude* – which is the common German expression for *The Wandering Jew*, and sublimer even than our own.

when first starting on thy endless pilgrimage of woe, thou when first flying through the gates of Jerusalem, and vainly yearning to leave the pursuing curse behind thee, couldst not more certainly have read thy doom of sorrow in the misgivings of thy troubled brain than I when passing for ever from my sister's room. The worm was at my heart: and, confining myself to that stage of life, I may say – the worm that could not die. For if, when standing upon the threshold of manhood, I had ceased to feel its perpetual gnawings, *that* was because a vast expansion of intellect, it was because new hopes, new necessities, and the frenzy of youthful blood, had translated me into a new creature. Man is doubtless *one* by some subtle *nexus* that we cannot perceive, extending from the new-born infant to the superannuated dotard: but as regards many affections and passions incident to his nature at different stages, he is *not* one; the unity of man in this respect is coextensive only with the particular stage to which the passion belongs. Some passions, as that of sexual love, are celestial by one half of their origin, animal and earthy by the other half. These will not survive their own appropriate stage. But love, which is *altogether* holy, like that between two children, will revisit undoubtedly by glimpses the silence and the darkness of old age: and I repeat my belief – that, unless bodily torment should forbid it, that final experience in my sister's bedroom, or some other in which her innocence was concerned, will rise again for me to illuminate the hour of death.

On the day following this which I have recorded, came a body of medical men to examine the brain, and the particular nature of the complaint, for in some of its symptoms it had shown perplexing anomalies. Such is the sanctity of death, and especially of death alighting on an innocent child, that even gossiping people do not gossip on such a subject. Consequently, I knew nothing of the purpose which drew together these surgeons, nor suspected any thing of the cruel changes which might have been wrought in my sister's head. Long after this I saw a similar case; I surveyed the corpse (it was that of a beautiful boy, eighteen years old,[29] who had died of the same complaint) one hour *after* the surgeons had laid the skull in ruins; but the dishonours of this scrutiny were hidden by bandages, and had not disturbed the repose of the countenance. So it might have been here; but, if it were *not* so, then I was happy in being spared the shock, from having that marble image of peace, icy and rigid as it was, unsettled by disfiguring images. Some hours after the strangers had withdrawn, I crept again to the room, but the door was now locked – the key was taken away – and I was shut out for ever.

Then came the funeral. I, as a point of decorum, was carried thither. I was put into a carriage with some gentlemen whom I did not know. They were kind to me; but naturally they talked of things disconnected with the occasion, and their conversation was a torment. At the church, I was told to hold a white handkerchief to my eyes. Empty hypocrisy! What need had *he* of masques or mockeries, whose heart died within him at every word that was uttered? During that part of the service which passed within the church, I made an effort to attend, but I sank back continually into my own solitary darkness, and I heard little consciously, except some fugitive strains from the sublime chapter of St Paul, which in England is always read at burials. And here I notice a profound error of our present illustrious Laureate.[30] When I heard those dreadful words – for dreadful they were to me – 'It is sown in corruption, it is raised in incorruption; it is sown in dishonour, it is raised in glory;' such was the recoil of my feelings, that I could even have shrieked out a protesting – 'Oh, no, no!' if I had not been restrained by the publicity of the occasion. In after years, reflecting upon this revolt of my feelings, which, being the voice of nature in a child, must be as true as any mere *opinion* of a child might probably be false, I saw at once the unsoundness of a passage in *The Excursion*.[31] The book is not here, but the substance I remember perfectly. Mr Wordsworth argues, that if it were not for the unsteady faith which people fix upon the beatific condition after death of those whom they deplore, nobody could be found so selfish, as even secretly to wish for the restoration to earth of a beloved object. A mother, for instance, could never dream of yearning for her child, and secretly calling it back by her silent aspirations from the arms of God, if she were but reconciled to the belief that really it *was* in those arms. But this I utterly deny.

To take my own case, when I heard those dreadful words of St Paul applied to my sister – viz. that she should be raised a spiritual body – nobody can suppose that selfishness, or any other feeling than that of agonizing love, caused the rebellion of my heart against them. I knew already that she was to come again in beauty and power. I did not now learn this for the first time. And that thought, doubtless, made my sorrow sublimer; but also it made it deeper. For here lay the sting of it, viz. in the fatal words – 'We shall be *changed*.' How was the unity of my interest in her to be preserved, if she were to be altered, and no longer to reflect in her sweet countenance the traces that were sculptured on my heart? Let a magician ask any woman whether she will permit him to improve her child, to raise it even from deformity to perfect beauty, if that must be done at the cost of its identity, and there is no loving mother but would reject his proposal with horror. Or, to take a case that has actually happened, if a mother were robbed of her child at two years old by gipsies, and the same child were restored to her at twenty, a fine young man, but divided by a sleep as it were of death from all remembrances that could restore the broken links of their once-tender connexion, would she not feel her grief unhealed, and her heart defrauded? Undoubtedly she would. All of us ask not of God for a better thing than that we have lost; we ask for the same, even with its faults and its frailties. It is true that the sorrowing person will also be changed eventually, but that must be by death. And a prospect so remote as that, and so alien from our present nature, cannot console us in an affliction which is not remote but present – which is not spiritual but human.

Lastly came the magnificent service which the English church performs at the side of the grave. There is exposed once again, and for the last time, the coffin. All eyes survey the record of name, of sex, of age, and the day of departure from earth – records how useless! and dropped into darkness as if messages addressed to worms. Almost at the very last comes the symbolic ritual, tearing and shattering the heart with volleying discharges, peal after peal, from the final artillery of woe. The coffin is lowered into its home; it has disappeared from the eye. The sacristan stands ready with his shovel of earth and stones. The priest's voice is heard once more – *earth to earth*, and the dread rattle ascends from the lid of the coffin; *ashes to ashes*, and again the killing sound is heard; *dust to dust*, and the farewell volley announces that the grave – the coffin – the face are sealed up for ever and ever.

Oh, grief! thou art classed amongst the depressing passions. And true it is, that thou humblest to the dust, but also thou exaltest to the clouds. Thou shakest as with ague, but also thou steadiest like frost. Thou sickenest the heart, but also thou healest its infirmities. Among the very foremost of mine was morbid sensibility to shame. And ten years afterwards, I used to reproach myself with this infirmity, by supposing the case, that, if it were thrown upon me to seek aid for a perishing fellow-creature, and that I could obtain that aid only by facing a vast company of critical or sneering faces, I might perhaps shrink basely from the duty. It is true, that no such case had ever actually occurred, so that it was a mere romance of casuistry to tax myself with cowardice so shocking. But to feel a doubt, was to feel condemnation; and the crime which *might* have been, was in my eyes the crime which *had* been. Now, however, all was changed; and for any thing which regarded my sister's memory, in one hour I received a new heart. Once in Westmoreland I saw a case resembling it. I saw a ewe suddenly put off and abjure her own nature, in a service of love – yes, slough it as completely, as ever serpent sloughed his skin. Her lamb had fallen into a deep trench, from which all escape was hopeless without the aid of man. And to a man she advanced boldly, bleating clamorously, until he followed her and rescued her beloved. Not less was the change in myself. Fifty thousand sneering faces would not have troubled me in any office of tenderness to my sister's memory. Ten legions would not have repelled me from seeking her, if there was a chance that she could be found. Mockery! it was lost upon me. Laugh at me, as one or two people did! I valued not their laughter. And when I was told insultingly to cease 'my girlish tears,' that word '*girlish*' had no sting for me, except as a verbal echo to the one eternal thought of my heart – that a girl was the sweetest thing I, in my short life, had known – that a girl it was who had crowned the earth with beauty, and had opened to my thirst fountains of pure celestial love, from which, in this world, I was to drink no more.

Interesting it is to observe how certainly all deep feelings agree in this, that they seek for solitude, and are nursed by solitude. Deep grief, deep love, how naturally do these ally themselves with religious feeling; and all three, love, grief, religion, are haunters of solitary places. Love, grief, the passion of reverie, or the mystery of devotion – what were these without solitude? All day long, when it was not impossible for me to do so, I sought the most silent and sequestered nooks in the grounds about the house, or in the neighbouring fields. The awful stillness occasionally of summer noons, when no winds were abroad, the appealing silence of grey or misty afternoons – these were fascinations as of witchcraft. Into the woods or the desert air I gazed as if some comfort lay hid in *them*. I wearied the heavens with my inquest of beseeching looks. I tormented the blue depths with obstinate scrutiny, sweeping them with my eyes and searching them for ever after one angelic face that might perhaps have permission to reveal itself for a moment. The faculty of shaping images in the distance out of slight elements, and grouping them after the yearnings of the heart, aided by a slight defect in my eyes, grew upon me at this time. And I recal at the present moment one instance of that sort, which may show how merely shadows, or a gleam of brightness, or nothing at all, could furnish a sufficient basis for this creative faculty. On Sunday mornings I was always taken to church: it was a church on the old and natural model of England, having aisles, galleries, organ, all things ancient and venerable, and the proportions majestic. Here, whilst the congregation knelt through the long Litany, as often as we came to that passage, so beautiful amongst many that are so, where God is supplicated on behalf of 'all sick persons and young children,' and that he would 'show his pity upon all prisoners and captives' – I wept in secret, and raising my streaming eyes to the windows of the galleries, saw, on days when the sun was shining, a spectacle as affecting as ever prophet can have beheld. The sides of the windows were rich with storied glass; through the deep purples and crimsons streamed the golden light; emblazonries of heavenly illumination mingling with the earthly emblazonries of what is grandest in man. There were the apostles that had trampled upon earth, and the glories of earth, out of celestial love to man. There were the martyrs that had borne witness to the truth through flames, through torments, and through armies of fierce insulting faces. There were the saints who, under intolerable pangs, had glorified God by meek submission to his will. And all the time, whilst this tumult of sublime memorials held on as the deep chords from an accompaniment in the bass, I saw through the wide central field of the window, where the glass was uncoloured, white fleecy clouds sailing over the azure depths of the sky; were it but a fragment or a hint of such a cloud, immediately under the flash of my sorrow-haunted eye, it grew and shaped itself into a vision of beds with white lawny curtains; and in the beds lay sick children, dying children, that were tossing in anguish, and weeping clamorously for death. God, for some mysterious reason, could not suddenly release them from their pain; but he suffered the beds, as it seemed, to rise slowly through the clouds; slowly the beds ascended into the chambers of the air; slowly, also, his arms descended from the heavens, that he and his young children whom in Judea, once and for ever, he had blessed, though they *must* pass slowly through the dreadful chasm of separation, might yet meet the sooner. These visions were self-sustained. These visions needed not that any sound should speak to me, or music mould my feelings. The hint from the Litany, the fragment from the clouds, those and the storied windows were sufficient. But not the less the blare of the tumultuous organ wrought its own separate creations. And oftentimes in anthems, when the mighty instrument threw its vast columns of sound, fierce yet melodious, over the voices of the choir – when it rose high in arches, as might seem, sur-mounting and overriding the strife of the vocal parts, and gather-ing by strong coercion the total storm into unity – sometimes I seemed to walk triumphantly upon those clouds which so recently I had looked up to as mementos of prostrate sorrow, and even as ministers of sorrow in its creations; yes, sometimes

under the transfigurations of music I felt* of grief itself as a fiery
chariot for mounting victoriously above the causes of grief.

I point so often to the feelings, the ideas, or the ceremonies of
religion, because there never yet was profound grief nor profound philosophy which did not inosculate at many points with
profound religion. But I request the reader to understand, that
of all things I was not, and could not have been, a child trained
to *talk* of religion, least of all to talk of it controversially or
polemically. Dreadful is the picture, which in books we sometimes find, of children discussing the doctrines of Christianity,
and even teaching their seniors the boundaries and distinctions
between doctrine and doctrine. And it has often struck me with
amazement, that the two things which God made most beautiful
among his works, viz. infancy and pure religion, should, by the
folly of man, (in yoking them together on erroneous principles,)
neutralize each other's beauty, or even form a combination positively hateful. The religion becomes nonsense, and the child
becomes a hypocrite. The religion is transfigured into cant, and
the innocent child into a dissembling liar.†

---

* '*I felt.*' – The reader must not forget, in reading this and other passages, that,
though a child's feelings are spoken of, it is not the child who speaks. *I* decipher
what the child only felt in cipher. And so far is this distinction or this explanation
from pointing to any thing metaphysical or doubtful, that a man must be grossly
unobservant who is not aware of what I am here noticing, not as a peculiarity
of this child or that, but as a necessity of all children. Whatsoever in a man's
mind blossoms and expands to his own consciousness in mature life, must have
pre-existed in germ during his infancy. I, for instance, did not, as a child,
consciously read in my own deep feelings these ideas. No, not at all; nor was it
possible for a child to do so. I the child had the feelings, I the man decipher them.
In the child lay the handwriting mysterious to *him*; in me the interpretation and
the comment.

† I except, however, one case – the case of a child dying of an organic disorder,
so therefore as to die slowly, and aware of its own condition. Because such a
child is solemnized, and sometimes, in a partial sense, inspired – inspired by the
depth of its sufferings, and by the awfulness of its prospect. Such a child having
put off the earthly mind in many things, may naturally have put off the childish
mind in all things. I therefore, speaking for myself only, acknowledge to have
read with emotion a record of a little girl, who, knowing herself for months to
be amongst the elect of death, became anxious even to sickness of heart for
what she called the *conversion* of her father. Her filial duty and reverence had
been swallowed up in filial love.

God, be assured, takes care for the religion of children wheresoever his Christianity exists. Wheresoever there is a national church established, to which a child sees his friends resorting; wheresoever he beholds all whom he honours periodically prostrate before those illimitable heavens which fill to overflowing his young adoring heart; wheresoever he sees the sleep of death falling at intervals upon men and women whom he knows, depth as confounding to the plummet of his mind as those heavens ascend beyond his power to pursue – *there* take you no thought for the religion of a child, any more than for the lilies how they shall be arrayed, or for the ravens how they shall feed their young.[32]

God speaks to children also in dreams, and by the oracles that lurk in darkness. But in solitude, above all things, when made vocal by the truths and services of a national church, God holds 'communion undisturbed' with children. Solitude, though silent as light, is, like light, the mightiest of agencies; for solitude is essential to man. All men come into this world *alone* – all leave it *alone*. Even a little child has a dread, whispering consciousness, that if he should be summoned to travel into God's presence, no gentle nurse will be allowed to lead him by the hand, nor mother to carry him in her arms, nor little sister to share his trepidations. King and priest, warrior and maiden, philosopher and child, all must walk those mighty galleries alone. The solitude, therefore, which in this world appals or fascinates a child's heart, is but the echo of a far deeper solitude through which already he has passed, and of another solitude deeper still, through which he *has* to pass: reflex of one solitude – prefiguration of another.

Oh, burthen of solitude, that cleavest to man through every stage of his being – in his birth, which *has* been – in his life, which *is* – in his death, which *shall* be – mighty and essential solitude! that wast, and art, and art to be; – thou broodest, like the spirit of God moving upon the surface of the deeps, over every heart that sleeps in the nurseries of Christendom. Like the vast laboratory of the air, which, seeming to be nothing, or less than the shadow of a shade, hides within itself the principles of all things, solitude for a child is the Agrippa's mirror[33] of the

unseen universe. Deep is the solitude in life of millions upon
millions who, with hearts welling forth love, have none to love
them. Deep is the solitude of those who, with secret griefs, have
none to pity them. Deep is the solitude of those who, fighting with
doubts or darkness, have none to counsel them. But deeper than
the deepest of these solitudes is that which broods over childhood,
bringing before it at intervals the final solitude which watches for
it, and is waiting for it within the gates of death. Reader, I tell you
a truth, and hereafter I will convince you of this truth, that for a
Grecian child solitude was nothing, but for a Christian child it
has become the power of God and the mystery of God. Oh,
mighty and essential solitude, that wast, and art, and art to be
– thou, kindling under the torch of Christian revelations, art
now transfigured for ever, and hast passed from a blank negation
into a secret hieroglyphic from God, shadowing in the hearts of
infancy the very dimmest of his truths!

'*But you forgot her*,' says the Cynic; '*you happened one day to
forget this sister of yours?*' – Why not? To cite the beautiful
words of Wallenstein,

> 'What pang
> Is permanent with man? From the highest
> As from the vilest thing of every day
> He learns to wean himself. For the strong hours
> Conquer him.'*

Yes, *there* lies the fountain of human oblivions. It is TIME,
the great conqueror, it is the 'strong hours' whose batteries
storm every passion of men. For, in the fine expression of
Schiller, '*Was verschmerzte nicht der mensch?*' What sorrow is
it in man that will not finally fret itself to sleep? Conquering, at
last, gates of brass, or pyramids of granite, why should it be a
marvel to us, or a triumph to Time, that he is able to conquer a
frail human heart?

* *Death of Wallenstein*, Act v. Scene 1, (Coleridge's Translation,) relating to
his remembrances of the younger Piccolomini.

However, for this once my Cynic must submit to be told –
that he is wrong. Doubtless, it is presumption in me to suggest
that his sneers can ever go awry, any more than the shafts of
Apollo.[34] But still, however impossible such a thing is, in this one
case it happens that they *have*. And when it happens that they do
not, I will tell you, reader, why in my opinion it is; and you will
see that it warrants no exultation in the Cynic. Repeatedly I have
heard a mother reproaching herself, when the birthday revolved
of the little daughter whom so suddenly she had lost, with her
own insensibility that could so soon need a remembrancer of the
day. But, besides, that the majority of people in this world (as
being people called to labour) have no time left for cherishing
grief by solitude and meditation, always it is proper to ask
whether the memory of the lost person were chiefly dependent
upon a visual image. No death is usually half so affecting as the
death of a young child from two to five years old.

But yet for the same reason which makes the grief more
exquisite, generally for such a loss it is likely to be more perishable. Wherever the image, visually or audibly, of the lost person
is more essential to the life of the grief, there the grief will be
more transitory.

Faces begin soon (in Shakspeare's fine expression) to 'dislimn:'[35] features fluctuate: combinations of feature unsettle.
Even the expression becomes a mere idea that you can describe
to another, but not an image that you can reproduce for yourself.
Therefore it is that the faces of infants, though they are divine
as flowers in a savanna of Texas, or as the carolling of birds in
a forest, are, like flowers in Texas, and the carolling of birds in
a forest, soon overtaken by the pursuing darkness that swallows
up all things human. All glories of flesh vanish; and this, the
glory of infantine beauty seen in the mirror of the memory,
soonest of all. But when the departed person worked upon
yourself by powers that were intellectual and moral – powers *in*
the flesh, though not *of* the flesh – the memorials in your own
heart become more steadfast, if less affecting at the first. Now,
in my sister were combined for me both graces – the graces
of childhood, and the graces of expanding thought. Besides
that, as regards merely the *personal* image, always the smooth

rotundity of baby features must vanish sooner, as being less individual than the features in a child of eight, touched with a pensive tenderness, and exalted into a characteristic expression by a premature intellect.

Rarely do things perish from my memory that are worth remembering. Rubbish dies instantly. Hence it happens that passages in Latin or English poets which I never could have read but once, (and *that* thirty years ago,) often begin to blossom anew when I am lying awake, unable to sleep. I become a distinguished compositor in the darkness; and, with my aërial composing-stick,[36] sometimes I 'set up' half a page of verses, that would be found tolerably correct if collated with the volume that I never had in my hand but once. I mention this in no spirit of boasting. Far from it; for, on the contrary, amongst my mortifications have been compliments to my memory, when, in fact, any compliment that I had merited was due to the higher faculty of an electric aptitude for seizing analogies, and by means of those aërial pontoons passing over like lightning from one topic to another. Still it is a fact, that this pertinacious life of memory for things that simply touch the ear without touching the consciousness, does in fact beset me. Said but once, said but softly, not marked at all, words revive before me in darkness and solitude; and they arrange themselves gradually into sentences, but through an effort sometimes of a distressing kind, to which I am in a manner forced to become a party. This being so, it was no great instance of that power – that three separate passages in the funeral service, all of which but one had escaped my notice at the time, and even that one as to the part I am going to mention, but all of which must have struck on my ear, restored themselves perfectly when I was lying awake in bed; and though struck by their beauty, I was also incensed by what seemed to me the harsh sentiment expressed in two of these passages. I will cite all the three in an abbreviated form, both for my immediate purpose, and for the indirect purpose of giving to those unacquainted with the English funeral service some specimen of its beauty.

The first passage was this, 'Forasmuch as it hath pleased Almighty God, of his great mercy, to take unto himself the soul of our dear sister here departed, we therefore commit her body to the ground, earth to earth, ashes to ashes, dust to dust, in sure and certain hope of the resurrection to eternal life.' * * *[37]

I pause to remark that a sublime effect arises at this point through a sudden rapturous interpolation from the Apocalypse, which, according to the rubric, 'shall be said or sung;' but always let it be sung, and by the full choir: –

'I heard a voice from heaven saying unto me, Write, from henceforth blessed are the dead which die in the Lord; even so saith the Spirit; for they rest from their labours.'

The second passage, almost immediately succeeding to this awful burst of heavenly trumpets, and the one which more particularly offended me, though otherwise even then, in my seventh year, I could not but be touched by its beauty, was this: – 'Almighty God, with whom do live the spirits of them that depart hence in the Lord, and with whom the souls of the faithful, after they are delivered from the burden of the flesh, are in joy and felicity; WE give thee hearty thanks that it hath pleased thee to deliver this our sister out of the miseries of this sinful world; beseeching thee, that it may please thee of thy gracious goodness shortly to accomplish the number of thine elect, and to hasten thy kingdom.' * *

In what world was I living when a man (calling himself a man of God) could stand up publicly and give God 'hearty thanks' that he had taken away my sister? But, young child, understand – taken her away from the miseries of this sinful world. Oh yes! I hear what you say; I understand *that*; but that makes no difference at all. She being gone, this world doubtless (as you say) is a world of unhappiness. But for me *ubi Cæsar, ibi Roma*[38] – where my sister was, there was paradise; no matter whether in heaven above, or on the earth beneath. And he had taken her away, cruel priest! of his *'great* mercy?' I did not presume, child though I was, to think rebelliously against *that*. The reason was not any hypocritical or canting submission where my heart yielded none, but because already my deep musing intellect had perceived a mystery and a labyrinth in the economies of this world. God, I saw, moved not as *we* moved – walked not as *we* walked – thought not as *we* think. Still I saw no mercy to myself, a poor frail dependent creature – torn away so suddenly from the prop on which altogether it depended. Oh yes! perhaps there was; and many years after I came to suspect it. Nevertheless it was a benignity that pointed far a-head; such as by a child could not have been perceived, because then the great arch had not come round; could not have been recognized if it *had* come round; could not have been valued if it had even been dimly recognized.

Finally, as the closing prayer in the whole service stood, this – which I acknowledged then, and now acknowledge, as equally beautiful and consolatory; for in this was no harsh peremptory challenge to the infirmities of human grief as to a thing not meriting notice in a religious rite. On the contrary, there was a gracious condescension from the great apostle to grief, as to a passion that he might perhaps himself have participated.

'Oh, merciful God! the father of our Lord Jesus Christ, who is the resurrection and the life, in whom whosoever believeth shall live, though he die; who also taught us by his holy apostle St Paul not to be sorry, as men without hope, for them that sleep in *him*; WE meekly beseech thee, O Father! to raise us from the death of sin unto the life of righteousness; that, when we shall depart this life, we may rest in *him* as our hope is – that this our sister doth.'

Ah, *that* was beautiful; that was heavenly! We might be sorry, we had leave to be sorry; only not without hope. And we were by hope to rest in *Him*, as this our sister doth. And howsoever a man may think that he is without hope, I, that have read the writing upon these great abysses of grief, and viewed their shadows under the correction of mightier shadows from deeper abysses since then, abysses of aboriginal fear and eldest darkness, in which yet I believe that all hope had not absolutely died, know that he is in a natural error. If, for a moment, I and so many others, wallowing in the dust of affliction, could yet rise up suddenly like the dry corpse* which stood upright in the glory of life when touched by the bones of the prophet; if in those vast choral anthems, heard by my childish ear, the voice of God wrapt itself as in a cloud of

* '*Like the dry corpse which stood upright.*' – See the *Second* Book of Kings, chap. xiii. v. 20 and 21. Thirty years ago this impressive incident was made the subject of a large altar-piece by Mr Alston,[39] an interesting American artist, then resident in London.

music, saying – 'Child, that sorrowest, I command thee to rise up and ascend for a season into my heaven of heavens' – then it was plain that despair, that the anguish of darkness, was not *essential* to such sorrow, but might come and go even as light comes and goes upon our troubled earth.

Yes! the light may come and go; grief may wax and wane; grief may sink; and grief again may rise, as in impassioned minds oftentimes it does, even to the heaven of heavens; but there is a necessity – that, if too much left to itself in solitude, finally it will descend into a depth from which there is no re-ascent; into a disease which seems no disease; into a languishing which, from its very sweetness, perplexes the mind and is fancied to be very health. Witchcraft has seized upon you, nympholepsy[40] has struck you. Now you rave no more. You acquiesce; nay, you are passionately delighted in your condition. Sweet becomes the grave, because you also hope immediately to travel thither: luxurious is the separation, because only perhaps for a few weeks shall it exist for you; and it will then prove but the brief summer night that had retarded a little, by a refinement of rapture, the heavenly dawn of reunion. Inevitable sometimes it is in solitude – that this should happen with minds morbidly meditative; that, when we stretch out our arms in darkness, vainly striving to draw back the sweet faces that have vanished, slowly arises a new stratagem of grief, and we say – 'Be it that they no more come back to us, yet what hinders but we should go to *them*?'

Perilous is that crisis for the young. In its effect perfectly the same as the ignoble witchcraft of the poor African *Obeah*,* this

---

* '*African Obeah.*' – Thirty years ago it would not have been necessary to say one word of the Obi or Obeah magic; because at that time several distinguished writers (Miss Edgeworth, for instance, in her Belinda) had made use of this superstition in fictions, and because the remarkable history of Three-finger'd Jack,[41] a story brought upon the stage, had made the superstition notorious as a fact. Now, however, so long after the case has probably passed out of the public mind, it may be proper to mention – that when an Obeah man, *i.e.*, a professor of this dark collusion with human fears and human credulity, had once woven his dreadful net of ghostly terrors, and had thrown it over his selected victim, vainly did that victim flutter, struggle, languish in the meshes; unless the spells were reversed, he generally perished; and without a wound except from his own too domineering fancy.

sublimer witchcraft of grief will, if left to follow its own natural course, terminate in the same catastrophe of death. Poetry, which neglects no phenomena that are interesting to the heart of man, has sometimes touched a little

'On the sublime attractions of the grave.'[42]

But you think that these attractions, existing at times for the adult, could not exist for the child. Understand that you are wrong. Understand that these attractions *do* exist for the child; and perhaps as much more strongly than they *can* exist for the adult, by the whole difference between the concentration of a childish love, and the inevitable distraction upon multiplied objects of any love that can affect an adult. There is a German superstition (well-known by a popular translation) of the Erl-king's Daughter,[43] who fixes her love upon some child, and seeks to wile him away into her own shadowy kingdom in forests.

'Who is it that rides through the forest so fast?'

It is a knight, who carries his child before him on the saddle. The Erl-king's Daughter rides on his right hand, and still whispers temptations to the infant audible only to *him*.

'If thou wilt, dear baby, with me go away,
We will see a fine show, we will play a fine play.'

The consent of the baby is essential to her success. And finally she *does* succeed. Other charms, other temptations, would have been requisite for me. My intellect was too advanced for those fascinations. But could the Erl-king's Daughter have revealed herself to me, and promised to lead me where my sister was, she might have wiled me by the hand into the dimmest forests upon earth. Languishing was my condition at that time. Still I languished for things 'which' (a voice from heaven seemed to answer through my own heart) 'cannot be granted;' and which, when again I languished, again the voice repeated, '*cannot* be granted.'

*

Well it was for me that, at this crisis, I was summoned to put on the harness of life, by commencing my classical studies under one of my guardians, a clergyman of the English Church,[44] and (so far as regarded Latin) a most accomplished scholar.

At the very commencement of my new studies, there happened an incident which afflicted me much for a short time, and left behind a gloomy impression, that suffering and wretchedness were diffused amongst all creatures that breathe. A person had given me a kitten. There are three animals which seem, beyond all others, to reflect the beauty of human infancy in two of its elements – viz. joy, and guileless innocence, though less in its third element of simplicity, because *that* requires language for its full expression: these three animals are the kitten, the lamb, and the fawn. Other creatures may be as happy, but they do not show it so much. Great was the love which poor silly I had for this little kitten; but, as I left home at ten in the morning, and did not return till near five in the afternoon, I was obliged, with some anxiety, to throw it for those seven hours upon its own discretion, as infirm a basis for reasonable hope as could be imagined. I did not wish the kitten, indeed, at all less foolish than it was, except just when I was leaving home, and then its exceeding folly gave me a pang. Just about that time, it happened that we had received, as a present from Leicestershire, a fine young Newfoundland dog, who was under a cloud of disgrace for crimes of his youthful blood committed in that county. One day he had taken too great a liberty with a pretty little cousin of mine, Emma H——, about four years old. He had, in fact, bitten off her cheek, which, remaining attached by a shred, was, through the energy of a governess, replaced, and subsequently healed without a scar. His name being *Turk*, he was immediately pronounced by the best Greek scholar of that neighbourhood, ἐπώνυμος (*i.e.* named significantly, or reporting his nature in his name.) But as Miss Emma confessed to having been engaged in taking away a bone from him, on which subject no dog can be taught to understand a joke, it did not strike our own authorities that he was to be considered in a state of reprobation; and as our gardens (near to a great town) were, on account chiefly of melons, constantly robbed, it was held that a moderate degree of fierceness was rather a favourable trait in his character. My poor kitten, it was supposed, had been engaged in the same playful trespass upon Turk's property as my Leicestershire cousin, and Turk laid her dead on the spot. It is impossible to describe my grief when the case was made known to me at five o'clock in the evening, by a man's holding out the little creature dead: she that I had left so full of glorious life – life which even in a kitten is infinite – was now stretched in motionless repose. I remember that there was a large coal stack in the yard. I dropped my Latin books, sat down upon a huge block of coal, and burst into a passion of tears. The man, struck with my tumultuous grief, hurried into the house; and from the lower regions deployed instantly the women of the laundry and the kitchen. No one subject is so absolutely sacred, and enjoys so *classical* a sanctity among servant girls, as 1. Grief; and 2. Love which is unfortunate. All the young women took me up in their arms and kissed me; and last of all, an elderly woman, who was the cook, not only kissed me, but wept so audibly, from some suggestion doubtless of grief personal to herself, that I threw my arms about her neck and kissed *her* also. It is probable, as I now suppose, that some account of my grief for my sister had reached them. Else I was never allowed to visit *their* region of the house. But, however *that* might be, afterwards it struck me, that if I had met with so much sympathy, or with any sympathy at all, from the servant chiefly connected with myself in the desolating grief I had suffered, possibly I should not have been so profoundly shaken.

But did I in the mean time feel anger towards Turk? Not the least. And the reason was this: – My guardian, who taught me Latin, was in the habit of coming over and dining at my mother's table whenever he pleased. On these occasions he, who like myself pitied *dependant* animals, went invariably into the yard of the offices, taking me with him, and unchained the dogs. There were two – *Grim*, a mastiff, and *Turk*, our young friend. My guardian was a bold athletic man, and delighted in dogs. He told me, which also my own heart told me, that these poor dogs languished out their lives under this confinement. The moment that I and my guardian (*ego et rex meus*)[45] appeared in

sight of the two kennels, it is impossible to express the joy of
the dogs. Turk was usually restless; Grim slept away his life in
surliness. But at the sight of us – of my little insignificant self
and my six-foot guardian – both dogs yelled with delight. We
unfastened their chains with our own hands, they licking our
hands; and as to myself, licking my miserable little face; and at
one bound they re-entered upon their natural heritage of joy.
Always we took them through the fields, where they molested
nothing, and closed with giving them a cold bath in the brook
which bounded my father's property. What despair must have
possessed our dogs when they were taken back to their hateful
prisons! and I, for my part, not enduring to see their misery,
slunk away when the rechaining commenced. It was in vain to
tell me that all people, who had property out of doors to protect,
chained up dogs in the same way; *this* only proved the extent of
the oppression; for a monstrous oppression it *did* seem, that
creatures, boiling with life and the desires of life, should be thus
detained in captivity until they were set free by death. That
liberation visited poor *Grim* and *Turk* sooner than any of us
expected, for they were both poisoned within the year that
followed by a party of burglars. At the end of that year I was
reading the Æneid; and it struck me, who remembered the
howling recusancy of *Turk*, as a peculiarly fine circumstance,
introduced amongst the horrors of Tartarus, that sudden gleam
of powerful animals, full of life and conscious rights, rebelling
against chains: –

> 'Iræque leonum
> Vincla recusantum.'*

Virgil had doubtless picked up that gem in his visits at feeding-
time to the *caveæ*[46] of the Roman amphitheatre. But the rights
of brute creatures to a merciful forbearance on the part of man,
could not enter into the feeblest conceptions of one belonging

---

* What follows, I think, (for book I have none of any kind where this paper is
proceeding,) viz. *et serâ sub nocte rudentum*, is probably a mistake of Virgil's;
the lions did not roar because night was approaching, but because night brought
with it their principal meal, and consequently the impatience of hunger.

to a nation that, (although too noble to be *wantonly* cruel,) yet in the same amphitheatre manifested so little regard even to human rights. Under Christianity, the condition of the brute has improved, and will improve much more. There is ample room. For I am sorry to say, that the commonest vice of Christian children, too often surveyed with careless eyes by mothers, that in their *human* relations are full of kindness, is cruelty to the inferior creatures thrown upon their mercy. For my own part, what had formed the groundwork of my happiness, (since joyous was my nature, though overspread with a cloud of sadness,) had been from the first a heart overflowing with love. And I had drunk in too profoundly the spirit of Christianity from our many nursery readings, not to read also in its divine words the justification of my own tendencies. That which I desired, was the thing which I ought to desire; the mercy that I loved was the mercy that God had blessed. From the sermon on the Mount resounded for ever in my ears – 'Blessed are the merciful!' I needed not to add – 'For they shall obtain mercy.' By lips so holy, and when standing in the atmosphere of truths so divine, simply to have been blessed – *that* was a sufficient ratification; every truth so revealed, and so hallowed by position, starts into sudden life, and becomes to itself its own authentication, needing no proof to convince, needing no promise to allure.

It may well be supposed, therefore, that, having so early awakened within me what may be philosophically called the *transcendental* justice of Christianity, I blamed not *Turk* for yielding to the coercion of his nature. He had killed the object of my love. But, besides that he was under the constraint of a primary appetite – Turk was himself the victim of a killing oppression. He was doomed to a fretful existence so long as he should exist at all. Nothing could reconcile this to my benignity, which at that time rested upon two pillars – upon the deep, deep heart which God had given to me at my birth, and upon exquisite health. Up to the age of two, and almost through that entire space of twenty-four months, I had suffered from ague; but when *that* left me, all germs and traces of ill health fled away for ever – except only such (and those how curable!) as I inherited from my schoolboy distresses in London, or had created by means of opium. Even the long ague was not without ministrations of favour to my prevailing temper; and on the whole, no subject for pity; since naturally it won for me the sweet caresses of female tenderness, both young and old. I was a little petted; but you see by this time, reader, that I must have been too much of a philosopher, even in the year one *ab urbe condita*[47] of my frail earthly tenement, to abuse such indulgence. It also won for me a ride on horseback whenever the weather permitted. I was placed on a pillow, in front of a cankered old man, upon a large white horse, not so young as *I* was, but still showing traces of blood. And even the old man, who was both the oldest and the worst of the three, talked with gentleness to myself, reserving his surliness – for all the rest of the world.

These things pressed with a gracious power of incubation upon my predispositions; and in my overflowing love I did things fitted to make the reader laugh, and sometimes fitted to bring myself into perplexity. One instance from a thousand may illustrate the combination of both effects. At four years old, I had repeatedly seen the housemaid raising her long broom and pursuing (generally destroying) a vagrant spider. The holiness of all life, in my eyes, forced me to devise plots for saving the poor doomed wretch; and thinking intercession likely to prove useless, my policy was – to draw off the housemaid on pretence of showing her a picture, until the spider, already *en route*, should have had time to escape. Very soon, however, the shrewd housemaid, marking the coincidence of these picture exhibitions with the agonies of fugitive spiders, detected my stratagem; so that, if the reader will pardon an expression borrowed from the street, henceforwards the picture was 'no go.' However, as she approved of my motive, she told me of the many murders that the spider had committed, and next (which was worse) of the many that he certainly *would* commit if reprieved. This staggered me. I could have gladly forgiven the past; but it *did* seem a false mercy to spare one spider in order to scatter death amongst fifty flies. I thought timidly for a moment, of suggesting that people sometimes repented, and that *he* might repent; but I checked myself, on considering that I had never read any account, and that she might laugh at the idea, of a penitent spider. To desist was a necessity in these circumstances. But the difficulty which the housemaid had suggested, did not depart; it troubled my musing mind to perceive, that the welfare of one creature might stand upon the ruin of another: and the case of the spider remained thenceforwards even more perplexing to my understanding than it was painful to my heart.

The reader is likely to differ from me upon the question, moved by recurring to such experiences of childhood, whether much value attaches to the perceptions and intellectual glimpses of a child. Children, like men, range through a gamut that is infinite, of temperaments and characters, ascending from the very dust below our feet to highest heaven. I have seen children that were sensual, brutal, devilish. But, thanks be to the *vis medicatrix* of human nature, and to the goodness of God, these are as rare exhibitions as all other monsters. People thought, when seeing such odious travesties and burlesques upon lovely human infancy, that perhaps the little wretches might be *kil-crops*.*[48] Yet, possibly, (it has since occurred to me,) even these children of the fiend, as they seemed, might have one chord in their horrible natures that answered to the call of some sublime purpose. There is a mimic instance of this kind, often found amongst ourselves in natures that are not really 'horrible,' but which *seem* such to persons viewing them from a station not sufficiently central: – Always there are mischievous boys in a neighbourhood, boys who tie canisters to the tails of cats belonging to ladies – a thing which *greatly* I disapprove; and who rob orchards – a thing which *slightly* I disapprove; and behold! the next day, on meeting the injured ladies, they say to me, 'Oh, my dear friend, never pretend to argue for him! This boy, we shall all see, will come to be hanged.' Well, *that* seems a disagreeable prospect for all parties; so I change the subject; and lo! five years later, there is an English frigate fighting with a frigate of heavier metal, (no matter of what nation.) The noble captain has man-œuvred, as only *his* countrymen can manœuvre; he has delivered

---

* '*Kilcrops*.' – See, amongst Southey's early poems, one upon this superstition. Southey argues *contra*; but for my part, I should have been more disposed to hold a brief on the other side.

his broadsides, as only the proud islanders can deliver them. Suddenly he sees the opening for a *coup-de-main*;[49] through his speaking-trumpet he shouts – '*Where are my boarders?*' And instantly rise upon the deck, with the gaiety of boyhood, in white shirt sleeves bound with black ribands, fifty men, the *élite* of the crew; and behold! at the very head of them, cutlass in hand, is our friend the tyer of canisters to the tails of ladies' cats – a thing which *greatly* I disapprove, and also the robber of orchards – a thing which *slightly* I disapprove. But here is a man that will not suffer you either greatly or slightly to disapprove him. Fire celestial burns in his eye; his nation, his glorious nation, is in his mind; himself he regards no more than the life of a cat, or the ruin of a canister. On the deck of the enemy he throws himself with rapture; and if *he* is amongst the killed, if he for an object so gloriously unselfish lays down with joy his life and glittering youth, mark this – that, perhaps, he will not be the least in heaven.

But coming back to the case of childhood, I maintain stead-fastly – that, into all the *elementary* feelings of man, children look with more searching gaze than adults. My opinion is, that where circumstances favour, where the heart is deep, where humility and tenderness exist in strength, where the situation is favourable as to solitude and as to genial feelings, children have a specific power of contemplating the truth, which departs as they enter the world. It is clear to me, that children, upon elementary paths which require no knowledge of the world to unravel, tread more firmly than men; have a more pathetic sense of the beauty which lies in justice; and, according to the immortal ode of our great laureate,[50] [ode 'On the Intimations of Immortality in Childhood,'] a far closer communion with God. I, if you observe, do not much intermeddle with religion, properly so called. My path lies on the interspace between religion and philo-sophy, that connects them both. Yet here for once I shall trespass on grounds not properly mine, and desire you to observe in St Matthew, chap. xxi., and v. 15, *who* were those that, crying in the temple, made the first public recognition of Christianity. Then, if you say, 'Oh, but children echo what they hear, and are no independent authorities!' I must request you to extend your reading into v. 16, where you will find that the testimony of these children, as bearing an *original* value, was ratified by the highest testimony; and the recognition of these children did itself receive a heavenly recognition. And this could *not* have been, unless there were children in Jerusalem who saw into truth with a far sharper eye than Sanhedrims and Rabbis.

It is impossible, with respect to any memorable grief, that it can be adequately exhibited so as to indicate the enormity of the convulsion which really it caused, without viewing it under a variety of aspects – a thing which is here almost necessary for the effect of proportion to what follows: 1st, for instance, in its immediate pressure, so stunning and confounding; 2dly, in its oscillations, as in its earlier agitations, frantic with tumults, that borrow the wings of the winds; or in its diseased impulses of sick languishing desire, through which sorrow transforms itself to a sunny angel, that beckons us to a sweet repose. These phases of revolving affection I have already sketched. And I shall also sketch a third, *i.e.* where the affliction, seemingly hushing itself to sleep, suddenly soars upwards again upon combining with *another* mode of sorrow; viz. anxiety without definite limits, and the trouble of a reproaching conscience. As sometimes,* upon the English lakes, waterfowl that have careered in the air until the eye is wearied with the eternal wheelings of their inimitable flight – Grecian simplicities of motion, amidst a labyrinthine infinity of curves that would baffle the geometry of Apollonius[51] – seek the water at last, as if with some settled purpose (you imagine) of reposing. Ah, how little have you understood the omnipotence of that life which they inherit! *They* want no rest; they laugh at resting; all is 'make believe,' as when an infant hides its laughing face behind its mother's shawl. For a moment it is still. Is it meaning to rest? Will its impatient heart endure to lurk there for long? Ask rather if a cataract will stop from fatigue. Will a sunbeam sleep on its travels? Or the Atlantic rest from its labours? As little can the infant, as little

* In this place I derive my feeling partly from a lovely sketch of the appearance, in verse, by Mr Wordsworth;[52] partly from my own experience of the case; and, not having the poems here, I know not how to proportion my acknowledgments.

can the waterfowl of the lakes, suspend their play, except as a variety of play, or rest unless when nature compels them. Suddenly starts off the infant, suddenly ascend the birds, to new evolutions as incalculable as the caprices of a kaleidoscope; and the glory of their motions, from the mixed immortalities of beauty and inexhaustible variety, becomes at least pathetic to survey. So also, and with such life of variation, do the *primary* convulsions of nature – such, perhaps, as only *primary** formations in the human system can experience – come round again and again by reverberating shocks.

The new intercourse with my guardian, and the changes of scene which naturally it led to, were of use in weaning my mind from the mere disease which threatened it in case I had been left any longer to my total solitude. But out of these changes grew an incident which restored my grief, though in a more troubled shape, and now for the first time associated with something like remorse and deadly anxiety. I can safely say that this was my earliest trespass, and perhaps a venial one – all things considered. Nobody ever discovered it; and but for my own frankness it would not be known to this day. But *that* I could not know; and for years, that is from seven or earlier up to ten, such was my simplicity, that I lived in constant terror. This, though it revived my grief, did me probably great service; because it was no longer a state of languishing desire tending to torpor, but of feverish irritation and gnawing care that kept alive the activity of my understanding. The case was this: – It happened that I had now, and commencing with my first introduction to Latin studies, a large weekly allowance of pocket-money, too large for my age,

* 'And so, then,' the Cynic objects, 'you rank your own mind (and you tell us so frankly) amongst the primary formations?' As I love to annoy him, it would give me pleasure to reply – 'Perhaps I do.' But as I never answer more questions than are necessary, I confine myself to saying, that this is not a necessary construction of the words. Some minds stand nearer to the type of the original nature in man, are truer than others to the great magnet in our dark planet. Minds that are impassioned on a more colossal scale than ordinary, deeper in their vibrations, and more extensive in the scale of their vibrations – whether, in other parts of their intellectual system, they had or had not a corresponding compass – will tremble to greater depths from a fearful convulsion, and will come round by a longer curve of undulations.

but safely entrusted to myself, who never spent or desired to spend one fraction of it upon any thing but books. But all proved too little for my colossal schemes. Had the Vatican, the Bodleian, and the *Bibliothèque du Roi*[53] been all emptied into one collection for my private gratification, little progress would have been made towards content in this particular craving. Very soon I had run ahead of my allowance, and was about three guineas deep in debt. There I paused; for deep anxiety now began to oppress me as to the course in which this mysterious (and indeed guilty) current of debt would finally flow. For the present it was frozen up; but I had some reason for thinking that Christmas thawed all debts whatsoever, and set them in motion towards innumerable pockets. Now *my* debt would be thawed with all the rest; and in what direction would it flow? There was no river that would carry it off to sea; to somebody's pocket it would beyond a doubt make its way; and who *was* that somebody? This question haunted me for ever. Christmas had come, Christmas had gone, and I heard nothing of the three guineas. But I was not easier for *that*. Far rather I *would* have heard of it; for this indefinite approach of a loitering catastrophe gnawed and fretted my feelings. No Grecian audience ever waited with more shuddering horror for the anagnorisis* of the Œdipus,[54] than I for the explosion of my debt. Had I been less ignorant, I should have proposed to mortgage my weekly allowance for the debt, or to form a sinking fund for redeeming it; for the *weekly* sum was nearly five per cent on the entire debt. But I had a mysterious awe of ever alluding to it. This arose from my want of some confidential friend; whilst my grief pointed continually to the remembrance – that *so* it had not always been. But was not the bookseller to blame in suffering a child scarcely seven years old to contract such a debt? Not in the least. He was both a rich man, who could not possibly care for my trifling custom, and notoriously an honourable man. Indeed the money which I myself spent every week in books, would reasonably have caused

---

* *i.e.* (As on account of English readers is added,) the recognition of his true identity, which in one moment, and by a horrid flash of revelation, connects him with acts incestuous, murderous, parricidal, in the past, and with a mysterious fatality of woe lurking in the future.

him to presume that so small a sum as three guineas might well be authorized by my family. He stood, however, on plainer ground. For my guardian, who was very indolent, (as people chose to call it,) that is, like his little melancholy ward, spent all his time in reading, often enough would send me to the bookseller's with a written order for books. This was to prevent my forgetting. But when he found that such a thing as 'forgetting' in the case of a book, was wholly out of the question for me, the trouble of writing was dismissed. And thus I had become factor-general on the part of my guardian, both for *his* books, and for such as were wanted on my own account in the natural course of my education. My private 'little account' had therefore in fact flowed homewards at Christmas, not (as I anticipated) in the shape of an independent current, but as a little tributary rill that was lost in the waters of some more important river. This I now know, but could not then have known with any certainty. So far, however, the affair would gradually have sunk out of my anxieties as time wore on. But there was another item in the case, which, from the excess of my ignorance, preyed upon my spirits far more keenly; and this, keeping itself alive, kept also the other incident alive. With respect to the debt, I was not so ignorant as to think it of much danger by the mere amount: my own allowance furnished a scale for preventing *that* mistake: it was the principle, the having presumed to contract debts on my own account, that I feared to have exposed. But this other case was a ground for anxiety even as regarded the amount; not really; but under the jesting representation made to me, which I (as ever before and after) swallowed in perfect faith. Amongst the books which I had bought, all English, was a history of Great Britain, commencing of course with Brutus and a thousand years of impossibilities;[55] these fables being generously thrown in as a little gratuitous *extra* to the mass of truths which were to follow. This was to be completed in sixty or eighty parts, I believe. But there was another work left more indefinite as to its ultimate extent, and which from its nature seemed to imply a far wider range. It was a general history of navigation, supported by a vast body of voyages. Now, when I considered with myself what a huge thing the sea was, and that so many thousands of captains, commodores, admirals, were eternally running up and down it, and scoring lines upon its face so rankly, that in some of the main 'streets' and 'squares' (as one might call them) their tracks would blend into one undistinguishable blot, – I began to fear that such a work tended to infinity. What was little England to the universal sea? And yet *that* went perhaps to fourscore parts. Not enduring the uncertainty that now besieged my tranquillity, I resolved to know the worst; and on a day ever memorable to me I went down to the bookseller's. He was a mild elderly man, and to myself had always shown a kind indulgent manner. Partly perhaps he had been struck by my extreme gravity; and partly, during the many conversations I had with him, on occasion of my guardian's orders for books, with my laughable simplicity. But there was another reason which had early won for me his paternal regard. For the first three or four months I had found Latin something of a drudgery; and the incident which for ever knocked away the 'shores,' at that time preventing my launch upon the general bosom of Latin literature, was this: – One day the bookseller took down a Beza's *Latin Testament*; and, opening it, asked me to translate for him the chapter which he pointed to. I was struck by perceiving that it was the great chapter of St Paul on the grave and resurrection.[56] I had never seen a Latin version: yet from the simplicity of the scriptural style in *any* translation, (though Beza's is far from good,) I could not well have failed in construing. But as it happened to be this particular chapter, which in English I had read again and again with so passionate a sense of its grandeur, I read it off with a fluency and effect like some great opera-singer uttering a rapturous *bravura*. My kind old friend expressed himself gratified, making me a present of the book as a mark of his approbation. And it is remarkable, that from this moment, when the deep memory of the English words had forced me into seeing the precise correspondence of the two concurrent streams – Latin and English – never again did any difficulty arise to check the velocity of my progress in this particular language. At less than eleven years of age, when as yet I was a very indifferent Grecian, I had become a brilliant master of Latinity, as my Alcaics and Choriambics[57] remain to testify: and the whole occasion of a change so memorable to a boy, was this casual summons to translate a composition with which my heart was filled. Ever after this he showed me a caressing kindness, and so condescendingly, that generally he would leave any people for a moment with whom he was engaged, to come and speak to me. On this fatal day, however, for such it proved to me, he could not do this. He saw me, indeed, and nodded, but could not leave a party of elderly strangers. This accident threw me unavoidably upon one of his young people. Now this was a market-day; and there was a press of country people present, whom I did not wish to hear my question. Never did human creature, with his heart palpitating at Delphi for the solution of some killing mystery, stand before the priestess of the oracle,[58] with lips that moved more sadly than mine, when now advancing to a smiling young man at a desk. His answer was to decide, though I could not exactly know *that*, whether for the next two years I was to have an hour of peace. He was a handsome, good-natured young man, but full of fun and frolic; and I dare say was amused with what must have seemed to *him* the absurd anxiety of my features. I described the work to him, and he understood me at once: how many volumes did he think it would extend to? There was a whimsical expression perhaps of drollery about his eyes, but which unhappily, under my preconceptions, I translated into scorn, as he replied, – 'How many volumes? Oh! really I can't say, maybe a matter of 15,000, be the same more or less.' '*More?*' I said in horror, altogether neglecting the contingency of 'less.' 'Why,' he said, 'we can't settle these things to a nicety. But, considering the subject,' [ay, *that* was the very thing which I myself considered,] 'I should say, there might be some trifle over, as suppose 400 or 500 volumes, be the same more or less.' What, then, here there might be supplements to supplements – the work might positively *never* end. On one pretence or another, if an author or publisher might add 500 volumes, he might add another round 15,000. Indeed it strikes one even now, that by the time all the one-legged commodores and yellow admirals of that generation had exhausted their long yarns, another generation would have grown another crop of the same gallant spinners. I asked no

more, but slunk out of the shop, and never again entered it with
cheerfulness, or propounded any frank questions as heretofore.
For I was now seriously afraid of pointing attention to myself
as one that, by having purchased some numbers, and obtained
others on credit, had silently contracted an engagement to take
all the rest, though they should stretch to the crack of doom.
Certainly I had never heard of a work that extended to 15,000
volumes; but still there was no natural impossibility that it
should; and, if in any case, in none so reasonably as one upon
the inexhaustible sea. Besides, any slight mistake as to the letter
of the number, could not affect the horror of the final prospect.
I saw by the imprint, and I heard, that this work emanated from
London, a vast centre of mystery to me, and the more so, as a
thing unseen at any time by my eyes, and nearly 200 miles
distant. I felt the fatal truth, that here was a ghostly cobweb
radiating into all the provinces from the mighty metropolis. I
secretly had trodden upon the outer circumference, had dam-
aged or deranged the fine threads and links, – concealment or
reparation there could be none. Slowly perhaps, but surely, the
vibration would travel back to London. The ancient spider that
sat there at the centre, would rush along the network through
all longitudes and latitudes, until he found the responsible caitiff,
author of so much mischief. Even, with less ignorance than
mine, there *was* something to appal a child's imagination in the
vast systematic machinery by which any elaborate work could
disperse itself, could levy money, could put questions and get
answers – all in profound silence, nay, even in darkness – searching every nook of every town, and of every hamlet in so populous
a kingdom. I had some dim terrors, also, connected with the
Stationers' Company.[59] I had often observed them in popular
works threatening unknown men with unknown chastisements,
for offences equally unknown; nay, to myself, absolutely incon-
ceivable. Could *I* be the mysterious criminal so long pointed
out, as it were, in prophecy? I figured the stationers, doubtless
all powerful men, pulling at one rope, and my unhappy self
hanging at the other end. But an image, which seems now
even more ludicrous than the rest, at that time was the one most
connected with the revival of my grief. It occurred to my subtlety,

that the Stationers' Company, or any other company, could
not possibly demand the money until they had delivered the
volumes. And, as no man could say that I had ever positively
refused to receive them, they would have no pretence for not
accomplishing this delivery in a civil manner. Unless I should
turn out to be no customer at all, at present it was clear that I
had a right to be considered a most excellent customer; one, in
fact, who had given an order for fifteen thousand volumes. Then
rose up before me this great opera-house 'scena' of the delivery.
There would be a ring at the front door. A waggoner in the
front, with a bland voice, would ask for 'a young gentleman
who had given an order to *their* house.' Looking out, I should
perceive a procession of carts and waggons, all advancing in
measured movements; each in turn would present its rear,
deliver its cargo of volumes, by shooting them, like a load of
coals, on the lawn, and wheel off to the rear, by way of clearing
the road for its successors. Then the impossibility of even asking
the servants to cover with sheets, or counterpanes, or table-
cloths, such a mountainous, such a 'star-y-pointing'[60] record of
my past offences lying in so conspicuous a situation! Men would
not know my guilt merely, they would see it. But the reason why
this form of the consequences, so much more than any other,
stuck by my imagination was, that it connected itself with one
of the Arabian nights which had particularly interested myself
and my sister. It was that tale, where a young porter, having his
ropes about his person, had stumbled into the special 'preserve'
of some old magician. He finds a beautiful lady imprisoned, to
whom (and not without prospects of success) he recommends
himself as a suitor, more in harmony with her own years than a
withered magician. At this crisis the magician returns. The
young man bolts, and for that day successfully; but unluckily
he leaves his ropes behind. Next morning he hears the magician,
too honest by half, enquiring at the front door, with much
expression of condolence, for the unfortunate young man who
had lost his ropes in his own zenana. Upon this story I used to
amuse my sister, by ventriloquizing to the magician from the
lips of the trembling young man – 'Oh, Mr Magician, these
ropes cannot be mine! They are far too good; and one wouldn't

like, you know, to rob some other poor young man. If you please, Mr Magician, I never had money enough to buy so beautiful a set of ropes.' But argument is thrown away upon a magician, and off he sets on his travels with the young porter – not forgetting to take the ropes along with him.

Here now was the case, that had once seemed so impressive to me in a mere fiction from a far-distant age and land, literally reproduced in myself. For what did it matter whether a magician dunned one with old ropes for his engines of torture, or Stationers' Hall with 15,000 volumes, (in the rear of which there might also be ropes?) Should *I* have ventriloquized, would my sister have laughed, had either of us but guessed the possibility that I myself, and within one twelve months, and, alas! standing alone in the world as regarded *confidential* counsel, should repeat within my own inner experience the shadowy panic of the young Bagdat intruder upon the privacy of magicians? It appeared, then, that I had been reading a legend concerning myself in the *Arabian Nights*. I had been contemplated in types a thousand years before on the banks of the Tigris. It was horror and grief that prompted that thought.

Oh, heavens! that the misery of a child should by possibility become the laughter of adults! – that even I, the sufferer, should be capable of amusing myself, as if it had been a jest, with what for three years had constituted the secret affliction of my life, and its eternal trepidation – like the ticking of a death-watch[61] to patients lying awake in the plague. I durst ask no counsel; there was no one to ask. Possibly my sister could have given me none in a case which neither of us should have understood, and where to seek for information from others, would have been at once to betray the whole reason for seeking it. But, if no advice, she would have given me her pity, and the expression of her endless love; and, with the relief of sympathy, that heals for a season all distresses, she would have given me that exquisite luxury – the knowledge that, having parted with my secret, yet also I had *not* parted with it, since it was in the power only of one that could much less betray me than I could betray myself. At this time, that is about the year when I suffered most, I was reading Cæsar. Oh, laurelled scholar – sun-bright intellect –

'foremost man of all this world'[62] – how often did I make out of
thy immortal volume a pillow to support my wearied brow, as
at evening, on my homeward road, I used to turn into some
silent field, where I might give way unobserved to the reveries
which besieged me! I wondered, and found no end of wondering,
at the revolution that one short year had made in my happiness.
I wondered that such billows *could* overtake me! At the beginning of that year how radiantly happy! At the end how insup-
portably alone!

> 'Into what depth thou see'st,
> From what height fallen.'[63]

For ever I searched the abysses with some wandering thoughts
unintelligible to myself. For ever I dallied with some obscure
notion, how my sister's love might be made in some dim way
available for delivering me from misery; or else how the misery
I had suffered and was suffering might be made, in some way
equally dim, the ransom for winning back her love.

Here pause, reader! Imagine yourself seated in some cloud-
scaling swing, oscillating under the impulse of lunatic hands;
for the strength of lunacy may belong to human dreams, the
fearful caprice of lunacy, and the malice of lunacy, whilst the
victim of those dreams may be all the more certainly removed
from lunacy; even as a bridge gathers cohesion and strength from
the increasing resistance into which it is forced by increasing
pressure. Seated in such a swing, fast as you reach the lowest
point of depression, may you rely on racing up to a starry
altitude of corresponding ascent. Ups and downs you will see,
heights and depths, in our fiery course together, such as will
sometimes tempt you to look shyly and suspiciously at me, your
guide, and the ruler of the oscillations. Here, at the point where
I have called a halt, the reader has reached the lowest depth
in my nursery afflictions. From that point, according to the
principles of *art* which govern the movement of these Confessions, I had meant to launch him upwards through the whole
arch of ascending visions which seemed requisite to balance the

sweep downwards, so recently described in his course. But accidents of the press have made it impossible to accomplish this purpose in the present month's journal. There is reason to regret that the advantages of position, which were essential to the full effect of passages planned for equipoise and mutual resistance, have thus been lost. Meantime, upon the principle of the mariner who rigs a *jury*-mast in default of his regular spars, I find my resource in a sort of 'jury' peroration – not sufficient in the way of a balance by its *proportions*, but sufficient to indicate the *quality* of the balance which I had contemplated. He who has *really* read the preceding parts of these present Confessions, will be aware that a stricter scrutiny of the past, such as was natural after the whole economy of the dreaming faculty had been convulsed beyond all precedents on record, led me to the conviction that not one agency, but two agencies, had co-operated to the tremendous result. The nursery experience had been the ally and the natural co-efficient of the opium. For that reason it was that the nursery experience has been narrated. Logically, it bears the very same relation to the convulsions of the dreaming faculty as the opium. The idealizing tendency existed in the dream-theatre of my childhood; but the preter-natural strength of its action and colouring was first developed after the confluence of the *two* causes. The reader must suppose me at Oxford: twelve years and a half are gone by; I am in the glory of youthful happiness; but I have now first tampered with opium; and now first the agitations of my childhood reopened in strength, now first they swept in upon the brain with power and the grandeur of recovered life, under the separate and the concurring inspirations of opium.

Once again, after twelve years' interval, the nursery of my childhood expanded before me – my sister was moaning in bed – I was beginning to be restless with fears not intelligible to myself. Once again the nurse, but now dilated to colossal pro-portions, stood as upon some Grecian stage with her uplifted hand, and like the superb Medea standing alone with her chil-dren in the nursery at Corinth,* smote me senseless to the

* Euripides.

ground.[64] Again, I was in the chamber with my sister's corpse –
again the pomps of life rose up in silence, the glory of summer,
the frost of death. Dream formed itself mysteriously within
dream; within these Oxford dreams remoulded itself continually
the trance in my sister's chamber, – the blue heavens, the everlasting vault, the soaring billows, the throne steeped in the
thought (but not the sight) of 'Him that sate thereon;'[65] the
flight, the pursuit, the irrecoverable steps of my return to earth.
Once more the funeral procession gathered; the priest in his
white surplice stood waiting with a book in his hand by the side
of an open grave, the sacristan with his shovel; the coffin sank;
the *dust to dust* descended. Again I was in the church on a
heavenly Sunday morning. The golden sunlight of God slept
amongst the heads of his apostles, his martyrs, his saints; the
fragment from the litany – the fragment from the clouds – awoke
again the lawny beds that went up to scale the heavens – awoke
again the shadowy arms that moved downwards to meet them.
Once again, arose the swell of the anthem – the burst of the
Hallelujah chorus – the storm – the trampling movement of the
choral passion – the agitation of my own trembling sympathy –
the tumult of the choir – the wrath of the organ. Once more I,
that wallowed, became he that rose up to the clouds. And now
in Oxford, all was bound up into unity; the first state and the
last were melted into each other as in some sunny glorifying
haze. For high above my own station, hovered a gleaming
host of heavenly beings, surrounding the pillows of the dying
children. And such beings sympathize equally with sorrow that
grovels and with sorrow that soars. Such beings pity alike the
children that are languishing in death, and the children that live
only to languish in tears.

THE PALIMPSEST

You know perhaps, masculine reader,[66] better than I can tell
you, what is a *Palimpsest*. Possibly you have one in your own
library. But yet, for the sake of others who may *not* know, or
may have forgotten, suffer me to explain it here: lest any female

reader, who honours these papers with her notice, should tax
me with explaining it once too seldom; which would be worse
to bear than a simultaneous complaint from twelve proud men,
that I had explained it three times too often. You therefore, fair
reader, understand that for *your* accommodation exclusively, I
explain the meaning of this word. It is Greek; and our sex enjoys
the office and privilege of standing counsel to yours, in all
questions of Greek. We are, under favour, perpetual and hereditary dragomans to you. So that if, by accident, you know the
meaning of a Greek word, yet by courtesy to us, your counsel
learned in that matter, you will always seem *not* to know it.

A palimpsest, then, is a membrane or roll cleansed of its
manuscript by reiterated successions.

What was the reason that the Greeks and the Romans had
not the advantage of printed books? The answer will be, from
ninety-nine persons in a hundred – Because the mystery of
printing was not then discovered. But this is altogether a mistake.
The secret of printing must have been discovered many thousands of times before it was used, or *could* be used. The inventive
powers of man are divine; and also his stupidity is divine – as
Cowper so playfully illustrates[67] in the slow development of the
sofa through successive generations of immortal dulness. It took
centuries of blockheads to raise a joint stool into a chair; and it
required something like a miracle of genius, in the estimate of
elder generations, to reveal the possibility of lengthening a chair
into a *chaise-longue*, or a sofa. Yes, these were inventions that
cost mighty throes of intellectual power. But still, as respects
printing, and admirable as is the stupidity of man, it was really
not quite equal to the task of evading an object which stared
him in the face with so broad a gaze. It did not require an
Athenian intellect to read the main secret of printing in many
scores of processes which the ordinary uses of life were *daily*
repeating. To say nothing of analogous artifices amongst various
mechanic artisans, all that is essential in printing must have been
known to every nation that struck coins and medals. Not,
therefore, any want of a printing art – that is, of an art for
multiplying impressions – but the want of a cheap material for
receiving such impressions, was the obstacle to an introduction

of printed books even as early as Pisistratus.[68] The ancients *did* apply printing to records of silver and gold; to marble and many other substances cheaper than gold and silver, they did *not*, since each monument required a *separate* effort of inscription. Simply this defect it was of a cheap material for receiving impresses, which froze in its very fountains the early resources of printing.

Some twenty years ago, this view of the case was luminously expounded by Dr Whately, the present archbishop of Dublin,[69] and with the merit, I believe, of having first suggested it. Since then, this theory has received indirect confirmation. Now, out of that original scarcity affecting all materials proper for durable books, which continued up to times comparatively modern, grew the opening for palimpsests. Naturally, when once a roll of parchment or of vellum had done its office, by propagating through a series of generations what once had possessed an interest for *them*, but which, under changes of opinion or of taste, had faded to their feelings or had become obsolete for their understandings, the whole *membrana* or vellum skin, the twofold product of human skill, costly material, and costly freight of thought, which it carried, drooped in value concurrently – supposing that each were inalienably associated to the other. Once it had been the impress of a human mind which stamped its value upon the vellum; the vellum, though costly, had contributed but a secondary element of value to the total result. At length, however, this relation between the vehicle and its freight has gradually been undermined. The vellum, from having been the setting of the jewel, has risen at length to be the jewel itself; and the burden of thought, from having given the chief value to the vellum, has now become the chief obstacle to its value; nay, has totally extinguished its value, unless it can be dissociated from the connexion. Yet, if this unlinking *can* be effected, then – fast as the inscription upon the membrane is sinking into rubbish – the membrane itself is reviving in its separate importance; and, from bearing a ministerial value, the vellum has come at last to absorb the whole value.

Hence the importance for our ancestors that the separation *should* be effected. Hence it arose in the middle ages, as a

considerable object for chemistry, to discharge the writing from
the roll, and thus to make it available for a new succession of
thoughts. The soil, if cleansed from what once had been hot-
house plants, but now were held to be weeds, would be ready
to receive a fresh and more appropriate crop. In that object the
monkish chemists succeeded; but after a fashion which seems
almost incredible; incredible not as regards the extent of their
success, but as regards the delicacy of restraints under which it
moved; so equally adjusted was their success to the immediate
interests of that period, and to the reversionary interests of our
own. They did the thing; but not so radically as to prevent
us, their posterity, from *un*doing it. They expelled the writing
sufficiently to leave a field for the new manuscript, and yet not
sufficiently to make the traces of the elder manuscript irrecoverable for us. Could magic, could Hermes Trismegistus,[70] have
done more? What would you think, fair reader, of a problem
such as this – to write a book which should be sense for your
own generation, nonsense for the next, should revive into sense
for the next after that, but again became nonsense for the fourth;
and so on by alternate successions, sinking into night or blazing
into day, like the Sicilian river Arethusa, and the English river
Mole – or like the undulating motions of a flattened stone which
children cause to skim the breast of a river, now diving below
the water, now grazing its surface, sinking heavily into darkness,
rising buoyantly into light, through a long vista of alternations?
Such a problem, you say, is impossible. But really it is a problem
not harder apparently than – to bid a generation kill, but so that
a subsequent generation may call back into life; bury, but so
that posterity may command to rise again. Yet *that* was what
the rude chemistry of past ages effected when coming into
combination with the reaction from the more refined chemistry
of our own. Had *they* been better chemists, had *we* been worse
– the mixed result, viz. that, dying for *them*, the flower should
revive for *us*, could not have been effected: They did the thing
proposed to them: they did it effectually; for they founded upon
it all that was wanted: and yet ineffectually, since we unravelled
their work; effacing all above which they had superscribed;
restoring all below which they had effaced.

Here, for instance, is a parchment which contained some Grecian tragedy, the Agamemnon of Æschylus, or the Phœnissæ of Euripides. This had possessed a value almost inappreciable in the eyes of accomplished scholars, continually growing rarer through generations. But four centuries are gone by since the destruction of the Western Empire. Christianity, with towering grandeurs of another class, has founded a different empire; and some bigoted yet perhaps holy monk has washed away (as he persuades himself) the heathen's tragedy, replacing it with a monastic legend; which legend is disfigured with fables in its incidents, and yet, in a higher sense, is true, because interwoven with Christian morals and with the sublimest of Christian revelations. Three, four, five, centuries more find man still devout as ever; but the language has become obsolete, and even for Christian devotion a new era has arisen, throwing it into the channel of crusading zeal or of chivalrous enthusiasm. The *membrana* is wanted now for a knightly romance – for 'my Cid,' or Cœur de Lion; for Sir Tristrem, or Lybæus Disconus.[71] In this way, by means of the imperfect chemistry known to the mediæval period, the same roll has served as a conservatory for three separate generations of flowers and fruits, all perfectly different, and yet all specially adapted to the wants of the successive possessors. The Greek tragedy, the monkish legend, the knightly romance, each has ruled its own period. One harvest after another has been gathered into the garners of man through ages far apart. And the same hydraulic machinery has distributed, through the same marble fountains, water, milk, or wine, according to the habits and training of the generations that came to quench their thirst.

Such were the achievements of rude monastic chemistry. But the more elaborate chemistry of our own days has reversed all these motions of our simple ancestors, with results in every stage that to *them* would have realized the most fantastic amongst the promises of thaumaturgy. Insolent vaunt of Paracelsus, that he would restore the original rose or violet out of the ashes settling from its combustion[72] – *that* is now rivalled in this modern achievement. The traces of each successive handwriting, regularly effaced, as had been imagined, have, in the inverse

order, been regularly called back: the footsteps of the game
pursued, wolf or stag, in each several chase, have been unlinked,
and hunted back through all their doubles; and, as the chorus
of the Athenian stage unwove through the antistrophe every
step that had been mystically woven through the strophe, so, by
our modern conjurations of science, secrets of ages remote from
each other have been exorcised* from the accumulated shadows
of centuries. Chemistry, a witch as potent as the Erictho of
Lucan,[73] (*Pharsalia*, lib. vi. or vii.,) has extorted by her torments,
from the dust and ashes of forgotten centuries, the secrets of a
life extinct for the general eye, but still glowing in the embers.
Even the fable of the Phœnix – that secular bird, who propagated
his solitary existence, and his solitary births, along the line of
centuries, through eternal relays of funeral mists – is but a type
of what we have done with Palimpsests. We have backed upon
each Phœnix in the long *regressus*, and forced him to expose his
ancestral Phœnix, sleeping in the ashes below his own ashes.
Our good old forefathers would have been aghast at our sor-
ceries; and, if they speculated on the propriety of burning Dr
Faustus, *us* they would have burned by acclamation. Trial there
would have been none; and they could no otherwise have satisfied their horror of the brazen profligacy marking our modern
magic, than by ploughing up the houses of all who had been
parties to it, and sowing the ground with salt.

Fancy not, reader, that this tumult of images, illustrative or
allusive, moves under any impulse or purpose of mirth. It is but
the coruscation of a restless understanding, often made ten times
more so by irritation of the nerves, such as you will first learn
to comprehend (its *how* and its *why*) some stage or two ahead.
The image, the memorial, the record, which for me is derived
from a palimpsest, as to one great fact in our human being, and
which immediately I will show you, is but too repellent of
laughter; or, even if laughter *had* been possible, it would have
been such laughter as oftentimes is thrown off from the fields of

---

* Some readers may be apt to suppose, from all English experience, that the
word *exorcise* means properly banishment to the shades. Not so. Citation *from*
the shades, or sometimes the torturing coercion of mystic adjurations, is more
truly the primary sense.

ocean* – laughter that hides, or that seems to evade mustering tumult; foam-bells that weave garlands of phosphoric radiance for one moment round the eddies of gleaming abysses; mimicries of earth-born flowers that for the eye raise phantoms of gaiety, as oftentimes for the ear they raise echoes of fugitive laughter, mixing with the ravings and choir-voices of an angry sea.

What else than a natural and mighty palimpsest is the human brain? Such a palimpsest is my brain; such a palimpsest, O reader! is yours. Everlasting layers of ideas, images, feelings, have fallen upon your brain softly as light. Each succession has seemed to bury all that went before. And yet in reality not one has been extinguished. And if, in the vellum palimpsest, lying amongst the other *diplomata* of human archives or libraries, there is any thing fantastic or which moves to laughter, as oftentimes there is in the grotesque collisions of those successive themes, having no natural connexion, which by pure accident have consecutively occupied the roll, yet, in our own heaven-created palimpsest, the deep memorial palimpsest of the brain, there are not and cannot be such incoherencies. The fleeting accidents of a man's life, and its external shows, may indeed be irrelate and incongruous; but the organizing principles which fuse into harmony, and gather about fixed predetermined centres, whatever heterogeneous elements life may have accumulated from without, will not permit the grandeur of human unity greatly to be violated, or its ultimate repose to be troubled in the retrospect from dying moments, or from other great convulsions.

Such a convulsion is the struggle of gradual suffocation, as in drowning; and, in the original Opium Confessions, I mentioned a case of that nature communicated to me by a lady from her

---

* '*Laughter from the fields of ocean.*' – Many readers will recall, though at the moment of writing my own thoughts did *not* recall, the well-known passage in the Prometheus –[74]

– ποντίων τε κυμάτων

'Oh multitudinous laughter of the ocean billows!' It is not clear whether Æschylus contemplated the laughter as addressing the ear or the eye.

own childish experience. The lady is still living, though now of unusually great age; and I may mention – that amongst her faults never was numbered any levity of principle, or carelessness of the most scrupulous veracity; but, on the contrary, such faults as arise from austerity, too harsh perhaps, and gloomy – indulgent neither to others nor herself. And, at the time of relating this incident, when already very old, she had become religious to asceticism. According to my present belief, she had completed her ninth year, when playing by the side of a solitary brook, she fell into one of its deepest pools. Eventually, but after what lapse of time nobody ever knew, she was saved from death by a farmer, who, riding in some distant lane, had seen her rise to the surface; but not until she had descended within the abyss of death, and looked into its secrets, as far, perhaps, as ever human eye *can* have looked that had permission to return. At a certain stage of this descent, a blow seemed to strike her – phos-phoric radiance sprang forth from her eye-balls; and immediately a mighty theatre expanded within her brain. In a moment, in the twinkling of an eye, every act – every design of her past life lived again – arraying themselves not as a succession, but as parts of a coexistence. Such a light fell upon the whole path of her life backwards into the shades of infancy, as the light perhaps which wrapt the destined apostle on his road to Damascus.[75] Yet that light blinded for a season; but hers poured celestial vision upon the brain, so that her consciousness became omni-present at one moment to every feature in the infinite review.

This anecdote was treated sceptically at the time by some critics. But besides that it has since been confirmed by other experiences essentially the same, reported by other parties in the same circumstances who had never heard of each other; the true point for astonishment is not the *simultaneity* of arrangement under which the past events of life – though in fact successive – had formed their dread line of revelation. This was but a second-ary phenomenon; the deeper lay in the resurrection itself, and the possibility of resurrection, for what had so long slept in the dust. A pall, deep as oblivion, had been thrown by life over every trace of these experiences; and yet suddenly, at a silent command, at the signal of a blazing rocket sent up from the brain, the pall draws up, and the whole depths of the theatre are exposed. Here was the greater mystery: now this mystery is liable to no doubt; for it is repeated, and ten thousand times repeated by opium, for those who are its martyrs.

Yes, reader, countless are the mysterious handwritings of grief or joy which have inscribed themselves successively upon the palimpsest of your brain; and, like the annual leaves of aboriginal forests, or the undissolving snows on the Himalaya, or light falling upon light, the endless strata have covered up each other in forgetfulness. But by the hour of death, but by fever, but by the searchings of opium, all these can revive in strength. They are not dead, but sleeping. In the illustration imagined by myself, from the case of some individual palimpsest, the Grecian tragedy had seemed to be displaced, but was *not* displaced, by the monkish legend; and the monkish legend had seemed to be displaced, but was *not* displaced, by the knightly romance. In some potent convulsion of the system, all wheels back into its earliest elementary stage. The bewildering romance, light tarnished with darkness, the semi-fabulous legend, truth celestial mixed with human falsehoods, these fade even of themselves as life advances. The romance has perished that the young man adored. The legend has gone that deluded the boy. But the deep deep tragedies of infancy, as when the child's hands were unlinked for ever from his mother's neck, or his lips for ever from his sister's kisses, these remain lurking below all, and these lurk to the last. Alchemy there is none of passion or disease that can scorch away these immortal impresses. And the dream which closed the preceding section, together with the succeeding dreams of this, (which may be viewed as in the nature of choruses winding up the overture contained in Part I.,)[76] are but illustrations of this truth, such as every man probably will meet experimentally who passes through similar convulsions of dreaming or delirium from any similar or equal disturbance in his nature.*

* This, it may be said, requires a corresponding duration of experience; but, as an argument for this mysterious power lurking in our nature, I may remind the reader of one phenomenon open to the notice of every body, viz. the tendency of very aged persons to throw back and concentrate the light of their memory

LEVANA AND OUR LADIES OF SORROW

Oftentimes at Oxford I saw Levana in my dreams. I knew her by her Roman symbols. Who is Levana? Reader, that do not pretend to have leisure for very much scholarship, you will not be angry with me for telling you. Levana was the Roman goddess that performed for the new-born infant the earliest office of ennobling kindness – typical, by its mode, of that grandeur which belongs to man every where, and of that benignity in powers invisible, which even in Pagan worlds sometimes descends to sustain it. At the very moment of birth, just as the infant tasted for the first time the atmosphere of our troubled planet, it was laid on the ground. *That* might bear different interpretations. But immediately, lest so grand a creature should grovel there for more than one instant, either the paternal hand, as proxy for the goddess Levana, or some near kinsman, as proxy for the father, raised it upright, bade it look erect as the king of all this world, and presented its forehead to the stars, saying, perhaps, in his heart – 'Behold what is greater than yourselves!' This symbolic act represented the function of Levana. And that mysterious lady, who never revealed her face, (except to me in dreams,) but always acted by delegation, had her name from the Latin verb (as still it is the Italian verb) *levare*, to raise aloft.

This is the explanation of Levana. And hence it has arisen that some people have understood by Levana the tutelary power that controls the education of the nursery. She, that would not suffer at his birth even a prefigurative or mimic degradation for her awful ward, far less could be supposed to suffer the real degradation attaching to the non-development of his powers. She therefore watches over human education. Now, the word *edŭco*, with the penultimate short, was derived (by a process often exemplified in the crystallization of languages) from the

---

upon scenes of early childhood, as to which they recall many traces that had faded even to *themselves* in middle life, whilst they often forget altogether the whole intermediate stages of their experience. This shows that naturally, and without violent agencies, the human brain is by tendency a palimpsest.

word *edūco*, with the penultimate long. Whatsoever *educes* or developes – educates. By the education of Levana, therefore, is meant – not the poor machinery that moves by spelling-books and grammars, but that mighty system of central forces hidden in the deep bosom of human life, which by passion, by strife, by temptation, by the energies of resistance, works for ever upon children – resting not day or night, any more than the mighty wheel of day and night themselves, whose moments, like restless spokes, are glimmering* for ever as they revolve.

If, then, *these* are the ministries by which Levana works, how profoundly must she reverence the agencies of grief! But you, reader! think – that children generally are not liable to grief such as mine. There are two senses in the word *generally* – the sense of Euclid[77] where it means *universally*, (or in the whole extent of the *genus*,) and a foolish sense of this word where it means *usually*. Now I am far from saying that children universally are capable of grief like mine. But there are more than you ever heard of, who die of grief in this island of ours. I will tell you a common case. The rules of Eton require that a boy on the *foundation*[78] should be there twelve years: he is superannuated at eighteen, consequently he must come at six. Children torn away from mothers and sisters at that age not unfrequently die. I speak of what I know. The complaint is not entered by the registrar as grief; but *that* it is. Grief of that sort, and at that age, has killed more than ever have been counted amongst its martyrs.

Therefore it is that Levana often communes with the powers

---

* '*Glimmering*.' – As I have never allowed myself to covet any man's ox nor his ass, nor any thing that is his, still less would it become a philosopher to covet other people's images, or metaphors. Here, therefore, I restore to Mr Wordsworth this fine image of the revolving wheel, and the glimmering spokes, as applied by him to the flying successions of day and night.[79] I borrowed it for one moment in order to point my own sentence; which being done, the reader is witness that I now pay it back instantly by a note made for that sole purpose. On the same principle I often borrow their seals from young ladies – when closing my letters. Because there is sure to be some tender sentiment upon them about 'memory,' or 'hope,' or 'roses,' or 'reunion:' and my correspondent must be a sad brute who is not touched by the eloquence of the seal, even if his taste is so bad that he remains deaf to mine.

that shake man's heart: therefore it is that she doats upon grief. 'These ladies,' said I softly to myself, on seeing the ministers with whom Levana was conversing, 'these are the Sorrows; and they are three in number, as the *Graces* are three, who dress man's life with beauty; the *Parcæ* are three, who weave the dark arras of man's life in their mysterious loom always with colours sad in part, sometimes angry with tragic crimson and black; the *Furies* are three, who visit with retributions called from the other side of the grave offences that walk upon this; and once even the *Muses*[80] were but three, who fit the harp, the trumpet, or the lute, to the great burdens of man's impassioned creations. These are the Sorrows, all three of whom I know.' The last words I say *now*; but in Oxford I said – 'one of whom I know, and the others too surely I *shall* know.' For already, in my fervent youth, I saw (dimly relieved upon the dark background of my dreams) the imperfect lineaments of the awful sisters. These sisters – by what name shall we call them?

If I say simply – 'The Sorrows,' there will be a chance of mistaking the term; it might be understood of individual sorrow – separate cases of sorrow, – whereas I want a term expressing the mighty abstractions that incarnate themselves in all individual sufferings of man's heart; and I wish to have these abstractions presented as impersonations, that is, as clothed with human attributes of life, and with functions pointing to flesh. Let us call them, therefore, *Our Ladies of Sorrow*. I know them thoroughly, and have walked in all their kingdoms. Three sisters they are, of one mysterious household; and their paths are wide apart; but of their dominion there is no end. Them I saw often conversing with Levana, and sometimes about myself. Do they talk, then? Oh, no! Mighty phantoms like these disdain the infirmities of language. They may utter voices through the organs of man when they dwell in human hearts, but amongst themselves is no voice nor sound – eternal silence reigns in *their* kingdoms. *They* spoke not as they talked to Levana. *They* whispered not. *They* sang not. Though oftentimes methought they *might* have sung; for I upon earth had heard their mysteries oftentimes deciphered by harp and timbrel, by dulcimer and organ. Like God, whose servants they are, they utter their pleasure, not by sounds that perish, or by words that go astray, but by signs in heaven – by changes on earth – by pulses in secret rivers – heraldries painted on darkness – and hieroglyphics written on the tablets of the brain. *They* wheeled in mazes; *I* spelled the steps. *They* telegraphed from afar; *I* read the signals. *They* conspired together; and on the mirrors of darkness *my* eye traced the plots. *Theirs* were the symbols, – *mine* are the words.

What is it the sisters are? What is it that they do? Let me describe their form, and their presence; if form it were that still fluctuated in its outline; or presence it were that for ever advanced to the front, or for ever receded amongst shades.

The eldest of the three is named *Mater Lachrymarum*, Our Lady of Tears. She it is that night and day raves and moans, calling for vanished faces. She stood in Rama, when a voice was heard of lamentation – Rachel weeping for her children, and refusing to be comforted. She it was that stood in Bethlehem on the night when Herod's sword swept its nurseries of Innocents,[81] and the little feet were stiffened for ever, which, heard at times as they tottered along floors overhead, woke pulses of love in household hearts that were not unmarked in heaven.

Her eyes are sweet and subtle, wild and sleepy by turns; oftentimes rising to the clouds; oftentimes challenging the heavens. She wears a diadem round her head. And I knew by childish memories that she could go abroad upon the winds, when she heard the sobbing of litanies or the thundering of organs, and when she beheld the mustering of summer clouds. This sister, the elder, it is that carries keys more than Papal at her girdle, which open every cottage and every palace. She, to my knowledge, sate all last summer by the bedside of the blind beggar, him that so often and so gladly I talked with, whose pious daughter, eight years old, with the sunny countenance, resisted the temptations of play and village mirth to travel all day long on dusty roads with her afflicted father. For this did God send her a great reward. In the spring-time of the year, and whilst yet her own spring was budding, he recalled her to himself. But her blind father mourns for ever over *her*; still he dreams at midnight that the little guiding hand is locked within his own; and still he wakens to a darkness that is *now* within a second and a deeper darkness. This *Mater Lachrymarum* also has been sitting all this winter of 1844-5 within the bedchamber of the Czar,[82] bringing before his eyes a daughter (not less pious) that vanished to God not less suddenly, and left behind her a darkness not less profound. By the power of her keys it is that Our Lady of Tears glides a ghostly intruder into the chambers of sleepless men, sleepless women, sleepless children, from Ganges to the Nile, from Nile to Mississippi. And her, because she is the first-born of her house, and has the widest empire, let us honour with the title of 'Madonna.'

The second sister is called *Mater Suspiriorum*, Our Lady of Sighs. She never scales the clouds, nor walks abroad upon the winds. She wears no diadem. And her eyes, if they were ever seen, would be neither sweet nor subtle; no man could read their story; they would be found filled with perishing dreams, and with wrecks of forgotten delirium. But she raises not her eyes; her head, on which sits a dilapidated turban, droops for ever; for ever fastens on the dust. She weeps not. She groans not. But she sighs inaudibly at intervals. Her sister, Madonna, is oftentimes stormy and frantic; raging in the highest against heaven; and demanding back her darlings. But Our Lady of Sighs never clamours, never defies, dreams not of rebellious aspirations. She is humble to abjectness. Hers is the meekness that belongs to the hopeless. Murmur she may, but it is in her sleep. Whisper she may, but it is to herself in the twilight. Mutter she does at times, but it is in solitary places that are desolate as she is desolate, in ruined cities, and when the sun has gone down to his rest. This sister is the visitor of the Pariah, of the Jew, of the bondsman to the oar in Mediterranean galleys, of the English criminal in Norfolk island,[83] blotted out from the books of remembrance in sweet far-off England, of the baffled penitent reverting his eye for ever upon a solitary grave, which to him seems the altar overthrown of some past and bloody sacrifice, on which altar no oblations can now be availing, whether towards pardon that he might implore, or towards reparation that he might attempt. Every slave that at noonday looks up to the tropical sun with timid reproach, as he points with one hand to the earth, our general mother, but for *him* a stepmother, as he points with the other hand to the Bible, our general teacher, but against *him* sealed and sequestered;* – every woman sitting in darkness, without love to shelter her head, or hope to illumine her solitude, because the heaven-born instincts kindling in her nature germs of holy affections, which God implanted in her womanly bosom, having been stifled by social necessities, now burn sullenly to waste, like sepulchral lamps amongst the ancients; – every nun defrauded of her unreturning May-time by wicked kinsmen, whom God will judge; – every captive in every dungeon; – all that are betrayed, and all that are rejected; outcasts by traditionary law, and children of *hereditary* disgrace – all these walk with 'Our Lady of Sighs.' She also carries a key; but she needs it little. For her kingdom is chiefly amongst the tents of Shem,[84] and the houseless vagrant of every clime. Yet in the very highest ranks of man she finds chapels of her own; and even in glorious England there are some that, to the world, carry their heads as proudly as the reindeer, who yet secretly have received her mark upon their foreheads.

But the third sister, who is also the youngest—! Hush! whisper, whilst we talk of *her*! Her kingdom is not large, or else no flesh should live; but within that kingdom all power is hers. Her head, turreted like that of Cybèle,[85] rises almost beyond the reach of sight. She droops not; and her eyes rising so high, *might* be hidden by distance. But, being what they are, they cannot be hidden; through the treble veil of crape which she wears, the fierce light of a blazing misery, that rests not for matins or for vespers – for noon of day or noon of night – for ebbing or for flowing tide – may be read from the very ground. She is the defier of God. She also is the mother of lunacies, and the suggestress of suicides. Deep lie the roots of her power; but narrow is the nation that she rules. For she can approach only those in whom a profound nature has been upheaved by central convulsions; in whom the heart trembles and the brain rocks under con-

---

* This, the reader will be aware, applies chiefly to the cotton and tobacco States of North America; but not to them only: on which account I have not scrupled to figure the sun, which looks down upon slavery, as *tropical* – no matter if strictly within the tropics, or simply so near to them as to produce a similar climate.

spiracies of tempest from without and tempest from within. Madonna moves with uncertain steps, fast or slow, but still with tragic grace. Our Lady of Sighs creeps timidly and stealthily. But this youngest sister moves with incalculable motions, bounding, and with a tiger's leaps. She carries no key; for, though coming rarely amongst men, she storms all doors at which she is permitted to enter at all. And *her* name is *Mater Tenebrarum* – Our Lady of Darkness.

These were the *Semnai Theai*, or Sublime Goddesses* – these were the *Eumenides*, or Gracious Ladies, (so called by antiquity in shuddering propitiation) – of my Oxford dreams. MADONNA spoke. She spoke by her mysterious hand. Touching my head, she beckoned to Our Lady of Sighs; and *what* she spoke, translated out of the signs which (except in dreams) no man reads, was this: –

'Lo! here is he, whom in childhood I dedicated to my altars. This is he that once I made my darling. Him I led astray, him I beguiled, and from heaven I stole away his young heart to mine. Through me did he become idolatrous; and through me it was, by languishing desires, that he worshipped the worm, and prayed to the wormy grave. Holy was the grave to him; lovely was its darkness; saintly its corruption. Him, this young idolater, I have seasoned for thee, dear gentle Sister of Sighs! Do thou take him now to *thy* heart, and season him for our dreadful sister. And thou' – turning to the *Mater Tenebrarum*, she said – 'wicked sister, that temptest and hatest, do thou take him from *her*. See that thy sceptre lie heavy on his head. Suffer not woman and her tenderness to sit near him in his darkness. Banish the frailties of hope – wither the relentings of love – scorch the fountains of tears: curse him as only thou canst curse. So shall he be accomplished in the furnace – so shall he see the things that ought *not* to be seen – sights that are abominable, and secrets that are unutterable. So shall he read elder truths, sad truths, grand truths, fearful truths. So shall he rise again *before*

---

* '*Sublime Goddesses.*' – The word σεμνός is usually rendered *venerable* in dictionaries; not a very flattering epithet for females. But by weighing a number of passages in which the word is used pointedly, I am disposed to think that it comes nearest to our idea of the *sublime*; as near as a Greek word *could* come.

he dies. And so shall our commission be accomplished which from God we had – to plague his heart until we had unfolded the capacities of his spirit.'*

THE APPARITION OF THE BROCKEN

Ascend with me on this dazzling Whitsunday the Brocken of North Germany.[86] The dawn opened in cloudless beauty; it is a dawn of bridal June; but, as the hours advance, her youngest sister April, that sometimes cares little for racing across both frontiers of May, frets the bridal lady's sunny temper with sallies of wheeling and careering showers – flying and pursuing, opening and closing, hiding and restoring. On such a morning, and reaching the summits of the forest-mountain about sunrise, we shall have one chance the more for seeing the famous Spectre of the Brocken.† Who and what is he? He is a solitary apparition,

* The reader, who wishes at all to understand the course of these Confessions, ought not to pass over this dream-legend. There is no great wonder that a vision, which occupied my waking thoughts in those years, should re-appear in my dreams. It was in fact a legend recurring in sleep, most of which I had myself silently written or sculptured in my daylight reveries. But its importance to the present Confessions is this – that it rehearses or prefigures their course. This FIRST part belongs to Madonna. The THIRD belongs to the 'Mater Suspiriorum,' and will be entitled *The Pariah Worlds*. The FOURTH, which terminates the work, belongs to the 'Mater Tenebrarum,' and will be entitled *The Kingdom of Darkness*. As to the SECOND, it is an interpolation requisite to the effect of the others; and will be explained in its proper place.

† '*Spectre of the Brocken*.' – This very striking phenomenon has been continually described by writers, both German and English, for the last fifty years. Many readers, however, will not have met with these descriptions: and on *their* account I add a few words in explanation; referring them for the best scientific comment on the case to Sir David Brewster's 'Natural Magic.' The spectre takes the shape of a human figure, or, if the visitors are more than one, then the spectres multiply; they arrange themselves on the blue ground of the sky, or the dark ground of any clouds that may be in the right quarter, or perhaps they are strongly relieved against a curtain of rock, at a distance of some miles, and always exhibiting gigantic proportions. At first, from the distance and the colossal size, every spectator supposes the appearance to be quite independent of himself. But very soon he is surprised to observe his own motions and gestures mimicked; and wakens to the conviction that the phantom is but a dilated reflection of himself. This Titan amongst the apparitions of earth is

in the sense of loving solitude; else he is not always solitary in
his personal manifestations, but on proper occasions has been
known to unmask a strength quite sufficient to alarm those who
had been insulting him.

Now, in order to test the nature of this mysterious apparition,
we will try two or three experiments upon him. What we fear,
and with some reason, is, that as he lived so many ages with
foul Pagan sorcerers, and witnessed so many centuries of dark
idolatries, his heart may have been corrupted; and that even
now his faith may be wavering or impure. We will try.

Make the sign of the cross, and observe whether he repeats
it, (as, on Whitsunday,*[87] he surely ought to do.) Look! he *does*
repeat it; but the driving showers perplex the images, and *that*,
perhaps, it is which gives him the air of one who acts reluctantly
or evasively. Now, again, the sun shines more brightly, and the

---

exceedingly capricious, vanishing abruptly for reasons best known to himself,
and more coy in coming forward than the Lady Echo of Ovid.[88] One reason
why he is seen so seldom must be ascribed to the concurrence of conditions
under which only the phenomenon can be manifested: the sun must be near to
the horizon, (which of itself implies a time of day inconvenient to a person
starting from a station as distant as Elbingerode;) the spectator must have his
back to the sun; and the air must contain some vapour – but *partially* distributed.
Coleridge ascended the Brocken on the Whitsunday of 1799, with a party of
English students from Goettingen, but failed to see the phantom; afterwards in
England (and under the same three conditions) he saw a much rarer phenomenon, which he described in the following eight lines. I give them from a
corrected copy: (the apostrophe in the beginning must be understood as
addressed to an ideal conception): –

> 'And art thou nothing? Such thou art as when
> The woodman winding westward up the glen
> At wintry dawn, when o'er the sheep-track's maze
> The viewless snow-mist weaves a glist'ning haze,
> Sees full before him, gliding without tread,
> An image with a glory round its head:
> This shade he worships for its golden hues,
> And *makes* (not knowing) that which he pursues.'[89]

* '*On Whitsunday.*' – It is singular, and perhaps owing to the temperature and
weather likely to prevail in that early part of summer, that more appearances
of the spectre have been witnessed on Whitsunday than on any other day.

showers have swept off like squadrons of cavalry to the rear. We will try him again.

Pluck an anemone, one of these many anemones which once was called the sorcerer's flower,* and bore a part perhaps in his horrid ritual of fear; carry it to that stone which mimics the outline of a heathen altar, and once was called the sorcerer's altar;* then bending your knee, and raising your right hand to God, say, – 'Father, which art in heaven – this lovely anemone, that once glorified the worship of fear, has travelled back into thy fold; this altar, which once reeked with bloody rites to Cortho, has long been rebaptized into thy holy service. The darkness is gone – the cruelty is gone which the darkness bred; the moans have passed away which the victims uttered; the cloud has vanished which once sate continually upon their graves – cloud of protestation that ascended for ever to thy throne from the tears of the defenceless, and the anger of the just. And lo! I thy servant, with this dark phantom, whom, for one hour on this thy festival of Pentecost, I make *my* servant, render thee united worship in this thy recovered temple.'

Look, now! the apparition plucks an anemone, and places it on an altar; he also bends his knee, he also raises his right hand to God. Dumb he is; but sometimes the dumb serve God acceptably. Yet still it occurs to you, that perhaps on this high festival of the Christian Church, he may be overruled by supernatural influence into confession of his homage, having so often been made to bow and bend his knee at murderous rites. In a service of religion he may be timid. Let us try him, therefore, with an earthly passion, where he will have no bias either from favour or from fear.

If, then, once in childhood you suffered an affliction that was ineffable; If once, when powerless to face such an enemy, you were summoned to fight with the tiger that couches within the

---

* 'The sorcerer's flower,' and 'the sorcerer's altar.' – These are names still clinging to the anemone of the Brocken, and to an altar-shaped fragment of granite near one of the summits; and it is not doubted that they both connect themselves through links of ancient tradition with the gloomy realities of Paganism, when the whole Hartz and the Brocken formed for a very long time the last asylum to a ferocious but perishing idolatry.

separations of the grave; in that case, after the example of Judæa (on the Roman coins)[90] – sitting under her palm-tree to weep, but sitting with her head veiled – do you also veil your head. Many years are passed away since then; and you were a little ignorant thing at that time, hardly above six years old; or perhaps (if you durst tell all the truth) not quite so much. But your heart was deeper than the Danube; and, as was your love, so was your grief. Many years are gone since that darkness settled on your head; many summers, many winters; yet still its shadows wheel round upon you at intervals, like these April showers upon this glory of bridal June. Therefore now, on this dovelike morning of Pentecost, do you veil your head like Judæa in memory of that transcendant woe, and in testimony that, indeed, it surpassed all utterance of words. Immediately you see that the apparition of the Brocken veils *his* head, after the model of Judæa weeping under her palm-tree, as if he also had a human heart, and that *he* also, in childhood, having suffered an affliction which was ineffable, wished by these mute symbols to breathe a sigh towards heaven in memory of that affliction, and by way of record, though many a year after, that it was indeed unutterable by words.

This trial is decisive. You are now satisfied that the apparition is but a reflex of yourself; and, in uttering your secret feelings to *him*, you make this phantom the dark symbolic mirror for reflecting to the daylight what else must be hidden for ever.

Such a relation does the Dark Interpreter, whom immediately the reader will learn to know as an intruder into my dreams, bear to my own mind. He is originally a mere reflex of my inner nature. But as the apparition of the Brocken sometimes is disturbed by storms or by driving showers, so as to dissemble his real origin, in like manner the Interpreter sometimes swerves out of my orbit, and mixes a little with alien natures. I do not always know him in these cases as my own parhelion. What he says, generally is but that which *I* have said in daylight, and in meditation deep enough to sculpture itself on my heart. But sometimes, as his face alters, his words alter; and they do not always seem such as I have used, or *could* use. No man can account for all things that occur in dreams. Generally I believe this – that he is a faithful representative of myself; but he also is at times subject to the action of the god *Phantasus*,[91] who rules in dreams.

Hailstone choruses* besides, and storms, enter my dreams. Hailstones and fire that run along the ground, sleet and blinding hurricanes, revelations of glory insufferable pursued by volleying darkness – these are powers able to disturb any features that originally were but shadow, and to send drifting the anchors of any vessel that rides upon deeps so treacherous as those of dreams. Understand, however, the Interpreter to bear generally the office of a tragic chorus at Athens. The Greek chorus is perhaps not quite understood by critics, any more than the Dark Interpreter by myself. But the leading function of both must be supposed this – not to tell you any thing absolutely new, *that* was done by the actors in the drama; but to recall you to your own lurking thoughts – hidden for the moment or imperfectly developed, and to place before you, in immediate connexion with groups vanishing too quickly for any effort of meditation on your own part, such commentaries, prophetic or looking back, pointing the moral or deciphering the mystery, justifying Providence, or mitigating the fierceness of anguish, as would or might have occurred to your own meditative heart – had only time been allowed for its motions.

The Interpreter is anchored and stationary in my dreams; but great storms and driving mists cause him to fluctuate uncertainly, or even to retire altogether, like his gloomy counterpart the shy Phantom of the Brocken – and to assume new features or strange features, as in dreams always there is a power not contented with reproduction, but which absolutely creates or transforms. This dark being the reader will see again in a further stage of my opium experience; and I warn him that he will not always be found sitting inside my dreams, but at times outside, and in open daylight.

---

* '*Hailstone choruses.*' – I need not tell any lover of Handel that his oratorio of 'Israel in Egypt' contains a chorus familiarly known by this name. The words are – 'And he gave them hailstones for rain; fire, mingled with the hail, ran along upon the ground.'

FINALE TO PART I – SAVANNAH-LA-MAR

God smote Savannah-la-Mar,[92] and in one night, by earthquake, removed her, with all her towers standing and population sleeping, from the steadfast foundations of the shore to the coral floors of ocean. And God said – 'Pompeii did I bury and conceal from men through seventeen centuries: this city I will bury, but not conceal. She shall be a monument to men of my mysterious anger; set in azure light through generations to come: for I will enshrine her in a crystal dome of my tropic seas.' This city, therefore, like a mighty galleon with all her apparel mounted, streamers flying, and tackling perfect, seems floating along the noiseless depths of ocean: and oftentimes in glassy calms, through the translucid atmosphere of water that now stretches like an air-woven awning above the silent encampment, mariners from every clime look down into her courts and terraces, count her gates, and number the spires of her churches. She is one ample cemetery, and *has* been for many a year; but in the mighty calms that brood for weeks over tropic latitudes, she fascinates the eye with a *Fata-Morgana*[93] revelation, as of human life still subsisting in submarine asylums sacred from the storms that torment our upper air.

Thither, lured by the loveliness of cerulean depths, by the peace of human dwellings privileged from molestation, by the gleam of marble altars sleeping in everlasting sanctity, oftentimes in dreams did I and the dark Interpreter cleave the watery veil that divided us from her streets. We looked into the belfries, where the pendulous bells were waiting in vain for the summons which should awaken their marriage peals; together we touched the mighty organ keys, that sang no *jubilates*[94] for the ear of Heaven – that sang no requiems for the ear of human sorrow; together we searched the silent nurseries, where the children were all asleep, and *had* been asleep through five generations. 'They are waiting for the heavenly dawn,' whispered the Interpreter to himself; 'and, when *that* comes, the bells and the organs will utter a *jubilate* repeated by the echoes of Paradise.' Then, turning to me, he said – 'This is sad: this is piteous: but less would not have sufficed for the purposes of God. Look here: put into a Roman clepsydra[95] one hundred drops of water; let these run out as the sands in an hourglass; every drop measuring the hundredth part of a second, so that each shall represent but the three-hundred-and-sixty-thousandth part of an hour. Now, count the drops as they race along; and, when the fiftieth of the hundred is passing, behold! forty-nine are not, because already they have perished; and fifty are not, because they are yet to come. You see, therefore, how narrow, how incalculably narrow, is the true and actual present. Of that time which we call the present, hardly a hundredth part but belongs either to a past which has fled, or to a future which is still on the wing. It has perished, or it is not born. It was, or it is not. Yet even this approximation to the truth is *infinitely* false. For again subdivide that solitary drop, which only was found to represent the present, into a lower series of similar fractions, and the actual present which you arrest measures now but the thirty-sixth millionth of an hour; and so by infinite declensions the true and very present, in which only we live and enjoy, will vanish into a mote of a mote, distinguishable only by a heavenly vision. Therefore the present, which only man possesses, offers less capacity for his footing than the slenderest film that ever spider twisted from her womb. Therefore, also, even this incalculable shadow from the narrowest pencil of moonlight, is more transitory than geometry can measure, or thought of angel can overtake. The time which *is*, contracts into a mathematic point; and even that point perishes a thousand times before we can utter its birth. All is finite in the present; and even that finite is infinite in its velocity of flight towards death. But in God there is nothing finite; but in God there is nothing transitory; but in God there *can* be nothing that tends to death. Therefore, it follows – that for God there can be no present. The future is the present of God; and to the future it is that he sacrifices the human present. Therefore it is that he works by earthquake. Therefore it is that he works by grief. Oh, deep is the ploughing of earthquake! Oh, deep,' [and his voice swelled like a *sanctus*[96] rising from the choir of a cathedral,] – 'oh, deep is the ploughing of grief! But oftentimes less would not suffice for the agriculture of God.

Upon a night of earthquake he builds a thousand years of pleasant habitations for man. Upon the sorrow of an infant, he raises oftentimes from human intellects glorious vintages that could not else have been. Less than these fierce ploughshares would not have stirred the stubborn soil. The one is needed for earth, our planet – for earth itself as the dwelling-place of man. But the other is needed yet oftener for God's mightiest instrument; yes,' [and he looked solemnly at myself,] 'is needed for the mysterious children of the earth!'

END OF PART I

PART II

The Oxford visions, of which some have been given, were but anticipations necessary to illustrate the glimpse opened of childhood, (as being its reaction.) In this SECOND part, returning from that anticipation, I retrace an abstract of my boyish and youthful days so far as they furnished or exposed the germs of later experiences in worlds more shadowy.

Upon me, as upon others scattered thinly by tens and twenties over every thousand years, fell too powerfully and too early the vision of life. The horror of life mixed itself already in earliest youth with the heavenly sweetness of life; that grief, which one in a hundred has sensibility enough to gather from the sad retrospect of life in its closing stage, for me shed its dews as a prelibation upon the fountains of life whilst yet sparkling to the morning sun. I saw from afar and from before what I was to see from behind. Is this the description of an early youth passed in the shades of gloom? No, but of a youth passed in the divinest happiness. And if the reader has (which so few have) the passion, without which there is no reading of the legend and super-scription upon man's brow, if he is not (as most are) deafer than the grave to every *deep* note that sighs upwards from the Delphic caves of human life, he will know that the rapture of life (or any thing which by approach can merit that name) does not arise, unless as perfect music arises – music of Mozart or

Beethoven – by the confluence of the mighty and terrific discords with the subtle concords. Not by contrast, or as reciprocal foils do these elements act, which is the feeble conception of many, but by union. They are the sexual forces in music: 'male and female created he them;'[97] and these mighty antagonists do not put forth their hostilities by repulsion, but by deepest attraction.

As 'in to-day already walks to-morrow,'[98] so in the past experience of a youthful life may be seen dimly the future. The collisions with alien interests or hostile views, of a child, boy, or very young man, so insulated as each of these is sure to be, – those aspects of opposition which such a person *can* occupy, are limited by the exceedingly few and trivial lines of connexion along which he is able to radiate any essential influence whatever upon the fortunes or happiness of others. Circumstances may magnify his importance for the moment; but, after all, any cable which he carries out upon other vessels is easily slipped upon a feud arising. Far otherwise is the state of relations connecting an adult or responsible man with the circles around him as life advances. The network of these relations is a thousand times more intricate, the jarring of these intricate relations a thousand times more frequent, and the vibrations a thousand times harsher which these jarrings diffuse. This truth is felt beforehand misgivingly and in troubled vision, by a young man who stands upon the threshold of manhood. One earliest instinct of fear and horror would darken his spirit if it could be revealed to itself and self-questioned at the moment of birth: a second instinct of the same nature would again pollute that tremulous mirror, if the moment were as punctually marked as physical birth is marked, which dismisses him finally upon the tides of absolute self-controul. A dark ocean would seem the total expanse of life from the first: but far darker and more appalling would seem that interior and second chamber of the ocean which called him away for ever from the direct accountability of others. Dreadful would be the morning which should say – 'Be thou a human child incarnate;' but more dreadful the morning which should say – 'Bear thou henceforth the sceptre of thy self-dominion through life, and the passion of life!' Yes, dreadful would be both: but without a basis of the dreadful there is no perfect rapture. It is a part through the sorrow of life, growing out of its events, that this basis of awe and solemn darkness slowly accumulates. *That* I have illustrated. But, as life expands, it is more through the *strife* which besets us, strife from conflicting opinions, positions, passions, interests, that the funereal ground settles and deposits itself, which sends upward the dark lustrous brilliancy through the jewel of life – else revealing a pale and superficial glitter. Either the human being must suffer and struggle as the price of a more searching vision, or his gaze must be shallow and without intellectual revelation.

Through accident it was in part, and, where through no accident but my own nature, not through features of it at all painful to recollect, that constantly in early life (that is, from boyish days until eighteen, when by going to Oxford, practically I became my own master) I was engaged in duels of fierce continual struggle, with some person or body of persons, that sought, like the Roman *retiarius*,[99] to throw a net of deadly coercion or constraint over the undoubted rights of my natural freedom. The steady rebellion upon my part in one-half, was a mere human reaction of justifiable indignation; but in the other half it was the struggle of a conscientious nature – disdaining to feel it as any mere right or discretional privilege – no, feeling it as the noblest of duties to resist, though it should be mortally, those that would have enslaved me, and to retort scorn upon those that would have put my head below their feet. Too much, even in later life, I have perceived in men that pass for good men, a disposition to degrade (and if possible to degrade through self-degradation) those in whom unwillingly they feel any weight of oppression to themselves, by commanding qualities of intellect or character. They respect you: they are compelled to do so: and they hate to do so. Next, therefore, they seek to throw off the sense of this oppression, and to take vengeance for it, by co-operating with any unhappy accidents in your life, to inflict a sense of humiliation upon you, and (if possible) to force you into becoming a consenting party to that humiliation. Oh, wherefore is it that those who presume to call themselves the 'friends' of this man or that woman, are so often those above all others, whom in the hour of death that man or woman is most likely to salute with the valediction – Would God I had never seen your face?

In citing one or two cases of these early struggles, I have chiefly in view the effect of these upon my subsequent visions under the reign of opium. And this indulgent reflection should accompany the mature reader through all such records of boyish inexperience. A good-tempered man, who is also acquainted with the world, will easily evade, without needing any artifice of servile obsequiousness, those quarrels which an upright simplicity, jealous of its own rights, and unpractised in the science of worldly address, cannot always evade without some loss of self-respect. Suavity in this manner may, it is true, be reconciled with firmness in the matter; but not easily by a young person who wants all the appropriate resources of knowledge, of adroit and guarded language, for making his good temper available. Men are protected from insult and wrong, not merely by their own skill, but also in the absence of any skill at all, by the general spirit of forbearance to which society has trained all those whom they are likely to meet. But boys meeting with no such forbearance or training in other boys, must sometimes be thrown upon feuds in the ratio of their own firmness, much more than in the ratio of any natural proneness to quarrel. Such a subject, however, will be best illustrated by a sketch or two of my own principal feuds.

The first, but merely transient and playful, nor worth noticing at all, but for its subsequent resurrection under other and awful colouring in my dreams, grew out of an imaginary slight, as I viewed it, put upon me by one of my guardians. I had four guardians: and the one of these who had the most knowledge and talent of the whole, a banker, living about a hundred miles from my home, had invited me when eleven years old to his house. His eldest daughter, perhaps a year younger than myself, wore at that time upon her very lovely face the most angelic expression of character and temper that I have almost ever seen. Naturally, I fell in love with her. It seems absurd to say so; and the more so, because two children more absolutely innocent than we were cannot be imagined, neither of us having ever been at any school; – but the simple truth is, that in the most chivalrous sense I was in love with her. And the proof that I was so showed itself in three separate modes: I kissed her glove on any rare occasion when I found it lying on a table; secondly, I looked out for some excuse to be jealous of her; and, thirdly, I did my very best to get up a quarrel. What I wanted the quarrel for was the luxury of a reconciliation; a hill cannot be had, you know, without going to the expense of a valley. And though I hated the very thought of a moment's difference with so truly gentle a girl, yet how, but through such a purgatory, could one win the paradise of her returning smiles? All this, however, came to nothing; and simply because she positively would *not* quarrel. And the jealousy fell through, because there was no decent subject for such a passion, unless it had settled upon an old music-master whom lunacy itself could not adopt as a rival. The quarrel meantime, which never prospered with the daughter, silently kindled on my part towards the father. His offence was this. At dinner, I naturally placed myself by the side of M., and it gave me great pleasure to touch her hand at intervals. As M. was my cousin, though twice or even three times removed, I did not feel taking too great a liberty in this little act of tenderness. No matter if three thousand times removed, I said, my cousin is my cousin: nor had I very much designed to conceal the act; or if so, rather on her account than my own. One evening, however, papa observed my manœuvre. Did he seem displeased? Not at all: he even condescended to smile. But the next day he placed M. on the side opposite to myself. In one respect this was really an improvement; because it gave me a better view of my cousin's sweet countenance. But then there was the loss of the hand to be considered, and secondly there was the affront. It was clear that vengeance must be had. Now there was but one thing in this world that I could do even decently: but *that* I could do admirably. This was writing Latin hexameters. Juvenal, though it was not very much of him that I had then read, seemed to me a divine model. The inspiration of wrath spoke through him as through a Hebrew prophet. The same inspiration spoke now in me. *Facit indignatio versum*,[100] said Juvenal. And it must be owned that Indignation has never made such good verses since as she did in that day. But still, even to me this agile passion proved a Muse of genial inspiration for a couple of paragraphs: and one line I will mention as worthy to have taken its place in Juvenal himself. I say this without scruple, having not a shadow of vanity, nor on the other hand a shadow of false modesty connected with such boyish accomplishments. The poem opened thus –

> 'Te nimis austerum, sacræ qui fœdera mensæ
> Diruis, insector Satyræ reboante flagello.'[101]

But the line, which I insist upon as of Roman strength, was the closing one of the next sentence. The general effect of the sentiment was – that my clamorous wrath should make its way even into ears that were past hearing:

> '– mea sæva querela
> Auribus insidet ceratis, auribus etsi
> Non audituris hybernâ nocte procellam.'[102]

The power, however, which inflated my verse, soon collapsed; having been soothed from the very first by finding – that except in this one instance at the dinner-table, which probably had been viewed as an indecorum, no further restraint of any kind whatever was meditated upon my intercourse with M. Besides, it was too painful to lock up good verses in one's own solitary breast. Yet how could I shock the sweet filial heart of my cousin by a fierce lampoon or *stylites*[103] against her father, had Latin even figured amongst her accomplishments? Then it occurred to me that the verses might be shown to the father. But was there not something treacherous in gaining a man's approbation under a mask to a satire upon himself? Or would he have always understood me? For one person a year after took the *sacræ mensæ* (by which I had meant the sanctities of hospitality) to mean the sacramental table. And on consideration I began to suspect, that many people would pronounce myself the party who had violated the holy ties of hospitality, which are equally binding on guest as on host. Indolence, which sometimes comes in aid of good impulses as well as bad, favoured these relenting thoughts; the society of M. did still more to wean me from further efforts of satire: and, finally, my Latin poem remained a *torso*. But upon the whole my guardian had a narrow escape of descending to posterity in a disadvantageous light, had he rolled down to it through my hexameters.

Here was a case of merely playful feud. But the same talent of Latin verses soon after connected me with a real feud that harassed my mind more than would be supposed, and precisely by this agency, viz. that it arrayed one set of feelings against another. It divided my mind as by domestic feud against itself. About a year after, returning from the visit to my guardian's, and when I must have been nearly completing my twelfth year, I was sent to a great public school. Every man has reason to rejoice who enjoys so great an advantage. I condemned and *do* condemn the practice of sometimes sending out into such stormy exposures those who are as yet too young, too dependent on female gentleness, and endowed with sensibilities too exquisite. But at nine or ten the masculine energies of the character are beginning to be developed: or, if not, no discipline will better aid in their developement than the bracing intercourse of a great English classical school. Even the selfish are forced into accommodating themselves to a public standard of generosity, and the effeminate into conforming to a rule of manliness. I was myself at two public schools; and I think with gratitude of the benefit which I reaped from both; as also I think with gratitude of the upright guardian in whose quiet household I learned Latin so effectually. But the small private schools which I witnessed for brief periods, containing thirty to forty boys, were models of ignoble manners as respected some part of the juniors, and of favouritism amongst the masters. Nowhere is the sublimity of public justice so broadly exemplified as in an English school. There is not in the universe such an areopagus for fair play and abhorrence of all crooked ways, as an English mob, or one of the English time-honoured public schools. But my own first introduction to such an establishment was under peculiar and contradictory circumstances. When my 'rating,' or graduation in the school, was to be settled, naturally my altitude (to speak astronomically) was taken by the proficiency in Greek. But I could then barely construe books so easy as the Greek Testament and the Iliad. This was considered quite well enough for my age; but still it caused me to be placed three steps below the highest rank in the school. Within one week, however, my talent for Latin verses, which had by this time gathered strength and expansion, became known. I was honoured as never was man or boy since Mordecai the Jew.[104] Not properly belonging to the flock of the head master, but to the leading section of the second, I was now weekly paraded for distinction at the supreme tribunal of the school; out of which at first grew nothing but a sunshine of approbation delightful to my heart, still brooding upon solitude. Within six weeks this had changed. The approbation indeed continued, and the public testimony of it. Neither would there, in the ordinary course, have been any painful reaction from jealousy or fretful resistance to the soundness of my pretensions; since it was sufficiently known to some of my schoolfellows, that I, who had no male relatives but military men, and those in India, could not have benefited by any clandestine aid. But, unhappily, the head master was at that time dissatisfied with some points in the progress of his head form; and, as it soon appeared, was continually throwing in their teeth the brilliancy of my verses at twelve, by comparison with theirs at seventeen, eighteen, and nineteen. I had observed him sometimes pointing to myself; and was perplexed at seeing this gesture followed by gloomy looks, and what French reporters call 'sensation,' in these young men, whom naturally I viewed with awe as my leaders, boys that were called young men, men that were reading Sophocles – (a name that carried with it the sound of something seraphic to my ears) – and who never had vouchsafed to waste a word on such a child as myself. The day was come, however, when all that would be changed. One of these leaders strode up to me in the public playgrounds, and delivering a blow on my shoulder, which was not intended to hurt me, but as a mere formula of introduction, asked me, 'What the d—l I meant by bolting out of the course, and annoying other people in that manner? Were other people to have no rest for me and my verses, which, after all, were horribly bad?' There might have

been some difficulty in returning an answer to this address, but
none was required. I was briefly admonished to see that I wrote
worse for the future, or else— At this *aposiopesis* [105] I looked
enquiringly at the speaker, and he filled up the chasm by saying,
that he would 'annihilate' me. Could any person fail to be aghast
at such a demand? I was to write worse than my own standard,
which, by his account of my verses, must be difficult; and I was
to write worse than himself, which might be impossible. My
feelings revolted, it may be supposed, against so arrogant a
demand, unless it had been far otherwise expressed; and on the
next occasion for sending up verses, so far from attending to
the orders issued. I double-shotted my guns; double applause
descended on myself; but I remarked with some awe, though
not repenting of what I had done, that double confusion seemed
to agitate the ranks of my enemies. Amongst them loomed out
in the distance my 'annihilating' friend, who shook his huge fist
at me, but with something like a grim smile about his eyes. He
took an early opportunity of paying his respects to me – saying,
'You little devil, do you call this writing your worst?' 'No,' I
replied; 'I call it writing my best.' The annihilator, as it turned
out, was really a good-natured young man; but he soon went
off to Cambridge; and with the rest, or some of them, I continued
to wage war for nearly a year. And yet, for a word spoken with
kindness, I would have resigned the peacock's feather in my cap
as the merest of baubles. Undoubtedly, praise sounded sweet in
my ears also. But *that* was nothing by comparison with what
stood on the other side. I detested distinctions that were connected with mortification to others. And, even if I could have got
over *that*, the eternal feud fretted and tormented my nature.
Love, that once in childhood had been so mere a necessity to
me, *that* had long been a mere reflected ray from a departed
sunset. But peace, and freedom from strife, if love were no
longer possible, (as so rarely it is in this world,) was the absolute
necessity of my heart. To contend with somebody was still my
fate; how to escape the contention I could not see; and yet for
itself, and the deadly passions into which it forced me, I hated
and loathed it more than death. It added to the distraction and
internal feud of my own mind – that I could not *altogether*

condemn the upper boys. I was made a handle of humiliation to them. And in the mean time, if I had an advantage in one accomplishment, which is all a matter of accident, or peculiar taste and feeling, they, on the other hand, had a great advantage over me in the more elaborate difficulties of Greek, and of choral Greek poetry. I could not altogether wonder at their hatred of myself. Yet still, as they had chosen to adopt this mode of conflict with me, I did not feel that I had any choice but to resist. The contest was terminated for me by my removal from the school, in consequence of a very threatening illness affecting my head; but it lasted nearly a year; and it did not close before several amongst my public enemies had become my private friends. They were much older, but they invited me to the houses of their friends, and showed me a respect which deeply affected me – this respect having more reference, apparently, to the firmness I had exhibited than to the splendour of my verses. And, indeed, these had rather drooped from a natural accident; several persons of my own class had formed the practice of asking me to write verses for *them*. I could not refuse. But, as the subjects given out were the same for all of us, it was not possible to take so many crops off the ground without starving the quality of all.

Two years and a half from this time, I was again at a public school of ancient foundation. Now I was myself one of the three who formed the highest class. Now I myself was familiar with Sophocles, who once had been so shadowy a name in my ear. But, strange to say, now in my sixteenth year, I cared nothing at all for the glory of Latin verse. All the business of school was slight and trivial in my eyes. Costing me not an effort, it could not engage any part of my attention; that was now swallowed up altogether by the literature of my native land. I still rever-enced the Grecian drama, as always I must. But else I cared little then for classical pursuits. A deeper spell had mastered me; and I lived only in those bowers where deeper passions spoke.

Here, however, it was that began another and more important struggle. I was drawing near to seventeen, and, in a year after *that*, would arrive the usual time for going to Oxford. To Oxford my guardians made no objection; and they readily agreed to make the allowance then universally regarded as the *minimum* for an Oxford student, viz. £200 per annum. But they insisted, as a previous condition, that I should make a positive and definitive choice of a profession. Now I was well aware that, if I *did* make such a choice, no law existed, nor could any obligation be created through deeds or signature, by which I could finally be compelled into keeping my engagement. But this evasion did not suit me. Here, again, I felt indignantly that the principle of the attempt was unjust. The object was certainly to do me service by saving money, since, if I selected the bar as my profession, it was contended by some persons, (misinformed, however,) that not Oxford, but a special pleader's office, would be my proper destination; but I cared not for arguments of that sort. Oxford I was determined to make my home; and also to bear my future course utterly untrammeled by promises that I might repent. Soon came the catastrophe of this struggle. A little before my seventeenth birthday, I walked off one lovely summer morning to North Wales – rambled there for months – and, finally, under some obscure hopes of raising money on my personal security, I went up to London. Now I was in my eighteenth year; and, during this period it was that I passed through that trial of severe distress, of which I gave some account in my former Confessions. Having a motive, however, for glancing backwards briefly at that period in the present series, I will do so at this point.

I saw in one journal an insinuation that the incidents in the *preliminary* narrative were possibly without foundation. To such an expression of mere gratuitous malignity, as it happened to be supported by no one argument except a remark, apparently absurd, but certainly false, I did not condescend to answer. In reality, the possibility had never occurred to me that any person of judgment would seriously suspect me of taking liberties with that part of the work, since, though no one of the parties concerned but myself stood in so central a position to the circumstances as to be acquainted with *all* of them, many were acquainted with each separate section of the memoir. Relays of witnesses might have been summoned to mount guard, as it were, upon the accuracy of each particular in the whole succession of incidents; and some of these people had an interest, more or less strong, in exposing any deviation from the strictest *letter* of the truth, had it been in their power to do so. It is now twenty-two years since I saw the objection here alluded to; and, in saying that I did not condescend to notice it, the reader must not find any reason for taxing me with a blamable haughtiness. But every man is entitled to be haughty when his veracity is impeached; and, still more, when it is impeached by a dishonest objection, or, if not *that*, by an objection which argues a careless-ness of attention almost amounting to dishonesty, in a case where it was meant to sustain an imputation of falsehood. Let a man read carelessly if he will, but not where he is meaning to use his reading for a purpose of wounding another man's honour. Having thus, by twenty-two years' silence, sufficiently expressed my contempt for the slander,* I now feel myself at liberty to draw it into notice, for the sake, *inter alia*,[106] of showing in how rash a spirit malignity often works. In the preliminary account of certain boyish adventures which had exposed me to suffering of a kind not commonly incident to persons in my station of life, and leaving behind a temptation to the use of opium under certain arrears of weakness, I had occasion to notice a disreputable attorney in London, who showed me some attentions, partly on my own account as a boy of some expectations, but much more with the purpose of fastening his professional grappling-hooks upon the young Earl of A—t,[107] my former companion, and my present correspon-dent. This man's house was slightly described, and, with more minuteness, I had exposed some interesting traits in his house-hold economy. A question, therefore, naturally arose in several

---

* Being constantly almost an absentee from London, and very often from other great cities, so as to command oftentimes no favourable opportunities for overlooking the great mass of public journals, it is possible enough that other slanders of the same tenor may have existed. I speak of what met my own eye, or was accidentally reported to me – but in fact all of us are exposed to this evil of calumnies lurking unseen – for no degree of energy, and no excess of disposable time, would enable any one man to exercise this sort of vigilant police over *all* journals. Better, therefore, tranquilly to leave all such malice to confound itself.

people's curiosity – Where was this house situated? and the more so because I had pointed a renewed attention to it by saying, that on that very evening, (viz. the evening on which that particular page of the Confessions was written,) I had visited the street, looked up at the windows, and, instead of the gloomy desolation reigning there when myself and a little girl were the sole nightly tenants, sleeping in fact (poor freezing creatures that we both were) on the floor of the attorney's law-chamber, and making a pillow out of his infernal parchments, I had seen with pleasure the evidences of comfort, respectability, and domestic animation, in the lights and stir prevailing through different stories of the house. Upon this the upright critic told his readers that I had described the house as standing in Oxford Street, and then appealed to their own knowledge of that street whether such a house could be *so* situated. Why not – he neglected to tell us. The houses at the east end of Oxford Street are certainly of too small an order to meet my account of the attorney's house; but why should it be at the east end? Oxford Street is a mile and a quarter long, and being built continuously on both sides, finds room for houses of *many* classes. Meantime it happens that, although the true house was most obscurely indicated, *any* house whatever in Oxford Street was most luminously excluded. In all the immensity of London there was but one single street that could be challenged by an attentive reader of the Confessions as peremptorily *not* the street of the attorney's house – and *that* one was Oxford Street; for, in speaking of my own renewed acquaintance with the outside of this house, I used some expression implying that, in order to make such a visit of reconnoissance, I had turned *aside* from Oxford Street. The matter is a perfect trifle in itself, but it is no trifle in a question affecting a writer's accuracy. If in a thing so absolutely impossible to be forgotten as the true situation of a house painfully memorable to a man's feelings, from being the scene of boyish distresses the most exquisite – nights passed in the misery of cold, and hunger preying upon him both night and day, in a degree which very many would not have survived, – he, when retracing his schoolboy annals, could have shown indecision even, far more dreaded inaccuracy, in identifying the house, not one syllable after *that*, which he could have said on any other subject, would have won any confidence, or deserved any, from a judicious reader. I may now mention – the Herod being dead whose persecutions I had reason to fear – that the house in question stands in Greek Street on the west, and is the house on that side nearest to Soho-Square, but without looking into the Square. This it was hardly safe to mention at the date of the published Confessions. It was my private opinion, indeed, that there were probably twenty-five chances to one in favour of my friend the attorney having been by that time hanged. But then this argued inversely; one chance to twenty-five that my friend might be *un*hanged, and knocking about the streets of London; in which case it would have been a perfect god-send to him that here lay an opening (of *my* contrivance, not *his*) for requesting the opinion of a jury on the amount of *solatium*[108] due to his wounded feelings in an action on the passage in the Confessions. To have indicated even the street would have been enough. Because there could surely be but one such Grecian in Greek Street, or but one that realized the other conditions of the unknown quantity. There was also a separate danger not absolutely so laughable as it sounds. Me there was little chance that the attorney should meet; but my book he might easily have met (supposing always that the warrant of *Sus. per coll.*[109] had not yet on *his* account travelled down to Newgate.) For he was literary; admired literature; and, as a lawyer, he wrote on some subjects fluently; Might he not publish *his* Confessions? Or, which would be worse, a supplement to mine – printed so as exactly to match? In which case I should have had the same affliction that Gibbon the historian dreaded so much; viz. that of seeing a refutation of himself, and his own answer to the refutation, all bound up in one and the same self-combating volume. Besides, he would have cross-examined me before the public in Old Bailey style; no story, the most straightforward that ever was told, could be sure to stand *that*. And my readers might be left in a state of painful doubt whether *he* might not, after all, have been a model of suffering innocence – I (to say the kindest thing possible) plagued with the natural treacheries of a schoolboy's memory.

In taking leave of this case and the remembrances connected with it, let me say that, although really believing in the probability of the attorney's having at least found his way to Australia,[110] I had no satisfaction in thinking of that result. I knew my friend to be the very perfection of a scamp. And in the running account between us, (I mean, in the ordinary sense, as to money,) the balance could not be in *his* favour; since I, on receiving a sum of money, (considerable in the eyes of us both,) had transferred pretty nearly the whole of it to *him*, for the purpose ostensibly held out to me (but of course a hoax) of purchasing certain law 'stamps;' for he was then pursuing a diplomatic correspondence with various Jews who lent money to young heirs, in some trifling proportion on my own insignificant account, but much more truly on the account of Lord A—t, my young friend. On the other side, he had given to me simply the reliques of his breakfast-table, which itself was hardly more than a relique. But in this he was not to blame. He could not give to me what he had not for himself, nor sometimes for the poor starving child whom I now suppose to have been his illegitimate daughter. So desperate was the running fight, yard-arm to yard-arm, which he maintained with creditors fierce as famine and hungry as the grave; so deep also was his horror (I know not for which of the various reasons supposable) against falling into a prison, that he seldom ventured to sleep twice successively in the same house. That expense of itself must have pressed heavily in London, where you pay half-a-crown at least for a bed that would cost only a shilling in the provinces. In the midst of his knaveries, and what were even more shocking to my remembrance, his confidential discoveries in his rambling conversations of knavish *designs*, (not always pecuniary,) there was a light of wandering misery in his eye at times, which affected me afterwards at intervals when I recalled it in the radiant happiness of nineteen, and amidst the solemn tranquillities of Oxford. That of itself was interesting; the man was worse by far than he had been meant to be; he had not the mind that reconciles itself to evil. Besides, he respected scholarship, which appeared by the deference he generally showed to myself, then about seventeen; he had an interest in literature; *that* argues something good; and was pleased at any time, or even cheerful, when I turned the conversation upon books; nay, he seemed touched with emotion, when I quoted some sentiment noble and impassioned from one of the great poets, and would ask me to repeat it. He would have been a man of memorable energy, and for good purposes, had it not been for his agony of conflict with pecuniary embarrassments. These probably had commenced in some fatal compliance with temptation arising out of funds confided to him by a client. Perhaps he had gained fifty guineas for a moment of necessity, and had sacrificed for that trifle *only* the serenity and the comfort of a life. Feelings of relenting kindness, it was not in my nature to refuse in such a case; and I wished to * * * But I never succeeded in tracing his steps through the wilderness of London until some years back, when I ascertained that he was dead. Generally speaking, the few people whom I have disliked in this world were flourishing people of good repute. Whereas the knaves whom I have known, one and all, and by no means few, I think of with pleasure and kindness.

Heavens! when I look back to the sufferings which I have witnessed or heard of even from this one brief London experience, I say if life could throw open its long suits of chambers to our eyes from some station *beforehand*, if from some secret stand we could look *by anticipation* along its vast corridors, and aside into the recesses opening upon them from either hand, halls of tragedy or chambers of retribution, simply in that small wing and no more of the great caravanserai[111] which we ourselves shall haunt, simply in that narrow tract of time and no more where we ourselves shall range, and confining our gaze to those and no others for whom personally we shall be interested, what a recoil we should suffer of horror in our estimate of life! What if those sudden catastrophes, or those inexpiable afflictions, which *have* already descended upon the people within my own knowledge, and almost below my own eyes, all of them now gone past, and some long past, had been thrown open before me as a secret exhibition when first I and they stood within the vestibule of morning hopes; when the calamities themselves had hardly begun to gather in their elements of

possibility, and when some of the parties to them were as yet no
more than infants! The past viewed not *as* the past, but by a
spectator who steps back ten years deeper into the rear, in
order that he may regard it as a future; the calamity of 1840
contemplated from the station of 1830 – the doom that rang
the knell of happiness viewed from a point of time when as yet
it was neither feared nor would even have been intelligible – the
name that killed in 1843, which in 1835 would have struck no
vibration upon the heart – the portrait that on the day of her
Majesty's coronation[112] would have been admired by you with
a pure disinterested admiration, but which if seen to-day would
draw forth an involuntary groan – cases such as these are
strangely moving for all who add deep thoughtfulness to deep
sensibility. As the hastiest of improvisations, accept – fair reader,
(for you it is that will chiefly feel such an invocation of the past)
– three or four illustrations from my own experience.

Who is this distinguished-looking young woman with her
eyes drooping, and the shadow of a dreadful shock yet fresh
upon every feature? Who is the elderly lady with her eyes flashing
fire? Who is the downcast child of sixteen? What is that torn
paper lying at their feet? Who is the writer? Whom does the
paper concern? Ah! if she, if the central figure in the group –
twenty-two at the moment when she is revealed to us – could,
on her happy birth-day at sweet seventeen, have seen the image
of herself five years onwards, just as *we* see it now, would she
have prayed for life as for an absolute blessing? or would she
not have prayed to be taken from the evil to come – to be taken
away one evening at least before this day's sun arose? It is true,
she still wears a look of gentle pride, and a relic of that noble
smile which belongs to *her* that suffers an injury which many
times over she would have died sooner than inflict. Womanly
pride refuses itself before witnesses to the total prostration of
the blow; but, for all *that*, you may see that she longs to be left
alone, and that her tears will flow without restraint when she is
so. This room is her pretty boudoir, in which, till to-night –
poor thing! – she has been glad and happy. There stands her
miniature conservatory, and there expands her miniature library; as we circumnavigators of literature are apt (you know) to

regard all female libraries in the light of miniatures. None of these will ever rekindle a smile on *her* face; and there, beyond, is her music, which only of all that she possesses, will now become dearer to her than ever; but not, as once, to feed a self-mocked pensiveness, or to cheat a half-visionary sadness. She will be sad indeed. But she is one of those that will suffer in silence. Nobody will ever detect *her* failing in any point of duty, or querulously seeking the support in others which she can find for herself in this solitary room. Droop she will not in the sight of men; and, for all beyond, nobody has any concern with *that* except God. You shall hear what becomes of her, before we take our departure; but now let me tell you what has happened. In the main outline I am sure you guess already without aid of mine, for we leaden-eyed men, in such cases, see nothing by comparison with you our quick-witted sisters. That haughty-looking lady with the Roman cast of features, who must once have been strikingly handsome – an Agrippina, even yet, in a favourable presentation – is the younger lady's aunt. She, it is rumoured, once sustained, in her younger days, some injury of that same cruel nature which has this day assailed her niece, and ever since she has worn an air of disdain, not altogether unsupported by real dignity, towards men. This aunt it was that tore the letter which lies upon the floor. It deserved to be torn; and yet she that had the best right to do so would *not* have torn it. That letter was an elaborate attempt on the part of an accomplished young man to release himself from sacred engagements. What need was there to argue the case of *such* engagements? Could it have been requisite with pure female dignity to plead any thing, or do more than *look* an indisposition to fulfil them? The aunt is now moving towards the door, which I am glad to see; and she is followed by that pale timid girl of sixteen, a cousin, who feels the case profoundly, but is too young and shy to offer an intellectual sympathy.

One only person in this world there is, who *could* to-night have been a supporting friend to our young sufferer, and *that* is her dear loving twin-sister, that for eighteen years read and wrote, thought and sang, slept and breathed, with the dividing-door open for ever between their bed-rooms, and never once a

separation between their hearts; but she is in a far distant land.
Who else is there at her call? Except God, nobody. Her aunt
had somewhat sternly admonished her, though still with a
relenting in her eye as she glanced aside at the expression in her
niece's face, that she must 'call pride to her assistance.' Ay, true;
but pride, though a strong ally in public, is apt in private to
turn as treacherous as the worst of those against whom she is
invoked. How could it be dreamed by a person of sense, that a
brilliant young man of merits, various and eminent, in spite of
his baseness, to whom, for nearly two years, this young woman
had given her whole confiding love, might be dismissed from a
heart like hers on the earliest summons of pride, simply because
she herself had been dismissed from *his*, or seemed to have been
dismissed, on a summons of mercenary calculation? Look! now
that she is relieved from the weight of an unconfidential presence, she has sat for two hours with her head buried in her
hands. At last she rises to look for something. A thought has
struck her; and, taking a little golden key which hangs by a
chain within her bosom, she searches for something locked up
amongst her few jewels. What is it? It is a Bible exquisitely
illuminated, with a letter attached, by some pretty silken artifice,
to the blank leaves at the end. This letter is a beautiful record,
wisely and pathetically composed, of maternal anxiety still
burning strong in death, and yearning, when all objects beside
were fast fading from *her* eyes, after one parting act of communion with the twin darlings of her heart. Both were thirteen
years old, within a week or two, as on the night before her death
they sat weeping by the bedside of their mother, and hanging
on her lips, now for farewell whispers, and now for farewell
kisses. They both knew that, as her strength had permitted
during the latter month of her life, she had thrown the last
anguish of love in her beseeching heart into a letter of counsel
to themselves. Through this, of which each sister had a copy,
she trusted long to converse with her orphans. And the last
promise which she had entreated on this evening from both,
was – that in either of two contingencies they would review her
counsels, and the passages to which she pointed their attention
in the Scriptures; namely, first, in the event of any calamity,

that, for one sister or for both, should overspread their paths
with total darkness; and secondly, in the event of life flowing in
too profound a stream of prosperity, so as to threaten them with
an alienation of interest from all spiritual objects. She had not
concealed that, of these two extreme cases, she would prefer for
her own children the first. And now had that case arrived indeed,
which she in spirit had desired to meet. Nine years ago, just as
the silvery voice of a dial in the dying lady's bedroom was
striking nine upon a summer evening, had the last visual ray
streamed from her seeking eyes upon her orphan twins, after
which, throughout the night, she had slept away into heaven.
Now again had come a summer evening memorable for unhappiness; now again the daughter thought of those dying lights
of love which streamed at sun-set from the closing eyes of her
mother; again, and just as she went back in thought to this
image, the same silvery voice of the dial sounded nine o'clock.
Again she remembered her mother's dying request; again her
own tear-hallowed promise – and with her heart in her mother's
grave she now rose to fulfil it. Here, then, when this solemn
recurrence to a testamentary counsel has ceased to be a mere
office of duty towards the departed, having taken the shape of
a consolation for herself, let us pause.

Now, fair companion in this exploring voyage of inquest into
hidden scenes, or forgotten scenes of human life – perhaps it
might be instructive to direct our glasses upon the false perfidi-
ous lover. It might. But do not let us do so. We might like him
better, or pity him more, than either of us would desire. His
name and memory have long since dropped out of every body's
thoughts. Of prosperity, and (what is more important) of
internal peace, he is reputed to have had no gleam from the
moment when he betrayed his faith, and in one day threw away
the jewel of good conscience, and 'a pearl richer than all his
tribe.' But, however that may be, it is certain that, finally, he
became a wreck; and of any *hopeless* wreck it is painful to talk
– much more so, when through him others also became wrecks.
   Shall we, then, after an interval of nearly two years has passed
over the young lady in the boudoir, look in again upon *her*?

You hesitate, fair friend: and I myself hesitate. For in fact she also has become a wreck; and it would grieve us both to see her altered. At the end of twenty-one months she retains hardly a vestige of resemblance to the fine young woman we saw on that unhappy evening with her aunt and cousin. On consideration, therefore, let us do this. We will direct our glasses to her room, at a point of time about six weeks further on. Suppose this time gone; suppose her now dressed for her grave, and placed in her coffin. The advantage of that is – that, though no change can restore the ravages of the past, yet (as often is found to happen with young persons) the expression has revived from her girlish years. The child-like aspect has revolved, and settled back upon her features. The wasting away of the flesh is less apparent in the face; and one might imagine that, in this sweet marble countenance, was seen the very same upon which, eleven years ago, her mother's darkening eyes had lingered to the last, until clouds had swallowed up the vision of her beloved *twins*. Yet, if that were in part a fancy, this at least is no fancy – that not only much of a child-like truth and simplicity has reinstated itself in the temple of her now reposing features, but also that tranquillity and perfect peace, such as are appropriate to eternity; but which from the *living* countenance had taken their flight for ever, on that memorable evening when we looked in upon the impassioned group – upon the towering and denouncing aunt, the sympathizing but silent cousin, the poor blighted niece, and the wicked letter lying in fragments at their feet.

Cloud, that hast revealed to us this young creature and her blighted hopes, close up again. And now, a few years later, not more than four or five, give back to us the latest arrears of the changes which thou concealest within thy draperies. Once more, 'open sesame!' and show us a third generation. Behold a lawn islanded with thickets. How perfect is the verdure – how rich the blossoming shrubberies that screen with verdurous walls from the possibility of intrusion, whilst by their own wandering line of distribution they shape and umbrageously embay, what one might call lawny saloons and vestibules – sylvan galleries and closets. Some of these recesses, which unlike themselves as fluently as snakes, and unexpectedly as the shyest nooks, watery cells, and crypts, amongst the shores of a forest-lake, being formed by the mere caprices and ramblings of the luxuriant shrubs, are so small and so quiet, that one might fancy them meant for *boudoirs*. Here is one that, in a less fickle climate, would make the loveliest of studies for a writer of breathings from some solitary heart, or of *suspiria* from some impassioned memory! And opening from one angle of this embowered study, issues a little narrow corridor, that, after almost wheeling back upon itself, in its playful mazes, finally widens into a little circular chamber; out of which there is no exit, (except back again by the entrance,) small or great; so that, adjacent to his study, the writer would command how sweet a bed-room, permitting him to lie the summer through, gazing all night long at the burning host of heaven. How silent *that* would be at the noon of summer nights, how grave-like in its quiet! And yet, need there be asked a stillness or a silence more profound than is felt at this present noon of day? One reason for such peculiar repose, over and above the tranquil character of the day, and the distance of the place from high-roads, is the outer zone of woods, which almost on every quarter invests the shrubberies – swathing them, (as one may express it,) belting them, and overlooking them, from a varying distance of two and three furlongs, so as oftentimes to keep the winds at a distance. But, however caused and supported, the silence of these fanciful lawns and lawny chambers is oftentimes oppressive in the depth of summer to people unfamiliar with solitudes, either mountain-ous or sylvan; and many would be apt to suppose that the villa, to which these pretty shrubberies form the chief dependencies, must be untenanted. But that is not the case. The house is inhabited, and by its own legal mistress – the proprietress of the whole domain; and not at all a silent mistress, but as noisy as most little ladies of five years old, for that is her age. Now, and just as we are speaking, you may hear her little joyous clamour as she issues from the house. This way she comes, bounding like a fawn; and soon she rushes into the little recess which I pointed out as a proper study for any man who should be weaving the deep harmonies of memorial *suspiria*. But I fancy that she will soon dispossess it of that character, for her *suspiria* are not many at this stage of her life. Now she comes dancing into sight; and you see that, if she keeps the promise of her infancy, she will be an interesting creature to the eye in after life. In other respects, also, she is an engaging child – loving, natural, and wild as any one of her neighbours for some miles round; viz. leverets, squirrels, and ring-doves. But what will surprise you most is – that, although a child of pure English blood, she speaks very little English; but more Bengalee than perhaps you will find it convenient to construe. That is her Ayah,[113] who comes up from behind at a pace so different from her youthful mistress's. But, if their paces are different, in other things they agree most cordially; and dearly they love each other. In reality, the child has passed her whole life in the arms of this ayah. She remembers nothing elder than *her*; eldest of things is the ayah in her eyes; and, if the ayah should insist on her worshipping herself as the goddess Railroadina or Steamboatina, that made England and the sea and Bengal, it is certain that the little thing would do so, asking no question but this – whether kissing would do for worshipping.

Every evening at nine o'clock, as the ayah sits by the little creature lying awake in bed, the silvery tongue of a dial tolls the hour. Reader, you know who she is. She is the grand-daughter of her that faded away about sunset in gazing at her twin orphans. Her name is Grace. And she is the niece of that elder and once happy Grace, who spent so much of her happiness in this very room, but whom, in her utter desolation, we saw in the boudoir with the torn letter at her feet. She is the daughter of that other sister, wife to a military officer, who died abroad. Little Grace never saw her grandmama, nor her lovely aunt that was her namesake, nor consciously her mama. She was born six months after the death of the elder Grace; and her mother saw her only through the mists of mortal suffering, which carried her off three weeks after the birth of her daughter.

This view was taken several years ago; and since then the younger Grace in her turn is under a cloud of affliction. But she is still under eighteen; and of her there may be hopes. Seeing such things in so short a space of years, for the grandmother died at thirty-two, we say – Death we can face: but knowing, as some of us do, what is human life, which of us is it that without shuddering could (if consciously we were summoned) face the hour of birth?

THE ENGLISH
MAIL-COACH

or The Glory of Motion

Some twenty or more years before I matriculated at Oxford, Mr Palmer, M.P. for Bath,[1] had accomplished two things, very hard to do on our little planet, the Earth, however cheap they may happen to be held by the eccentric people in comets: he had invented mail-coaches, and he had married the daughter* of a duke. He was, therefore, just twice as great a man as Galileo, who certainly invented (or *discovered*) the satellites of Jupiter, those very next things extant to mail-coaches in the two capital points of speed and keeping time, but who did *not* marry the daughter of a duke.

These mail-coaches, as organized by Mr Palmer, are entitled to a circumstantial notice from myself – having had so large a share in developing the anarchies of my subsequent dreams, an agency which they accomplished, first, through velocity, at that time unprecedented; they first revealed the glory of motion: suggesting, at the same time, an under-sense, not unpleasurable, of possible though indefinite danger; secondly, through grand effects for the eye between lamp-light and the darkness upon solitary roads; thirdly, through animal beauty and power so often displayed in the class of horses selected for this mail service; fourthly, through the conscious presence of a central intellect, that, in the midst of vast distances,† of storms, of darkness, of night, overruled all obstacles into one steady

* Lady Madeline Gordon.
† '*Vast distances.*' – One case was familiar to mail-coach travellers, where two mails in opposite directions, north and south, starting at the same minute from points six hundred miles apart, met almost constantly at a particular bridge which exactly bisected the total distance.

co-operation in a national result. To my own feeling, this Post-office service recalled some mighty orchestra, where a thousand instruments, all disregarding each other, and so far in danger of discord, yet all obedient as slaves to the supreme *baton* of some great leader, terminate in a perfection of harmony like that of heart, veins, and arteries, in a healthy animal organization. But, finally, that particular element in this whole combination which most impressed myself, and through which it is that to this hour Mr Palmer's mail-coach system tyrannizes by terror and terrific beauty over my dreams, lay in the awful political mission which at that time it fulfilled. The mail-coaches it was that distributed over the face of the land, like the opening of apocalyptic vials, the heart-shaking news of Trafalgar, of Salamanca, of Vittoria, of Waterloo.[2] These were the harvests that, in the grandeur of their reaping, redeemed the tears and blood in which they had been sown. Neither was the meanest peasant so much below the grandeur and the sorrow of the times as to confound these battles, which were gradually moulding the destinies of Christendom, with the vulgar conflicts of ordinary warfare, which are often-times but gladiatorial trials of national prowess. The victories of England in this stupendous contest rose of themselves as natural *Te Deums*[3] to heaven; and it was felt by the thoughtful that such victories, at such a crisis of general prostration, were not more beneficial to ourselves than finally to France, and to the nations of western and central Europe, through whose pusillanimity it was that the French domination had prospered.

The mail-coach, as the national organ for publishing these mighty events, became itself a spiritualized and glorified object to an impassioned heart; and naturally, in the Oxford of that day, all hearts were awakened. There were, perhaps, of us gownsmen, two thousand *resident** in Oxford, and dispersed through five-and-twenty colleges. In some of these the custom permitted the student to keep what are called 'short terms;' that is, the four terms of Michaelmas, Lent, Easter, and Act, were

---

* 'Resident.' – The number on the books was far greater, many of whom kept up an intermitting communication with Oxford. But I speak of those only who were steadily pursuing their academic studies, and of those who resided constantly as *fellows*.

kept severally by a residence, in the aggregate, of ninety-one days, or thirteen weeks. Under this interrupted residence, accordingly, it was possible that a student might have a reason for going down to his home four times in the year. This made eight journeys to and fro. And as these homes lay dispersed through all the shires of the island, and most of us disdained all coaches except his majesty's mail, no city out of London could pretend to so extensive a connexion with Mr Palmer's establishment as Oxford. Naturally, therefore, it became a point of some interest with us, whose journeys revolved every six weeks on an average, to look a little into the executive details of the system. With some of these Mr Palmer had no concern; they rested upon bye-laws not unreasonable, enacted by posting-houses for their own benefit, and upon others equally stern, enacted by the inside passengers for the illustration of their own exclusiveness. These last were of a nature to rouse our scorn, from which the transition was not *very long* to mutiny. Up to this time, it had been the fixed assumption of the four inside people, (as an old tradition of all public carriages from the reign of Charles II,) that they, the illustrious quaternion, constituted a porcelain variety of the human race, whose dignity would have been compromised by exchanging one word of civility with the three miserable delf ware[4] outsides. Even to have kicked an outsider might have been held to attaint the foot concerned in that operation; so that, perhaps, it would have required an act of parliament to restore its purity of blood. What words, then, could express the horror, and the sense of treason, in that case, which *had* happened, where all three outsides, the trinity of Pariahs, made a vain attempt to sit down at the same breakfast-table or dinner-table with the consecrated four? I myself witnessed such an attempt; and on that occasion a benevolent old gentleman endeavoured to soothe his three holy associates, by suggesting that, if the outsides were indicted for this criminal attempt at the next assizes, the court would regard it as a case of lunacy (or *delirium tremens*) rather than of treason. England owes much of her grandeur to the depth of the aristocratic element in her social composition. I am not the man to laugh at it. But sometimes it expressed itself in extravagant shapes. The course taken with the infatuated outsiders, in the particular attempt which I have noticed, was, that the waiter, beckoning them away from the privileged *salle-à-manger*,[5] sang out, 'This way, my good men;' and then enticed them away off to the kitchen. But that plan had not always answered. Sometimes, though very rarely, cases occurred where the intruders, being stronger than usual, or more vicious than usual, resolutely refused to move, and so far carried their point, as to have a separate table arranged for themselves in a corner of the room. Yet, if an Indian screen could be found ample enough to plant them out from the very eyes of the high table, or *dais*, it then became possible to assume as a fiction of law – that the three delf fellows, after all, were not present. They could be ignored by the porcelain men, under the maxim, that objects not appearing, and not existing, are governed by the same logical construction.

Such now being, at that time, the usages of mail-coaches, what was to be done by us of young Oxford? We, the most aristocratic of people, who were addicted to the practice of looking down superciliously even upon the insides themselves as often very suspicious characters, were we voluntarily to court indignities? If our dress and bearing sheltered us, generally, from the suspicion of being 'raff,' (the name at that period for 'snobs,'*) we really *were* such constructively, by the place we assumed. If we did not submit to the deep shadow of eclipse, we entered at least the skirts of its penumbra. And the analogy of theatres was urged against us, where no man can complain of the annoyances incident to the pit or gallery, having his instant remedy in paying the higher price of the boxes. But the soundness of this analogy we disputed. In the case of the theatre, it cannot be pretended that the inferior situations have any separate attractions, unless the pit suits the purpose of the dramatic reporter. But the reporter or critic is a rarity. For most people, the sole benefit is in the price. Whereas, on the contrary, the outside of the mail had its own incommunicable advantages.

* 'Snobs,' and its antithesis, 'nobs,' arose among the internal factions of shoe-makers perhaps ten years later. Possibly enough, the terms may have existed much earlier; but they were then first made known, picturesquely and effectively, by a trial at some assizes which happened to fix the public attention.

These we could not forego. The higher price we should willingly
have paid, but *that* was connected with the condition of riding
inside, which was insufferable. The air, the freedom of prospect,
the proximity to the horses, the elevation of seat – these were
what we desired; but, above all, the certain anticipation of
purchasing occasional opportunities of driving.

Under coercion of this great practical difficulty, we instituted
a searching inquiry into the true quality and valuation of the
different apartments about the mail. We conducted this inquiry
on metaphysical principles; and it was ascertained satisfactorily,
that the roof of the coach, which some had affected to call the
attics, and some the garrets, was really the drawing-room, and
the box was the chief ottoman or sofa in that drawing-room;
whilst it appeared that the inside, which had been traditionally
regarded as the only room tenantable by gentlemen, was, in fact,
the coal-cellar in disguise.

Great wits jump. The very same idea had not long before
struck the celestial intellect of China. Amongst the presents
carried out by our first embassy to that country was a state-
coach. It had been specially selected as a personal gift by George
III; but the exact mode of using it was a mystery to Pekin. The
ambassador, indeed, (Lord Macartney,)[6] had made some dim
and imperfect explanations upon the point; but as his excellency
communicated these in a diplomatic whisper, at the very
moment of his departure, the celestial mind was very feebly
illuminated; and it became necessary to call a cabinet council
on the grand state question – 'Where was the emperor to sit?'
The hammer-cloth[7] happened to be unusually gorgeous; and
partly on that consideration, but partly also because the box
offered the most elevated seat, and undeniably went foremost,
it was resolved by acclamation that the box was the imperial
place, and, *for the scoundrel who drove, he might sit where he
could find a perch*. The horses, therefore, being harnessed, under
a flourish of music and a salute of guns, solemnly his imperial
majesty ascended his new English throne, having the first lord
of the treasury on his right hand, and the chief jester on his left.
Pekin gloried in the spectacle; and in the whole flowery people,
constructively present by representation, there was but one

discontented person, which was the coachman. This mutinous individual, looking as blackhearted as he really was, audaciously shouted – 'Where am *I* to sit?' But the privy council, incensed by his disloyalty, unanimously opened the door, and kicked him into the inside. He had all the inside places to himself; but such is the rapacity of ambition, that he was still dissatisfied. 'I say,' he cried out in an extempore petition, addressed to the emperor through a window, 'how am I to catch hold of the reins?' – 'Any how,' was the answer; 'don't trouble *me*, man, in my glory; through the windows, through the key-holes – how you please.' Finally, this contumacious coachman lengthened the check-strings into a sort of jury-reins, communicating with the horses; with these he drove as steadily as may be supposed. The emperor returned after the briefest of circuits: he descended in great pomp from his throne, with the severest resolution never to remount it. A public thanks-giving was ordered for his majesty's prosperous escape from the disease of a broken neck; and the state-coach was dedicated for ever as a votive offering to the God Fo, Fo – whom the learned more accurately call Fi, Fi.

A revolution of this same Chinese character did young Oxford of that era effect in the constitution of mail-coach society. It was a perfect French revolution; and we had good reason to say, *Ca ira*.[8] In fact, it soon became *too* popular. The 'public,' a well-known character, particularly disagreeable, though slightly respectable, and notorious for affecting the chief seats in syna-gogues, had at first loudly opposed this revolution; but when all opposition showed itself to be ineffectual, our disagreeable friend went into it with headlong zeal. At first it was a sort of race between us; and, as the public is usually above 30, (say generally from 30 to 50 years old,) naturally we of young Oxford, that averaged about 20, had the advantage. Then the public took to bribing, giving fees to horse-keepers, &c., who hired out their persons as warming-pans on the box-seat. *That*, you know, was shocking to our moral sensibilities. Come to bribery, we observed, and there is an end to all morality, Aris-totle's, Cicero's, or anybody's. And, besides, of what use was it? For *we* bribed also. And as our bribes to those of the public being demonstrated out of Euclid to be as five shillings to sixpence, here again young Oxford had the advantage. But the contest was ruinous to the principles of the stable-establishment about the mails. The whole corporation was constantly bribed, rebribed, and often sur-rebribed; so that a horse-keeper, ostler, or helper, was held by the philosophical at that time to be the most corrupt character in the nation.

There was an impression upon the public mind, natural enough from the continually augmenting velocity of the mail, but quite erroneous, that an outside seat on this class of carriages was a post of danger. On the contrary, I maintained that, if a man had become nervous from some gipsy prediction in his childhood, allocating to a particular moon now approaching some unknown danger, and he should inquire earnestly, – 'Whither can I go for shelter? Is a prison the safest retreat? Or a lunatic hospital? Or the British Museum?' I should have replied – 'Oh, no; I'll tell you what to do. Take lodgings for the next forty days on the box of his majesty's mail. Nobody can touch you there. If it is by bills at ninety days after date[9] that you are made unhappy – if noters and protesters are the sort of wretches whose astrological shadows darken the house of life – then note you what I vehemently protest, viz., that no matter though the sheriff in every county should be running after you with his *posse*, touch a hair of your head he cannot whilst you keep house, and have your legal domicile, on the box of the mail. It's felony to stop the mail; even the sheriff cannot do that. And an *extra* (no great matter if it grazes the sheriff) touch of the whip to the leaders at any time guarantees your safety.' In fact, a bed-room in a quiet house seems a safe enough retreat; yet it is liable to its own notorious nuisances, to robbers by night, to rats, to fire. But the mail laughs at these terrors. To robbers, the answer is packed up and ready for delivery in the barrel of the guard's blunderbuss. Rats again! there *are* none about mail-coaches, any more than snakes in Von Troil's Iceland;[10] except, indeed, now and then a parliamentary rat, who always hides his shame in the 'coal-cellar.' And, as to fire, I never knew but one in a mail-coach, which was in the Exeter mail, and caused by an obstinate sailor bound to Devonport. Jack, making light of the law and the lawgiver that had set their faces against his offence, insisted on taking up a forbidden seat in the rear of the roof, from which he could exchange his own yarns with those of the guard. No greater offence was then known to mail-coaches; it was treason, it was *læsa majestas*,[11] it was by tendency arson; and the ashes of Jack's pipe, falling amongst the straw of the hinder boot, containing the mail-bags, raised a flame which (aided by the wind of our motion) threatened a revolution in the republic of letters. But even this left the sanctity of the box unviolated. In dignified repose, the coachman and myself sat on, resting with benign composure upon our knowledge – that the fire would have to burn its way through four inside passengers before it could reach ourselves. With a quotation rather too trite, I remarked to the coachman, –

—'Jam proximus ardet
Ucalegon.'[12]

But, recollecting that the Virgilian part of his education might have been neglected, I interpreted so far as to say, that perhaps at that moment the flames were catching hold of our worthy brother and next-door neighbour Ucalegon. The coachman said nothing, but by his faint sceptical smile he seemed to be thinking that he knew better; for that in fact, Ucalegon, as it happened, was not in the way-bill.

No dignity is perfect which does not at some point ally itself with the indeterminate and mysterious. The connexion of the mail with the state and the executive government – a connexion obvious, but yet not strictly defined – gave to the whole mail establishment a grandeur and an official authority which did us service on the roads, and invested us with seasonable terrors. But perhaps these terrors were not the less impressive, because their exact legal limits were imperfectly ascertained. Look at those turnpike gates; with what deferential hurry, with what an obedient start, they fly open at our approach! Look at that long line of carts and carters ahead, audaciously usurping the very crest of the road: ah! traitors, they do not hear us as yet, but as soon as the dreadful blast of our horn reaches them with the proclamation of our approach, see with what frenzy of trepida-

tion they fly to their horses' heads, and deprecate our wrath by
the precipitation of their crane-neck quarterings. Treason they
feel to be their crime; each individual carter feels himself under
the ban of confiscation and attainder: his blood is attainted
through six generations, and nothing is wanting but the heads-
man and his axe, the block and the sawdust, to close up the
vista of his horrors. What! shall it be within benefit of clergy, to
delay the king's message on the highroad? – to interrupt the
great respirations, ebb or flood, of the national intercourse – to
endanger the safety of tidings running day and night between
all nations and languages? Or can it be fancied, amongst the
weakest of men, that the bodies of the criminals will be given
up to their widows for Christian burial? Now, the doubts which
were raised as to our powers did more to wrap them in terror,
by wrapping them in uncertainty, than could have been effected
by the sharpest definitions of the law from the Quarter Sessions.
We, on our parts, (we, the collective mail, I mean,) did our
utmost to exalt the idea of our privileges by the insolence with
which we wielded them. Whether this insolence rested upon law
that gave it a sanction, or upon conscious power, haughtily
dispensing with that sanction, equally it spoke from a potential
station; and the agent in each particular insolence of the
moment, was viewed reverentially, as one having authority.

Sometimes after breakfast his majesty's mail would become
frisky; and in its difficult wheelings amongst the intricacies of
early markets, it would upset an apple-cart, a cart loaded with
eggs, &c. Huge was the affliction and dismay, awful was the
smash, though, after all, I believe the damage might be levied
upon the hundred. I, as far as was possible, endeavoured in such
a case to represent the conscience and moral sensibilities of the
mail; and, when wildernesses of eggs were lying poached under
our horses' hoofs, then would I stretch forth my hands in sorrow,
saying (in words too celebrated in those days from the false*

---

* 'False echoes' – yes, false! for the words ascribed to Napoleon, as breathed
to the memory of Desaix, never were uttered at all. They stand in the same
category of theatrical inventions as the cry of the foundering *Vengeur*, as the
vaunt of General Cambronne at Waterloo, '*La Garde meurt, mais ne se rend
pas,*' as the repartees of Talleyrand.[13]

echoes of Marengo) – 'Ah! wherefore have we not time to weep over you?' which was quite impossible, for in fact we had not even time to laugh over them. Tied to post-office time, with an allowance in some cases of fifty minutes for eleven miles, could the royal mail pretend to undertake the offices of sympathy and condolence? Could it be expected to provide tears for the accidents of the road? If even it seemed to trample on humanity, it did so, I contended, in discharge of its own more peremptory duties.

Upholding the morality of the mail, *à fortiori*[14] I upheld its rights, I stretched to the uttermost its privilege of imperial precedency, and astonished weak minds by the feudal powers which I hinted to be lurking constructively in the charters of this proud establishment. Once I remember being on the box of the Holyhead mail, between Shrewsbury and Oswestry, when a tawdry thing from Birmingham, some *Tallyho* or *Highflier*, all flaunting with green and gold, came up alongside of us. What a contrast to our royal simplicity of form and colour is this plebeian wretch! The single ornament on our dark ground of chocolate colour was the mighty shield of the imperial arms, but emblazoned in proportions as modest as a signet-ring bears to a seal of office. Even this was displayed only on a single pannel, whispering, rather than proclaiming, our relations to the state; whilst the beast from Birmingham had as much writing and painting on its sprawling flanks as would have puzzled a decipherer from the tombs of Luxor.[15] For some time this Birmingham machine ran along by our side, – a piece of familiarity that seemed to us sufficiently jacobinical. But all at once a movement of the horses announced a desperate intention of leaving us behind. 'Do you see *that*?' I said to the coachman. 'I see,' was his short answer. He was awake, yet he waited longer than seemed prudent; for the horses of our audacious opponent had a disagreeable air of freshness and power. But his motive was loyal; his wish was that the Birmingham conceit should be full-blown before he froze it. When *that* seemed ripe, he unloosed, or, to speak by a stronger image, he sprang his known resources, he slipped our royal horses like cheetas, or hunting leopards after the affrighted game. How they could retain such a reserve of fiery power after the work they had accomplished, seemed hard to explain. But on our side, besides the physical superiority, was a tower of strength, namely, the king's name, 'which they upon the adverse faction wanted.'[16] Passing them without an effort, as it seemed, we threw them into the rear with so lengthening an interval between us, as proved in itself the bitterest mockery of their presumption; whilst our guard blew back a shattering blast of triumph, that was really too painfully full of derision.

I mention this little incident for its connexion with what followed. A Welshman, sitting behind me, asked if I had not felt my heart burn within me during the continuance of the race? I said – No; because we were not racing with a mail, so that no glory could be gained. In fact, it was sufficiently mortifying that such a Birmingham thing should dare to challenge us. The Welshman replied, that he didn't see *that*; for that a cat might look at a king, and a Brummagem coach might lawfully race the Holyhead mail. '*Race* us perhaps,' I replied, 'though even *that* has an air of sedition, but not *beat* us. This would have been treason; and for its own sake I am glad that the Tallyho was disappointed.' So dissatisfied did the Welshman seem with this opinion, that at last I was obliged to tell him a very fine story from one of our elder dramatists, viz. – that once, in some Oriental region, when the prince of all the land, with his splendid court, were flying their falcons, a hawk suddenly flew at a majestic eagle; and in defiance of the eagle's prodigious advantages, in sight also of all the astonished field-sportsmen, spectators, and followers, killed him on the spot. The prince was struck with amazement at the unequal contest, and with burning admiration for its unparalleled result. He commanded that the hawk should be brought before him; caressed the bird with enthusiasm, and ordered that, for the commemoration of his matchless courage, a crown of gold should be solemnly placed on the hawk's head; but then that, immediately after this coronation, the bird should be led off to execution, as the most valiant indeed of traitors, but not the less a traitor that had dared to rise in rebellion against his liege lord the eagle. 'Now,' said I to the Welshman, 'how painful it would have been to you

and me as men of refined feelings, that this poor brute, the
Tallyho, in the impossible case of a victory over us, should have
been crowned with jewellery, gold, with Birmingham ware, or
paste diamonds, and then led off to instant execution.' The
Welshman doubted if that could be warranted by law. And
when I hinted at the 10th of Edward III chap. 15,[17] for regulating
the precedency of coaches, as being probably the statute relied
on for the capital punishment of such offences, he replied drily
– That if the attempt to pass a mail was really treasonable, it
was a pity that the Tallyho appeared to have so imperfect an
acquaintance with law.

These were among the gaieties of my earliest and boyish
acquaintance with mails. But alike the gayest and the most
terrific of my experiences rose again after years of slumber,
armed with preternatural power to shake my dreaming sensibilities; sometimes, as in the slight case of Miss Fanny on the Bath
road, (which I will immediately mention,) through some casual
or capricious association with images originally gay, yet opening
at some stage of evolution into sudden capacities of horror;
sometimes through the more natural and fixed alliances with
the sense of power so various lodged in the mail system.

The modern modes of travelling cannot compare with the
mail-coach system in grandeur and power. They boast of more
velocity, but not however as a consciousness, but as a fact
of our lifeless knowledge, resting upon *alien* evidence; as, for
instance, because somebody *says* that we have gone fifty miles
in the hour, or upon the evidence of a result, as that actually we
find ourselves in York four hours after leaving London. Apart
from such an assertion, or such a result, I am little aware of the
pace. But, seated on the old mail-coach, we needed no evidence
out of ourselves to indicate the velocity. On this system the word
was – *Non magna loquimur*, as upon railways, but *magna
vivimus*.[18] The vital experience of the glad animal sensibilities
made doubts impossible on the question of our speed; we heard
our speed, we saw it, we felt it as a thrilling; and this speed
was not the product of blind insensate agencies, that had no
sympathy to give, but was incarnated in the fiery eyeballs of an
animal, in his dilated nostril, spasmodic muscles, and echoing

hoofs. This speed was incarnated in the *visible* contagion amongst brutes of some impulse, that, radiating into *their* natures, had yet its centre and beginning in man. The sensibility of the horse uttering itself in the maniac light of his eye, might be the last vibration in such a movement; the glory of Salamanca[19] might be the first – but the intervening link that connected them, that spread the earthquake of the battle into the eyeball of the horse, was the heart of man – kindling in the rapture of the fiery strife, and then propagating its own tumults by motions and gestures to the sympathies, more or less dim, in his servant the horse.

But now, on the new system of travelling, iron tubes and boilers have disconnected man's heart from the ministers of his locomotion. Nile nor Trafalgar has power any more to raise an extra bubble in a steam-kettle. The galvanic cycle[20] is broken up for ever; man's imperial nature no longer sends itself forward through the electric sensibility of the horse; the interagencies are gone in the mode of communication between the horse and his master, out of which grew so many aspects of sublimity under accidents of mists that hid, or sudden blazes that revealed, of mobs that agitated, or midnight solitudes that awed. Tidings, fitted to convulse all nations, must henceforwards travel by culinary process; and the trumpet that once announced from afar the laurelled mail, heart-shaking, when heard screaming on the wind, and advancing through the darkness to every village or solitary house on its route, has now given way for ever to the pot-wallopings of the boiler.

Thus have perished multiform openings for sublime effects, for interesting personal communications, for revelations of impressive faces that could not have offered themselves amongst the hurried and fluctuating groups of a railway station. The gatherings of gazers about a mail-coach had one centre, and acknowledged only one interest. But the crowds attending at a railway station have as little unity as running water, and own as many centres as there are separate carriages in the train.

How else, for example, than as a constant watcher for the dawn, and for the London mail that in summer months entered about dawn into the lawny thickets of Marlborough Forest, couldst thou, sweet Fanny of the Bath road, have become known to myself? Yet Fanny, as the loveliest young woman for face and person that perhaps in my whole life I have beheld, merited the station which even *her* I could not willingly have spared; yet (thirty-five years later) she holds in my dreams; and though, by an accident of fanciful caprice, she brought along with her into those dreams a troop of dreadful creatures, fabulous and not fabulous, that were more abominable to a human heart than Fanny and the dawn were delightful.

Miss Fanny of the Bath road, strictly speaking, lived at a mile's distance from that road, but came so continually to meet the mail, that I on my frequent transits rarely missed her, and naturally connected her name with the great thoroughfare where I saw her; I do not exactly know, but I believe with some burthen of commissions to be executed in Bath, her own residence being probably the centre to which these commissions gathered. The mail coachman, who wore the royal livery, being one amongst the privileged few,* happened to be Fanny's grandfather. A good man he was, that loved his beautiful granddaughter; and, loving her wisely, was vigilant over her deportment in any case where young Oxford might happen to be concerned. Was I then vain enough to imagine that I myself individually could fall within the line of his terrors? Certainly not, as regarded any physical pretensions that I could plead; for Fanny (as a chance passenger from her own neighbourhood once told me) counted in her train a hundred and ninety-nine professed admirers, if not open aspirants to her favour; and probably not one of the whole brigade but excelled myself in personal advantages. Ulysses even, with the unfair advantage of his accursed bow,[21] could hardly have undertaken that amount of suitors. So the

---

* 'Privileged few.' – The general impression was that this splendid costume belonged of right to the mail coachmen as their professional dress. But that was an error. To the guard it *did* belong as a matter of course, and was essential as an official warrant, and a means of instant identification for his person, in the discharge of his important public duties. But the coachman, and especially if his place in the series did not connect him immediately with London and the General Post Office, obtained the scarlet coat only as an honorary distinction after long or special service.

danger might have seemed slight – only that woman is universally aristocratic: it is amongst her nobilities of heart that she *is* so. Now, the aristocratic distinctions in my favour might easily with Miss Fanny have compensated my physical deficiencies. Did I then make love to Fanny? Why, yes; *mais oui donc;*[22] as much love as one *can* make whilst the mail is changing horses, a process which ten years later did not occupy above eighty seconds; but *then*, viz. about Waterloo, it occupied five times eighty. Now, four hundred seconds offer a field quite ample enough for whispering into a young woman's ear a great deal of truth; and (by way of parenthesis) some trifle of falsehood. Grandpapa did right, therefore, to watch me. And yet, as happens too often to the grandpapas of earth, in a contest with the admirers of granddaughters, how vainly would he have watched me had I meditated any evil whispers to Fanny! She, it is my belief, would have protected herself against any man's evil suggestions. But he, as the result showed, could not have intercepted the opportunities for such suggestions. Yet he was still active; he was still blooming. Blooming he was as Fanny herself.

'Say, all our praises why should lords –'[23]

No, that's not the line:

'Say, all our roses why should girls engross?'

The coachman showed rosy blossoms on his face deeper even than his granddaughter's, – *his* being drawn from the ale-cask, Fanny's from youth and innocence, and from the fountains of the dawn. But, in spite of his blooming face, some infirmities he had; and one particularly, (I am very sure, no *more* than one,) in which he too much resembled a crocodile. This lay in a monstrous inaptitude for turning round. The crocodile, I presume, owes that inaptitude to the absurd *length* of his back; but in our grandpapa it arose rather from the absurd *breadth* of his back; combined, probably, with some growing stiffness in his legs. Now upon this crocodile infirmity of his I planted an easy opportunity for tendering my homage to Miss Fanny. In defiance of all his honourable vigilance, no sooner had he presented to us his mighty Jovian back, (what a field for displaying to mankind his royal scarlet!) whilst inspecting professionally the buckles, the straps, and the silver turrets of his harness, than I raised Miss Fanny's hand to my lips, and, by the mixed tenderness and respectfulness of my manner, caused her easily to understand how happy it would have made me to rank upon her list as No. 10 or 12, in which case a few casualties amongst her lovers (and observe – they *hanged* liberally in those days) might have promoted me speedily to the top of the tree; as, on the other hand, with how much loyalty of submission I acquiesced in her allotment, supposing that she had seen reason to plant me in the very rearward of her favour, as No. 199+1. It must not be supposed that I allowed any trace of jest, or even of playfulness, to mingle with these expressions of my admiration; that would have been insulting to her, and would have been false as regarded my own feelings. In fact, the utter shadowyness of our relations to each other, even after our meetings through seven or eight years had been very numerous, but of necessity had been very brief, being entirely on mail-coach allowance – timed, in reality, by the General Post-Office – and watched by a crocodile belonging to the antepenultimate generation, left it easy for me to do a thing which few people ever *can* have done – viz., to make love for seven years, at the same time to be as sincere as ever creature was, and yet never to compromise myself by overtures that might have been foolish as regarded my own interests, or misleading as regarded hers. Most truly I loved this beautiful and ingenuous girl; and had it not been for the Bath and Bristol mail, heaven only knows what might have come of it. People talk of being over head and ears in love – now, the mail was the cause that I sank only over ears in love, which, you know, still left a trifle of brain to overlook the whole conduct of the affair. I have mentioned the case at all for the sake of a dreadful result from it in after years of dreaming. But it seems, *ex abundanti*,[24] to yield this moral – viz. that as, in England, the idiot and the half-wit are held to be under the guardianship of Chancery, so the man making love, who is often but a variety of the same imbecile class, ought to be made a ward of the General Post-Office, whose severe course of *timing* and periodical interruption might intercept many a foolish declaration, such as lays a solid foundation for fifty years' repentance.

Ah, reader! when I look back upon those days, it seems to me that all things change or perish. Even thunder and lightning, it pains me to say, are not the thunder and lightning which I seem to remember about the time of Waterloo. Roses, I fear, are degenerating, and, without a Red revolution, must come to the dust. The Fannies of our island – though this I say with reluctance – are not improving; and the Bath road is notoriously superannuated. Mr Waterton[25] tells me that the crocodile does *not* change – that a cayman, in fact, or an alligator, is just as good for riding upon as he was in the time of the Pharaohs. *That* may be; but the reason is, that the crocodile does not live fast – he is a slow coach. I believe it is generally understood amongst naturalists, that the crocodile is a blockhead. It is my own impression that the Pharaohs were also blockheads. Now, as the Pharaohs and the crocodile domineered over Egyptian society, this accounts for a singular mistake that prevailed on the Nile. The crocodile made the ridiculous blunder of supposing man to be meant chiefly for his own eating. Man, taking a different view of the subject, naturally met that mistake by another; he viewed the crocodile as a thing sometimes to worship, but always to run away from. And this continued until Mr Waterton changed the relations between the animals. The mode of escaping from the reptile he showed to be, not by running away, but by leaping on its back, booted and spurred. The two animals had misunderstood each other. The use of the crocodile has now been cleared up – it is to be ridden; and the use of man is, that he may improve the health of the crocodile by riding him a fox-hunting before breakfast. And it is pretty certain that any crocodile, who has been regularly hunted through the season, and is master of the weight he carries, will take a six-barred gate now as well as ever he would have done in the infancy of the Pyramids.

Perhaps, therefore, the crocodile does *not* change, but all things else *do*: even the shadow of the Pyramids grows less. And often the restoration in vision of Fanny and the Bath road, makes me too pathetically sensible of that truth. Out of the darkness, if I happen to call up the image of Fanny from thirty-five years back, arises suddenly a rose in June; or, if I think for an instant of the rose in June, up rises the heavenly face of Fanny. One after the other, like the antiphonies in a choral service, rises Fanny and the rose in June, then back again the rose in June and Fanny. Then come both together, as in a chorus; roses and Fannies, Fannies and roses, without end – thick as blossoms in paradise. Then comes a venerable crocodile, in a royal livery of scarlet and gold, or in a coat with sixteen capes; and the crocodile is driving four-in-hand from the box of the Bath mail. And suddenly we upon the mail are pulled up by a mighty dial, sculptured with the hours, and with the dreadful legend TOO LATE. Then all at once we are arrived in Marl-borough forest, amongst the lovely households* of the roe-deer: these retire into the dewy thickets; the thickets are rich with roses; the roses call up (as ever) the sweet countenance of Fanny, who, being the granddaughter of a crocodile, awakens a dread-ful host of wild semi-legendary animals – griffins, dragons, basilisks, sphinxes – till at length the whole vision of fighting images crowds into one towering armorial shield, a vast emblaz-onry of human charities and human loveliness that have per-ished, but quartered heraldically with unutterable horrors of monstrous and demoniac natures; whilst over all rises, as a surmounting crest, one fair female hand, with the fore-finger pointing, in sweet, sorrowful admonition, upwards to heaven, and having power (which, without experience, I never could have believed) to awaken the pathos that kills in the very bosom of the horrors that madden the grief that gnaws at the heart, together with the monstrous creations of darkness that shock the belief, and make dizzy the reason of man. This is the pecu-liarity that I wish the reader to notice, as having first been made

---

* 'Households.' – Roe-deer do not congregate in herds like the fallow or the red deer, but by separate families, parents, and children; which feature of approximation to the sanctity of human hearths, added to their comparatively miniature and graceful proportions, conciliate to them an interest of a peculiarly tender character, if less dignified by the grandeurs of savage and forest life.

known to me for a possibility by this early vision of Fanny on the Bath road. The peculiarity consisted in the confluence of two different keys, though apparently repelling each other, into the music and governing principles of the same dream; horror, such as possesses the maniac, and yet, by momentary transitions, grief, such as may be supposed to possess the dying mother when leaving her infant children to the mercies of the cruel. Usually, and perhaps always, in an unshaken nervous system, these two modes of misery exclude each other – here first they met in horrid reconciliation. There was also a separate peculiarity in the quality of the horror. This was afterwards developed into far more revolting complexities of misery and incomprehensible darkness; and perhaps I am wrong in ascribing any value as a *causative* agency to this particular case on the Bath road – possibly it furnished merely an *occasion* that accidentally introduced a mode of horrors certain, at any rate, to have grown up, with or without the Bath road, from more advanced stages of the nervous derangement. Yet, as the cubs of tigers or leopards, when domesticated, have been observed to suffer a sudden development of their latent ferocity under too eager an appeal to their playfulness – the gaieties of sport in *them* being too closely connected with the fiery brightness of their murderous instincts – so I have remarked that the caprices, the gay arabesques, and the lovely floral luxuriations of dreams, betray a shocking tendency to pass into finer maniacal splendours. That gaiety, for instance, (for such at first it was,) in the dreaming faculty, by which one principal point of resemblance to a crocodile in the mail-coachman was soon made to clothe him with the form of a crocodile, and yet was blended with accessory circumstances derived from his *human* functions, passed rapidly into a further development, no longer gay or playful, but terrific, the most terrific that besieges dreams, viz. – the horrid inoculation upon each other of incompatible natures. This horror has always been secretly felt by man; it was felt even under pagan forms of religion, which offered a very feeble, and also a very limited gamut for giving expression to the human capacities of sublimity or of horror. We read it in the fearful composition of the sphinx. The dragon, again, is the snake inoculated upon the scorpion. The basilisk unites the mysterious malice of the evil eye, unintentional on the part of the unhappy agent, with the intentional venom of some other malignant natures. But these horrid complexities of evil agency are but *objectively* horrid; they inflict the horror suitable to their compound nature; but there is no insinuation that they *feel* that horror. Heraldry is so full of these fantastic creatures, that, in some zoologies, we find a separate chapter or a supplement dedicated to what is denominated heraldic zoology. And why not? For these hideous creatures, however visionary,* have a real traditionary ground in medieval belief – sincere and partly reasonable, though adulterating with mendacity, blundering, credulity, and intense superstition. But the dream-horror which I speak of is far more frightful. The dreamer finds housed within himself – occupying, as it were, some separate chamber in his brain – holding, perhaps, from that station a secret and detestable commerce with his own heart – some horrid alien nature. What if it were his own nature repeated, – still, if the duality were distinctly perceptible, even *that* – even this mere numerical

---

* '*However visionary.*' – But *are* they always visionary? The unicorn, the kraken, the sea-serpent, are all, perhaps, zoological facts. The unicorn, for instance, so far from being a lie, is rather *too* true; for, simply as a *monokeras*,[26] he is found in the Himalaya, in Africa, and elsewhere, rather too often for the peace of what in Scotland would be called the *intending* traveller. That which really *is* a lie in the account of the unicorn – viz., his legendary rivalship with the lion – which lie may God preserve, in preserving the mighty imperial shield that embalms it – cannot be more destructive to the zoological pretensions of the unicorn, than are to the same pretensions in the lion our many popular crazes about his goodness and magnanimity, or the old fancy (adopted by Spenser,[27] and noticed by so many among our elder poets) of his graciousness to maiden innocence. The wretch is the basest and most cowardly among the forest tribes; nor has the sublime courage of the English bull-dog ever been so memorably exhibited as in his hopeless fight at Warwick with the cowardly and cruel lion called Wallace.[28] Another of the traditional creatures, still doubtful, is the mermaid, upon which Southey once remarked to me, that, if it had been differently named, (as, suppose, a mer-ape,) nobody would have questioned its existence any more than that of sea-cows, sea-lions, &c. The mermaid has been discredited by her human name and her legendary human habits. If she would not coquette so much with melancholy sailors, and brush her hair so assiduously upon solitary rocks, she would be carried on our books for as honest a reality, as decent a female, as many that are assessed to the poor-rates.

double of his own consciousness – might be a curse too mighty
to be sustained. But how, if the alien nature contradicts his own,
fights with it, perplexes, and confounds it? How, again, if not
one alien nature, but two, but three, but four, but five, are
introduced within what once he thought the inviolable sanctuary of himself? These, however, are horrors from the kingdoms
of anarchy and darkness, which, by their very intensity, challenge the sanctity of concealment, and gloomily retire from
exposition. Yet it was necessary to mention them, because the
first introduction to such appearances (whether causal, or
merely casual) lay in the heraldic monsters, which monsters were
themselves introduced (though playfully) by the transfigured
coachman of the Bath mail.

GOING DOWN WITH VICTORY

But the grandest chapter of our experience, within the whole
mail-coach service, was on those occasions when we went down
from London with the news of victory. A period of about ten
years stretched from Trafalgar to Waterloo: the second and
third years of which period (1806 and 1807) were comparatively
sterile; but the rest, from 1805 to 1815 inclusively, furnished a
long succession of victories; the least of which, in a contest of
that portentous nature, had an inappreciable value of position
– partly for its absolute interference with the plans of our enemy,
but still more from its keeping alive in central Europe the sense
of a deep-seated vulnerability in France. Even to tease the coasts
of our enemy, to mortify them by continual blockades, to insult
them by capturing if it were but a baubling schooner under the
eyes of their arrogant armies, repeated from time to time a sullen
proclamation of power lodged in a quarter to which the hopes
of Christendom turned in secret. How much more loudly must
this proclamation have spoken in the audacity* of having

* '*Audacity!*' – Such the French accounted it; and it has struck me that Soult[29]
would not have been so popular in London, at the period of her present
Majesty's coronation, or in Manchester, on occasion of his visit to that town,
if they had been aware of the insolence with which he spoke of us in notes

bearded the *élite* of their troops, and having beaten them in pitched battles! Five years of life it was worth paying down for the privilege of an outside place on a mail-coach, when carrying down the first tidings of any such event. And it is to be noted that, from our insular situation, and the multitude of our frigates disposable for the rapid transmission of intelligence, rarely did any unauthorized rumour steal away a prelibation from the aroma of the regular despatches. The government official news was generally the first news.

From eight P.M. to fifteen or twenty minutes later, imagine the mails assembled on parade in Lombard Street, where, at that time, was seated the General Post-Office. In what exact strength we mustered I do not remember; but, from the length of each separate *attelage*,[30] we filled the street, though a long one, and though we were drawn up in double file. On *any* night the spectacle was beautiful. The absolute perfection of all the appointments about the carriages and the harness, and the magnificence of the horses, were what might first have fixed the attention. Every carriage, on every morning in the year, was taken down to an inspector for examination – wheels, axles, linchpins, pole, glasses, &c., were all critically probed and tested. Every part of every carriage had been cleaned, every horse had been groomed, with as much rigour as if they belonged to a private gentleman; and that part of the spectacle offered itself always. But the night before us is a night of victory; and behold! to the ordinary display, what a heart-shaking addition! – horses, men, carriages – all are dressed in laurels and flowers, oak leaves and ribbons. The guards, who are his Majesty's servants, and the coachmen, who are within the privilege of the Post-Office, wear the royal liveries of course; and as it is summer (for all the *land* victories were won in summer,) they wear, on

---

written at intervals from the field of Waterloo. As though it had been mere felony in our army to look a French one in the face, he said more than once – 'Here are the English – we have them: they are caught *en flagrant delit*.'[31] Yet no man should have known us better; no man had drunk deeper from the cup of humiliation than Soult had in the north of Portugal, during his flight from an English army, and subsequently at Albuera, in the bloodiest of recorded battles.

this fine evening, these liveries exposed to view, without any covering of upper coats. Such a costume, and the elaborate arrangement of the laurels in their hats, dilated their hearts, by giving to them openly an *official* connection with the great news, in which already they have the general interest of patriotism. That great national sentiment surmounts and quells all sense of ordinary distinctions. Those passengers who happen to be gentlemen are now hardly to be distinguished as such except by dress. The usual reserve of their manner in speaking to the attendants has on this night melted away. One heart, one pride, one glory, connects every man by the transcendant bond of his English blood. The spectators, who are numerous beyond precedent, express their sympathy with these fervent feelings by continual hurrahs. Every moment are shouted aloud by the Post-Office servants the great ancestral names of cities known to history through a thousand years, – Lincoln, Winchester, Portsmouth, Gloucester, Oxford, Bristol, Manchester, York, Newcastle, Edinburgh, Perth, Glasgow – expressing the grandeur of the empire by the antiquity of its towns, and the grandeur of the mail establishment by the diffusive radiation of its separate missions. Every moment you hear the thunder of lids locked down upon the mail-bags. That sound to each individual mail is the signal for drawing off, which process is the finest part of the entire spectacle. Then come the horses into play; – horses! can these be horses that (unless powerfully reined in) would bound off with the action and gestures of leopards? What stir! – what sea-like ferment! – what a thundering of wheels, what a trampling of horses! – what farewell cheers – what redoubling peals of brotherly congratulation, connecting the name of the particular mail – 'Liverpool for ever!' – with the name of the particular victory – 'Badajoz for ever!' or 'Salamanca for ever!'[32] The half-slumbering consciousness that, all night long and all the next day – perhaps for even a longer period – many of these mails, like fire racing along a train of gunpowder, will be kindling at every instant new successions of burning joy, has an obscure effect of multiplying the victory itself, by multiplying to the imagination into infinity the stages of its progressive diffusion. A fiery arrow seems to be let loose, which from that moment is destined to travel, almost without intermission, westwards for three hundred* miles – northwards for six hundred; and the sympathy of our Lombard Street friends at parting is exalted a hundredfold by a sort of visionary sympathy with the approaching sympathies, yet unborn, which we were going to evoke.

Liberated from the embarrassments of the city, and issuing into the broad uncrowded avenues of the northern suburbs, we begin to enter upon our natural pace of ten miles an hour. In the broad light of the summer evening, the sun perhaps only just at the point of setting, we are seen from every storey of every house. Heads of every age crowd to the windows – young and old understand the language of our victorious symbols – and

---

* 'Three hundred.' – Of necessity this scale of measurement, to an American, if he happens to be a thoughtless man, must sound ludicrous. Accordingly, I remember a case in which an American writer indulges himself in the luxury of a little lying, by ascribing to an Englishman a pompous account of the Thames, constructed entirely upon American ideas of grandeur, and concluding in something like these terms: – 'And, sir, arriving at London, this mighty father of rivers attains a breadth of at least two furlongs, having, in its winding course, traversed the astonishing distance of 170 miles.' And this the candid American thinks it fair to contrast with the scale of the Mississippi. Now, it is hardly worth while to answer a pure falsehood gravely, else one might say that no Englishman out of Bedlam ever thought of looking in an island for the rivers of a continent; nor, consequently, could have thought of looking for the peculiar grandeur of the Thames in the length of its course, or in the extent of soil which it drains: yet, if he *had* been so absurd, the American might have recollected that a river, not to be compared with the Thames even as to volume of water – viz. the Tiber – has contrived to make itself heard of in this world for twenty-five centuries to an extent not reached, nor likely to be reached very soon, by any river, however corpulent, of his own land. The glory of the Thames is measured by the density of the population to which it ministers, by the commerce which it supports, by the grandeur of the empire of which, though far from the largest, it is the most influential stream. Upon some such scale, and not by a transfer of Columbian standards, is the course of our English mails to be valued. The American may fancy the effect of his own valuations to our English ears, by supposing the case of a Siberian glorifying his country in these terms: – 'Those rascals, sir, in France and England, cannot march half a mile in any direction without finding a house where food can be had and lodging: whereas, such is the noble desolation of our magnificent country, that in many a direction for a thousand miles, I will engage a dog shall not find shelter from a snow-storm, nor a wren find an apology for breakfast.'

rolling volleys of sympathizing cheers run along behind and before our course. The beggar, rearing himself against the wall, forgets his lameness – real or assumed – thinks not of his whining trade, but stands erect, with bold exulting smiles, as we pass him. The victory has healed him, and says – Be thou whole! Women and children, from garrets alike and cellars, look down or look up with loving eyes upon our gay ribbons and our martial laurels – sometimes kiss their hands, sometimes hang out, as signals of affection, pocket handkerchiefs, aprons, dusters, anything that lies ready to their hands. On the London side of Barnet,[33] to which we draw near within a few minutes after nine, observe that private carriage which is approaching us. The weather being so warm, the glasses are all down; and one may read, as on the stage of a theatre, everything that goes on within the carriage. It contains three ladies, one likely to be 'mama,' and two of seventeen or eighteen, who are probably her daughters. What lovely animation, what beautiful unpre-meditated pantomime, explaining to us every syllable that passes, in these ingenuous girls! By the sudden start and raising of the hands, on first discovering our laurelled equipage – by the sudden movement and appeal to the elder lady from both of them – and by the heightened colour on their animated countenances, we can almost hear them saying – 'See, see! Look at their laurels. Oh, mama! there has been a great battle in Spain; and it has been a great victory.' In a moment we are on the point of passing them. We passengers – I on the box, and the two on the roof behind me – raise our hats, the coachman makes his professional salute with the whip; the guard even, though punctilious on the matter of his dignity as an officer under the crown, touches his hat. The ladies move to us, in return, with a winning graciousness of gesture: all smile on each side in a way that nobody could misunderstand, and that nothing short of a grand national sympathy could so instantaneously prompt. Will these ladies say that we are nothing to *them*? Oh, no; they will not say *that*. They cannot deny – they do not deny – that for this night they are our sisters: gentle or simple, scholar or illiterate servant, for twelve hours to come – we on the outside have the honour to be their brothers. Those poor women again, who stop to gaze upon us with delight at the entrance of Barnet, and seem by their air of weariness to be returning from labour – do you mean to say that they are washerwomen and charwomen? Oh, my poor friend, you are quite mistaken; they are nothing of the kind. I assure you, they stand in a higher rank: for this one night they feel themselves by birthright to be daughters of England, and answer to no humbler title.

Every joy, however, even rapturous joy – such is the sad law of earth – may carry with it grief, or fear of grief, to some. Three miles beyond Barnet, we see approaching us another private carriage, nearly repeating the circumstances of the former case. Here also the glasses are all down – here also is an elderly lady seated; but the two amiable daughters are missing; for the single young person, sitting by the lady's side, seems to be an attendant – so I judge from her dress, and her air of respectful reserve. The lady is in mourning; and her countenance expresses sorrow. At first she does not look up; so that I believe she is not aware of our approach, until she hears the measured beating of our horses' hoofs. Then she raises her eyes to settle them painfully on our triumphal equipage. Our decorations explain the case to her at once; but she beholds them with apparent anxiety, or even with terror. Some time before this, I, finding it difficult to hit a flying mark, when embarrassed by the coachman's person and reins intervening, had given to the guard a *Courier* evening paper, containing the gazette, for the next carriage that might pass. Accordingly he tossed it in so folded that the huge capitals expressing some such legend as – GLORIOUS VICTORY, might catch the eye at once. To see the paper, however, at all, interpreted as it was by our ensigns of triumph, explained everything; and, if the guard were right in thinking the lady to have received it with a gesture of horror, it could not be doubtful that she had suffered some deep personal affliction in connexion with this Spanish war.

Here now was the case of one who, having formerly suffered, might, erroneously perhaps, be distressing herself with anticipations of another similar suffering. That same night, and hardly three hours later, occurred the reverse case. A poor woman, who too probably would find herself, in a day or two, to have suffered the heaviest of afflictions by the battle, blindly allowed herself to express an exultation so unmeasured in the news, and its details, as gave to her the appearance which amongst Celtic Highlanders is called *fey*.[34] This was at some little town, I forget what, where we happened to change horses near midnight. Some fair or wake had kept the people up out of their beds. We saw many lights moving about as we drew near; and perhaps the most impressive scene on our route was our reception at this place. The flashing of torches and the beautiful radiance of blue lights (technically Bengal lights)[35] upon the heads of our horses; the fine effect of such a showery and ghostly illumination falling upon flowers and glittering laurels, whilst all around the massy darkness seemed to invest us with walls of impenetrable black-ness, together with the prodigious enthusiasm of the people, composed a picture at once scenical and affecting. As we staid for three or four minutes, I alighted. And immediately from a dismantled stall in the street, where perhaps she had been presid-ing at some part of the evening, advanced eagerly a middle-aged woman. The sight of my newspaper it was that had drawn her attention upon myself. The victory which we were carrying down to the provinces on *this* occasion was the imperfect one of Talavera.[36] I told her the main outline of the battle. But her agitation, though not the agitation of fear, but of exultation rather, and enthusiasm, had been so conspicuous when listening, and when first applying for information, that I could not but ask her if she had not some relation in the Peninsular army. Oh! yes: her only son was there. In what regiment? He was a trooper in the 23d Dragoons. My heart sank within me as she made that answer. This sublime regiment, which an Englishman should never mention without raising his hat to their memory, had made the most memorable and effective charge recorded in military annals. They leaped their horses – *over* a trench, where they could *into* it, and with the result of death or mutilation when they could *not*. What proportion cleared the trench is nowhere stated. Those who *did*, closed up and went down upon the enemy with such divinity of fervour – (I use the word *divinity* by design: the inspiration of God must have prompted this movement to those whom even then he was calling to his presence) – that two results followed. As regarded the enemy, this 23d Dragoons, not, I believe, originally 350 strong, paralysed a French column, 6000 strong, then ascending the hill, and fixed the gaze of the whole French army. As regarded themselves, the 23d were supposed at first to have been all but annihilated; but eventually, I believe, not so many as one in four survived. And this, then, was the regiment – a regiment already for some hours known to myself and all London as stretched, by a large majority, upon one bloody aceldama[37] – in which the young trooper served whose mother was now talking with myself in a spirit of such hopeful enthusiasm. Did I tell her the truth? Had I the heart to break up her dream? No. I said to myself, To-morrow, or the next day, she will hear the worst. For this night, wherefore should she not sleep in peace? After to-morrow, the chances are too many that peace will forsake her pillow. This brief respite, let her owe this to *my* gift and *my* forbearance. But, if I told her not of the bloody price that had been paid, there was no reason for suppressing the contributions from her son's regiment to the service and glory of the day. For the very few words that I had time for speaking, I governed myself accordingly. I showed her not the funeral banners under which the noble regiment was sleeping. I lifted not the overshadowing laurels from the bloody trench in which horse and rider lay mangled together. But I told her how these dear children of England, privates and officers, had leaped their horses over all obstacles as gaily as hunters to the morning's chase. I told her how they rode their horses into the mists of death, (saying to myself, but not saying to *her*,) and laid down their young lives for thee, O mother England! as willingly – poured out their noble blood as cheerfully – as ever, after a long day's sport, when infants, they had rested their wearied heads upon their mothers' knees, or had sunk to sleep in her arms. It is singular that she seemed to have no fears, even after this knowledge that the 23d Dragoons had been conspicuously engaged, for her son's safety: but so much was she enraptured by the knowledge that *his* regiment, and therefore *he*, had rendered eminent service in the trying conflict – a service which had actually made them the foremost topic of conversation in London – that in the mere simplicity of her fervent nature, she threw her arms round my neck, and, poor woman, kissed me.

THE VISION OF SUDDEN DEATH[38]

What is to be thought of sudden death? It is remarkable that, in different conditions of society, it has been variously regarded, as the consummation of an earthly career most fervently to be desired, and, on the other hand, as that consummation which is most of all to be deprecated. Cæsar the Dictator, at his last dinner party,[39] (*cæna,*) and the very evening before his assassination, being questioned as to the mode of death which, in *his* opinion, might seem the most eligible, replied – 'That which should be most sudden.' On the other hand, the divine Litany of our English Church, when breathing forth supplications, as if in some representative character for the whole human race prostrate before God, places such a death in the very van of horrors. 'From lightning and tempest; from plague, pestilence, and famine; from battle and murder, and from sudden death, – *Good Lord, deliver us.*' Sudden death is here made to crown the climax in a grand ascent of calamities; it is the last of curses; and yet, by the noblest of Romans, it was treated as the first of blessings. In that difference, most readers will see little more than the difference between Christianity and Paganism. But there I hesitate. The Christian church may be right in its estimate of sudden death; and it is a natural feeling, though after all it may also be an infirm one, to wish for a quiet dismissal from life – as that which *seems* most reconcilable with meditation, with penitential retrospects, and with the humilities of farewell prayer. There does not, however, occur to me any direct scriptural warrant for this earnest petition of the English Litany. It seems rather a petition indulged to human infirmity, than exacted from human piety. And, however *that* may be, two remarks suggest themselves as prudent restraints upon a doctrine, which else *may* wander; and *has* wandered, into an uncharitable superstition. The first is this: that many people are likely to exaggerate the horror of a sudden death, (I mean the *objective* horror to him who contemplates such a death, not the *subjective* horror to him who suffers it) from the false disposition to lay a stress upon words or acts, simply because by an accident they have become words or acts. If a man dies, for instance, by some sudden death when he happens to be intoxicated, such a death is falsely regarded with peculiar horror; as though the intoxication were suddenly exalted into a blasphemy. But *that* is unphilosophic. The man was, or he was not, *habitually* a drunkard. If not, if his intoxication were a solitary accident, there can be no reason at all for allowing special emphasis to this act, simply because through misfortune it became his final act. Nor, on the other hand, if it were no accident, but one of his *habitual* transgressions, will it be the more habitual or the more a transgression, because some sudden calamity, surprising him, has caused this habitual transgression to be also a final one? Could the man have had any reason even dimly to foresee his own sudden death, there would have been a new feature in his act of intemperance – a feature of presumption and irreverence, as in one that by possibility felt himself drawing near to the presence of God. But this is no part of the case supposed. And the only new element in the man's act is not any element of extra immorality, but simply of extra misfortune.

The other remark has reference to the meaning of the word *sudden*. And it is a strong illustration of the duty which for ever calls us to the stern valuation of words – that very possibly Cæsar and the Christian church do not differ in the way supposed; that is, do not differ by any difference of doctrine as between Pagan and Christian views of the moral temper appropriate to death, but that they are contemplating different cases. Both contemplate a violent death; a βιαθάνατος – death that is βίαιος:[40] but the difference is – that the Roman by the word 'sudden' means an *unlingering* death: whereas the Christian litany by 'sudden' means a death *without warning*, consequently without any available summons to religious preparation. The poor mutineer, who kneels down to gather into his heart the bullets from twelve firelocks of his pitying comrades, dies by a most sudden death in Cæsar's sense: one shock, one mighty spasm, one (possibly *not* one) groan, and all is over. But, in the sense of the Litany,

his death is far from sudden; his offence originally, his imprisonment, his trial, the interval between his sentence and its
execution, having all furnished him with separate warnings of
his fate – having all summoned him to meet it with solemn
preparation.

Meantime, whatever may be thought of a sudden death as a
mere variety in the modes of dying, where death in some shape
is inevitable – a question which, equally in the Roman and the
Christian sense, will be variously answered according to each
man's variety of temperament – certainly, upon one aspect of
sudden death there can be no opening for doubt, that of all
agonies incident to man it is the most frightful, that of all
martyrdoms it is the most freezing to human sensibilities –
namely, where it surprises a man under circumstances which
offer (or which seem to offer) some hurried and inappreciable
chance of evading it. Any effort, by which such an evasion can
be accomplished, must be as sudden as the danger which it
affronts. Even *that*, even the sickening necessity for hurrying
in extremity where all hurry seems destined to be vain, self-
baffled, and where the dreadful knell of *too late* is already
sounding in the ears by anticipation – even that anguish is liable
to a hideous exasperation in one particular case, namely, where
the agonizing appeal is made not exclusively to the instinct of
self-preservation, but to the conscience, on behalf of another
life besides your own, accidentally cast upon *your* protection.
To fail, to collapse in a service merely your own, might seem
comparatively venial; though, in fact, it is far from venial. But
to fail in a case where Providence has suddenly thrown into
your hands the final interests of another – of a fellow-creature
shuddering between the gates of life and death; this, to a man
of apprehensive conscience, would mingle the misery of an
atrocious criminality with the misery of a bloody calamity. The
man is called upon, too probably, to die; but to die at the very
moment when, by any momentary collapse, he is self-denounced
as a murderer. He had but the twinkling of an eye for his effort,
and that effort might, at the best, have been unavailing; but
from this shadow of a chance, small or great, how if he has
recoiled by a treasonable *lâcheté*?[41] The effort *might* have been

without hope; but to have risen to the level of that effort – would have rescued him, though not from dying, yet from dying as a traitor to his duties.

The situation here contemplated exposes a dreadful ulcer, lurking far down in the depths of human nature. It is not that men generally are summoned to face such awful trials. But potentially, and in shadowy outline, such a trial is moving subterraneously in perhaps all men's natures – muttering under ground in one world, to be realized perhaps in some other. Upon the secret mirror of our dreams such a trial is darkly projected at intervals, perhaps, to every one of us. That dream, so familiar to childhood, of meeting a lion, and, from languishing prostration in hope and vital energy, that constant sequel of lying down before him, publishes the secret frailty of human nature – reveals its deep-seated Pariah falsehood to itself – records its abysmal treachery. Perhaps not one of us escapes that dream; perhaps, as by some sorrowful doom of man, that dream repeats for every one of us, through every generation, the original temptation in Eden. Every one of us, in this dream, has a bait offered to the infirm places of his own individual will; once again a snare is made ready for leading him into captivity to a luxury of ruin; again, as in aboriginal Paradise, the man falls from innocence; once again, by infinite iteration, the ancient Earth groans to God, through her secret caves, over the weakness of her child; 'Nature from her seat, sighing through all her works,' again 'gives signs of woe that all is lost;'[42] and again the counter sigh is repeated to the sorrowing heavens of the endless rebellion against God. Many people think that one man, the patriarch of our race, could not in his single person execute this rebellion for all his race. Perhaps they are wrong. But, even if not, perhaps in the world of dreams every one of us ratifies for himself the original act. Our English rite of 'Confirmation,' by which, in years of awakened reason, we take upon us the engagements contracted for us in our slumbering infancy, – how sublime a rite is that! The little postern gate, through which the baby in its cradle had been silently placed for a time within the glory of God's countenance, suddenly rises to the clouds as a triumphal arch, through which, with banners displayed and martial pomps, we make our second entry as crusading soldiers militant for God, by personal choice and by sacramental oath. Each man says in effect – 'Lo! I rebaptize myself; and that which once was sworn on my behalf, now I swear for myself.' Even so in dreams, perhaps, under some secret conflict of the midnight sleeper, lighted up to the consciousness at the time, but darkened to the memory as soon as all is finished, each several child of our mysterious race completes for himself the aboriginal fall.

As I drew near to the Manchester post-office, I found that it was considerably past midnight; but to my great relief, as it was important for me to be in Westmorland by the morning, I saw by the huge saucer eyes of the mail, blazing through the gloom of overhanging houses, that my chance was not yet lost. Past the time it was; but by some luck, very unusual in my experience, the mail was not even yet ready to start. I ascended to my seat on the box, where my cloak was still lying as it had lain at the Bridgewater Arms. I had left it there in imitation of a nautical discoverer, who leaves a bit of bunting on the shore of his discovery, by way of warning off the ground the whole human race, and signalizing to the Christian and the heathen worlds, with his best compliments, that he has planted his throne for ever upon that virgin soil; henceforward claiming the *jus dominii* to the top of the atmosphere above it, and also the right of driving shafts to the centre of the earth below it; so that all people found after this warning, either aloft in the atmosphere, or in the shafts, or squatting on the soil, will be treated as trespassers – that is, decapitated by their very faithful and obedient servant, the owner of the said bunting. Possibly my cloak might not have been respected, and the *jus gentium*[43] might have been cruelly violated in my person – for, in the dark, people commit deeds of darkness, gas being a great ally of morality – but it so happened that, on this night, there was no other outside passenger; and the crime, which else was but too probable, missed fire for want of a criminal. By the way, I may as well mention at this point, since a circumstantial accuracy is essential to the effect of my narrative, that there was no other person of any description whatever about the mail – the guard, the coachman, and myself being allowed for – except only one – a

horrid creature of the class known to the world as insiders, but
whom young Oxford called sometimes 'Trojans,' in opposition
to our Grecian selves, and sometimes 'vermin.' A Turkish
Effendi, who piques himself on good-breeding, will never mention by name a pig. Yet it is but too often that he has reason to
mention this animal; since constantly, in the streets of Stamboul,[44] he has his trousers deranged or polluted by this vile
creature running between his legs. But under any excess of hurry
he is always careful, out of respect to the company he is dining
with, to suppress the odious name, and to call the wretch 'that
other creature,' as though all animal life beside formed one
group, and this odious beast (to whom, as Chrysippus observed,
salt serves as an apology for a soul) formed another and alien
group on the outside of creation. Now I, who am an English
Effendi, that think myself to understand good-breeding as well
as any son of Othman,[45] beg my reader's pardon for having
mentioned an insider by his gross natural name. I shall do so no
more: and, if I should have occasion to glance at so painful a
subject, I shall always call him 'that other creature.' Let us hope,
however, that no such distressing occasion will arise. But, by
the way, an occasion arises at this moment; for the reader will
be sure to ask, when we come to the story, 'Was this other
creature present?' He was *not*; or more correctly, perhaps, *it*
was not. We dropped the creature – or the creature, by natural
imbecility, dropped itself – within the first ten miles from Manchester. In the latter case, I wish to make a philosophic remark
of a moral tendency. When I die, or when the reader dies, and
by repute suppose of fever, it will never be known whether we
died in reality of the fever or of the doctor. But this other
creature, in the case of dropping out of the coach, will enjoy a
coroner's inquest; consequently he will enjoy an epitaph. For I
insist upon it, that the verdict of a coroner's jury makes the best
of epitaphs. It is brief, so that the public all find time to read it;
it is pithy, so that the surviving friends (if any *can* survive such
a loss) remember it without fatigue; it is upon oath, so that
rascals and Dr Johnsons cannot pick holes in it. 'Died through
the visitation of intense stupidity, by impinging on a moonlight
night against the off hind wheel of the Glasgow mail! Deodand[46]

upon the said wheel – two-pence.' What a simple lapidary inscription! Nobody much in the wrong but an off-wheel; and with few acquaintances; and if it were but rendered into choice Latin, though there would be a little bother in finding a Ciceronian word for 'off-wheel,' Morcellus[47] himself, that great master of sepulchral eloquence, could not show a better. Why I call this little remark *moral*, is, from the compensation it points out. Here, by the supposition, is that other creature on the one side, the beast of the world; and he (or it) gets an epitaph. You and I, on the contrary, the pride of our friends, get none.

But why linger on the subject of vermin? Having mounted the box, I took a small quantity of laudanum, having already travelled two hundred and fifty miles – viz., from a point seventy miles beyond London, upon a simple breakfast. In the taking of laudanum there was nothing extraordinary.[48] But by accident it drew upon me the special attention of my assessor on the box, the coachman. And in *that* there was nothing extraordinary. But by accident, and with great delight, it drew my attention to the fact that this coachman was a monster in point of size, and that he had but one eye. In fact he had been foretold by Virgil as –

'Monstrum horrendum, informe, ingens, cui lumen ademptum.'

He answered in every point – a monster he was – dreadful, shapeless, huge, who had lost an eye. But why should *that* delight me? Had he been one of the Calendars in the Arabian Nights,[49] and had paid down his eye as the price of his criminal curiosity, what right had *I* to exult in his misfortune? I did *not* exult: I delighted in no man's punishment, though it were even merited. But these personal distinctions identified in an instant an old friend of mine, whom I had known in the south for some years as the most masterly of mail-coachmen. He was the man in all Europe that could best have undertaken to drive six-in-hand full gallop over *Al Sirat*[50] – that famous bridge of Mahomet across the bottomless gulf, backing himself against the Prophet and twenty such fellows. I used to call him *Cyclops mastigophorus*, Cyclops the whip-bearer, until I observed that his skill made whips useless, except to fetch off an impertinent fly from a leader's head; upon which I changed his Grecian name to Cyclops *diphrélates* (Cyclops the charioter.) I, and others known to me, studied under him the diphrelatic art. Excuse, reader, a word too elegant to be pedantic. And also take this remark from me, as a *gage d'amitié*[51] – that no word ever was or *can* be pedantic which, by supporting a distinction, supports the accuracy of logic; or which fills up a chasm for the understanding. As a pupil, though I paid extra fees, I cannot say that I stood high in his esteem. It showed his dogged honesty, (though, observe, not his discernment,) that he could not see my merits. Perhaps we ought to excuse his absurdity in this particular by remembering his want of an eye. *That* made him blind to my merits. Irritating as this blindness was, (surely it could not be envy?) he always courted my conversation, in which art I certainly had the whip-hand of him. On this occasion, great joy was at our meeting. But what was Cyclops doing here? Had the medical men recommended northern air, or how? I collected, from such explanations as he volunteered, that he had an interest at stake in a suit-at-law pending at Lancaster; so that probably he had got himself transferred to this station, for the purpose of connecting with his professional pursuits an instant readiness for the calls of his law-suit.

Meantime, what are we stopping for? Surely we've been waiting long enough. Oh, this procrastinating mail, and oh, this procrastinating post-office! Can't they take a lesson upon that subject from *me*? Some people have called *me* procrastinating. Now you are witness, reader, that I was in time for *them*. But can *they* lay their hands on their hearts, and say that they were in time for me? I, during my life, have often had to wait for the post-office: the post-office never waited a minute for me. What are they about? The guard tells me that there is a large extra accumulation of foreign mails this night, owing to irregularities caused by war and by the packet-service, when as yet nothing is done by steam. For an *extra* hour, it seems, the post-office has been engaged in threshing out the pure wheaten correspondence of Glasgow, and winnowing it from the chaff of all baser intermediate towns. We can hear the flails going at this moment. But at last all is finished. Sound your horn, guard. Manchester, good bye; we've lost an hour by your criminal conduct at the post-office: which, however, though I do not mean to part with a serviceable ground of complaint, and one which really *is* such for the horses, to me secretly is an advantage, since it compels us to recover this last hour amongst the next eight or nine. Off we are at last, and at eleven miles an hour: and at first I detect no changes in the energy or in the skill of Cyclops.

From Manchester to Kendal, which virtually (though not in law) is the capital of Westmoreland, were at this time seven stages of eleven miles each. The first five of these, dated from Manchester, terminated in Lancaster, which was therefore fifty-five miles north of Manchester, and the same distance exactly from Liverpool. The first three terminated in Preston (called, by way of distinction from other towns of that name, *proud* Preston,) at which place it was that the separate roads from Liverpool and from Manchester to the north became confluent. Within these first three stages lay the foundation, the progress, and termination of our night's adventure. During the first stage, I found out that Cyclops was mortal: he was liable to the shocking affection of sleep – a thing which I had never previously suspected. If a man is addicted to the vicious habit of sleeping, all the skill in aurigation of Apollo himself, with the horses of Aurora[52] to execute the motions of his will, avail him nothing. 'Oh, Cyclops!' I exclaimed more than once, 'Cyclops, my friend; thou art mortal. Thou snorest.' Through this first eleven miles, however, he betrayed his infirmity – which I grieve to say he shared with the whole Pagan Pantheon – only by short stretches. On waking up, he made an apology for himself, which, instead of mending the matter, laid an ominous foundation for coming disasters. The summer assizes were now proceeding at Lancaster: in consequence of which, for three nights and three days, he had not lain down in a bed. During the day, he was waiting for his uncertain summons as a witness on the trial in which he was interested; or he was drinking with the other witnesses, under the vigilant surveillance of the attorneys. During the night, or that part of it when the least temptations existed to conviviality, he was driving. Throughout the second stage he grew more and more drowsy. In the second mile of the third stage, he surrendered himself finally and without a struggle to his perilous temptation. All his past resistance had but deepened the weight of this final oppression. Seven atmospheres of sleep seemed resting upon him; and, to consummate the case, our worthy guard, after singing 'Love amongst the Roses,' for the fiftieth or sixtieth time, without any invitation from Cyclops or myself, and without applause for his poor labours, had moodily resigned himself to slumber – not so deep doubtless as the coachman's, but deep enough for mischief; and having, probably, no similar excuse. And thus at last, about ten miles from Preston, I found myself left in charge of his Majesty's London and Glasgow mail then running about eleven miles an hour.

What made this negligence less criminal than else it must have been thought, was the condition of the roads at night during the assizes. At that time all the law business of populous Liverpool, and of populous Manchester, with its vast cincture of populous rural districts, was called up by ancient usage to the tribunal of Lilliputian Lancaster. To break up this old traditional usage required a conflict with powerful established interests, a large system of new arrangements, and a new parliamentary statute. As things were at present, twice in the year so vast a body of business rolled northwards, from the southern quarter of the county, that a fortnight at least occupied the severe exertions of two judges for its despatch. The consequence of this was – that every horse available for such a service, along the whole line of road, was exhausted in carrying down the multitudes of people who were parties to the different suits. By sunset, therefore, it usually happened that, through utter exhaustion amongst men and horses, the roads were all silent. Except exhaustion in the vast adjacent county of York from a contested election, nothing like it was ordinarily witnessed in England.

On this occasion, the usual silence and solitude prevailed along the road. Not a hoof nor a wheel was to be heard. And to strengthen this false luxurious confidence in the noiseless roads, it happened also that the night was one of peculiar solemnity and peace. I myself, though slightly alive to the possibilities of peril, had so far yielded to the influence of the mighty calm as to sink into a profound reverie. The month was August, in which lay my own birth-day; a festival to every thoughtful man suggesting solemn and often sigh-born thoughts.* The county was my own native county – upon which, in its southern section, more than upon any equal area known to man past or present, had descended the original curse of labour in its heaviest form, not mastering the bodies of men only as of slaves, or criminals in mines, but working through the fiery will. Upon no equal space of earth, was, or ever had been, the same energy of human power put forth daily. At this particular season also of the assizes, that dreadful hurricane of flight and pursuit, as it might have seemed to a stranger, that swept to and from Lancaster all day long, hunting the county up and down, and regularly subsiding about sunset, united with the permanent distinction of Lancashire as the very metropolis and citadel of labour, to point the thoughts pathetically upon that counter vision of rest, of saintly repose from strife and sorrow, towards which, as to their secret haven, the profounder aspirations of man's heart are continually travelling. Obliquely we were nearing the sea upon our left, which also must, under the present circumstances, be repeating the general state of halcyon repose. The sea, the atmosphere, the light, bore an orchestral part in this universal lull. Moonlight, and the first timid tremblings of the dawn, were now blending; and the blendings were brought into a still more exquisite state of unity, by a slight silvery mist, motionless and dreamy, that covered the woods and fields, but with a veil of equable transparency. Except the feet of our own horses, which, running on a sandy margin of the road, made little disturbance, there was no sound abroad. In the clouds, and on the earth, prevailed the same majestic peace; and in spite of all that the villain of a schoolmaster has done for the ruin of our sublimer thoughts, which are the thoughts of our infancy, we still believe in no such nonsense as a limited atmosphere. Whatever we may swear with our false feigning lips, in our faithful hearts we still

---

* 'Sigh-born.' – I owe the suggestion of this word to an obscure remembrance of a beautiful phrase in Giraldus Cambrensis,[53] viz., *suspiriosæ cogitationes*.

believe, and must for ever believe, in fields of air traversing the total gulf between earth and the central heavens. Still, in the confidence of children that tread without fear *every* chamber in their father's house, and to whom no door is closed, we, in that Sabbatic vision which sometimes is revealed for an hour upon nights like this, ascend with easy steps from the sorrow-stricken fields of earth, upwards to the sandals of God.

Suddenly from thoughts like these, I was awakened to a sullen sound, as of some motion on the distant road. It stole upon the air for a moment; I listened in awe; but then it died away. Once roused, however, I could not but observe with alarm the quickened motion of our horses. Ten years' experience had made my eye learned in the valuing of motion; and I saw that we were now running thirteen miles an hour. I pretend to no presence of mind. On the contrary, my fear is, that I am miserably and shamefully deficient in that quality as regards action. The palsy of doubt and distraction hangs like some guilty weight of dark unfathomed remembrances upon my energies, when the signal is flying for *action*. But, on the other hand, this accursed gift I have, as regards *thought*, that in the first step towards the possibility of a misfortune, I see its total evolution: in the radix, I see too certainly and too instantly its entire expansion; in the first syllable of the dreadful sentence, I read already the last. It was not that I feared for ourselves. What could injure *us*? Our bulk and impetus charmed us against peril in any collision. And I had rode through too many hundreds of perils that were frightful to approach, that were matter of laughter as we looked back upon them, for any anxiety to rest upon *our* interests. The mail was not built, I felt assured, nor bespoke, that could betray *me* who trusted to its protection. But any carriage that we could meet would be frail and light in comparison of ourselves. And I remarked this ominous accident of our situation. We were on the wrong side of the road. But then the other party, if other there was, might also be on the wrong side; and two wrongs might make a right. *That* was not likely. The same motive which had drawn *us* to the right-hand side of the road, viz., the soft beaten sand, as contrasted with the paved centre, would prove attractive to others. Our lamps, still lighted, would give the impression of vigilance on our part. And every creature that met us, would rely upon *us* for quartering.* All this, and if the separate links of the anticipation had been a thousand times more, I saw – not discursively or by effort – but as by one flash of horrid intuition.

Under this steady though rapid anticipation of the evil which *might* be gathering ahead, ah, reader! what a sullen mystery of fear, what a sigh of woe, seemed to steal upon the air, as again the far-off sound of a wheel was heard! A whisper it was – a whisper from, perhaps, four miles off – secretly announcing a ruin that, being foreseen, was not the less inevitable. What could be done – who was it that could do it – to check the storm-flight of these maniacal horses? What! could I not seize the reins from the grasp of the slumbering coachman? You, reader, think that it would have been in *your* power to do so. And I quarrel not with your estimate of yourself. But, from the way in which the coachman's hand was viced between his upper and lower thigh, this was impossible. The guard subsequently found it impossible, after this danger had passed. Not the grasp only, but also the position of this Polyphemus,[54] made the attempt impossible. You still think otherwise. See, then, that bronze equestrian statue. The cruel rider has kept the bit in his horse's mouth for two centuries. Unbridle him, for a minute, if you please, and wash his mouth with water. Or stay, reader, unhorse me that marble emperor: knock me those marble feet from those marble stirrups of Charlemagne.

The sounds ahead strengthened, and were now too clearly the sounds of wheels. Who and what could it be? Was it industry in a taxed cart? – was it youthful gaiety in a gig? Whoever it was, something must be attempted to warn them. Upon the other party rests the active responsibility, but upon *us* – and, woe is me! that *us* was my single self – rests the responsibility of warning. Yet, how should this be accomplished? Might I not seize the guard's horn? Already, on the first thought, I was making my way over the roof to the guard's seat. But this, from

* '*Quartering*.' – this is the technical word; and, I presume, derived from the French *cartayer*, to evade a rut or any obstacle.

the foreign mails being piled upon the roof, was a difficult, and even dangerous attempt, to one cramped by nearly three hundred miles of outside travelling. And, fortunately, before I had lost much time in the attempt, our frantic horses swept round an angle of the road, which opened upon us the stage where the collision must be accomplished, the parties that seemed summoned to the trial, and the impossibility of saving them by any communication with the guard.

Before us lay an avenue, straight as an arrow, six hundred yards, perhaps, in length; and the umbrageous trees, which rose in a regular line from either side, meeting high overhead, gave to it the character of a cathedral aisle. These trees lent a deeper solemnity to the early light; but there was still light enough to perceive, at the further end of this gothic aisle, a light, reedy gig, in which were seated a young man, and, by his side, a young lady. Ah, young sir! what are you about? If it is necessary that you should whisper your communications to this young lady – though really I see nobody at this hour, and on this solitary road, likely to overhear your conversation – is it, therefore, necessary that you should carry your lips forward to hers? The little carriage is creeping on at one mile an hour; and the parties within it, being thus tenderly engaged, are naturally bending down their heads. Between them and eternity, to all human calculation, there is but a minute and a half. What is it that I shall do? Strange it is, and to a mere auditor of the tale, might seem laughable, that I should need a suggestion from the *Iliad* to prompt the sole recourse that remained. But so it was. Suddenly I remembered the shout of Achilles, and its effect. But could I pretend to shout like the son of Peleus, aided by Pallas?[55] No, certainly: but then I needed not the shout that should alarm all Asia militant; a shout would suffice, such as should carry terror into the hearts of two thoughtless young people, and one gig horse. I shouted – and the young man heard me not. A second time I shouted – and now he heard me, for now he raised his head.

Here, then, all had been done that, by me, *could* be done: more on *my* part was not possible. Mine had been the first step: the second was for the young man: the third was for God. If, said I, the stranger is a brave man, and if, indeed, he loves the young girl at his side – or, loving her not, if he feels the obligation pressing upon every man worthy to be called a man, of doing his utmost for a woman confided to his protection – he will at least make some effort to save her. If *that* fails, he will not perish the more, or by a death more cruel, for having made it; and he will die, as a brave man should, with his face to the danger, and with his arm about the woman that he sought in vain to save. But if he makes no effort, shrinking, without a struggle, from his duty, he himself will not the less certainly perish for this baseness of poltroonery. He will die no less: and why not? Wherefore should we grieve that there is one craven less in the world? No; *let* him perish, without a pitying thought of ours wasted upon him; and, in that case, all our grief will be reserved for the fate of the helpless girl, who, now, upon the least shadow of failure in *him*, must, by the fiercest of translations – must, without time for a prayer – must, within seventy seconds, stand before the judgment-seat of God.

But craven he was not: sudden had been the call upon him, and sudden was his answer to the call. He saw, he heard, he comprehended, the ruin that was coming down: already its gloomy shadow darkened above him; and already he was meas-uring his strength to deal with it. Ah! what a vulgar thing does courage seem, when we see nations buying it and selling it for a shilling a-day: ah! what a sublime thing does courage seem, when some fearful crisis on the great deeps of life carries a man, as if running before a hurricane, up to the giddy crest of some mountainous wave, from which, accordingly as he chooses his course, he descries two courses, and a voice says to him audibly – 'This way lies hope; take the other way and mourn for ever!' Yet, even then, amidst the raving of the seas and the frenzy of the danger, the man is able to confront his situation – is able to retire for a moment into solitude with God, and to seek all his counsel from *him*! For seven seconds, it might be, of his seventy, the stranger settled his countenance steadfastly upon us, as if to search and value every element in the conflict before him. For five seconds more he sate immovably, like one that mused on some great purpose. For five he sate with eyes upraised, like one that prayed in sorrow, under some extremity of doubt, for wisdom to guide him towards the better choice. Then suddenly he rose; stood upright; and, by a sudden strain upon the reins, raising his horse's forefeet from the ground, he slewed him round on the pivot of his hind legs, so as to plant the little equipage in a position nearly at right-angles to ours. Thus far his condition was not improved; except as a first step had been taken towards the possibility of a second. If no more were done, nothing was done; for the little carriage still occupied the very centre of our path, though in an altered direction. Yet even now it may not be too late: fifteen of the twenty seconds may still be unexhausted; and one almighty bound forward may avail to clear the ground. Hurry then, hurry! for the flying moments – *they* hurry! Oh hurry, hurry, my brave young man! for the cruel hoofs of our horses – *they* also hurry! Fast are the flying moments, faster are the hoofs of our horses. Fear not for *him*, if human energy can suffice: faithful was he that drove, to his terrific duty; faithful was the horse to *his* command. One blow, one impulse given with voice and hand by the stranger, one rush from the horse, one bound as if in the act of rising to a fence, landed the docile creature's fore-feet upon the crown or arching centre of the road. The larger half of the little equipage had then cleared our over-towering shadow: *that* was evident even to my own agitated sight. But it mattered little that one wreck should float off in safety, if upon the wreck that perished were embarked the human freightage. The rear part of the carriage – was *that* certainly beyond the line of absolute ruin? What power could answer the question? Glance of eye, thought of man, wing of angel, which of these had speed enough to sweep between the question and the answer, and divide the one from the other? Light does not tread upon the steps of light more indivisibly, than did our all-conquering arrival upon the escaping efforts of the gig. *That* must the young man have felt too plainly. His back was now turned to us; not by sight could he any longer communicate with the peril; but by the dreadful rattle of our harness, too truly had his ear been instructed – that all was finished as regarded any further effort of *his*. Already in resignation he had rested from his struggle; and perhaps, in his heart he was whispering – 'Father, which art above, do thou finish in heaven what I on earth have attempted.' We ran past them faster than ever mill-race in our inexorable flight. Oh, raving of hurricanes that must have sounded in their young ears at the moment of our transit! Either with the swingle-bar, or with the haunch of our near leader, we had struck the off-wheel of the little gig, which stood rather obliquely and not quite so far advanced as to be accurately parallel with the near wheel. The blow, from the fury of our passage, resounded terrifically. I rose in horror, to look upon the ruins we might have caused. From my elevated station I looked down, and looked back upon the scene, which in a moment told its tale, and wrote all its records on my heart for ever.

The horse was planted immovably, with his fore-feet upon the paved crest of the central road. He of the whole party was alone untouched by the passion of death. The little cany carriage – partly perhaps from the dreadful torsion of the wheels in its recent movement, partly from the thundering blow we had given to it – as if it sympathized with human horror, was all alive with tremblings and shiverings. The young man sat like a rock. He stirred not at all. But *his* was the steadiness of agitation frozen into rest by horror. As yet he dared not to look round; for he knew that, if anything remained to do, by him it could no longer be done. And as yet he knew not for certain if their safety were accomplished. But the lady—

But the lady—! Oh heavens! will that spectacle ever depart from my dreams, as she rose and sank upon her seat, sank and rose, threw up her arms wildly to heaven, clutched at some visionary object in the air, fainting, praying, raving, despairing! Figure to yourself, reader, the elements of the case; suffer me to recal before your mind the circumstances of the unparalleled situation. From the silence and deep peace of this saintly summer night, – from the pathetic blending of this sweet moonlight, dawnlight, dreamlight, – from the manly tenderness of this flattering, whispering, murmuring, love, – suddenly as from the woods and fields, – suddenly as from the chambers of the air opening in revelation, – suddenly as from the ground yawning at her feet, leaped upon her, with the flashing of cataracts, Death the crownèd phantom, with all the equipage of his terrors, and the tiger roar of his voice.

The moments were numbered. In the twinkling of an eye our flying horses had carried us to the termination of the umbrageous aisle; at right-angles we wheeled into our former direction; the turn of the road carried the scene out of my eyes in an instant, and swept it into my dreams for ever.

DREAM-FUGUE

On the above theme of sudden death

'Whence the sound
Of instruments, that made melodious chime,
Was heard, of harp and organ; and who mov'd
Their stops and chords, was seen; his volant touch
Instinct through all proportions, low and high,
Fled and pursued transverse the resonant fugue.'
    Par. Lost, B. xi.

Tumultuosissimamente[56]

Passion of Sudden Death! that once in youth I read and interpreted by the shadows of thy averted* signs; – Rapture of panic taking the shape, which amongst tombs in churches I have seen, of woman bursting her sepulchral bonds – of woman's Ionic form bending forward from the ruins of her grave, with arching foot, with eyes upraised, with clasped adoring hands – waiting, watching, trembling, praying, for the trumpet's call to rise from dust for ever; – Ah, vision too fearful of shuddering humanity on the brink of abysses! vision that didst start back – that didst reel away – like a shrivelling scroll from before the wrath of fire racing on the wings of the wind! Epilepsy so brief of horror – wherefore is it that thou canst not die? Passing so suddenly into

---

* '*Averted* signs.' – I read the course and changes of the lady's agony in the succession of her involuntary gestures; but let it be remembered that I read all this from the rear, never once catching the lady's full face, and even her profile imperfectly.

darkness, wherefore is it that still thou sheddest thy sad funeral
blights upon the gorgeous mosaics of dreams? Fragment of
music too stern, heard once and heard no more, what aileth thee
that thy deep rolling chords come up at intervals through all
the worlds of sleep, and after thirty years have lost no element
of horror?

I

Lo, it is summer, almighty summer! The everlasting gates of life
and summer are thrown open wide; and on the ocean, tranquil
and verdant as a savannah, the unknown lady from the dreadful
vision and I myself are floating: she upon a fairy pinnace, and I
upon an English three-decker. But both of us are wooing gales
of festal happiness within the domain of our common country
– within that ancient watery park – within that pathless chase
where England takes her pleasure as a huntress through winter
and summer, and which stretches from the rising to the setting
sun. Ah! what a wilderness of floral beauty was hidden, or was
suddenly revealed, upon the tropic islands through which the
pinnace moved. And upon her deck what a bevy of human
flowers – young women how lovely, young men how noble, that
were dancing together, and slowly drifting towards *us* amidst
music and incense, amidst blossoms from forests and gorgeous
corymbi[57] from vintages, amidst natural caroling and the echoes
of sweet girlish laughter. Slowly the pinnace nears us, gaily she
hails us, and slowly she disappears beneath the shadow of our
mighty bows. But then, as at some signal from heaven, the music
and the carols, and the sweet echoing of girlish laughter – all
are hushed. What evil has smitten the pinnace, meeting or
overtaking her? Did ruin to our friends couch within our own
dreadful shadow? Was our shadow the shadow of death? I
looked over the bow for an answer; and, behold! the pinnace
was dismantled; the revel and the revellers were found no more;
the glory of the vintage was dust; and the forest was left without
a witness to its beauty upon the seas. 'But where,' and I turned
to our own crew – 'where are the lovely women that danced
beneath the awning of flowers and clustering corymbi? Whither

have fled the noble young men that danced with *them*?' Answer
there was none. But suddenly the man at the mast-head, whose
countenance darkened with alarm, cried aloud – 'Sail on the
weather-beam! Down she comes upon us; in seventy seconds
she will founder!'

2

I looked to the weather-side, and the summer had departed. The
sea was rocking, and shaken with gathering wrath. Upon its
surface sate mighty mists, which grouped themselves into arches
and long cathedral aisles. Down one of these, with the fiery pace
of a quarrel from a cross-bow, ran a frigate right athwart our
course. 'Are they mad?' some voice exclaimed from our deck.
'Are they blind? Do they woo their ruin?' But in a moment, as
she was close upon us, some impulse of a heady current or
sudden vortex gave a wheeling bias to her course, and off she
forged without a shock. As she ran past us, high aloft amongst
the shrouds stood the lady of the pinnace. The deeps opened
ahead in malice to receive her, towering surges of foam ran after
her, the billows were fierce to catch her. But far away she was
borne into desert spaces of the sea: whilst still by sight I followed
her, as she ran before the howling gale, chased by angry sea-birds
and by maddening billows; still I saw her, as at the moment
when she ran past us, amongst the shrouds, with her white
draperies streaming before the wind. There she stood with hair
dishevelled, one hand clutched amongst the tackling – rising,
sinking, fluttering, trembling, praying – there for leagues I saw
her as she stood, raising at intervals one hand to heaven, amidst
the fiery crests of the pursuing waves and the raving of the
storm; until at last, upon a sound from afar of malicious laughter
and mockery, all was hidden for ever in driving showers; and
afterwards, but when I know not, and how I know not,

3

Sweet funeral bells from some incalculable distance, wailing over the dead that die before the dawn, awakened me as I slept in a boat moored to some familiar shore. The morning twilight even then was breaking; and, by the dusky revelations which it spread, I saw a girl adorned with a garland of white roses about her head for some great festival, running along the solitary strand with extremity of haste. Her running was the running of panic; and often she looked back as to some dreadful enemy in the rear. But when I leaped ashore, and followed on her steps to warn her of a peril in front, alas! from me she fled as from another peril; and vainly I shouted to her of quicksands that lay ahead. Faster and faster she ran; round a promontory of rock she wheeled out of sight; in an instant I also wheeled round it, but only to see the treacherous sands gathering above her head. Already her person was buried; only the fair young head and the diadem of white roses around it were still visible to the pitying heavens; and, last of all, was visible one marble arm. I saw by the early twilight this fair young head, as it was sinking down to darkness – saw this marble arm, as it rose above her head and her treacherous grave, tossing, faultering, rising, clutching as at some false deceiving hand stretched out from the clouds – saw this marble arm uttering her dying hope, and then her dying despair. The head, the diadem, the arm, – these all had sunk; at last over these also the cruel quicksand had closed; and no memorial of the fair young girl remained on earth, except my own solitary tears, and the funeral bells from the desert seas, that, rising again more softly, sang a requiem over the grave of the buried child, and over her blighted dawn.

I sate, and wept in secret the tears that men have ever given to the memory of those that died before the dawn, and by the treachery of earth, our mother. But the tears and funeral bells were hushed suddenly by a shout as of many nations, and by a roar as from some great king's artillery advancing rapidly along the valleys, and heard afar by its echoes among the mountains. 'Hush!' I said, as I bent my ear earthwards to listen – 'hush! – this either is the very anarchy of strife, or else' – and then I listened more profoundly, and said as I raised my head – 'or else, oh heavens! it is *victory* that swallows up all strife.'

4

Immediately, in trance, I was carried over land and sea to some distant kingdom, and placed upon a triumphal car, amongst companions crowned with laurel. The darkness of gathering midnight, brooding over all the land, hid from us the mighty crowds that were weaving restlessly about our carriage as a centre – we heard them, but we saw them not. Tidings had arrived, within an hour, of a grandeur that measured itself against centuries; too full of pathos they were, too full of joy that acknowledged no fountain but God, to utter themselves by other language than by tears, by restless anthems, by reverberations rising from every choir, of the *Gloria in excelsis*.[58] These tidings we that sate upon the laurelled car had it for our privilege to publish amongst all nations. And already, by signs audible through the darkness, by snortings and tramplings, our angry horses, that knew no fear of fleshly weariness, upbraided us with delay. Wherefore *was* it that we delayed? We waited for a secret word, that should bear witness to the hope of nations, as now accomplished for ever. At midnight the secret word arrived; which word was – Waterloo and Recovered Christendom! The dreadful word shone by its own light; before us it went; high above our leaders' heads it rode, and spread a golden light over the paths which we traversed. Every city, at the presence of the secret word, threw open its gates to receive us. The rivers were silent as we crossed. All the infinite forests, as we ran along their margins, shivered in homage to the secret word. And the darkness comprehended it.

Two hours after midnight we reached a mighty minster. Its gates, which rose to the clouds, were closed. But when the dreadful word, that rode before us, reached them with its golden light, silently they moved back upon their hinges; and at a flying gallop our equipage entered the grand aisle of the cathedral. Headlong was our pace; and at every altar, in the little chapels and oratories to the right hand and left of our course, the lamps, dying or sickening, kindled anew in sympathy with the secret word that was flying past. Forty leagues we might have run in the cathedral, and as yet no strength of morning light had reached us, when we saw before us the aërial galleries of the organ and the choir. Every pinnacle of the fret-work, every station of advantage amongst the traceries, was crested by white-robed choristers, that sang deliverance; that wept no more tears, as once their fathers had wept; but at intervals that sang together to the generations, saying –

'Chaunt the deliverer's praise in every tongue,'

and receiving answers from afar,

– 'such as once in heaven and earth were sung.'[59]

And of their chaunting was no end; of our headlong pace was neither pause nor remission.

Thus, as we ran like torrents – thus, as we swept with bridal rapture over the Campo Santo* of the cathedral graves – suddenly we became aware of a vast necropolis rising upon the far-off horizon – a city of sepulchres, built within the saintly cathedral for the warrior dead that rested from their feuds on earth. Of purple granite was the necropolis; yet, in the first minute, it lay like a purple stain upon the horizon – so mighty was the distance. In the second minute it trembled through many changes, growing into terraces and towers of wondrous altitude, so mighty was the pace. In the third minute already, with our

---

* *Campo Santo.* – It is probable that most of my readers will be acquainted with the history of the Campo Santo at Pisa – composed of earth brought from Jerusalem for a bed of sanctity, as the highest prize which the noble piety of crusaders could ask or imagine. There is another Campo Santo at Naples, formed, however, (I presume,) on the example given by Pisa. Possibly the idea may have been more extensively copied. To readers who are unacquainted with England, or who (being English) are yet unacquainted with the cathedral cities of England, it may be right to mention that the graves within-side the cathedrals often form a flat pavement over which carriages and horses might roll; and perhaps a boyish remembrance of one particular cathedral, across which I had seen passengers walk and burdens carried, may have assisted my dream.

dreadful gallop, we were entering its suburbs. Vast sarcophagi rose on every side, having towers and turrets that, upon the limits of the central aisle, strode forward with haughty intrusion, that ran back with mighty shadows into answering recesses. Every sarcophagus showed many bas-reliefs – bas-reliefs of battles – bas-reliefs of battle-fields; of battles from forgotten ages – of battles from yesterday – of battle-fields that, long since, nature had healed and reconciled to herself with the sweet oblivion of flowers – of battle-fields that were yet angry and crimson with carnage. Where the terraces ran, there did *we* run; where the towers curved, there did *we* curve. With the flight of swallows our horses swept round every angle. Like rivers in flood, wheeling round headlands; like hurricanes that ride into the secrets of forests; faster than ever light unwove the mazes of darkness, our flying equipage carried earthly passions – kindled warrior instincts – amongst the dust that lay around us; dust oftentimes of our noble fathers that had slept in God from Créci[60] to Trafalgar. And now had we reached the last sarco-phagus, now were we abreast of the last bas-relief, already had we recovered the arrow-like flight of the illimitable central aisle, when coming up this aisle to meet us we beheld a female infant that rode in a carriage as frail as flowers. The mists, which went before her, hid the fawns that drew her, but could not hide the shells and tropic flowers with which she played – but could not hide the lovely smiles by which she uttered her trust in the mighty cathedral, and in the cherubim that looked down upon her from the topmost shafts of its pillars. Face to face she was meeting us; face to face she rode, as if danger there were none. 'Oh baby!' I exclaimed, 'shalt thou be the ransom for Waterloo? Must we, that carry tidings of great joy to every people, be messengers of ruin to thee?' In horror I rose at the thought; but then also, in horror at the thought, rose one that was sculptured on the bas-relief – a Dying Trumpeter. Solemnly from the field of battle he rose to his feet; and, unslinging his stony trumpet, carried it, in his dying anguish, to his stony lips – sounding once, and yet once again; proclamation that, in *thy* ears, oh baby! must have spoken from the battlements of death. Immediately deep shadows fell between us, and aboriginal silence. The choir had ceased to sing. The hoofs of our horses, the rattling of our harness, alarmed the graves no more. By horror the bas-relief had been unlocked into life. By horror we, that were so full of life, we men and our horses, with their fiery fore-legs rising in mid air to their everlasting gallop, were frozen to a bas-relief. Then a third time the trumpet sounded; the seals were taken off all pulses; life, and the frenzy of life, tore into their channels again; again the choir burst forth in sunny grandeur, as from the muffling of storms and darkness; again the thunderings of our horses carried temptation into the graves. One cry burst from our lips as the clouds, drawing off from the aisle, showed it empty before us – 'Whither has the infant fled? – is the young child caught up to God?' Lo! afar off, in a vast recess, rose three mighty windows to the clouds; and on a level with their summits, at height insuperable to man, rose an altar of purest alabaster. On its eastern face was trembling a crimson glory. Whence came *that*? Was it from the reddening dawn that now streamed *through* the windows? Was it from the crimson robes of the martyrs that were painted *on* the windows? Was it from the bloody bas-reliefs of earth? Whencesoever it were – there, within that crimson radiance, suddenly appeared a female head, and then a female figure. It was the child – now grown up to woman's height. Clinging to the horns of the altar,[61] there she stood – sinking, rising, trembling, fainting – raving, despairing; and behind the volume of incense that, night and day, streamed upwards from the altar, was seen the fiery font, and dimly was descried the outline of the dreadful being that should baptize her with the baptism of death. But by her side was kneeling her better angel, that hid his face with wings; that wept and pleaded for *her*; that prayed when *she* could *not*; that fought with heaven by tears for *her* deliverance; which also, as he raised his immortal countenance from his wings, I saw, by the glory in his eye, that he had won at last.

5

Then rose the agitation, spreading through the infinite cathedral, to its agony; then was completed the passion of the mighty fugue. The golden tubes of the organ, which as yet had but sobbed and muttered at intervals – gleaming amongst clouds and surges of incense – threw up, as from fountains unfathomable, columns of heart-shattering music. Choir and anti-choir were filling fast with unknown voices. Thou also, Dying Trumpeter! – with thy love that was victorious, and thy anguish that was finishing, didst enter the tumult: trumpet and echo – farewell love, and farewell anguish – rang through the dreadful *sanctus*. We, that spread flight before us, heard the tumult, as of flight, mustering behind us. In fear we looked round for the unknown steps that, in flight or in pursuit, were gathering upon our own. Who were these that followed? The faces, which no man could count – whence were *they*? 'Oh, darkness of the grave!' I exclaimed, 'that from the crimson altar and from the fiery font wert visited with secret light – that wert searched by the effulgence in the angel's eye – were these indeed thy children? Pomps of life, that, from the burials of centuries, rose again to the voice of perfect joy, could it be *ye* that had wrapped me in the reflux of panic?' What ailed me, that I should fear when the triumphs of earth were advancing? Ah! Pariah heart within me, that couldst never hear the sound of joy without sullen whispers of treachery in ambush; that, from six years old, didst never hear the promise of perfect love, without seeing aloft amongst the stars fingers as of a man's hand writing the secret legend – '*ashes to ashes, dust to dust!*' – wherefore shouldst *thou* not fear, though all men should rejoice? Lo! as I looked back for seventy leagues through the mighty cathedral, and saw the quick and the dead that sang together to God, together that sang to the generations of man – ah! raving, as of torrents that opened on every side: trepidation, as of female and infant steps that fled – ah! rushing, as of wings that chased! But I heard a voice from heaven, which said – 'Let there be no reflux of panic – let there be no more fear, and no more sudden death! Cover them with joy as the tides cover the shore!' *That* heard the children of the choir, *that* heard the children of the grave. All the hosts of jubilation made ready to move. Like armies that ride in pursuit, they moved with one step. Us, that, with laurelled heads, were passing from the cathedral through its eastern gates, they overtook, and, as with a garment, they wrapped us round with thunders that overpowered our own. As brothers we moved together; to the skies we rose – to the dawn that advanced – to the stars that fled: rendering thanks to God in the highest – that, having hid his face through one generation behind thick clouds of War, once again was ascending – was ascending from Waterloo – in the visions of Peace: – rendering thanks for thee, young girl! whom having overshadowed with his ineffable passion of Death – suddenly did God relent; suffered thy angel to turn aside his arm; and even in thee, sister unknown! shown to me for a moment only to be hidden for ever, found an occasion to glorify his goodness. A thousand times, amongst the phantoms of sleep, has he shown thee to me, standing before the golden dawn, and ready to enter its gates – with the dreadful Word going before thee – with the armies of the grave behind thee; shown thee to me, sinking, rising, fluttering, fainting, but then suddenly reconciled, adoring: a thousand times has he followed thee in the worlds of sleep – through storms; through desert seas; through the darkness of quicksands; through fugues and the persecution of fugues; through dreams, and the dreadful resurrections that are in dreams – only that at the last, with one motion of his victorious arm, he might record and emblazon the endless resurrections of his love!

Appendix: Opium in the Nineteenth Century

For centuries before medical theories of addiction began to emerge in the latter third of the nineteenth century, opium was an unremarkable part of daily existence in Britain. During the first two-thirds of the century, opium was the active ingredient in folk remedies made from seed capsules of the poppy, or 'poppy-heads', and a number of opium-based medicines were available commercially. Before the Pharmacy Act of 1868 made the sale of opium and other so-called poisons the exclusive right of licensed pharmacists and chemists, wholesale opium was available to any retailer, including grocers, bakers, tailors, publicans and street vendors.

In Britain, people could buy opium in pills, powders and poultices, liniments, lozenges and laudanum, syrups, suppositories and seed-pods straight off the poppy stalk. And it was relatively cheap. In fact it was cheaper than gin, a circumstance to which many detractors attributed its widespread use among workers in the Lancashire industrial centres and the Fens in the 1830s and 1840s. Patent medicines containing opium were a staple of British homes almost regardless of class and included such familiar brands as Godfrey's Cordial, Collis Browne's Chlorodyne, Mrs Winslow's Soothing Syrup, and the Kendal Black Drop favoured by Coleridge and Byron. These medicines were used to treat a long list of common afflictions including ague (a malaria-like fever), bronchitis, cancer, cholera, diabetes, diarrhoea, delirium tremens, depression, fatigue, gangrene, gout, insanity, intestinal obstruction, menstrual symptoms, neuralgia, pneumonia, sciatica, sleeplessness, tetanus, tuberculosis and ulcers. In short, opium was as unexceptional in the early nineteenth-century home as are aspirin or ibuprofen in today's.

Although many of the phenomena we now associate with addiction or drug dependence were also evident in the nineteenth century, it is important to note that the terms now used to describe them were not yet available and the social context in which they might have been observed was significantly different. In modern parlance, the terms 'addiction' and 'drug dependence' are virtually interchangeable and usually refer to a range of physiological, psychological and social effects associated with the habitual use of certain substances, including opiates. The chief physiological effects in question are generally agreed to be (1) tolerance, or the necessity for ever greater dosages of the substance to produce the original effect, and (2) the withdrawal syndrome, which is the onset of pronounced and uncomfortable physical symptoms when dosages of the substance are decreased or halted. Opium has both of these effects, as do a number of other substances including caffeine, nicotine and alcohol. The rate at which tolerance develops and the kind and severity of withdrawal symptoms vary with individuals and circumstances, but they include, in the four to six hours after the last dose, frequent yawning, sneezing, runny nose, goose bumps and, from the twelfth hour to the third day, violent diarrhoea, alternating chills and sweats, hypersensitivity to touch, irritability, depression and spontaneous orgasms.

A few specialized treatises on opium had noted effects like tolerance and withdrawal as early as 1700,[1] but in general, these phenomena were much less remarked upon than they are now. This is due in part to the fact that opium's alkaloids (especially morphine), which have much more pronounced addictive tendencies than the opium from which they come, were not readily available in isolated form until later in the century. Thus the symptoms simply were not as marked as they later came to be. Furthermore, the symptoms of dependence appear only when prolonged use is suddenly halted or reduced, an inconvenience for which there was little occasion when the drug was so easy to get. When the average user suffered such symptoms between doses, he or she was likely to regard them as an illness for which opium was the appropriate remedy, and it was thus possible to perpetuate the cycle without recognizing it. Self-medication with opium was frequently a means of avoiding the expense of professional medical care, so doctors did not have consistent opportunities to observe the processes of dependence in motion. It was only after mid-century that medical professionals began to formulate modern ideas of addiction. The watershed was the rise of hypodermic morphine injection, which leads to much more pronounced withdrawal symptoms and which initially was almost always supervised by a medical professional.

OPIUM AND THE MEDICAL PROFESSIONS

Isolated in 1803 and introduc_d into general usage by the early 1820s, morphine was from the beginning more a medical professional tool than a popular one as it was less familiar, less readily available and more expensive than unrefined opium. And although it presented the significant advantage of predictable strength – the isolated alkaloid was of a consistent concentration whereas different batches of raw opium could vary radically in the proportions of their constituents – no one was certain at first how best to use it. But with the introduction in the mid-1850s of an even more exclusive device, the hypodermic syringe, morphine became at once more effective and more restricted to professional medical practice. An injection of 'morphia solution' quickly became the doctor's silver bullet, and the treatment's unprecedented efficacy in all cases of severe pain became even more evident as the new technology swept through military theatres in Europe and the United States during the 1860s. By the 1880s, the therapy was so woven into the fabric of daily medical practice that, as the author of a standard British medical textbook proclaimed, 'The hypodermic syringe and the morphia solution are now almost as indispensable accompaniments of the physician as the stethoscope and thermometer.'[2] Indeed the image of the doctor as the hierophant of arcane healing technologies in the latter third of the century – a trope largely responsible for the steadily increasing status of medicine as a profession – was inextricably linked to his administration of morphine injections. Said one American practitioner of the new therapy, 'The patient . . . gives you credit for a miracle.'[3]

By 1870, however, some practitioners were warning that 'injections of morphia, though free from the ordinary evils of opium eating, might, nevertheless, create the same artificial want and gain credit for assuaging a restlessness and depression of which it was itself the cause'.[4] As the 1870s progressed, European medical professionals began to define a new disease known primarily as 'morphinism' or 'morphinomania', a set of symptoms associated with the prolonged hypodermic injection of morphine. Interest in this new disease was aroused in Britain by the translation of treatises on the subject written in German, and discussions of morphinism were closely linked to debates about the treatment and legal control of alcoholism. The treatment of addiction quickly emerged as a new medical speciality complete with its own experts, professional organizations, sanatoriums and so forth.

A dense network of implication thus spans the development of addiction as a medical phenomenon, the rise of governmental control of opium sales and the evolution of the medical professions in the latter third of the nineteenth century. Earlier, orthodox medical practice (as opposed to hydropathy, mesmerism, patent-medicine peddling and other types of so-called quackery) had been divided between three types of professional. From bottom to top in terms of prestige, they were (1) apothecaries, who were originally only dispensers of drugs but ultimately secured the legal prerogative also to prescribe, make house calls and order treatments, as long as they did not charge for their services but only for the drugs they dispensed; (2) surgeons, who were systematically educated in anatomy, performed invasive operations and treated their patients with external medicines, but were not legally entitled to prescribe internal medications (unless they had also qualified as apothecaries, as they often did); and (3) physicians, who had earned university degrees and thus were learned in the classics but typically had an unsystematic education in anatomy and other sciences, and who advised and prescribed for their patients rather than actually performing operations or hands-on treatments.

The boundaries between these orders were sometimes clear, as they usually were between physicians and the other two orders. But in other instances the distinctions could be fuzzy – as in the case of surgeon-apothecaries who were the forerunners of today's general practitioners – or even hotly disputed, as they often were between apothecaries and other sellers of drugs who did not fit neatly into any of the three professional classifications. This latter type of conflict gave rise to the Apothecaries' Act of 1815, which granted the Society of Apothecaries the right to examine and license members and denied the right to prescribe and sell certain medicines to anyone not so licensed (the Royal Colleges of Surgeons and Physicians already had similar authority over their turfs).

But there were still a number of popular medicines that could at least be sold, if not prescribed, by any retailer, of which opium was the most significant. The continued availability, versatility and inexpensiveness of opium meant a loss of potential business not only for apothecaries but also for physicians and surgeons, as a significant number of people simply bought opium from their local grocer, tailor or publican and treated themselves at home without ever consulting a medical professional. This all changed with the 1858 Medical Act, which officially grouped qualifying British physicians, surgeons and apothecaries under the General Medical Council's levelling imprimatur as 'Registered Medical Practitioners'. The newly unified profession in effect struck an alliance with the next rank down, chemists and druggists, when the 1868 Pharmacy Act limited the legal sale of opiates exclusively to licensed chemists, druggists and pharmacists. This dealt a blow to professional medicine's stiffest competition, popular self-medication.

With the new-found claims to power and authority represented by both the Pharmacy Act and the hypodermic injection of morphine, late-century medical practitioners had more invested than ever in the exclusive control of opium. Many doctors felt strongly that morphine injection should remain solely a medical professional tool. But even as doctors writing in such cutting-edge medical publications as the *Lancet* were decrying the 'vicious habit' of morphinism, medical literature on the subject increasingly emphasized that most cases began with hypodermic injections, which were almost always either given by medical professionals or self-administered by patients whom doctors had personally trained in the use of the needle. This ironic circularity was enhanced by the fact that by far the greatest incidence of habitual hypodermic morphine use was among medical professionals themselves.

OPIUM AND THE ORIENT

Over the course of the nineteenth century, opium also came to be inextricably associated with the Orient. When a nineteenth-century Briton referred to 'the Orient', he or she might have meant any or all of Asia and its surrounding islands, what is now commonly called the Middle East and much of north Africa and Eastern Europe. This huge Orient functioned on a number of levels in nineteenth-century British culture. It included not only the biblical lands but also the settings of the popular *Arabian Nights* and the inspiration for the fashionable decor of Oriental rugs and Japan-lacquered furniture. It was also the fountainhead of exotic commodities such as tea, silk and spices. The development of British attitudes towards the Orient during the eighteenth and nineteenth centuries was intertwined with the growing study of Eastern languages, literatures and religions, or 'Orientalism'. Perceptions of this Orient were both reflected and structured by a long literary tradition that was still thriving in the nineteenth century. From the medieval accounts of the East through the first English translations of the *Arabian Nights* in the early eighteenth century to the rash of Romantic poems on Oriental themes, the English reading public proved eager for cunning caliphs, sensual sultans and other exotic characters in Oriental settings thick with an atmosphere of magic and violence.

It is noteworthy, however, that the Orient of these tales almost never included China. Before Coleridge's and De Quincey's opium-tinged narratives modified the English sense of the Orient, China was associated with a set of cultural phenomena somewhat different from those of the popular Oriental tales. A fantasized version of China, often referred to as the Isle of Cathay, undergirded eighteenth- and nineteenth-century English chinoiserie – the omnipresent decorative artifacts ranging from porcelain teapots and lacquered furniture to pseudo-Chinese suites of rooms and gardens complete with pagodas. The fantasy China reflected in these designs owed much to the exaggerated European travel narratives that thrived in the Middle Ages, such as the memoirs of Marco Polo. Once it gained a cultural foothold it was hard to shake off, and the persistence of Chinese isolationism made more down-to-earth accounts difficult to come by even as late as the mid-nineteenth century.

Western contact was severely limited by the Chinese imperial government until after the Anglo-Chinese opium wars (1839–42 and 1856–60; see below), and the few traders and diplomats who were grudgingly allowed to enter China at all rarely made it beyond the outlying port of Canton. The British East India Company worked during the first part of the century with several smaller organizations to smuggle Indian opium into China, thus circumventing China's highly restrictive foreign trade regulations and creating a tense relationship between Britain and China. In the late 1790s, when Coleridge claimed to have experienced the fantastic and threatening opium vision that inspired 'Kubla Khan', Anglo-Chinese relations had recently been strained almost to breaking point when the Macartney embassy of 1795 (see note 6 to 'The English Mail-Coach') had been pressured to participate in the ceremony of the *kotou* (from which is derived the modern 'kowtow'), which cast the Chinese emperor as the 'Son of Heaven' and 'Lord of the World', and made Western emissaries pay tribute to him by crawling on their bellies as if they were 'Outer Barbarians come from the darkness to worship the light'. Macartney predictably refused. It is partly because of a growing sense of British rivalry with China that Coleridge's and De Quincey's opium-dream versions of the country resemble the violent and mysterious land of the Oriental tales at least as much as the serene and beautiful Cathay implicit in chinoiserie.

In British culture, opium itself was strongly associated with the Orient by the beginning of the nineteenth century. This was partly because the familiar Oriental travellers' tales routinely featured exotic Orientals either eating or smoking opium. The association was cemented by the fact that the opium in domestic use came chiefly from Oriental sources. Most of the opium consumed in Britain came from Turkey and smaller quantities originated in Persia and Egypt. Despite the East India Company's monopoly over the vast poppy crops of Bengal, imports from India rarely supplied more than 12 per cent and usually accounted for less than 3 per cent.[5] None the less, the Indian opium industry reinforced the cultural association of opium and the Orient, especially the Company's illicit trade with China, which accounted for most of its profits. The sale of smuggled opium to the Chinese served British commercial interests by counterbalancing the deficit of trade in Chinese tea and silk and feeding the East India Company's chief source of revenue in Bengal. When the outraged Chinese government destroyed all the opium in British warehouses in Canton in 1839, British forces retaliated with a military campaign to 'open' China to free trade with the West. Thus began the first of the so-called opium wars (1839–42). It ended with the Treaty of Nanking, which opened five ports to British trade and ceded Hong Kong to Britain. The second opium war (1856–60) forced further Chinese territorial and trade concessions, including the reluctant legalization of opium in 1858.

In England, there had been for many years a rising tide of concern about the 'immoral' Indo-Chinese opium traffic; already in 1840, the future prime minister Gladstone had condemned the 'pernicious article' in the House of Commons. But active resistance to the trade was narrowly based before the rise of anti-opium leagues such as the Quaker-founded Society for the Suppression of the Opium Trade in the 1870s. The increased incidence of opium-smoking in China after the opium wars provided fodder for the anti-opium press and fuelled the controversy in England. When the anti-opium front piled on additional arguments about the alleged ill effects of opium on the Indian population, the Crown launched a royal commission to inquire into the production and consumption of opium in India and to ascertain whether prohibitions were warranted.

While debates over the opium trade raged within the Houses of Parliament, such popular media as newspapers, magazines and novels also conducted a sustained dialogue on the subject. The anti-opium movement was both borrowing from and influencing newspaper coverage – for instance, with its alarmist representations of opium-eating and -smoking in the Society for the Suppression of the Opium Trade's organ, the *Friend of China*. Both sides also consistently resorted to Coleridge and De Quincey as evidence either for or against the deleterious effects of habitual opium use, and those authors were themselves influenced by popular perceptions of Anglo-Oriental relations during the early days of the Indo-Chinese opium trade.

Moralistic conceptions pervaded many popular representations of opium as early as the first publication of Coleridge's 'Kubla Khan' (1816) and were even more pronounced in the later decades of the century, partly because of the combined activities of the anti-opium movement and the medical professions. When the *Friend of China* warned, for instance, that the British would someday suffer the consequences of their domineering treatment of China, this apprehension was both fuel for and evidence of anxieties about the influx of Chinese immigrants in the 1860s. These fears gained cultural currency in the latter half of the century, figuring prominently in the many journalistic and fictional representations of the allegedly innumerable opium dens in London's East End, despite evidence that there were probably only a couple of modest establishments with any claim to the title when the accounts first began to proliferate.

NOTES

1. For instance, under the heading 'The Effects of sudden Leaving off the Use of Opium, after a long, and lavish Use thereof' John Jones included 'Great and even intolerable Distresses and Anxieties, and Depressions of Spirits, which in few days commonly end in a most miserable Death, attended with strange Agonies, unless Men return to the Use of Opium' (*The Mysteries of Opium Reveal'd* (Richard Smith: London, 1700), p. 249). Jones's work seems to have been little read, however.

2. William Aitken, *The Science and Practice of Medicine*, 2 vols. (Charles Griffin and Co.: London, 1880), vol. 2, p. 115.

3. Henry Gibbons, 'Notes on the Hypodermic Treatment of Diseases', *Pacific Medical and Surgical Journal* 9 (October 1866), 183–4, quoted in H. Wayne Morgan, *Drugs in America: A Social History, 1800–1980* (Syracuse University Press; Syracuse, NY, 1981), p. 25.

4. Clifford Allbutt, 'On the Abuse of Hypodermic Injections of Morphia', *Practitioner* 5 (1870), 329.

5. Berridge and Edwards, *Opium and the People*, pp. 272–3.

Glossary

Act A thesis defended by a university student in public. At Oxford, Acts were heard in early July; thus the summer term was sometimes called 'Act' term, and De Quincey uses the word in this sense in 'Suspiria'.

Areopagus The hill where the highest court of Athens convened. Figuratively, it refers to any unusually rigorous and powerful tribunal.

attainder As De Quincey uses the term, the loss of all civil rights, including the right to pass on property to descendants, a penalty added to that of death in capital cases.

benefit of clergy From the twelfth century, members of the Church in England were exempt from punishment by ordinary courts, and the policy gradually evolved to the point where even lay people who could recite a verse from the Latin Bible might be entitled to benefit of clergy insofar as they could invoke it once to avert the death penalty. Beginning in the sixteenth century, certain crimes were deemed punishable 'without benefit of clergy', and the privilege was abolished in 1825.

Brummagem A provincial term for the city of Birmingham. Derived by parodying local pronunciation, it was and is used both affectionately and scornfully.

Catholic De Quincey sometimes uses the term in its general sense of 'universal' rather than as referring to the Church of Rome.

crane-neck An iron bar that united the front and back axles of a coach. It curved upward and then downward again at its union with the front axle, thus resembling a crane's neck. Coaches built in this manner were more finely manoeuvrable than those with a straight horizontal union (see *quartering*).

diplomata Plural of 'diploma', an official document such as a charter or, in its most familiar modern sense, an institution's official record of a student's completion of a course of study.

dragoman An interpreter of Arabic, Turkish or Persian, usually employed by travellers in the Near East.

Eclectic De Quincey uses the word (in the *Confessions*) in its ancient sense as applying to philosophers who attached themselves to no specific school or defined system, but instead picked and chose what pleased them from many different schools of thought.

factor-general Chief agent or representative.

four-in-hand A carriage pulled by four horses and driven by one person. The term is also used as an adverb to describe the act of driving such a carriage.

furlong Originally equivalent to the length of a furrow in a ploughed field, the furlong was an imprecise measurement for centuries, but by De Quincey's day it was standardized at one eighth of a mile, or 220 yards.

the hundred From the tenth to the nineteenth century, an administrative subdivision of an English (and later, Irish) county.

intercalary Describes days or months added to a calendar to harmonize it with the solar year. In the *Confessions* De Quincey refers to an 'intercalary year' as a kind of serendipitous bonus.

Ionic Of or pertaining to Ionia, a region of ancient Greece (now part of Turkey). It is also the name of one of the three orders of ancient Greek architecture (Ionic, Doric, Corinthian), distinguishable most notably by their characteristic columns.

jury-reins The prefix 'jury-' originates in nautical terminology, where it indicates a temporary replacement fashioned from whatever is available to meet the purpose, as in 'jury-rigging', 'jury-mast'. Thus 'jury-reins' are horses' reins cobbled together to meet the need of the moment.

laudanum A solution of opium dissolved in alcohol, the most popular form in which opium was dispensed in the nineteenth century. As different batches of raw opium could vary significantly in the relative concentrations of their constitutive alkaloids, and as different chemists used different recipes, different preparations could vary radically in strength. De Quincey eventually took to making his own.

lustrum A period of four or five years.

Magdalen A euphemism for a prostitute, after Mary Magdalene of the New Testament. Calling a woman a Magdalen – rather than a 'whore' or a 'harlot', for instance – implies that she is a 'fallen woman', pure at heart despite her bodily sin.

materia medica Medicines and other remedial substances employed in the practice of medicine.

membrana A skin or parchment (the Latin word for 'membrane'). De

Quincey uses it in reference to sheets of vellum (specially prepared sheepskin) that served as book pages in the Middle Ages. When the sheets were incompletely erased and reused, the resulting shadowy collage of texts was known as a palimpsest, a central metaphor in 'Suspiria'.

negus A popular drink in the nineteenth century, usually consisting of sherry and lemon juice sweetened and warmed, often by placing a red-hot poker in it until it steamed. The name was sometimes used generically for any hot, sweet alcoholic drink.

Newgate A prison in the City of London (the original square mile enclosed by the Roman wall) from the twelfth century until 1881. Executions took place there from 1783; *The Newgate Calendar*, published in 1773, detailed the most sensational crimes of Newgate inmates of the previous seventy years and provided source material for innumerable penny dreadfuls and shilling shockers. Twice rebuilt (once after the Great Fire of 1666), Newgate was demolished in 1902.

nexus A connection.

Nilotic Of or relating to the River Nile and its region in Egypt.

nob A wealthy person or one otherwise distinguished socially. The opposite of *snob* and *raff*.

parhelion A bright spot at the edge of the sun, once thought to be a reflection or 'mock sun'. Often used figuratively to indicate a lesser image of an original; De Quincey uses it in this sense.

prolegomena An introduction or prologue. Immanuel Kant, De Quincey's favourite philosopher, wrote a *Prolegomena to any Future Metaphysic* (1783), and De Quincey's use of the term hearkens to that usage.

public schools Originally referring to English schools that were subject to some degree of public management and oversight, the term has evolved to designate a handful of elite boarding schools including Eton, Harrow, Rugby, Winchester, Charterhouse. The term is often confusing to citizens of the United States, where a 'public school' is the equivalent of a British state school.

quartering Manoeuvring a coach or wagon to a quarter of the road – i.e., one of the outermost of four imaginary lanes – so as to accommodate oncoming traffic. 'Crane-neck quartering' is manoeuvring to the side of the road in the deft manner possible only with the agile crane-neck.

quartern loaf A 'quartern' is a quarter of something. A quartern loaf was a standard-size loaf made from a quarter of a stone (or three and a half pounds) of flour.

quaternion A group of four persons or things.

Quarter Sessions Convenings of English and Welsh courts four times annually by Justices of the Peace to hear criminal charges and civil and criminal appeals. Instituted in 1363 and abolished in 1971.

radix Root.

raff The lowest class of people (cf. the modern 'riff-raff'). Oxford and Cambridge students used it as a term of contempt for townspeople (see *snob* and *nob*).

regressus The course backward from a given point over a succession of developments. The ideas of 'regressus' and 'progressus' (the course forward) in relation to time and space are invoked in Immanuel Kant's *Critique of Pure Reason* (1787), a work that De Quincey often referred to.

revulsion Although the word is often used now as a synonym for disgust, De Quincey uses it in its older sense of a sudden violent change of sentiment. He might also be punning upon the medical sense of the word as 'counter-irritation', or the practice of treating a symptom in one part of the body by acting upon another, as in blood-letting.

snob Originally referring to a shoemaker's apprentice, this term evolved into Oxford and Cambridge slang for a townsman as opposed to a 'gownsman' (see *raff* and *nob*).

stamp In De Quincey's day, usually an embossed mark made on a document to signify that duties had been paid, as in the case of legal documents. (Adhesive stamps, such as postage stamps, are a more recent development.)

swingle-bar The cross-bar on a coach or wagon to which the horses are attached.

sympathetic ink Usually called 'invisible ink' today; any substance that can be written with and is invisible until heated.

taxed cart A small cart used mainly for farming or commerce, subject to a reduced duty.

tintinnabulous The *Oxford English Dictionary* defines this as 'characterized by or pertaining to bell-ringing', and cites De Quincey's usage of it in the *Confessions*. Edgar Allan Poe's famous use of variations on the word in his poem 'The Bells' is one of many indications of De Quincey's influence upon him.

torso Used figuratively to refer to something mutilated and incomplete, after the many classical statues of human figures that are missing head and limbs.

12mo. Abbreviation of 'duodecimo', which designates a size of book. Folio pages were made from full print sheets (about the size of an unfolded newspaper) folded in half. Quarto pages were folded in fourths, octavos in eighths and duodecimos in twelfths, so a '12mo. volume' was pocket-sized.

viz. Abbreviation of the Latin *videlicet* (literally, 'it is permissible'), meaning 'that is to say' or 'to wit'; used to introduce an elaboration of a previous statement.

water A jeweller's measurement of the transparency and lustre of gems, the highest grades of which are first, second and third water. Thus, to say something is of the first water is a figurative way of saying it is of the highest quality.

way-bill A list of passengers booked for seats on a coach.

zenana Harem.

Notes

CONFESSIONS OF AN ENGLISH OPIUM-EATER

Definitions of words that might be unfamiliar to modern readers may be found in the Glossary.

1. *demireps*: Women of only partial repute, of doubtful virtue. The colloquialism was current from the mid-eighteenth century to the mid-nineteenth.

2. *French literature . . . sensibility of the French*: The foremost implicit reference here is to Jean-Jacques Rousseau's *Confessions* (published posthumously in 1781), which unapologetically details the most damning as well as the most flattering details of its author's life. Even though Rousseau was Swiss, his writings exerted a profound influence upon the leaders of the French Revolution and were a cornerstone of nineteenth-century French sensibility. De Quincey's sneering dismissal thus ironically contradicts the focus of his own *Confessions*, whose title even conspicuously echoes Rousseau's.

3. *Humbly to express / A penitential loneliness*: Paraphrased from William Wordsworth (1770–1850), 'The White Doe of Rylstone': 'guilt, that humbly would express / A penitential loneliness' (176–7).

4. *the accursed chain which fettered me*: Although the notion of opiate addiction did not exist in its now familiar form for most of the nineteenth century, the idea of an opium habit was not uncommon (see the Appendix). De Quincey overstates the degree of his triumph, though; he never was able entirely to give up opium, as he woefully relates in both an appendix to the first book edition of the *Confessions* and 'Suspiria de Profundis'.

5. *one celebrated man*: Samuel Taylor Coleridge (1772–1834), poet, critic and philosopher who was already notorious among literati for his tremendous opium habit when the *Confessions* initially appeared.

De Quincey was a great admirer of Coleridge's work and became personally acquainted with him in 1807.

6. *the eloquent and benevolent . . . tedious to mention*: In his 1856 revision, De Quincey supplied the names, complaining that 'not through any fault of my own, but on the motion of some absurd coward having a voice potential at the press, all the names were struck out behind my back in the first edition of the book'. The 'eloquent and benevolent ——' was William Wilberforce (1759–1833), member of Parliament, evangelical philanthropist and campaigner against slavery. 'The late dean of ——' was Dr Isaac Milner (1750–1820), '*nominally* known to the public as Dean of Carlisle, being colloquially always called *Dean* Milner; but virtually he was best known in his own circle as the head of Queen's College, Cambridge, where he usually resided' (De Quincey's note). 'Lord ——' was Thomas, first Lord Erskine (1750–1823), famous legal advocate and Lord Chancellor of England (1806–7). The 'late under-secretary of state' was Henry Unwin Addington (1790–1870), permanent under-secretary for foreign affairs and brother of the prime minister (1801–4) and home secretary (1812–21) Henry Addington, first Viscount Sidmouth (1757–1844). 'Mr ——' was identified as Coleridge (see note 5 above). Of the other shadowy figure De Quincey said, 'Who is Mr Dash, the philosopher? Really I have forgot.' Reconstructing the list from the initials in the original manuscript (not full names, despite De Quincey's claim), Grevel Lindop argues that in fact 'Mr ——, the philosopher' was Coleridge and that 'Mr ——' was Charles Lloyd (1775–1839), minor poet and novelist and sometime associate of the Wordsworth circle.

7. *with a view to suicide . . . disputes*: The widespread fear that opium was being used in poisonings – accidental or deliberate, for suicidal or homicidal purposes – led to its first regulation in 1868 as one of the Pharmacy Act's 'poisons' (see the Appendix).

8. *one, two, or three grains . . . the evening*: This account of working-class opium use in Manchester was treated as gospel in a number of contexts for most of the remainder of the century. Although the reference to the number of grains is typical of De Quincey's seeming precision regarding quantities, it is (and would have been then) difficult to translate his grains and drops into actual dosages of opiates. Different chemists used different methods and proportions in their preparations, and even different lots of raw opium could vary in the concentrations of their constitutive alkaloids.

9. *That those eat now . . . eat the more*: The lines derive ultimately from the refrain in the anonymous *Pervigilium Veneris* ('Vigil of Venus'), a popular poem written probably sometime between the second and

fourth centuries AD: *cras amet qui numquam amavit, quique amavit cras amet* (literally, 'may he love tomorrow who has never loved before, and may he who has loved before love tomorrow'). 'The Vigil of Venus' by Thomas Parnell (1679–1718) translates the lines thus: 'Let those love now, who never lov'd before, / Let those who always lov'd, now love the more.'

10. *Mead*: Dr Richard Mead (1673–1754), a physician at St Thomas's Hospital in London, whose patients included George I, Queen Anne, Alexander Pope and Isaac Newton. His *A Mechanical Account of Poisons* (1702) was long respected as authoritative, and it is presumably to this work that Awsiter refers in the passage De Quincey quotes.

11. φωνᾶντα συνετοῖσι: An ancient Greek commonplace referring to '[sayings] that speak to the wise'.

12. *the Turks themselves*: Popular eighteenth-century travellers' tales often represented Turks eating opium. In fact, the insistence in De Quincey's title on '*English* Opium-Eater' is undoubtedly meant in part to pre-empt the more obvious adjective, 'Turkish'.

13. *'whose talk is of oxen'*: Misquoted from Ecclesiasticus 38:25: 'How can he get wisdome that holdeth the plough, and that glorieth in the goad; that driveth oxen, and is occupied in their labours, and whose talke is of bullocks?'

14. *Humani nihil a se alienum putat*: 'He deems nothing that is human foreign to him.'

15. *David Ricardo*: (1772–1823) Former stockjobber and member of Parliament who wrote the influential *On the Principles of Political Economy and Taxation* (1817), one of De Quincey's favourite books, as he details later in the *Confessions* (see note 149).

16. *A third exception*: All the succeeding specifics point to William Hazlitt (1778–1830), essayist, painter and disaffected former associate of Coleridge and the Lake circle.

17. *of whom indeed I know only one*: John Wilson (1785–1854), professor of moral philosophy at the University of Edinburgh, editor of *Blackwood's Edinburgh Magazine* and close friend of De Quincey's. He later authored the popular *Blackwood's* series 'Noctes Ambrosianae' ('Ambrosian Nights'), which featured a character called 'the Opium-Eater' based on De Quincey.

18. *to renew the pleasurable sensations*: De Quincey here alludes to the phenomenon now known as 'tolerance' (not yet systematically understood by medical professionals at the time), whereby larger quantities of the drug are required with each dose in order to attain the same effects. The onset of opiate tolerance is slower with more widely spaced doses (see the Appendix).

19. *one of my masters . . . a blockhead . . . a respectable scholar*: Respectively, John Morgan, headmaster of Bath Grammar School; the Revd Edward Spencer, Rector of Winkfield in Wiltshire and headmaster of a private school there; Charles Lawson, headmaster of Manchester Grammar School, whose appointment was in the gift of Brasenose College, Oxford.

20. *'Archididascalus'*: 'Headmaster'.

21. *a woman of high rank*: Lady Susan Carbery, a De Quincey family friend with whom Thomas enjoyed a strong rapport.

22. *a just remark of Dr Johnson's . . . when I came to leave* ——: In the last of his *Idler* essays (no. 103, 5 April 1760), Samuel Johnson (1709–84) bids a reluctant farewell to his readers, observing that 'There are few things not purely evil, of which we can say, without some emotion of uneasiness, "this is the last". Those who never could agree together, shed tears when mutual discontent has determined them to final separation; of a place which has been frequently visited, tho' without pleasure, the last look is taken with heaviness of heart.' The dash is for Manchester Grammar School.

23. *the ancient . . . 'drest in earliest light'*: The 'ancient towers' (since reconstructed) were of the fifteenth-century church of St Mary, Manchester, which became a cathedral in 1848. The quotation is from *The Revolt of Islam* by Percy Bysshe Shelley (1792–1822): 'the summit shone / Like Athos seen from Samothracia, dressed / In earliest light' (*Works of Shelley Including Materials Never Before Printed in Any Edition of the Poems*, ed. Thomas Hutchinson (Oxford: Clarendon Press, 1904), V, xliii). The poem, quoted several times in the *Confessions*, had been sent to De Quincey to review for *Blackwood's* in 1818. Although he did not review the volume, his letter praising the poem prompted John Wilson to write a very favourable notice.

24. *'pensive citadel'*: From the opening lines of an untitled sonnet published in 1807 by Wordsworth: 'Nuns fret not at their convent's narrow room; / And hermits are contented with their cells; / And students with their pensive citadels.'

25. *a picture of the lovely* ——: A copy of a Van Dyck portrait of a woman (a seventeenth-century Duchess of Somerset, according to Grevel Lindop), reportedly a benefactress of Manchester Grammar School and of Brasenose College, Oxford.

26. *Of Atlantean shoulders . . . mightiest monarchies*: John Milton (1608–74), *Paradise Lost*, II, 306–7.

27. *contretems*: Today *contretemps*, meaning 'an inconvenience', 'a hitch in plans'.

28. *the Seven Sleepers*: Various versions of the legend of the Seven

Sleepers more or less agree that the emperor Decius (AD 249–51), on a campaign of persecution in Ephesus, walled up seven noble young Christians in a cave as they slept there in hiding. During the reign of either Theodosius the Great (379–95) or Theodosius the Younger (408–50), the cave was opened and the seven men awoke believing they had slept for only one night. The incident was regarded as new proof of the resurrection of the body. The men then died praising God and were subsequently canonized.

29. *étourderie*: 'A careless mistake' or 'absent-mindedness', 'heed-lessness'.

30. *'with Providence my guide'*: Adapted from the closing lines of Milton's *Paradise Lost*, which describe Adam and Eve leaving Eden:

> The World was all before them, where to choose
> Thir place of rest, and Providence thir guide:
> They hand in hand with wandring steps and slow,
> Through Eden took thir solitarie way.

31. *a favourite English poet . . . on other personal accounts*: To meet William Wordsworth, the 'favourite English poet' whose volume De Quincey carried in his pocket. After several years of friendly correspondence, De Quincey travelled in 1807 to meet the poet at his home in Grasmere in the Lake District.

32. *B——*: Bangor.

33. *'Not to know them . . . unknown'*: Adapted from Satan's speech to the Angels Ithuriel and Zephon in *Paradise Lost*, IV, 830–1: 'Not to know mee argues your selves unknown, / The lowest of your throng.'

34. *noli me tangere*: 'Touch me not.'

35. οἱ πολλοί: 'The masses'.

36. *the Bishop of ——*: Dr William Cleaver (1742–1815), Bishop of Bangor and Master of Brasenose College, Oxford.

37. *the Head*: Holyhead, which was (and still is) the port for frequent ferries between England and Ireland.

38. *Llan-y-styndw (or some such name)*: Probably Llanystumdwy near the south coast of the Lleyn Peninsula in North Wales.

39. *prize-money*: All members of a British naval ship's crew received a share of the value of any goods confiscated from conquered enemy vessels during wartime. Over the course of the Napoleonic Wars, many naval officers amassed considerable fortunes by this means as the size of the share increased with rank.

40. *Sapphics or Alcaics*: Forms of ancient Greek poetry whose names come from their characteristic metres, which are associated, respect-

ively, with the poets Sappho and Alcaeus. Both poets were from the island of Lesbos and flourished in the seventh century BC.

41. *Mr Shelley . . . about old age*: De Quincey is referring to Shelley's *The Revolt of Islam*, II, xxxiii (*Works of Shelley*, ed. Hutchinson):

> . . . old age, with its gray hair,
> And wrinkled legends of unworthy things,
> And icy sneers, is . . . .
> . . . . cold and cruel, and is made
> The careless slave of that dark Power which brings
> Evil, like blight, on man.

42. *the plan of Cromwell*: In his *History of the Rebellion* (1702), Edward Hyde, first Earl of Clarendon (1609–74), reports that Oliver Cromwell 'never had the same serenity of mind he had been used to, after he refused the crown', but grew 'much more apprehensive of danger to his person' and 'rarely lodged two nights together in one chamber, but had many furnished and prepared' (XV, 143).

43. *the Blue-beard room of the house*: In the fairy-tale, Duke Bluebeard gives his new wife free rein of his huge castle except for one room, in which she ultimately discovers the corpses of several previous wives he has murdered.

44. *Mr* ——: In the 1856 revision, De Quincey describes the shady lawyer, here *Mr* ——, as 'an attorney who called himself, on most days of the week, by the name of Brunell, but occasionally (might it perhaps be on *red-letter* days?) by the more common name of Brown'. Red-letter days are associated with bills coming due, so De Quincey thus coyly hints at Brunell's assumption of aliases in order to evade creditors. Brunell also resurfaces in 'Suspiria de Profundis'.

45. *the dismal Tartarus*: In Greek mythology, Tartarus was the region below Hades where the Titans were confined. It was reserved for punishment of those who most displeased the gods.

46. *'cycle and epicycle, orb in orb'*: Milton, *Paradise Lost*, VIII, 80–4: foreseeing that God will laugh at humanity's attempts to explain the universe through intricate models, the angel Raphael predicts

> how they will weild
> The mightie frame, how build, unbuild, contrive
> To save appeerances, how gird the Sphear
> With Centric and Eccentric scribl'd o're,
> Cycle and Epicycle, Orb in Orb.

47. *as Dr Johnson ... could eat*: In her *Anecdotes of the Late Dr Samuel Johnson, Lld.* (1786), Hester Lynch Piozzi reminisces, 'I have heard him protest that he never had quite as much as he wished of wall-fruit, except once in his life, and that was when we were all together at Ombersley, the seat of my Lord Sandys' (2nd ed., p. 103).

48. *'the world was all before us'*: De Quincey paraphrases from *Paradise Lost*: see note 30.

49. *in a well-known part of London*: In the 1856 revision De Quincey gave the house's address as 38 Greek Street, Soho.

50. *'Sine Cerere,' &c. ... more Socratico*: *Sine Cerere et Libero friget Venus*: 'Without bread and wine lust grows cold'; *more Socratico*: 'in the Socratic manner'.

51. *'too deep for tears'*: Closing words of Wordsworth, 'Ode: Intimations of Immortality'.

52. *a gentleman of his late Majesty's household*: A courtier of the previous king, George III (1738–1820, reigned 1760–1820); at the time De Quincey wrote the *Confessions*, George IV (1762–1830, reigned 1820–30) was on the throne.

53. *a 10l. Bank-note*: De Quincey uses '*l.*' here as the abbreviation for the Latin *libra*, meaning 'pound'. Thus '10l.' is an alternative way of writing '£10'.

54. *a Jew named D——*: In the 1856 revision, De Quincey gives the man's full name as Dell, and adds, 'like all the other Jews with whom I have had negotiations, he was frank and honourable in his mode of conducting business. What he promised, he performed; and if his terms were high, as naturally they could not *but* be, to cover his risks, he avowed them from the first.'

55. *Doctor's Commons ... the second son of ——*: Doctors' Commons was technically the title given to the common table and dining-hall of the College (i.e., Association) of Doctors of Civil Law in London. But in popular parlance, the name referred more generally to the site and buildings occupied by that association from 1565 to 1858, when the labyrinthine complex was demolished to make way for Queen Victoria Street and the Underground's District Line. Located just south of St Paul's Cathedral, Doctors' Commons housed several courts, one of which handled testamentary affairs. Thus wills were filed there and available for public examination. —— was Thomas Quincey, whose second son was De Quincey himself.

56. *materialiter ... formaliter*: 'Materially ... formally'.

57. *the Earl of —— ... the Marquis of —— ... counties of M—— and Sl——*: The Earl of Altamont was a schoolfellow and boyhood friend of De Quincey's at Bath. His father, the Marquess of Sligo, had extensive land holdings, in the Irish counties of Mayo and Sligo.

58. *Sherrard-street*: Now Gerrard Street in Soho.

59. *the Gloucester Coffee-house*: A regular stop for westbound mail-coaches from London.

60. *a Roman poet*: Juvenal (first–second century AD). The passage in question appears in his *Satires*, X, 23: 'when broke, the traveller will whistle in the robber's face'.

61. *Lord of my learning and no land beside ... Lord ——*: The quotation is possibly adapted from Shakespeare's *King John*: amidst a dispute over whether 'Philip the Bastard' is the legitimate son of the wealthy Faulconbridge or the bastard of Richard Coeur de Lion, Queen Elinor asks him (I, i, 134–7):

> Whether hadst thou rather be a Faulconbridge,
> And like thy brother, to enjoy thy land,
> Or the reputed son of Cordelion,
> Lord of thy presence and no land beside?

However, the phrase is more similar in sentiment, if not quite as similar in wording, to the penultimate line of 'Character of a Happy Life' by Sir Henry Wotton (1568–1639), the final stanza of which reads:

> This man is freed from servile bands
> Of hope to rise, or fear to fall:
> Lord of himself, though not of Lands;
> And having nothing: yet hath all.

'Lord ——' in the next line is again Lord Altamont (see note 57).

62. *To slacken virtue ... merit praise*: Slightly altered (or misremembered) from Milton, *Paradise Regained*, II, 455–6 (which has 'prompt' instead of 'tempt').

63. *Pote's*: A well-known bookseller in Eton High Street.

64. *the University of —— . 'Ibi omnis effusus labor!'*: The university is Cambridge. The quotation is from Virgil, *Georgics*, IV, 491–2: 'Then all his work was for nothing!'

65. *the Earl of D——*: The second Earl of Desart, Lord Altamont's cousin.

66. *he was himself ... an author*: De Quincey's father, Thomas Quincey, anonymously published a travel memoir in 1775, *A Short Tour in the Midland Counties of England; Performed in the Summer of 1772. Together With an Account of a Similar Excursion, Undertaken September 1774*.

67. *those of Lady M. W. Montague*: Lady Mary Wortley Montagu (1689–1762) was a famous wit, poet and cosmopolitan. Her letters written from Turkey while her husband was ambassador there were published in 1763 and remained popular for several generations.

68. *'good man's table'*: Probably misquoted for 'good man's feast', from Shakespeare, *As You Like It*, II, vii, 115. The desperate Orlando enters Duke Senior's dining hall with sword drawn. Surprised and moved to find that the Duke offers him food anyway, he says:

> If ever you have look'd on better days,
> If ever been where bells have knoll'd to church,
> If ever sat at any good man's feast,
> If ever from your eyelids wip'd a tear,
> And know what 'tis to pity and be pitied,
> Let gentleness my strong enforcement be;
> In the which hope I blush, and hide my sword. (113–19)

69. *the story about Otway*: In his *Lives of the Poets*, Samuel Johnson recounts an apocryphal tale of the death of the playwright Thomas Otway (1651–85): 'He went out, as is reported, almost naked, in the rage of hunger, and finding a gentleman in a neighbouring coffee-house, asked him for a shilling. The gentleman gave him a guinea; and Otway going away bought a roll, and was choked with the first mouthful.'

70. *an address to —— in ——shire*: St John's Priory, Cheshire.

71. *begun*: Part I of the *Confessions* ended here with a note from the *London Magazine*'s editor promising that 'The remainder of this very interesting Article will be given in the next Number.'

72. *'the road to the North . . . fly for comfort' . . . in that very house*: The road to the north leads to Grasmere in the Lake District. Then follows a paraphrase of Psalms 55:6: 'O that I had wings like a dove! for then would I fly away, and be at rest!' Wordsworth was living at that time in the cottage at Town End (*that very house*), later known as Dove Cottage. De Quincey took up residence there in 1809, the Wordsworths having moved across Grasmere to Allan Bank, and maintained his tenancy until 1835, though he did not actually live there after 1820.

73. *haunted the couch of an Orestes*: Throughout the following pages, De Quincey refers repeatedly to the story of Orestes, best known from the *Oresteia*, a trilogy of plays (*Agamemnon*, *The Libation-Bearers*, *Eumenides*) by Aeschylus (c. 525–c. 456 BC), tragedian of Athens' Golden Age. Orestes is caught in an unresolvable cycle of vengeance.

His father, Agamemnon, sacrificed Orestes' sister Iphigenia at the behest of the gods; his mother, Clytemnestra, avenged that death by killing Agamemnon; and Orestes in turn avenged his father by killing his mother. Orestes is tormented day and night by the hideous avenging Furies, and his sole comfort through it all is the support of his sister Electra. De Quincey thus represents himself as alienated, perpetually tortured and with only one ally, his wife Margaret.

74. φίλον ὕπνου θέλγητρον, ἐπίκουρον νόσου: '[O] sweet charm of sleep, helper in times of sickness' (Euripides, *Orestes*, 211).

75. *'sleep no more'*: *Macbeth*, II, ii, 32. Wordsworth also used the phrase powerfully in describing his state of mind during the Terror in France in *The Prelude* (1850), X, 87. The passage also appears in the 1805 draft of the poem, which De Quincey probably heard or read when it was in manuscript.

76. *thou art sitting . . . that very house*: De Quincey wrote most of the *Confessions* while hiding from creditors in various lodgings around London. His dismal finances had kept him for months from returning to Grasmere, where his wife Margaret was still living in Dove Cottage (see note 72).

77. ἡδὺ δούλευμα: 'Sweet service' (Euripides, *Orestes*, 221).

78. ἄναξ ἀνδρῶν Ἀγαμέμνων: 'Agamemnon, King of Men', an epithet used frequently by Homer in his *Iliad*.

79. ὄμμα θεῖσ' εἴσω πέπλων: A slight misquotation of κρᾶτα θεῖσ' ἔσω πέπλων, 'putting her head inside her robe', i.e., 'covering her face with her robe' (Euripides, *Orestes*, 280).

80. *of manna or of Ambrosia*: Food of the gods. Manna was the miraculous bread from heaven that sustained the Israelites as they wandered in the wilderness (Exodus 16). Ambrosia was served along with nectar on Mount Olympus in Greek mythology.

81. *a duller spectacle . . . Sunday in London . . . the stately Pantheon*': De Quincey facetiously inverts the opening of Wordsworth's famous celebration of London's beauty, the sonnet 'Composed upon Westminster Bridge, Sept. 3, 1802': 'Earth has not anything to shew more fair.' The Pantheon, a London landmark on the south side of Oxford Street just west of Poland Street, was a grandiose building housing fashionable public assembly rooms. The description is quoted from Wordsworth's 'Power of Music', 3.

82. *tincture of opium*: Opium dissolved in alcohol, otherwise known as laudanum. (See the Appendix for more detailed information on opium in the nineteenth century.)

83. *Kings should disdain to die, and only disappear*: Misquoted from 'On the Much Lamented Death of Our Late Sovereign Lord King

Charles II, of Blessed Memory, a Pindarique Ode' by Thomas Flatman (1637–88), 21–5:

> But Princes (like the wondrous *Enoch*) should be free
>> From Death's Unbounded Tyranny,
>> And when their Godlike Race is run,
>> And nothing glorious left undone,
> Never submit to Fate, but only disappear.

84. φάρμαχον νηπενθές: A 'drug that assuages sorrow' (compare Homer, *Odyssey*, IV, 220–1).

85. *l'Allegro . . . Il Penseroso*: Two poems by Milton portraying, respectively, the sunny, active state of mind and the nocturnal, pensive mood.

86. *anti-mercurial*: The mercurial temperament corresponds to that of the Greek god Mercury, who was fleet-footed and lighthearted. But 'mercurial' also describes a class of medicines used in De Quincey's time as 'purgatives' (i.e., laxatives). Opium is of the opposite class, as its effects are constipative. De Quincey thus uses the adjective to pun on several of opium's effects.

87. *ex cathedra*: Literally 'from the chair', meaning by virtue of office or position rather than, for instance, reasoned argument or empirical evidence.

88. *Tuesday and Saturday*: When the London papers published the list of bankrupts, which both warned potential creditors of bad risks and added public humiliation to the punishment of those listed. The 'satiric author' is untraced.

89. *meo periculo*: 'At my peril', 'on my head be it if I am wrong'.

90. *'ponderibus librata suis'*: 'balanced by its own weight' (Latin). Throughout these pages, De Quincey takes a decisive stand in a then raging medical debate surrounding opium. Some medical professionals held that opium was a stimulant while others maintained that it was a narcotic. De Quincey insists that it is a stimulant.

91. *Athenæus*: Author of the *Deipnosophistae* (*Banquet of the Sophists*, c. AD 200), a lengthy fictional dinner conversation among a group of intellectuals who quote extensively from earlier ancient authors.

92. ἑαυτοὺς ἐμφανίζουσιν οἵτινες εἰσίν: '[Men] display who they really are.'

93. *of which church . . . the only member*: In his 1856 revision, De Quincey altered the wording to 'of which I acknowledge myself to be the Pope (consequently infallible), and self-appointed *legate a latere* to all degrees of latitude and longitude', indicating the increased number

of opium-eaters since 1821 (see the Introduction for discussion of De Quincey's escalating claims to authority regarding opium).

94. *Anastasius*: *Anastasius, or, Memoirs of a Greek* (1819), a novel by Thomas Hope (?1770–1831). The relevant context is made clear by De Quincey's succeeding quotations and explanation.

95. *a surgeon*: It is impossible to say for certain who was the particular surgeon De Quincey had in mind here, but he did expand upon the extenuating circumstances of the case in his 1856 revision, relating that the surgeon in question 'had himself taken opium largely for a most miserable affection (past all hope of cure)' which he 'had fought for more (I believe) than twenty years; fought victoriously, if victory it were, to make life supportable for himself, and during all that time to maintain in respectability a wife and a family of children altogether dependent on him'. He also noted that it was this surgeon 'who first made me aware of the dangerous variability of opium as to strength under the shifting proportions of its combination with alien impurities'.

96. *primâ facie*: 'At first appearance'.

97. *the numerous pictures of Turkish opium-eaters*: See note 12.

98. *The late Duke of* ——: Charles Howard, eleventh Duke of Norfolk (1746–1815), famed for his various excesses and eccentricities.

99. *Grassini*: Giuseppina Grassini (1773–1850), an Italian contralto who performed in London many times early in the century. She was admired for her beauty and acting skill as well as her singing voice, and rumour had it that she had been the mistress of both Napoleon and Wellington. The eminent surgeon Sir Charles Bell (1774–1842) voiced representative sentiments in a letter of 1805: 'It is only Signora Grassini who conveys the idea of the united power of music and action. She dies not only without being ridiculous, but with an effect equal to Mrs Siddons [see note 145]. The 'O Dio!' of Mrs Billington [Elizabeth Billington (?1768–1818), a very successful British soprano] is a bar of music, but in the strange, almost unnatural voice of Grassini, it goes to your soul' (*Letters* [1870], 40).

100. *that subject in Twelfth Night*: The famous passage on music in *Twelfth Night*, I, i, 1–7:

> If music be the food of love, play on,
> Give me excess of it; that surfeiting,
> the appetite may sicken, and so die.
> That strain again, it had a dying fall;
> O, it came o'er my ear like the sweet sound
> That breathes upon a bank of violets,
> Stealing and giving odor.

101. *a passage in the Religio Medici of Sir T. Brown*: A passage in *Religio Medici*, II (1642), by Sir Thomas Browne (1605–82) reads 'even that vulgar and Taverne Musicke which makes one man merry, another mad, strikes in me so deep a fit of devotion, and a profound contemplation of my Maker; there is something in it of Divinity more than the eare discovers . . . it is a sensible fit of that Harmony, which intellectually sounds in the eares of God, it unties the ligaments of my frame, takes me to pieces, dilates me out of my selfe, and by degrees, me thinkes, resolves me into Heaven.' (1st edn., II, pp. 169–70)

102. *Weld the traveller*: Isaac Weld (1774–1856) was a writer of noted travel books, including *Travels Through the States of North America and the Provinces of Upper and Lower Canada, During the Years 1795, 1796, and 1797* (1799), in which he says Native American women 'speak with the utmost ease, and the language, as pronounced by them, appears as soft as the Italian. They have, without exception, the most delicate harmonious voices I ever heard, and the most pleasing gentle laugh it is possible to conceive. I have oftentimes sat amongst a group of them for an hour or two together, merely from the pleasure of listening to their conversation, on account of its wonderful softness and delicacy.' (3rd edn. (1800), II, p. 288)

103. *Marinus in his life of Proclus*: Proclus (AD ?410–485) was a Greek Neoplatonist philosopher whose biography was written by one of his students, Marinus.

104. *the bee . . . chimneys*: In 1856, De Quincey added an explanatory note: 'In the large capacious chimneys of the rustic cottages throughout the Lake district, you can see up the entire cavity from the seat which you occupy, as an honoured visitor, in the chimney corner. There I used often to hear (though not to see) bees. Their murmuring was audible, though their bodily forms were too small to be visible at that altitude. On inquiry, I found that soot (chiefly from wood and peats) was useful in some stage of their wax or honey manufacture.'

105. *terræ incognitæ*: 'Unknown lands'.

106. *the cave of Trophonius*: According to various Greek legends, the renowned architect Trophonius was swallowed up by the earth at Lebadea in Boeotia. The resulting hole in the earth became the site of a famous oracle, which suppliants would enter in an elaborate ritual that allowed them to communicate with their own destiny. After consulting the oracle, visitors would become so profoundly dejected that it became a byword for deep melancholia that the subject had been visiting the cave of Trophonius.

107. *the great town of L——*: Liverpool, a suburb of which, Everton, was one of De Quincey's favourite holiday spots.

108. *mysticism, Behmenism, quietism, &c.... Sir H. Vane, the younger*: Behmenists were followers of Jakob Boehme (1575–1624), a German mystic who believed the universe was the product of conflict between opposing pairs of forces. Quietism is a form of Christian mysticism that ennobles passive contemplation and disengagement from the sensual world as the standards of perfection. Henry Vane (1613–62) was an ardent puritan, committed republican and adroit politician. His writings, on both political and religious issues, show pronounced mystical leanings.

109. *Oh! just, subtle, and mighty opium! ... 'the pangs that tempt the spirit to rebel'*: The first is adapted from the penultimate paragraph of the *History of the World* (1614) by Sir Walter Raleigh (c. 1554–1618): 'O eloquent, just and mightie Death!' The second is from the dedicatory poem (line 36) prefacing Wordsworth's 'The White Doe of Rylstone'.

110. *Wrongs unredress'd, and insults unavenged*: Wordsworth, *The Excursion*, III, 374.

111. *Phidias and Praxiteles ... Babylon and Hekatómpylos ... '... dreaming sleep' ... 'dishonours of the grave'*: Phidias and Praxiteles were highly influential Athenian artists whose sculptures (known mostly through literary descriptions and later facsimiles) help to define the classical era of Greek art (c. 480–320 BC). The work of Phidias (c. 465–425 BC) is associated with the High Classical style of the fifth century, that of Praxiteles (active c. 375–330 BC) with the Late Classical style of the fourth. Phidias, also an architect, directed construction of the Parthenon and executed its reputedly magnificent gold and ivory statue of Athena. Praxiteles is best known for his smaller-scale statues of divinities and especially of satyrs, one of which was an inspiration for Nathaniel Hawthorne's novel *The Marble Faun*. Babylon was legendary for its lavish architecture, as was the ancient Egyptian city of Thebes, known also as Hekatompylos ('hundred-gated') to distinguish it from the contemporary Greek city of the same name. *'from the anarchy of dreaming sleep'* is from Wordsworth, *The Excursion*, IV, 87. *'dishonours of the grave'* is paraphrased (or misremembered) from Thomas Flatman's 'On the Death of the Truly Valiant George Duke of Albemarle, Pindarique Ode', 160–1: 'That Sanctuary shall thee save, / From the dishonours of a Regal Grave.'

112. *the Bodleian*: The main library of Oxford University.

113. *frailer vessels ... bed-makers, &c.*: In the King James Version of the New Testament, women are described as 'the weaker vessel' (I Peter 3:7); 'frailer vessel' is probably either De Quincey's own translation of the original Greek or his imperfectly remembered version of the more familiar rendering. A bed-maker was a menial chambermaid and a

byword for a woman of easy virtue. (The poem 'Nancy the Bed-Maker' by William Pattison (1706–27), for instance, is a sort of soft-core pornographic account of a sexual tryst.) Thus De Quincey's inclusion of bed-makers in a list of 'frailer vessels' he 'once possessed' is probably a thinly veiled bawdy joke.

114. *the writings of Kant, Fichte, Schelling*: Immanuel Kant (1724–1804), Johann Gottlieb Fichte (1762–1814) and Friedrich Wilhelm Joseph von Schelling (1774–1854), German Idealist philosophers. The latter two were followers of Kant, whom De Quincey also studied and admired immensely.

115. *honi soit qui mal y pense*: 'dishonour to him who thinks evil', the motto of the Most Noble Order of the Garter.

116. *X.Y.Z., esquire . . . Custos Rotulorum*: The first was De Quincey's alias for the *Confessions* and other early articles. The *custos rotulorum* is a county's chief Justice of the Peace and custodian of the rolls and records.

117. *in the straw*: 'In childbed'.

118. *Dr Buchan*: William Buchan's *Domestic Medicine; or, the Family physician . . . Chiefly Calculated to Recommend a Proper Attention to Regimen and Simple Medicines* (1769) was immensely popular, having gone through more than twenty editions by the time De Quincey wrote the *Confessions*, and continued to be republished until the mid-nineteenth century. The recommendation regarding laudanum dosage sarcastically alluded to here is first mentioned in De Quincey's footnote on p. 45.

119. *a very melancholy event*: The death of William and Mary Wordsworth's daughter Kate. An awkward child, she was something of a black sheep in the Wordsworth family and enjoyed an unusually strong attachment to the small and self-conscious De Quincey. When she died of viral encephalitis in June 1812 before she was four years old, De Quincey caused something of a scandal in Grasmere with the intensity of his grief.

120. *à force d'ennuyer, by mere dint of pandiculation*: 'From sheer boredom', by the mere force of yawning.

121. *Eudæmonist*: Believer in the pursuit of happiness and personal well-being above all else.

122. *the Stoic philosophy*: A school of thought emphasizing strength of will and control of passions, emotions and appetites. Zeno of Citium (335–263 BC), mentioned in De Quincey's note, established the philosophy through his teaching in the 'Painted Stoa', a public colonnade in central Athens.

123. *'sweet men . . . to give absolution'*: Recast from lines 221–2 of

the General Prologue to *The Canterbury Tales* by Geoffrey Chaucer (c. 1343–1400): 'Ful swetely herde he confessioun, / And pleasant was his absolucioun.'

124. *opium that has not been boiled*: In its raw form, opium is the dried milk of the poppy seed-pod. Its preparation usually includes boiling and filtering. This process removes a number of impurities and heavier components, some of which can be semi-poisonous, but some impurities typically remain until the opium is further refined. For many years, De Quincey boiled crude opium himself and mixed the resulting extract with wine or brandy to make his own laudanum.

125. *'with a snow-white beard,'* ... *'... the pernicious drug'*: Another reference to Hope's *Anastasius* (see note 94).

126. *Lent or Ramadan*: Christian and Moslem periods of religious observance, marked by several weeks of fasting.

127. *from 320 grains of opium ... to forty*: De Quincey acknowledges several barriers to such precision in the accompanying note, but the situation was even more complex than he details (see note 8 above and the Appendix).

128. νυχθήμερον: 'A night and a day', or twenty-four hours.

129. *That moveth altogether, if it move at all*: Adapted from Wordsworth, 'Resolution and Independence', 77.

130. *Adelung's Mithridates*: *Mithridates oder allgemeine Sprachenkunde: mit dem Vater unser als Sprachprobe: in beynahe Fünfhundert Sprachen und Mundarten* (*Mithridates, or the Universal Table of Languages: with the Lord's Prayer as a Language Sample in Five Hundred Languages and Dialects*, 1806), by Johann Christoph Adelung (1732–1806), German philologist.

131. *A French surgeon ... hydrophobia*: De Quincey's medical history is rather loose here, perhaps even wholly apocryphal. The French surgeon might be, as Grevel Lindop speculates, a 'Dr A. White, who inoculated himself with plague in Alexandria in 1798'. But the most that is known of the other two medical heroes is what De Quincey added in his 1856 revision: the third 'was a surgeon who lived at Brighton'. Hydrophobia is another name for rabies.

132. *Let there be a cottage ... 'a cottage with a double coach-house'*: The description is of Dove Cottage in the vale of Grasmere. The quotation is from Coleridge, 'The Devil's Thoughts', 21.

133. *And at the doors ... secure in massy hall*: James Thomson (1700–48), *The Castle of Indolence*, I, xliii, 6–9. (De Quincey substitutes line 5 for line 7, which is properly 'The demons of the tempest, growling fell.')

134. *(as Mr —— says) '... like a post'*: In his 1856 revision, De

Quincey attributed the remark to 'Mr Anti-slavery Clarkson', otherwise known as Thomas Clarkson (1760–1846), the famous English
abolitionist.

135. *fee-simple*: Full legal ownership.

136. *St Thomas's day*: 21 December, the winter solstice, the longest
night of the year.

137. *I would have joined . . . Jonas Hanway*: Samuel Johnson criticized
the *Essay on Tea* (1757) by Jonas Hanway (1712–86), which attacks
the beverage as unhealthful. The dispute continued through a series of
published letters. A *bellum internecium* is a war of extermination.

138. *'a double debt to pay'*: Oliver Goldsmith (?1730–74), 'The
Deserted Village', 229–30: 'The chest contrived a double debt to pay, /
A bed by night, a chest of drawers by day.'

139. *à parte ante and à parte post*: 'Beforehand and afterwards'.

140. *her arms . . . like Hebe's*: Aurora was the Roman goddess of the
dawn, whose rosy arms brought morning light to the world. Hebe was
the goddess of youth and the charming cupbearer who served nectar
to the gods.

141. *as when some great painter . . . eclipse*: Shelley, *The Revolt of
Islam*, V, xxiii, 8–9.

142. *the hands . . . of an amanuensis*: Those of his wife, Margaret.

143. *feelings such as . . . at my command*: The feelings to which De
Quincey here alludes are now known as the withdrawal syndrome (see
the Appendix).

144. *'in medias res' . . . acmé*: 'Into the thick of things' . . . 'the highest
point'.

145. —— *reads vilely: and Mrs* ——: John Philip Kemble (1757–1823)
and his sister, Sarah Siddons (1755–1831), two of the most celebrated
actors of the age. De Quincey filled in their names in the 1856 revision
and added that 'Neither Coleridge nor Southey is a good reader of
verse. Southey is admirable almost in all things, but not in this. Both
he and Coleridge read as if crying, or at least wailing lugubriously.'

146. *overstep the modesty of nature*: Adapted from Hamlet's exhor-
tation to the troupe of players who are to perform at the court of
Denmark: 'Suit the action to the word, the word to the action; with
this special observance, that you o'erstep not the modesty of nature'
(Shakespeare, *Hamlet*, III, ii, 17–19).

147. *at her request and M.'s . . . W——'s poems*: M. is Margaret;
W—— is Wordsworth.

148. *De emendatione humani intellectûs*: *On the Correction of the
Human Intellect*. The unfinished work, *Tractatus de Intellectus Emendatione*, was by the Dutch philosopher Baruch Spinoza (1632–77).

149. *Mr Ricardo's book . . . 'Thou art the Man'*: John Wilson sent a copy of Ricardo's *On the Principles of Political Economy and Taxation* (see note 15 above) for De Quincey to review in *Blackwood's*. The quotation is from 2 Samuel 12:7.

150. *à priori*: Derived by deductive reasoning – rather than experiment or evidence, for instance – from elementary propositions.

151. *'the inevitable eye'*: The phrase occurs in an obscure poem by Shakerley Marmion (1603–39), 'Cupid and Psiche: Or an Epick Poem of Cupid, and his Mistress, As it was lately presented to the Prince Elector', II, 120–1: 'What darknesse can protect me? what disguise / Hide me from her inevitable eyes?' It might also be adapted from Wordsworth's 'When, to the attractions of the busy world', 82, which speaks of 'an inevitable ear'.

152. *A Scotchman of eminent name has lately told us*: De Quincey presumably refers here to a personal communication, probably from one of his many learned friends in Edinburgh.

153. *Œdipus or Priam . . . Tyre . . . Memphis*: Oedipus was a king of Grecian Thebes immortalized in Sophocles' (c. 496–406 BC) most famous tragedy; Priam was king of Troy during the siege recounted in Homer's *Iliad*; Tyre was an ancient Phoenician city in what is now southern Lebanon; Memphis, south of Cairo, was the capital of ancient Egypt during the Old Kingdom (3100–2242 BC).

154. *Livy*: Titus Livius (?64 BC–AD 17). His history of Rome from its foundation to his own age has long been regarded as a literary masterpiece as well as an essential historical document.

155. *Parliamentary War*: The English Civil War (1642–51), between Parliamentarians and Royalists.

156. *Marston Moor . . . Newbury . . . Naseby*: All battles of the English Civil War. Marston Moor (2 July 1644) and Naseby (14 June 1645) were Parliamentary victories. Two battles were fought at Newbury: the first (20 September 1643) was won by the Parliamentarians, the second (27 October 1644) by the Royalists.

157. *'sweeping by' . . . paludaments*: The quotation is from Milton's 'Il Penseroso', 97–8: 'Sometime let Gorgeous Tragedy / In Sceptred Pall come sweeping by'; paludaments are Roman military cloaks.

158. *alalagmos*: Transliteration of the Greek word ἀλαλαγμός, meaning 'shouting'.

159. *Piranesi's . . . Dreams*: Giovanni Battista Piranesi (1720–78), Italian engraver, chiefly of subjects inspired by ancient Roman architecture. The plates De Quincey calls his *Dreams* are Piranesi's famous *Carceri d'Invenzione* (*Imaginary Prisons*, 1745), surreal representations of vast classical dungeons.

160. *The appearance . . . a cerulean sky. &c. &c.*: From Wordsworth's nine-book poem *The Excursion*, II, 834–51.

161. *Dryden . . . Fuseli . . . Shadwell . . . Homer*: The poet, dramatist and poet laureate John Dryden (1631–1700); the Anglo-Swiss painter Henry Fuseli (1741–1825), most famous for striking dream images such as *The Nightmare* and *The Shepherd's Dream* (see cover); the poet and dramatist Thomas Shadwell (1642–92), who was well known to have used opium regularly. Homer's famous passage on the drink that brings forgetfulness is often taken as a reference to opium (see note 84).

162. *the last Lord Orford*: Horace Walpole, fourth Earl of Orford (1717–97), whose *The Castle of Otranto* (1764) originated the fantastic gothic novel genre to which De Quincey's style is in many ways indebted.

163. *some part of my London life . . . this*: In his 1856 revision, De Quincey added parenthetically that the specific part of his London life he blamed here was 'the searching for Ann amongst fluctuating crowds'.

164. *officina gentium*: Literally 'the factory of nations', the place where peoples are made.

165. *Brama . . . Vishnu . . . Seeva . . . Isis . . . Osiris*: In Hindu tradition, Brahma is the creator, Vishnu the preserver and Shiva the destroyer. Ancient Egyptians worshipped the married siblings Isis and Osiris as the female and male productive forces in nature, respectively. Osiris also ruled the land of the dead.

166. *cæteris paribus*: 'Other things being equal'.

167. *a child whom I had tenderly loved*: Kate Wordsworth (see note 119).

168. *Coronation Anthem*: George Frideric Handel (1685–1759) composed four anthems that were performed at the coronation of George II at Westminster Abbey in 1727. They have since been popularly regarded as some of Handel's most sublime music.

169. *'Deeper than ever plummet sounded'*: Shakespeare, *The Tempest*, III, iii, 100–01: 'my son i' th' ooze is bedded; and / I'll seek him deeper than e'er plummet sounded, / And with him there lie mudded.'

170. *when the incestuous mother . . . death*: In Milton's *Paradise Lost*, X, 602, Sin, Satan's daughter, is referred to as 'th' incestuous Mother' because she has borne him a child, Death. She describes her cataclysmic utterance of the name in II, 787–9: 'I fled and cri'd out *Death*; / Hell trembl'd at the hideous Name, and sigh'd / From all her Caves, and back resounded *Death*.'

171. *an Edinburgh surgeon of great eminence*: Robert Morrison convincingly argues that the eminent surgeon in question was George Bell

(1777–1832), known frequently to prescribe tincture of valerian for similar conditions (' "An Edinburgh Surgeon of Great Eminence" in De Quincey's *Confessions of an English Opium-Eater'*, *Notes and Queries* 46 (1999), 47–8).

172. *proof that opium . . . may still be renounced*: De Quincey again overstates his case (see note 4).

173. *William Lithgow*: Scottish author (1582–1645) of *A Most Delectable, and True Discourse, of an Admired and Painefull Peregrination from Scotland to the Most Famous Kingdomes in Europe, Asia, and Affricke, etc.* (1614). A collection of his writings called *The Travels and Adventures of William Lithgow in Europe, Asia, and Africa, During Nineteen Years* (1814) was reprinted several times in the nineteenth century. Thus De Quincey's reference to his 'Travels, &c.'.

174. *Jeremy Taylor*: In the 1856 revision, De Quincey admitted this attribution was erroneous, noting that 'the exact passage moving in my mind had evidently been this which follows, from Lord Bacon's "Essay on Death:" – "It is as natural to die as to be born; and to a little infant perhaps the one is as painful as the other." ' Francis Bacon (1561–1626), first Baron Verulam and Viscount St Albans, was a famous lawyer, philosopher and essayist sometimes credited with the authorship of Shakespeare's plays.

175. *With dreadful faces throng'd and fiery arms*: Milton, *Paradise Lost*, XII, 644.

SUSPIRIA DE PROFUNDIS

1. *Suspiria de Profundis*: 'Sighs from the Depths'.

2. *Daguerreotype, &c.*: One of the earliest means of preserving photographic images, introduced in France by Louis Daguerre in 1839.

3. *præmissis præmittendis*: 'Assuming the appropriate presuppositions'.

4. *sine quâ non*: 'An absolutely necessary element'.

5. *a striking incident in a modern novel*: The succeeding plot summary could formulaically describe many of the popular but ephemeral gothic novels that influenced De Quincey's own writing.

6. *Holy Office*: The Inquisition; the official body within the Roman Catholic Church charged with protecting morals and the faith in general and eradicating Protestantism in particular.

7. *in extenso*: 'At length'.

8. τὸ *brevity*: 'The very idea of brevity.' De Quincey here uses (rather gratuitously) a Greek device for creating abstract nouns.

9. *caduceus*: A staff encircled by two snakes and bearing wings at the top. It is associated with the god Mercury, messengers and physicians.

10. *Cheapside*: A street in the City of London (the original square mile enclosed by Roman walls), near St Paul's Cathedral. A bustling market-place in Saxon and medieval London, it had evolved by De Quincey's day into a centre for jewellers, goldsmiths, haberdashers, drapers, perfumers, lacemakers and other up-market shops.

11. *'viridantem floribus hastas'*: Literally, 'making [his] spears verdant with flowers', i.e., 'binding his spears with fresh flowers'. The phrase is lifted from the *Argonautica* (VI, 136) of Valerius Flaccus, a minor epic poet of the first century AD. It refers to a distinguishing characteristic of the Thyrsagetae, one of the Scythian tribes arrayed against the Colchians and the Argonauts.

12. *Cicero . . . Ethics*: In his *De Officiis* (*On Moral Obligations*), I, 42, Cicero claims the dealer cannot succeed unless he is deceitful – the most disgraceful thing it is possible to be. A large-scale importer can be respectable, he says, if he is honest in the distribution of his goods and retires when he has made enough money to be comfortable.

13. *The prayer of Agar*: Agur's prayer, Proverbs 30:8.

14. *the model of the emperor Marcus Aurelius*: In his *Meditations* (the ancient title translates simply as *To Himself*), a collection of Stoic-influenced reflections on moral, ethical and metaphysical issues, the Roman emperor Marcus Aurelius (AD 121–80) details, among other things, the modest blessings of his childhood.

15. *The first who died was Jane*: An echo of Wordsworth's 'We are Seven', 49: 'The first that died was sister Jane'.

16. *Dr Percival . . . Condorcet, D'Alembert . . . Mr Charles White*: The physician Thomas Percival (1740–1804) and the surgeon Charles White (1728–1813), both of Manchester, were distinguished for furthering the cause of public health, among other professional achievements. Marie Jean Antoine Nicolas de Caritat, Marquis de Condorcet (1743–94), and Jean le Rond d'Alembert (1717–83) were eminent mathematicians and philosophers. Condorcet made significant contributions to probability theory and the structure of the French educational system. D'Alembert also made important discoveries in physics and was co-editor (with the philosopher Diderot (1713–84)) of the *Encyclopédie*, a focal point of the French Enlightenment.

17. *If God should make another Eve'*: This (misquoted) line and the following quotations from Milton's *Paradise Lost* are taken from the latter part of Book IX.

18. *'Love . . . was most intense'*: Misquoted from Wordsworth's 'Tribute to the memory of the same dog', 27–8: 'For love, that comes

wherever life and sense / Are given by God, in thee was most intense.'

19. *John Paul, (Richter)*: Johann Paul Friedrich Richter (1763–1825), German author who published under the pen-name Jean Paul and was known to English audiences partly through De Quincey's translations. It is not clear what specific passage in his works De Quincey has in mind here.

20. *ex-officio*: 'Proceeding from office', 'by virtue of position'.

21. *Speech of Alhadra in Coleridge's Remorse*: Coleridge, *Remorse*, IV, 411.

22. *the guard*: The protective screen in front of the fireplace.

23. *Memnonian*: Memnon, king of Ethiopia and semi-divine son of Eos (goddess of the dawn) and Tithonus (a prince of Troy), was killed in the Trojan War and commemorated by a statue near Thebes in Egypt which was said to moan at sunrise.

24. *Æolian intonation*: Aeolus was the Greek god of the winds. A favourite Romantic symbol of a unifying spirit suffusing creation was the Aeolian harp, a stringed instrument that made music when the wind blew across it.

25. *some Sarsar wind of death*: The Arabic *çarçar* is a cold wind. In Robert Southey's (1774–1843) popular 'Oriental' romance *Thalaba the Destroyer*, I, xxxvi, 'the Sarsar' is called 'the Icy Wind of Death'.

26. φυγὴ μόνου πρὸς μόνον: Literally, 'the flight of the alone to the Alone', perhaps the most famous words (vol. VI, Ennead 9, ch. 11, line 51) in all the writings which make up the *Enneads* of the neo-Platonist Plotinus (third century AD). The phrase refers to the mystical union between the true devotee of the philosophical and spiritual life, who has succeeded in escaping from the emptiness of the sensory world, and the ultimate first principle of the cosmos, 'the One' or 'the Alone'.

27. *everlasting Jew*: As the most familiar version of the legend has it, Ahasuerus heckled Jesus as he carried the cross and consequently was cursed to wander the earth until the second coming. The Wandering Jew was a familiar motif in gothic novels in particular and Romantic literature in general.

28. *The thoughts . . . in final notes*: De Quincey planned a larger scope for 'Suspiria' than was ever realized and the notes referred to here never appeared.

29. *a beautiful boy, eighteen years old*: In 1834, De Quincey's son William died of encephalitis, the same illness that had killed De Quincey's sister Elizabeth in 1792 (the death he recalls so vividly in this first portion of *Suspiria*).

30. *sublime chapter of St Paul . . . illustrious Laureate*: The chapter referred to is 1 Corinthians 15: 42–4. The 'Laureate' is Wordsworth.

31. *a passage in The Excursion*: From IV, 153–61:

> For who could sink and settle to that point
> Of selfishness; so senseless who could be
> As long and perseveringly to mourn
> For any object of his love, removed
> From this unstable world, if he could fix
> A satisfying view upon that state
> Of pure, imperishable, blessedness,
> Which reason promises, and holy writ
> Ensures all believers?

32. *the lilies . . . feed their young*: An allusion to Luke 12:24–7.

33. *Agrippa's mirror*: In his *De Occulta Philosophia*, Henricus Cornelius Agrippa (German occultist philosopher, 1486–1535) compares the air to a looking-glass that receives images of all things and so provides bases for dreams and divinations.

34. *shafts of Apollo*: In Greek mythology, Apollo was the bright and shining patron deity of music and poetry. He was also an unerring archer.

35. *(in Shakspeare's fine expression) to 'dislimn'*: From *Antony and Cleopatra*, IV, xiv, 10.

36. *composing-stick*: A tray in which a compositor assembled type.

37. * * *: It is not known what was omitted here; the same is true of the similar asterisks below and on p. 182.

38. *ubi Cæsar, ibi Roma*: 'Where Caesar is, there is Rome'.

39. *Mr Alston*: Washington Allston (1779–1843), American artist, friend and portraitist of Coleridge, painted *The Dead Man Revived by Touching the Bones of the Prophet Elisha* (1811–14) while living in London. Often regarded as Allston's masterpiece, the painting (13 by 10 feet) is not actually an altarpiece, as De Quincey claims.

40. *nympholepsy*: According to Greek myth, a mortal who had seen a nymph was stricken with a diseased frenzy.

41. *Obeah magic . . . Three-finger'd Jack*: The plot of the novel *Belinda* (1801) by Maria Edgeworth (1768–1849) involved obeah (or obia), a form of witchcraft similar in many respects to voodoo, that originated in Africa and thrived in the Caribbean. Three-Fingered Jack was the nickname of Jack Mansong, a Jamaican bandit who, like Dick Turpin, became one of the notorious outlaw–heroes of eighteenth-century popular culture.

42. *'On the sublime attractions of the grave'*: From Wordsworth, *The Excursion*, IV, 238.

43. *the Erl-king's Daughter*: The popular German legend was the subject of several poems including the one by Johann Wolfgang von Goethe (1749–1832) which De Quincey quotes here in translation. Franz Schubert composed what was to become a popular musical setting of the same poem in 1815.

44. *one of my guardians . . . English Church*: Samuel Hall, vicar of St Peter's, Manchester. A family friend named as a guardian in Thomas Quincey Snr's will, Hall christened young Thomas while vicar at St Anne's, Manchester, and tutored Thomas and his brother William in Latin and Greek from 1793 until the Quincey family moved to Bath in 1796.

45. *ego et rex meus*: 'I and my patron'.

46. *Iræque leonum / Vincla recusantum . . . caveæ*: The complete passage reads (as De Quincey correctly indicates in his footnote) '*iraeque leonum / vincla recusantum et sera sub nocte rudentum*': 'The raging growls of lions straining against their chains and roaring at midnight' (Virgil (Roman poet, 70–19 BC), *Aeneid*, VI, 15–16). The *caveae* were the cages or stalls where lions were housed in Roman amphitheatres.

47. *ab urbe condita*: 'From the city's foundation'. Roman dating was relative to the establishment of the city of Rome, which Romans dated at 753 BC (in modern terms).

48. *vis medicatrix . . . kilcrops*: *vis medicatrix* means 'healing force'; kilcrops were ravenous children thought to be demon changelings. The Southey poem in question is 'The Killcrop. A Scene Between Benedict, a German Peasant, and Father Karl, an Old Neighbour'.

49. *coup-de-main*: Literally a 'blow of the hand'; a sudden, all-out attack.

50. *ode of our great laureate*: Wordsworth's 'Ode: Intimations of Immortality from Recollections of Early Childhood'.

51. *the geometry of Apollonius*: Apollonius of Perge, a Greek mathematician who flourished in Alexandria c. 200 BC, was known as 'the Great Geometer' and wrote a ground-breaking treatise on conic sections.

52. *a lovely sketch . . . by Mr Wordsworth*: 'Water Fowl', which includes the lines (10–14):

> Their jubilant activity evolves
> Hundreds of curves and circlets, to and fro,
> Upward and downward, progress intricate
> Yet unperplexed, as if one spirit swayed
> Their indefatigable flight.

53. *the Vatican, the Bodleian, and the Bibliothèque du Roi*: Three of the world's great book collections: the Vatican Library, the main library of Oxford University and what is now the National Library of France.

54. *the Œdipus*: Sophocles' tragedy *Oedipus Tyrannus* (*Oedipus the King*), which was probably written and first performed in the 420s BC. The title character ultimately discovers that, despite strenuous attempts to avoid it, he has fulfilled a prophecy of the oracle at Delphi (see note 58 below): he has unwittingly killed his father and married his mother. At the end of the play, after his mother/wife has committed suicide, he blinds himself and resolves to go into exile from Thebes for the rest of his life.

55. *Brutus and a thousand years of impossibilities*: Geoffrey of Monmouth's twelfth-century history attributed the foundation of Britain to Brutus, supposed great-grandson of Aeneas of Troy. According to Monmouth, Brutus landed in southwest England, conquered a race of giants inhabiting the island, founded London as New Troy, and sired a line of noble descendants including King Arthur, accounts of whose exploits were equally fanciful. Despite a complete lack of historical support, the legends proved remarkably persistent and continued to appear in histories for centuries.

56. *Beza's Latin Testament ... the great chapter ... resurrection*: Théodore de Bèze (1519–1605) was a French theologian who succeeded John Calvin as leader of the Protestant Reformation centred in Geneva. His Latin translation of the New Testament served as a source for both the Geneva Bible and the King James Version. *the great chapter of St Paul* is I Corinthians 15, in which St Paul proclaims that the faithful are resurrected after death, then attempts to prove logically that it is impossible for his proclamation not to be true.

57. *Alcaics and Choriambics*: Alcaics are odes of the type originated by the Greek lyric poet Alcaeus (620–580 BC), usually consisting of four stanzas (or strophes) of four lines each. Each strophe is based on a strict and intricate pattern of long and short syllables. A choriambic is another complex verse form in which each line consists of one trochee (a long syllable followed by a short one), three choriambs (a long syllable followed by two short syllables and another long one) and an iambus (a short syllable followed by a long one).

58. *priestess of the oracle*: The ancient Greeks believed that the Pythia, the priestess of the oracle of Apollo at Delphi, spoke the words of Apollo himself. Delphi was the most important oracle in the ancient Greek world, and the Pythia was consulted by individuals and states

on a wide range of issues from cult practices to the foundation of colonies.

59. *the Stationers' Company*: The printers' guild. Popular works some-times carried warnings that they were registered with the Stationers' Company, that unauthorized copiers would be punished, etc.

60. *'star-y-pointing'*: From Milton, 'On Shakespear,' 4.

61. *the ticking of a death-watch*: The death-watch beetle makes a noise like a watch ticking. Popular superstition had it that the noise foretold a death.

62. *'foremost man of all this world'*: From Shakespeare, *Julius Caesar*, IV, iii, 22.

63. *'Into what depth thou see'st, / From what height fallen'*: Slightly misquoted from Milton, *Paradise Lost*, I, 91–2: 'into what Pit thou seest / From what highth fall'n'.

64. *like the superb Medea . . . senseless to the ground*: The sorceress Medea helped Jason steal the golden fleece from her father in return for his pledge of eternal fidelity. When he violated that pledge by falling in love with the princess of Corinth, she killed the two sons she had borne him.

65. *'Him that sate thereon'*: Slightly misquoted from Milton, 'At a Solemn Music', 8: 'him that sits thereon'.

66. *masculine reader*: It was customary until well into the twentieth century for only middle-class and more affluent boys to receive a classical education (a curriculum emphasizing Latin and Greek). Thus De Quincey's patronizing attitude towards women here reflects the biases of his culture.

67. *as Cowper so playfully illustrates*: William Cowper (1731–1800), in *The Task*, I, 1–102.

68. *Pisistratus*: Peisistratus, 'tyrant' in Athens 545–527 BC. His domi-nation of the Athenian political scene was continued by his sons Hippias and Hipparchus until 510 BC, when they were forcibly expelled from the city. The reforms that sowed the seeds of democracy in Athens followed about three years later.

69. *Dr Whately, the present archbishop of Dublin*: Richard Whately (1787–1863), Oxford professor of political economy, educational reformer and philosopher most remembered for his writings on logic and rhetoric.

70. *Hermes Trismegistus*: 'Thrice-Great Hermes', a mythical ancient sage associated with the Egyptian god Thoth, and the supposed author of foundational works on alchemy, astrology and magic.

71. *'my Cid,' . . . Cœur de Lion . . . Sir Tristrem . . . Lybæus Disconus*:

Examples of the 'knightly romance' De Quincey cites as the next literary fashion leading to the recycling of vellum sheets. 'My Cid' is 'El Cantar de mio Cid' (usually translated as 'The Lay of the Cid' but more literally, 'The Song of My Cid'; 'Cid' derives from the Arabic for 'Lord'), a twelfth-century Spanish verse romance about the Castilian warrior hero, Rodrigo Díaz de Vivar (?1043–99). Richard I of England (reigned 1189–99) was nicknamed 'Coeur de Lion' ('Lion-Hearted') chiefly because of his bravery in the Crusades, and appeared in several chivalric romances. Tristram of Lyonesse was a legendary knight of King Arthur's court most famous for his doomed love affair with the beautiful Iseult (or Isolde), the story of which appears in several Arthurian romances. 'Libeaus Desconus' is a late fourteenth-century English romance about Gingelein, the son of Dame Ragnell and Sir Gawain, the famous knight of Arthur's court. As his name is unknown, he is knighted by Arthur as Libeaus Desconus (le bel inconnu, 'the fair unknown'). The romance concerns his rescue of the imprisoned Lady of Sinadoune. Chaucer also includes it in a list of representative (and implicitly ridiculous) romances in 'Sir Thopas' of The Canterbury Tales.

72. *Insolent vaunt of Paracelsus ... combustion*: In his *De Rerum Natura* (*On the Nature of Things*), VI, German alchemist and physician Paracelsus (1493–1541) gave instructions for regenerating vegetable matter from its own ashes.

73. *Erictho of Lucan*: The Roman poet Lucan (AD 39–65) wrote the epic *Pharsalia*, in the sixth book of which appears Erictho, a witch who feeds on rotting corpses and is able to entomb living souls and raise the newly dead.

74. *the well-known passage in the Prometheus*: ποντίων τε κυμάτων / Ἀνήριθμον γέλασμα, 'the boundless laughter of the ocean waves' (Aeschylus, *Prometheus Bound*, 89–90). The words form part of an address to nature, Prometheus' first utterance after being chained to a rock for stealing fire from the gods and giving it to humans.

75. *the destined apostle on his road to Damascus*: As the story is told in the New Testament, Saul of Tarsus, afterwards St Paul, was engaged in a campaign of persecution against Christians when Jesus appeared to him in a blinding light on the road to Damascus, inspiring his conversion to Christianity and subsequent ministry (Acts 22:6–11; 26:12–18).

76. *Part I.*: De Quincey's terminology is confusing here; by 'Part I.' he presumably means the previous instalment in *Blackwood's*, which fits his description of the content, rather than the designated 'Part I' of 'Suspiria de Profundis', which is not yet concluded at this point. Even

at that, however, De Quincey seems further confused, as the instalment matching his description was the second rather than the first.

77. *Euclid*: Perhaps the greatest mathematician of the classical world (flourished c. 300 BC in Alexandria, Egypt), Euclid is best known as the father of geometry.

78. *a boy on the foundation*: A boy attending Eton on an Eton-sponsored scholarship.

79. *I restore to Mr Wordsworth ... day and night*: Wordsworth, 'Conclusion: To ——', 9–11, from 'Miscellaneous Sonnets': 'Life flies: now every day / Is but a glimmering spoke in the swift wheel / Of the revolving week.'

80. *Graces ... Parcæ ... Furies ... Muses*: These trios of Greek and Roman goddesses were responsible for bestowing beauty, charm and grace (Graces), spinning, measuring and cutting the thread of human life (Parcae or Fates), punishing crimes beyond the reach of human justice (Furies) and inspiring artists, musicians, writers and astronomers (Muses, of whom there were ultimately nine).

81. *Rachel weeping ... its nurseries of Innocents*: Matthew 2:16–18.

82. *within the bedchamber of the Czar*: The Grand Duchess Alexandra Nikolaevna, youngest daughter of Czar Nicholas I (1796–1855), died in 1845 only a year after her marriage to the Prince of Hesse-Kassel. According to his biographer, the Czar loved Alexandra 'as the image of her mother', who was also near death at the time. (W. Bruce Lincoln, *Nicholas I: Emperor and Autocrat of All the Russias* (Indiana University Press: Bloomington, 1978), p. 272).

83. *Norfolk island*: Thousands of convicted British felons were sent to Australian penal colonies between 1788 and 1868. The infamously harsh punishment centres in Van Diemen's Land (later Tasmania) and Norfolk Island (northeast of Sydney) were reserved for those who committed further crimes after being transported to one of the other settlements.

84. *the tents of Shem*: Genesis 9:27.

85. *Cybèle*: A Phrygian goddess imported by the Greeks and Romans, known as 'the Great Mother' or 'Mother of the Gods'. De Quincey's reference to her turreted head relates to her appearance in ancient sculpture, where her mural headdress represented her role as protectress of cities.

86. *the Brocken of North Germany*: A peak in the Hartz Mountains.

87. *Whitsunday*: The Anglican name for the day of Pentecost, the festival observed on the seventh Sunday after Easter, a traditional time for baptisms. Whitsunday = 'White Sunday', after the white clothing worn by the newly baptized.

88. *the Lady Echo of Ovid*: In Book III of the *Metamorphoses* of the Roman poet Ovid (43 BC–AD 17), Echo hides from Narcissus, merely repeating back to him portions of his calls to her. When she finally shows herself, he spurns her, after which she refuses to be seen ever again.

89. *'And art thou nothing? . . . that which he pursues'*: From Coleridge, 'Constancy to an Ideal Object', 25–32. The last two lines of the published version are 'The enamoured rustic worships its fair hues, / Nor knows he makes the shadow he pursues!' (*The Complete Political Works of Samuel Taylor Coleridge*, ed. Ernest Hartley Coleridge (Oxford: Clarendon Press, 1912)). De Quincey claims to be quoting from a 'corrected copy', though, so perhaps his version reflects his friend Coleridge's thoughts at some time after the poem's publication in 1826.

90. *after the example of Judæa (on the Roman coins)*: To commemorate the capture and destruction of Jerusalem by his son Titus in AD 70, the emperor Vespasian (ruled AD 69–79) struck coins picturing Judea as a woman mourning beneath a palm tree.

91. *Phantasus*: One of the sons of Hypnos, god of sleep in Greek mythology, Phantasus (Phantasos) was responsible for bringing dreams of inanimate things. His brothers, Morpheus and Ikelos (or Phobetor), brought dreams of men and animals, respectively.

92. *Savannah-la-Mar*: A port in Jamaica engulfed by a hurricane in 1780.

93. *Fata-Morgana*: A mirage effect observed over water in which objects appear doubled, elongated and suspended in the air. It is seen most often in the Straits of Messina in Italy and over the Great Lakes in the United States. Popular legend has it that fairies are responsible for these images.

94. *jubilates*: Songs of religious exultation.

95. *clepsydra*: A water clock.

96. *sanctus*: The part of Christian liturgy spoken or sung ('Holy, holy, holy', in English) before the prayer of consecration and the administration of the sacrament.

97. *'male and female created he them'*: Genesis 1:27.

98. *'in to-day already walks to-morrow'*: Coleridge, *The Death of Wallenstein*, V, i, 102.

99. *the Roman retiarius*: A gladiator who attempted to ensnare his opponent by swinging a net at him.

100. *Facit indignatio versum*: 'Indignation inspires my poetry', from Juvenal, *Satires*, I, 79.

101. *'Te nimis austerum . . . flagello'*: 'You, who violate the compacts

of the sacred table with your excessive severity, I pursue with the reverberating scourge of satire.'

102. *mea sæva querela . . . nocte procellam*: 'My raging plaint shall take root in your waxy ears, even if those ears cannot hear a storm on a wintry night.'

103. *stylites*: The Stylites were an idiosyncratic sect of Christian ascetics who sat atop pillars, often for years at a time. De Quincey's reasons for using the word here – where he apparently intends it as a synonym for a satire, harangue, or other form of harshly critical utterance – are obscure.

104. *Mordecai the Jew*: Mordecai was lavishly and publicly honoured for averting an attempted assassination of King Ahasuerus (Esther 6:2–11).

105. *aposiopesis*: The omission of the end of a thought by a sudden breaking off, usually for rhetorical effect.

106. *inter alia*: 'Among other things'.

107. *Earl of A—t*: The Earl of Altamont (see *Confessions*, note 57).

108. *solatium*: 'Consolation in a time of emotional distress'.

109. *Sus. per coll.*: '*Suspendatur per collum*', 'Let him be hanged by the neck.'

110. *found his way to Australia*: Meaning he was sent there as a convicted criminal (see note 83).

111. *caravanserai*: An inn surrounding a courtyard where camel caravans would rest for the night.

112. *her Majesty's coronation*: The coronation of Queen Victoria on 28 June 1838, just over seven years before 'Suspiria' was published.

113. *Ayah*: A Hindu nursemaid employed by European families living in India.

THE ENGLISH MAIL-COACH

1. *Mr Palmer, M.P. for Bath*: John Palmer (1742–1818), whose fortune was founded on his thriving theatres in Bath and Bristol, successfully enlisted the support of Prime Minister Pitt in 1784–6 to establish a mail service with uniform government stage-coaches instead of mounted post-boys and other irregular conveyances. Launched between Bath and London, the service soon connected all of England's major cities, bringing about unprecedented speed, economy and safety of communication. Palmer's subsequent attempts to gain power and remuneration from his scheme were fraught with controversy, but he was elected twice as mayor of Bath and four times as MP for the district. *The*

Dictionary of National Biography, however, does not mention his marriage to Lady Madeline Gordon (who was married to a Charles Palmer) or any other duke's daughter.

2. *of Trafalgar, of Salamanca, of Vittoria, of Waterloo*: British victories in the Napoleonic Wars.

3. *Te Deums*: The Te Deum is the part of the Christian liturgy that praises God: *Te deum laudamus*, 'Thee, God, we praise.'

4. *delf ware*: A cheap variety of earthenware, also known as Delft, originally produced in that region of Holland.

5. *salle-à-manger*: 'Dining room'.

6. *Lord Macartney*: The Macartney embassy of 1795 travelled to Peking in the hope of improving Anglo-Chinese trade relations. The relationship had been strained by British attempts to market Indian opium in China against the wishes of the imperial government, a situation that ultimately led to the opium wars of the mid-nineteenth century. Although De Quincey embroiders his tale of the gift coach, it is based in fact; the entire visit was plagued by the question of who would take precedence (see the Appendix, under 'Opium and the Orient').

7. *hammer-cloth*: A cloth covering the coach box.

8. *Ca ira*: '*Ça ira, ça tiendra*' ('That will go, that will hold') was the chorus of a popular song of the French Revolution and became a popular revolutionary cry.

9. *bills at ninety days after date*: Bills that had come due and thus rendered the debtor liable to collection or, if he was unable to pay, imprisonment.

10. *snakes in Von Troil's Iceland*: When revising his works for the collected edition in 1854, De Quincey added this note: 'The allusion is to a well-known chapter in Von Troil's work, entitled, "Concerning the Snakes of Iceland". The entire chapter consists of these six words – "*There are no snakes in Iceland*."'

11. *læsa majestas*: 'Violated majesty', *lèse-majesté*, a flouting of what should be revered authority.

12. *'Jam proximus ardet / Ucalegon'*: 'Now his neighbour Ucalegon is aflame' (Virgil, *Aeneid*, II, 311–12). Here 'Ucalegon' means 'the house of Ucalegon', a famous example of metonymy cited by both Horace and Juvenal. The passage appears in the section of the *Aeneid* describing the sack of Troy by the Greeks. Ucalegon was a friend of the Trojan king, Priam.

13. *'False echoes'* ... *Talleyrand*: The 'false echoes of Marengo' are the words De Quincey quotes ('Ah! wherefore have we not time to weep over you?'), which, as he says, were erroneously attributed to

Napoleon upon the death of his officer Desaix at the Battle of Marengo (1800). *Le Vengeur* was a French warship that sank after being captured by the British in 1794. The popular French account had it that, after being reduced to splinters, the ship fired one last broadside as the crew cried 'Vive la République! ('Long live the Republic!'). 'La Garde meurt, mais ne se rend pas' means 'The Guard dies, but does not surrender.' Charles Maurice de Talleyrand-Périgord (1754–1838) was Napoleon's foreign minister and a career statesman and diplomat to whom were ascribed many legendary witticisms.

14. *à fortiori*: 'With stronger reason'.

15. *the tombs of Luxor*: The phrase often refers in general to the unparalleled archaeological finds (including many notable hieroglyphic inscriptions) in the area encompassing Luxor, Thebes and Karnak to the east of the Nile in Egypt.

16. *'which they upon the adverse faction wanted'*: Adapted from Shakespeare, *Richard III*, V, iii, 12–13: 'Besides, the King's name is a tower of strength / Which they upon the adverse faction want.'

17. *the 10th of Edward III chap. 15*: De Quincey is here pulling the Welshman's leg, as no such law exists. He may also have fabricated the 'story from one of our elder dramatists' about the Oriental king, the hawk and the eagle.

18. *Non magna loquimur . . . magna vivimus*: 'We do not speak great things . . . we live great things.'

19. *the glory of Salamanca*: In conjunction with Spanish guerrilla forces, the British army defeated the French at Salamanca in 1812, hastening France's loss of the Peninsular War in 1813 and the ultimate British victory.

20. *galvanic cycle*: A galvanic cell was the nineteenth-century forerunner of the modern battery. It was often used in spectacular scientific demonstrations, sometimes to animate dead limbs by attaching the battery to muscle tissue. Thus when De Quincey speaks of the galvanic cycle having been broken, he casts the horseman and his reins as the battery and leads that used to animate the 'ministers of his locomotion', the horses. This circuit has been broken in the new system of train travel, with its 'iron tubes and boilers'.

21. *Ulysses . . . his accursed bow*: In Homer's *Odyssey*, XXII, Ulysses fights off the suitors of his wife Penelope, succeeding against overwhelming odds through his famous skill with bow and arrow, a dubious distinction in ancient Greek culture as archery was considered a cowardly alternative to hand-to-hand combat.

22. *mais oui donc*: 'But of course'.

23. *'Say, all our praises why should lords'*: Altered from 'But all our

praises why should Lords engross?', Alexander Pope (1688–1744),
'Epistle III, To the Right Honourable Allen Lord Bathurst, Of the Use of
Riches', 249. De Quincey playfully rewrites the line in the next sentence.
24. *ex abundanti*: 'From an abundance'.
25. *Mr Waterton*: Charles Waterton (1782–1865), a wealthy eccentric
and naturalist perhaps most enduringly famous for the nature reserve
he established at his estate, Walton Park, in Yorkshire. In his *Wanderings in South America* (1825, 1st edn.), pp. 231–2, he described capturing a cayman (a tropical American crocodilian closely related to the
alligator) during his third expedition in 1820: 'I . . . jumped on his
back, turning half round as I vaulted, so that I gained my seat with my
face in the right position. I immediately seized his fore legs, and, by
main force, twisted them on his back; thus they served me for a bridle
. . . Should it be asked, how I managed to keep my seat, I would answer,
– I hunted some years with Lord Darlington's fox hounds.'
26. *monokeras*: Greek for 'one horn'. De Quincey is probably misremembering a bit of natural history when he asserts that such an animal
lives in the Himalayas and Africa. The kraken is a huge sea monster of
Scandinavian legend most familiar to modern audiences from the poem
of the same name by Alfred, Lord Tennyson (1809–92).
27. *the old fancy . . . Spenser*: *The Faerie Queene* by Sir Edmund
Spenser (?1552–99), I, iii, 5–6, describes a lion submitting to a virgin:

> It fortuned out of the thickest wood
>> A ramping Lyon rushed suddainly,
>> Hunting full greedie after saluage blood;
>> Soone as the royall virgin he did spy,
>> With gaping mouth at her ran greedily,
>> To have attonce deuour'd her tender corse:
>> But to the pray when as he drew more ny,
>> His bloudie rage asswaged with remorse,
> And with the sight amazd, forgat his furious forse.
>
> In stead thereof he kist her wearie feet,
>> And lickt her lilly hands with fawning tong,
>> As he her wronged innocence did weet.

>> *The Works of Edmund Spenser: A Variorum
>> Edition*, ed. Edwin Greenlaw, Charles Grosvenor
>> Osgood, Frederick Morgan Padelford, Ray
>> Heffner, 10 vols. (Baltimore: Johns Hopkins
>> Press, 1932–49).

28. *the cowardly and cruel lion called Wallace*: In *A History of War-wick and Its People* (1905), Thomas Kemp reports that a lion named Wallace killed two bulldogs in a fight on 30 July 1825. The event was so celebrated that a street in that part of Warwick was later named after the lion.

29. *Soult*: Marshal Nicolas Jean de Dieu Soult (1769–1851), Duke of Dalmatia, was one of Napoleon's most able and respected commanders and a prominent figure in French politics and diplomacy even after supporting Napoleon during the infamous 'Hundred Days' after his return from Elba. The British admired his bravery and ability in the Peninsular War, and even his arch-nemesis, the Duke of Wellington, greeted him with respect when he represented France at Victoria's coronation in 1837.

30. *attelage*: Harness, coupling, hitch.

31. *en flagrant delit*: French (today, *délit*) for the Latin *in flagrante delicto*, 'in the act of committing a misdeed', 'red-handed'.

32. *Badajoz . . . Salamanca for ever*: The night attack on the medieval fortress town of Badajoz in April 1812 was one of the more savage battles of the Peninsular War. Wellington also defeated Marmont's Army of Portugal in July of the same year at Salamanca (see note 19).

33. *Barnet*: On the main road between London and St Alban's, Barnet was a popular stopping point for coaches. In 1965 the name was given to a borough of northwest London that includes the area.

34. *fey*: 'Marked for imminent death', in one common Scottish usage, but also 'otherworldly', 'fairy-like', 'crazed'.

35. *Bengal lights*: Blue flare-like lights used for signalling and illumination.

36. *Talavera*: Wellington's victory at Talavera (1809) was marred by the fact that he afterwards had to retreat to Portugal, having been abandoned by Spanish reinforcements. Nevertheless, it was as a reward for this achievement that he was created Viscount Wellington.

37. *aceldama*: Aceldama (*Akeldama* is the Greek rendering of an Aramaic phrase meaning 'field of blood') was the name later given to the plot of land Judas bought with the money he earned by betraying Jesus. According to Acts 1:15–19, Judas fell in the middle of the field, bursting open so that his bowels and blood gushed out over the ground.

38. *The Vision of Sudden Death*: 'The English Mail-Coach' was published in two instalments in *Blackwood's* (in October and December 1849), and the second began here with a bracketed note, clearly by De Quincey, immediately following the section title:

The reader is to understand this present paper, in its two sections of *The Vision,*

&c., and *The Dream-Fugue*, as connected with a previous paper on *The English Mail-Coach*, published in the Magazine for October. The ultimate object was the Dream-Fugue, as an attempt to wrestle with the utmost efforts of music in dealing with a colossal form of impassioned horror. The Vision of Sudden Death contains the mail-coach incident, which did really occur, and did really suggest the variations of the Dream, here taken up by the Fugue, as well as other variations not now recorded. Confluent with these impressions, from the terrific experience on the Manchester and Glasgow mail, were other and more general impressions, derived from long familiarity with the English mail, as developed in the former paper; impressions, for instance, of animal beauty and power, of rapid motion, at that time unprecedented, of connexion with the government and public business of a great nation, but above all, of connexion with the national victories at an unexampled crisis, – the mail being the privileged organ for publishing and dispersing all news of that kind. From this function of the mail, arises naturally the introduction of Waterloo into the fourth variation of the Fugue; for the mail itself having been carried into the dreams by the incident in the Vision, naturally all the accessory circumstances of pomp and grandeur investing this national carriage followed in the train of the principal image.

39. *Cæsar the Dictator, at his last dinner party*: The incident is reported by Plutarch (c. AD 46–120) in his *Life of Julius Caesar*.
40. βιαθάνατος . . . βίαιος: 'Violent death' and 'violent' respectively.
41. *lâcheté*: 'Cowardice'.
42. *'Nature from her seat . . . all is lost'*: Adapted from Milton, *Paradise Lost*, IX, 782–4: 'Nature from her seat / Sighing through all her Works gave signs of woe, / That all was lost.'
43. *jus dominii . . . jus gentium*: *jus dominii* means 'property right'; *jus gentium* means 'law of nations', a phrase used by ancient Romans meaning that part of private law applying to citizens and non-citizens alike, or a 'universal' or 'natural' law applying to all peoples, or laws prevailing between states. De Quincey seems to invoke the second sense here.
44. *Effendi . . . Stamboul*: '*Effendi*' was an honorific title for a man of property, education or authority in eastern Mediterranean countries; *Stamboul* is a hilly peninsula at the heart of the ancient city of Istanbul (formerly Constantinople), abutting on to the Bosporus and the Sea of Marmara.
45. *Chrysippus . . . any son of Othman*: Chrysippus of Soli (c. 280–207 BC) came to Athens c. 260, then succeeded Cleanthes as head of the Stoa in 232. His voluminous writings, which survive only in fragments, helped to define and refine orthodox Stoic belief, being second in importance only to those of Zeno, the founder of Stoicism

(see note 122, *Confession*). Cicero (106–43 BC, Roman orator, statesman and man of letters) reports in his *De natura deorum* (*The Nature
of the Gods*), II, Chrysippus' view that life was bestowed on the pig as
salt to keep it from spoiling. *Son of Othman* means scion of the
Ottoman dynasty, native of Turkey.

46. *Dr Johnsons ... Deodand*: Samuel Johnson wrote a critical, at
times sardonic, 'Essay upon Epitaphs' (1740). A deodand was originally an offering to the gods of a belonging that had caused someone's
death, but later a fine levied against the owner of such an object.

47. *Morcellus*: Stefano Antonio Morcelli (1737–1822), Italian Jesuit
renowned as an authority on Latin inscriptions.

48. *simple breakfast ... extraordinary*: One of opium's effects is to
suppress both appetite and sensitivity to fatigue, which is presumably
why De Quincey cites the distance he had travelled on a small breakfast
as the reason for taking laudanum on this occasion.

49. *'Monstrum ... ademptum' ... the Arabian Nights*: The quotation
is from Virgil, *Aeneid*, III, 658, and refers to the Cyclops Polyphemus
(see note 54 below). De Quincey integrates a translation of all the
elements of the quotation into the following sentence. The three calendars (wandering ascetic dervishes) in the *Arabian Nights* tell of how
they lost their eyes, but for only one of them was curiosity the cause:
entering a forbidden room as the princess did in the tale of Bluebeard,
he found a winged horse who impaled his eye with its wing.

50. *Al Sirat*: Arabic for 'the path', the bridge to Paradise in Muslim
tradition. Narrower than a spider's thread and sharper than a sword,
it is navigable only by the morally pure, who pass easily. The wicked
who attempt to cross fall to damnation below.

51. *gage d'amitié*: 'Token of friendship'.

52. *aurigation ... Aurora*: The *Oxford English Dictionary* defines
'aurigation' as 'the action or art of driving a chariot or coach', citing
De Quincey's usage here. Among his other responsibilities, the Greek
god Apollo pulled the sun across the sky with his chariot, a task no
other god had sufficient skill to perform. Aurora was the Roman
goddess of the dawn (Eos, in the Greek Pantheon), and is often depicted
riding her chariot and horses across the sky.

53. *Giraldus Cambrensis*: Welsh historian and geographer (c. 1146–
c. 1220), chiefly of Ireland and Wales.

54. *Polyphemus*: The giant Cyclops that Odysseus tricked and blinded
in order to escape from his cave in the *Odyssey*, IX. Aeneas also
encounters Polyphemus in the *Aeneid*, III.

55. *the shout of Achilles ... Peleus ... Pallas*: Achilles' 'loud cry' or
'terrible cry' is mentioned several times in Homer's *Iliad* (especially in

Books XVIII–XX), including once when it is heard by his mother Thetis and her sisters at the bottom of the sea (XVIII). Peleus, king of the Myrmidons of Thessaly, was Achilles' mortal father. Pallas is an epithet of Athena, goddess of war, who fights on the side of the Greeks and often aids Achilles in the *Iliad*.

56. *Tumultuosissimamente*: 'With the greatest tumultuousness'. De Quincey here parodies stylistic indicators in concert music scores, which are conventionally in Italian.

57. *corymbi*: De Quincey borrows the word from the Latin form of the Greek *korumbos* (κόρυμβος), meaning 'peak' and, by extension, 'a cluster of ivy flowers' or 'a cluster of flowers/fruit' generally. The *Oxford English Dictionary* offers a second definition of the word 'corymb' as 'a cluster of ivy-berries or grapes' and cites De Quincey's usage here as one of only three.

58. *Gloria in excelsis*: 'Glory in the highest'.

59. *'Chaunt the deliverer's praise ... in heaven and earth were sung'*: Misquoted from Wordsworth's 'The Siege of Vienna Raised by John Sobieski' (ll. 11–14):

> Chant the Deliverer's praise in every tongue!
> The cross shall spread, the crescent hath waxed dim;
> He conquering, as in joyful Heaven is sung,
> He conquering through God, and God by him.

60. *Créci*: The Battle of Crécy, or Cressy (1346), in which Edward III's army triumphed over the French, was the first great English victory of the Hundred Years War.

61. *Clinging to the horns of the altar*: In the Old Testament, the sacrificial altar is represented as having horns. Clinging to them was apparently a rough equivalent of the later custom of seeking sanctuary within a church. In I Kings 1:50–53, for instance, Adonijah grasps the horns of the altar until Solomon swears he will not harm him.

PENGUIN ⊕ CLASSICS

The Classics Publisher

'Penguin Classics, one of the world's greatest series' JOHN KEEGAN

'I have never been disappointed with the Penguin Classics. All I have read is a model of academic seriousness and provides the essential information to fully enjoy the master works that appear in its catalogue' MARIO VARGAS LLOSA

'Penguin and Classics are words that go together like horse and carriage or Mercedes and Benz. When I was a university teacher I always prescribed Penguin editions of classic novels for my courses: they have the best introductions, the most reliable notes, and the most carefully edited texts' DAVID LODGE

'Growing up in Bombay, expensive hardback books were beyond my means, but I could indulge my passion for reading at the roadside bookstalls that were well stocked with all the Penguin paperbacks ... Sometimes I would choose a book just because I was attracted by the cover, but so reliable was the Penguin imprimatur that I was never once disappointed by the contents.

Such access certainly broadened the scope of my reading, and perhaps it's no coincidence that so many Merchant Ivory films have been adapted from great novels, or that those novels are published by Penguin' ISMAIL MERCHANT

'You can't write, read, or live fully in the present without knowing the literature of the past. Penguin Classics opens the door to a treasure house of pure pleasure, books that have never been bettered, which are read again and again with increased delight' JOHN MORTIMER

CLICK ON A CLASSIC
www.penguinclassics.com

The world's greatest literature at your fingertips

Constantly updated information on over 1600 titles, from
Icelandic sagas to ancient Indian epics, Russian drama to
Italian romance, American greats to African masterpieces

•

The latest news on recent additions to the list, updated
editions and specially commissioned translations

•

Original scholarly essays by leading writers: Elaine Showalter
on Zola, Laurie R. King on Arthur Conan Doyle, Frank
Kermode on Shakespeare, Lisa Appignanesi on Tolstoy

•

A wealth of background material, including biographies
of every classic author from Aristotle to Zamyatin, plot
synopses, readers' and teachers' guides, useful web links

•

Online desk and examination copy assistance for academics

•

Trivia quizzes, competitions, giveaways, news on
forthcoming screen adaptations

•

eBooks available to download

READ MORE IN PENGUIN

In every corner of the world, on every subject under the sun, Penguin represents quality and variety – the very best in publishing today.

For complete information about books available from Penguin – including Puffins and Penguin Classics – and how to order them, write to us at the appropriate address below. Please note that for copyright reasons the selection of books varies from country to country.

In the United Kingdom: *Please write to* Dept EP, Penguin Books Ltd, Bath Road, Harmondsworth, West Drayton, Middlesex UB7 0DA

In the United States: *Please write to* Consumer Services, Penguin Putnam Inc., 405 Murray Hill Parkway, East Rutherford, New Jersey 07073-2136. *VISA and MasterCard holders call 1-800-631-8571 to order Penguin titles*

In Canada: *Please write to* Penguin Books Canada Ltd, 10 Alcorn Avenue, Suite 300, Toronto, Ontario M4V 3B2

In Australia: *Please write to* Penguin Books Australia Ltd, 487 Maroondah Highway, Ringwood, Victoria 3134

In New Zealand: *Please write to* Penguin Books (NZ) Ltd, Private Bag 102902, North Shore Mail Centre, Auckland 10

In India: *Please write to* Penguin Books India Pvt Ltd, 11, Community Centre, Panchsheel Park, New Delhi 110017

In the Netherlands: *Please write to* Penguin Books Netherlands bv, Postbus 3507, NL-1001 AH Amsterdam

In Germany: *Please write to* Penguin Books Deutschland GmbH, Metzlerstrasse 26, 60594 Frankfurt am Main

In Spain: *Please write to* Penguin Books S. A., Bravo Murillo 19, 1°B, 28015 Madrid

In Italy: *Please write to* Penguin Italia s.r.l., Via Vittoria Emanuele 45 1a, 20094 Corsico, Milano

In France: *Please write to* Penguin France, 12, Rue Prosper Ferradou, 31700 Blagnac

In Japan: *Please write to* Penguin Books Japan Ltd, Iidabashi KM-Bldg, 2-23-9 Koraku, Bunkyo-Ku, Tokyo 112-0004

In South Africa: *Please write to* Penguin Books South Africa (Pty) Ltd, P.O. Box 751093, Gardenview, 2047 Johannesburg

HENRY JAMES

The Turn of the Screw *and* The Aspern Papers

*'The apparition had reached the landing
half-way up and was therefore on the spot
nearest the window, where, at the sight of me,
it stopped short'*

Oscar Wilde called James's chilling 'The Turn of the Screw' 'a
most wonderful, lurid poisonous little tale'. It tells of a young
governess sent to a country house to take charge of two
orphans, Miles and Flora. Unsettled by a sense of intense evil
within the house, she soon becomes obsessed with the belief that
malevolent forces are stalking the children in her care.
Obsession of a more worldly variety lies at the heart of 'The
Aspern Papers', the tale of a literary historian determined to get
his hands on some letters written by a great poet – and prepared
to use trickery and deception to achieve his aims. Both show
James's mastery of the short story and his genius for creating
haunting atmosphere and unbearable tension.

Anthony Curtis's wide-ranging introduction traces the development of the two stories from initial inspiration to finished work
and examines their critical reception.

Edited with an introduction by ANTHONY CURTIS

OSCAR WILDE

The Picture of Dorian Gray

*'The horror, whatever it was, had not yet entirely
spoiled that marvellous beauty'*

Enthralled by his own exquisite portrait, Dorian Gray
exchanges his soul for eternal youth and beauty. Influenced by
his friend Lord Henry Wotton, he is drawn into a corrupt
double life, indulging his desires in secret while remaining a
gentleman in the eyes of polite society. Only his portrait bears
the traces of his decadence. *The Picture of Dorian Gray* was a
succès de scandale. Early readers were shocked by its hints at
unspeakable sins, and the book was later used as evidence
against Wilde at his trial at the Old Bailey in 1895.

This definitive edition includes a selection of contemporary
reviews condemning the novel's immorality, and the introduction to the first Penguin Classics edition by Peter Ackroyd.

Edited with an introduction and notes by ROBERT MIGHALL

ROBERT LOUIS STEVENSON

The Strange Case of Dr Jekyll and Mr Hyde and Other Tales of Terror

*'He put the glass to his lips and drank at one gulp
... his face became suddenly black and the
features seemed to melt and alter'*

Published as a 'shilling shocker', Robert Louis Stevenson's dark psychological fantasy gave birth to the idea of the split personality. The story of respectable Dr Jekyll's strange association with 'damnable young man' Edward Hyde; the hunt through fog-bound London for a killer; and the final revelation of Hyde's true identity is a chilling exploration of humanity's basest capacity for evil. The other stories in this volume also testify to Stevenson's inventiveness within the Gothic tradition: 'Olalla', a tale of vampirism and tainted family blood, and 'The Body Snatcher', a gruesome fictionalization of the exploits of the notorious Burke and Hare.

This edition contains a critical introduction by Robert Mighall, which discusses class, criminality and the significance of the story's London setting. It also includes an essay on the scientific contexts of the novel and the development of the idea of the Jekyll-and-Hyde personality.

Edited with an introduction and notes by ROBERT MIGHALL

JONATHAN SWIFT
Gulliver's Travels

*'I felt something alive moving on my left Leg ...
when bending my Eyes downwards as much as I
could, I perceived it to be a human Creature not
six Inches high'*

Shipwrecked and cast adrift, Lemuel Gulliver wakes to find himself on Lilliput, an island inhabited by little people, whose height makes their quarrels over fashion and fame seem ridiculous. His subsequent encounters – with the crude giants of Brobdingnag, the philosophical Houyhnhnms and the brutish Yahoos – give Gulliver new, bitter insights into human behaviour. Swift's savage satire views mankind in a distorted hall of mirrors as a diminished, magnified and finally bestial species, presenting us with an uncompromising reflection of ourselves.

This text, based on the first edition of 1726, reproduces all its original illustrations and includes an introduction by Robert Demaria, Jr, which discusses the ways *Gulliver's Travels* has been interpreted since its first publication.

'A masterwork of irony ... that contains both a dark and bitter meaning and a joyous, extraordinary creativity of imagination. That is why it has lived for so long' MALCOLM BRAD-BURY

Edited with an introduction and notes by
ROBERT DEMARIA, JR

DANIEL DEFOE

A Journal of the Plague Year

*'It was a most surprising thing, to see those
Streets, which were usually so thronged, now
grown desolate'*

In 1665 the Great Plague swept through London, claiming
nearly 100,000 lives. In *A Journal*, written nearly sixty years
later, Defoe vividly chronicled the progress of the epidemic. We
follow his fictional narrator through a city transformed: the
streets and alleyways deserted; the houses of death with crosses
daubed on their doors; the dead-carts on their way to the pits.
And he recounts the horrifying stories of the citizens he encounters, as fear, isolation and hysteria take hold. *A Journal* is
both a fascinating historical document and a supreme work of
imaginative reconstruction.

This edition, based on the original 1722 text, contains a new
introduction, an appendix on the plague, a topographical index
and maps of contemporary London, and includes Anthony
Burgess's original introduction.

'The most reliable and comprehensive account of the Great
Plague that we possess' ANTHONY BURGESS

'Within the texture of Defoe's prose London becomes a living
and suffering being' PETER ACKROYD

Edited with an introduction and notes by CYNTHIA WALL